FOUNDATIONS OF

WORKFORCE EDUCATION

Second Edition

EDITED BY BETH WINFREY FREEBURG AND MARION E. HALL

Taken from:

Career Information, Career Counseling, and Career Development, Ninth Edition
by Duane Brown

Workforce Education: The Basics
by Kenneth C. Gray and Edwin L. Herr

Foundations of American Education: Perspectives on Education in a Changing World,
Fourteenth Edition
by James A. Johnson, Diann Musial, Gene E. Hall, Donna M. Gollnick, and Victor L. Dupuis

The Economics of Women, Men, and Work, Fifth Edition
by Francine D. Blau, Marianne A. Ferber, and Anne E. Winkler

Understanding Public Policy, Twelfth Edition
by Thomas R. Dye

Custom Publishing

New York   Boston   San Francisco
London   Toronto   Sydney   Tokyo   Singapore   Madrid
Mexico City   Munich   Paris   Cape Town   Hong Kong   Montreal

Cover Art: Courtesy of PhotoDisc/Getty Images.

Excerpts taken from:

Career Information, Career Counseling, and Career Development, Ninth Edition
by Duane Brown
Copyright © 2007, 2003, 2000, 1997, 1993, 1986, 1977, 1971, 1966 by Pearson Education, Inc.
Published by Allyn & Bacon
Boston, Massachusetts 02116

Workforce Education: The Basics
by Kenneth C. Gray and Edwin L. Herr
Copyright © 1998 by Allyn & Bacon
A Pearson Education Company

Foundations of American Education: Perspectives on Education in a Changing World, Fourteenth Edition
by James A. Johnson, Diann Musial, Gene E. Hall, Donna M. Gollnick, and Victor L. Dupuis
Copyright © 2008, 2005, 2002, 1999, 1996, 1994, 1991, 1988, 1985, 1982, 1979, 1976, 1973, 1969 by Pearson
Education, Inc.
Published by Allyn & Bacon

The Economics of Women, Men, and Work, Fifth Edition
by Francine D. Blau, Marianne A. Ferber, and Anne E. Winkler
Copyright © 2006, 2002, 1998, 1992, 1986 by Pearson Education, Inc.
Published by Prentice Hall
Upper Saddle River, New Jersey 07458

Understanding Public Policy, Twelfth Edition
by Thomas R. Dye
Copyright © 2008, 2005, 2002, 1998, 1995, 1992 by Pearson Education
Published by Prentice Hall

Copyright © 2008, 2005 by Pearson Custom Publishing
All rights reserved.

Printed in the United States of America

10 9 8 7 6 5 4 3

2008420006

MP/SB

**Pearson
Custom Publishing**
is a division of

www.pearsonhighered.com

ISBN10: 0-555-01508-4
ISBN13: 978-0-555-01508-7

CONTENTS

UNIT 3 Sociological Foundations   127

UNIT 4 Psychological Foundations   173

UNIT 5 Legislative Foundations 215

INTRODUCTION

This is the revised custom textbook for WED 466–Foundations of Work Education. We have located and synthesized new, improved, and current informational resources in efforts to build learners' understanding of the foundations of preparing and developing people for work.

WED 466 is a professional major course required for the Bachelor of Science Degree in Workforce Education and Development and also required for graduate work in the Department. The purpose of the course is to examine the historical, social, economic, and psychological foundations of work education, and the nature and role of education and training in preparing people for the world of work. Upon completion of the course learners will: (a) understand the five foundational areas for workforce education initiatives; (b) apply the economic concepts of supply and demand to high growth job training initiatives; (c) apply the concepts of continuing professional development; and (d) analyze a workforce development policy statement.

Preparing people for work has through history been a way to develop citizens who are prepared to work in the public and private economic sectors. Further, workforce development is directly related to productivity, entrepreneurship, and employee motivation and commitment. Secondary and post-secondary institutions of all types, business and industry, community-based organizations, and government entities prepare people for work.

Workforce education includes the development of clusters of knowledge, skills, attitudes, and behaviors. These clusters include basic literacy and job-specific knowledge and skills. In addition, the clusters include broad knowledge, skills, attitudes, and behaviors important to the success of workers in all jobs. Workforce education also includes meta-cognitive competencies, that is an individual focus on learning how to learn and to reflect on one's career choices.

The revised text, like the original, contains five units. These include: Unit 1 – Historical, Ethical, and Philosophical Foundations; Unit 2 – Labor and Economic Foundations; Unit 3 – Sociological Foundations; Unit 4 – Psychological Foundations; and Unit 5 – Legislative Foundations.

HISTORICAL, PHILOSOPHICAL, AND ETHICAL FOUNDATIONS

Historical, ethical, and philosophical foundations include key events, rationale for behaviors, and ways of thinking that influenced the development of education for work. This unit has been updated to include a more comprehensive overview of historical events that influence current workforce education and development in the public and private sectors. Important events include requirements of the pre- and post-industrial revolution and the evolution of apprenticeships as a timeline for the development of skilled craftsman. In addition, the text provides an overview of the evolution of apprenticeable occupations. Concurrent with these events was the evolution of high school vocational education and government employment and training programs. In addition, the passage of the GI Bill in 1944 provided educational funding for returning veterans and continues to shape the look at working America. The availability of funds targeted on worker preparation greatly influenced workforce education programs.

Ethics are principles or standards of human conduct. Societal norms or standards related to thought, action, and attitudes. Standards of human conduct at work are communicated formally and informally by employers. In addition, professional organizations maintain codes of ethics that reflect what its members believe to be the standards of performance. Thus, workforce education includes and is influenced by standards of human conduct.

Philosophy is the analysis of the fundamental ways of thinking about the world. Four major schools of thought that have influenced the development and practice education are idealism, realism, pragmatism, and existentialism. In addition, other influences on education are Eastern and Native American cultures. A philosophical viewpoint becomes a filter that affects actions of its followers.

ECONOMIC AND LABOR FOUNDATIONS

Labor and economic foundations of workforce education are grounded in labor market basics. Jobs generated by current economic conditions determine the skill sets needed by successful workers. This unit contains new content related to the terms, concepts, and statistical measures specific to the study of work. Supply and demand analysis, human capital investment theory, and the concept of labor market advantage provide models for understanding how jobs are generated. International labor markets influence the required skills and abilities of workers. Additionally, technology and innovation are shaping how work is accomplished. Thus, the emerging role of entrepreneurship influences worker productivity and preparation.

SOCIOLOGICAL FOUNDATIONS

Sociological foundations are those environmental considerations that influence the organization and delivery of workforce education. New and improved material is included in this unit. Specific contents include those environmental considerations that are external to the worker. Included are the context of work, worker interaction, and how organizations manage work process and product. Factors that lay the sociological foundations include perspectives of work and labor markets, contemporary work trends. In addition, social class, family influence on work, and status attainment affect workforce education.

PSYCHOLOGICAL FOUNDATIONS

Psychological foundations are internal factors that influence the organization and delivery of workforce education. Specifically, career development theory provides a look at how individuals choose jobs and then, advance and develop specific skills within the context of their career. This unit contains an updated look at the several categories of career development theories. These include trait and factor theories, developmental theories, learning theories, socioeconomic theories, and recent theoretical statements. An examination of decision making theory is equally important to understanding career development.

LEGISLATIVE FOUNDATIONS

Legislative foundations are based in the development of public policy which reflects decisions made by governing bodies for the public benefit. A conceptual framework for analyzing public policy have been added to this text. The legislative overview is much more comprehensive than the first edition. Initial federal legislation molding workforce education was the Smith-Hughes Act of 1917. That Act provided guidelines for preparing young people at the high school and post secondary (sub-baccalaureate) for work. Current and pending public policies regarding workforce education may be categorized and relate to career and technical education (CTE) or government employment and training (E & T). The Carl Perkins Vocational and Applied Technology Act of 1998 funds CTE programs that prepare students to enter the workforce with the academic and vocational skills needed to compete successfully in a world market.

The Workforce Investment Act of 1998 funds employment and training programs that provide the framework for a nationwide workforce preparation and employment system designed to meet both the needs of the nation's businesses, the needs of job seekers, and individuals wanting to further their careers. Programs funded by workforce legislation are delivered in various venues including high schools, post secondary institutions—community, career, and technical colleges, and in community based organizations and agencies.

SUMMARY

Increased understanding of the foundations of work education leads to improved competencies of all professionals whether working in the nation's high schools, community colleges, universities, trade schools, federal employment and training programs, or in private business and industry. Improved competencies lead to success across jobs in the workplace learning and performance fields.

Beth Winfrey Freeburg
Marion Eugene Hall

HISTORICAL, PHILOSOPHICAL, AND ETHICAL FOUNDATIONS

OBJECTIVES

After completing this unit the reader should be able to accomplish the following:

1. Describe education in colonial America.
2. Describe American apprenticeship.
3. Discuss the beginnings of universal education in America.
4. Describe the early educational efforts of adults including the mechanics institute, American Lyceum, and manual labor movements.
5. Describe early American technical schools, trade schools, and corporate schools.
6. Identify and describe the three major educational reform movements in the common school.
7. Describe charity schools and the effects they had on the development and organization of public schools.
8. Describe the Lancasterian system of instruction used in many charity schools.
9. Describe faculty psychology and how it led to the inclusion of manual training in the schools of the day.
10. Identify and describe the three aspects of the common school that made it different from other school models of the period.
11. Describe early American kindergartens and how they differed from those operating in Europe.

12. Discuss the social-efficiency movement and how it affected the organization and curricula of early schools.
13. Describe the work of the two NEA committees on education and how their reports affected the development of the comprehensive high schools.
14. Describe why junior high schools were created and the purposes they were to serve.
15. Describe the exclusion of African-American women from mainstream domestic science and later home economics and the contributions they made to the field.
16. Discuss how the movement of women from the home into industrial jobs added to the importance of general education home economics programs.
17. Discuss why home economics was an attractive field for young African-American women despite the barriers they encountered in the field.
18. Discuss the plight of the industrial worker in the late 1800s and early 1900s.
19. Discuss why the philosophy of John Dewey has gained favor among many academic and career and technical educators of today.
20. Discuss the manual training movement in America.
21. Discuss the American sloyd system of education.
22. Discuss the arts and crafts movement in America and the concept of manual arts.
23. Discuss the development of industrial arts and how this program operates.
24. Describe the status of agriculture, home economics, and business education prior to 1917.
25. Discuss the status of practical arts programs in 1900.
26. Discuss the impact of the Douglas Commission on the vocational education movement.
27. Discuss the impact of the National Society for the Promotion of Industrial Education and the Commission for National Aid to Vocational Education on passage of the Smith-Hughes Act.
28. Compare and contrast the educational philosophies of John Dewey and Charles Prosser.

EARLY CAREER AND TECHNICAL EDUCATION IN AMERICA

Education in the colonies fell chiefly to the church and family. These entities shouldered the responsibility of teaching children how to read and participate in church services. In addition, families served as the center for apprenticeship training, the only means of education available for most American families. Most families were engaged in agriculture or in trades such as blacksmithing, carpentry, leather tanning, spinning, etc., and imparted their skills through the father-son, mother-daughter informal apprenticeship system. Wealthy families established private schools for their children or hired tutors, and some even sent their children to Europe for formal schooling. Churches provided elementary education in reading, writing, and church doctrine so that children could read and understand the Bible and church theology, but the amount of elementary

Taken from Scott, J.L. and Sarkees-Wircenski, M. (2008) *Overview of Career and Technical Education.* Homewood, IL: American Technical Publishers. pp. 149–202.

education many children received from their parents was limited because many parents were illiterate and therefore could only provide training in the things required to provide sustenance for the family. From the beginning, colonists supported the idea of literacy for their children, first as a means of purifying the soul and later to promote social equality through the belief that literacy was the right of all people (Barlow, 1976).

American Apprenticeship

The early colonists imported the concept of apprenticeship to America and adjusted the concept to meet their needs. Two forms of apprenticeship emerged: voluntary and involuntary or compulsory. Voluntary apprenticeship involved an individual agreeing to be bound to a master to learn a trade or craft. Involuntary or compulsory apprenticeship involved a master becoming responsible for poor children and orphans, thus providing a means of meeting their personal and occupational needs. In general, apprenticeship in colonial America followed the traditions of Europe, but town governments instead of guilds controlled apprenticeship through laws. These laws ensured that the children would receive an education and be prepared for productive work. It was only natural that town governments would regulate apprenticeship because all decisions regarding the town, e.g. political, educational, economic, and social, were made at the town meetings where people were invited and encouraged to attend and participate. Apprenticeship agreements provided for room and board; clothing; religious training; general education; knowledge, understanding, and experience in the trade skills; and finally, instruction in the "mysteries" of the trade or practices that had an elementary scientific basis. Both boys and girls were apprenticed beginning at age eight or nine for varying periods of time, with the norm being from five to ten years. Girls usually served until the age of eighteen or until they married.

Apprenticeship declined in importance in the colonial period and was dealt the heaviest blow by the factory system in the nineteenth century. There were a number of reasons for its decline: (1) the abundance of land, which encouraged young men and women to establish their own lives, (2) the long periods of apprenticeship (up to 10 years) in which marriage was forbidden, (3) the confusion of apprentices with indentured servants (individuals who were sold into binding work agreements to pay their way to America), (4) the mobility and freedom of the people, (5) the willingness of the frontier people to make do with handmade furniture and implements, (6) the immigration of mechanics and craftsworkers from Europe, and (7) the division of labor in household factories that no longer required workers to make complete products from scratch.

Apprenticeship served as the chief source of education and training for the masses for over 150 years. New systems of education and training were beginning to surface in a progressive America that would relegate apprenticeship to only a small number of people. While a small number of workers continued to be thoroughly trained through apprenticeship, most workers learned job skills from their parents or through on-the-job training (learning job skills through observation and imitation).

Beginnings of Universal Education

Apprenticeship in America was considered an educational institution and not solely a means to prepare skilled craftsworkers. Very early on, however, colonial town leaders recognized that many masters could not read and write well enough to provide adequate instruction in these subjects, which lead to the development of schools to meet this educational need. In 1647, the general court of Massachusetts ordered towns of more than 50 households to employ a teacher to provide basic instruction in reading, writing, and arithmetic. Other colonies began to recognize the importance of elementary education to the survival and progress of a free society. In 1685, Thomas Budd developed an educational plan calling for seven years of compulsory education in Pennsylvania and New Jersey, which was to be funded by rent from 1,000 acres of land donated to the community to support a school. The proposed curriculum was a common core of reading, writing, arithmetic, and specialty areas for girls (spinning, weaving, sewing) and boys (joinery, turning, shoemaking). His proposal for education was not well accepted, but in 1747 the Moravian Brethren established a public school based on Budd's plan in Bethlehem, Pennsylvania (Walter, 1993).

Ben Franklin was concerned with broadening educational opportunities for common people and expanding the curriculum beyond the classics and religion to include in the same school instruction in the common trades. The Franklin Academy of Philadelphia opened its doors in 1751 but this new educational experiment was short lived, and in 1775 the school changed direction toward serving the elite. This academy later became the University of Pennsylvania (Barlow, 1976).

Franklin's experiment in combining academic subjects and those of a practical nature in the academy spread to other parts of the country and has continued into today. A takeoff on the concept of an academy is the career academies that are currently operating in some states. Career academies are programs designed to integrate academic and CTE curricula organized around a theme (occupation areas such as health, aerospace, etc.), which are taught as a "school within a school" where students take a sequence of courses together. Career academy programs encompass a set of jobs ranging from those that require no postsecondary education to those requiring an advanced degree.

Following the Revolutionary War, the need for a common system of education emerged as an essential element of a democratic society. Leaders of the new independent nation of America viewed education as important in promoting nationalism and balancing freedom and order. Very early leaders saw the need for the development of moral character in its citizens in order to promote a good society that would have social and political order. According to Spring (1990), a new belief grew out of the Lancasterian system of instruction, which contended that moral character was shaped by the way students interacted in schools as well as through the learning of didactic materials. This belief of the importance of institutional arrangements in the development of moral character led to the conclusion that all children should be educated in a common school system. The notion of the development of moral character as well as intelligence through common schooling was supported by proponents of faculty psychology. Faculty psychology maintained that the human mind was divided into different parts, such as intelligence and morality, and that these different parts (faculties) were natural components of the individual and could be influenced by environment (schooling). Powerful leaders like Benjamin Rush, the leading physician of the late 1700s and the father of American psychiatry, and Horace Mann, the father of the common school, were strong supporters of faculty psychology and the belief that virtuous functioning of the moral faculty is dependent upon how it is cultivated. Both of these leaders argued that discipline and exercise of the various faculties of the mind where necessary for proper development toward the goal of the perfectibility of the human being and that controlling the institutional environment was critical to this process (Spring, 1990).

Post–Revolutionary War formal education was chiefly supported and conducted by the church or through special schools (charity schools) established for poor and orphaned children by wealthy individuals or societies. At the same time, a process of change resulting from a variety of forces (philanthropic, political, economic, social) and moving control of education from churches and private ownership to the state was underway. According to Spring (1990) a number of charity schools and juvenile reformatories developed in the United States in the early 1800s to help reduce the crime and poverty that resulted from a large concentration of people in urban areas working long hours at industrial jobs and thus failing to provide a nurturing family environment. This charity school movement was important for it provided the framework for the later development of public schools and was the first attempt to use schools as a means of socializing children and preparing them for an industrious way of life.

Charity schools were established as a way of providing students with instruction to create good moral character and to replace a weak family structure as well as a way of keeping children off the streets and away from criminal associations. Many charity schools adopted the Lancasterian system of instruction, which featured students seated in rows receiving instruction from monitors. These monitors had previously received instruction from the master teacher who was seated at the front of the room. Monitors were selected from among the better students in a class and wore badges indicating their achievement rank. The Lancasterian system of instruction for students was similar to the factory system of production for adults and was called a "manufactory of knowledge" (Spring, 1990).

A student's submission to this factory system of education was supposed to result in a sense of orderliness and obedience. Students were constantly moving through materials with monitors that required discipline and order. Students who did not comply or were idle suffered some unique punishment. Business and industry leaders advocated this system of instruction, for the virtues of submission, order, and industriousness were considered essential for functioning in the workplace. In addition, this system was appreciated because it was efficient, was inexpensive to operate, and could serve a large number of students with one teacher. However, charity schools presented a problem in the socialization process; they created a division between the social classes—the poor attended charity schools and the economically fortunate attended other private schools and public institutions.

According to Spring (1990), the belief in the ameliorating power of schooling became an essential part of the common school movement in the 1830s and 1840s. Charity schools provided a working model for the establishment of common school systems. It was hoped that the negative aspect of the charity schools, which reinforced social class differences, would be overcome in the common school, where students from different social classes would be mixed together in the same school facility. The emphasis on moral development that was the chief outcome of charity schools could be offered to all social classes in common schools. The Lancasterian system of factory-type education also carried over to the common school movement, resulting in the seating arrangement of students and strict disciplinary control of instruction. Charity schools also paved the way for the belief that schools could be one of the best institutions to solve the problems of society and that belief continues to receive strong support from the general public today. Charity schools embodied the belief that education could and poverty and crime in society and this belief also carried over to the common school system that followed.

The American constitution had not addressed education directly. Education was considered a state responsibility. In time, education in America came to be viewed as a "concern of the Federal Government, a function of the state, and a responsibility of the local government" (Barlow, 1976). In the late 1700s and early 1800s church schools and private schools, including schools for the well-to-do as well as the charity and reform schools mentioned earlier, served those whose parents desired an education for them and those who needed a moral education to escape poverty and crime. There were no compulsory school laws, so the vast majority of children did not attend school and were taught the basics of living by their parents or through apprenticeship. Vast numbers of immigrants were coming from Germany, France, and other European countries and their children needed instruction in the American way of life. There were considerable debate as to the type of education that was to be provided to students of the new republic, but everyone agreed that democracy required an educated citizenry. The private schools simply could not handle all of these students and leaders like Benjamin Franklin, Thomas Jefferson, Benjamin Rush, Samuel Harrison Smith, Samuel Knox, and later Horace Mann began to propose the formation of a common school system for all children.

Thomas Jefferson furthered the ideas and concepts proposed earlier by Benjamin Franklin that education should prepare a person for life in the business and social world. His plan for a universal, secular, public education system was proposed in 1779 in a bill to the Virginia Legislature entitled "A Bill for the More General Infusion of Knowledge." He believed in educational equality, secularization of school curriculum, separation of church and state, state systems of education, local educational initiative, and academic freedom. His bill, finally passed in 1796, was never implemented by the Virginia Government. Jefferson's terms "public school" and "universal education" had different meanings to the thirteen early states, and these two educational concepts received much discussion among educational philosophers and statesmen. While the idea of universal education and public expense continued to be debated, the movement to meet the basic educational needs of poor children through private or philanthropic efforts and apprenticeship continued (Martin, 1981).

According to Edwards and Richey (1963), three important occurrences that were landmarks in the movement to establish universal public education at public expense were (1) the development of a system of public primary schools in Boston in 1818, (2) the establishment of a public high school in Boston in 1821, and (3) the passage in 1827 of a law in Massachusetts requiring the establishment of high schools in cities, towns, and districts of 500 families or more. These three events, coupled with the semiprivate academies initiated by Benjamin Franklin that featured diversified and flexible curricula including English, classical studies, and practical studies, paved the way for a universal, public-supported educational system at the elementary and high school levels. Academies attracted all types of students, but they charged tuition. This made it impossible for many working-class families to afford the kind of education they wanted for their children. What was needed for most American youth was a system of free public elementary and secondary education (Martin, 1981).

According to Spring (1990), the 1830s and 1840s are known as the decades of the common school movement in the United States. Before the common school period, a variety of public and private school organizations existed. For example Boston had established the first system of urban education in the 1790s. States like New York and Pennsylvania supported a system of charity schools since a majority of students in those states attended private schools. In 1821, Ohio law permitted the taxation of all property in a district for the support of schools and the state created a permanent school fund in 1827. While these states and others had taken action to provide support for public education, they did not approximate the distinct features of the common school: a school under state control teaching a common body of knowledge to students from diverse social and economic backgrounds.

Spring (1990) points out the three distinct aspects of the common school movement that made it different from other educational ventures. The first was an emphasis on educating all children in a common schoolhouse. It was argued that if students attended a common school in which a common political and social ideology was taught, they would be prepared to deal with political and social problems and meet the expectation of national unity among diverse populations. A second aspect of the common school movement was the idea of using schools as a means of conveying government policies. Earlier schools were created to provide leaders and responsible citizens for the new republic, but the common school movement took this idea a step further by implementing government policy to solve and control social, economic, and political problems. This idea led to the concept of the common school as a panacea for society's problems. The third distinctive feature of the common school movement was the creation of state agencies to control local schools. This feature was necessary to carry out government social, political, and economic policies and to maintain some sense of uniformity in the ways schools were formed and operated.

While New York was the first state to create a position of state school superintendent in 1812 and while other states followed that lead, it was not until the 1830s that state supervision and control of schools was widely implemented (due in part to the tireless work of Horace Mann, the first secretary of the Massachusetts Board of Education in 1837). These three aspects of the common school originated with the idea that human nature could be formed, shaped, and given direction if students were educated in a formally organized institution. The concept of a common school had popular support from most segments of society. The African-American community saw schooling as a means for economic and social improvement. Leaders of educational reform saw the government-operated common school as a place where children could be educated for a more perfect society. Political factions like liberals and conservatives battled over the creation of a school system that would be beneficial to all members of society (Spring, 1990).

From the early 1800s until the passage of the famous Kalamazoo Case in 1872, which paved the way for the right of states to collect taxes to support education, the movement to establish universal elementary and secondary education at public expense gained momentum under the untiring efforts of educational leaders like Horace Mann from Massachusetts. Mann was a firm believer in public support and control of education and felt that only through free, public, popular education could the excesses of a capitalistic democracy be eliminated. He believed strongly that education should be equally available to all classes and delivered through non-authoritarian and non-sectarian means. He further believed that the emphasis of school studies should be on the practical needs of the individual and that the individual should be actively involved in the learning process. Beginning in 1851with Massachusetts, state after state began to pass legislation requiring the attendance of youth in state-supported schools until the eighth grade. By 1875, the nation's educational system became firmly established and attention began to focus on the high school curriculum, which was viewed by many to be too narrow and traditional. The high school was viewed as the "peoples" school and the belief was that courses should be offered that met the needs of all students. Some educational reformers were advocating expanding the curriculum to include the introduction of many new practical subjects like those offered in the early academies. It was through this reform movement, many years later, that vocational education (now CTE) had its beginning in the public schools of our nation (Martin, 1981).

Early Educational Efforts for Adults

While many children were receiving elementary education through church schools, secular Sunday schools serving all classes of students, private academies, philanthropic institutions, apprenticeships, and eventually state-supported schools, older youth and adults also needed access to education to learn the basics and to improve their knowledge of democracy, citizenship, and work. The American labor force strongly supported the concept of free, public-supported schools for their children and the development of schools that could provide the educational advantages offered through apprenticeship. They also recognized the need to develop educational opportunities for employed workers.

Mechanics Institute Movement

In the early 1800s in large towns and cities, a number of societies for mechanics and tradesworkers came into existence to meet the work preparation needs of their members. These societies were patterned after the mechanics institutes that originated in England. Another adult educational opportunity developed to serve the widely separated small towns of our country in the form of the American Lyceum (Martin, 1981).

The mechanics institute movement in Europe and America arose as part of an effort to improve the economic and social conditions of industrial and agricultural workers and to provide a pool of educated and efficient workers for the merchant and manufacturing ruling class. The first mechanics institute in America was introduced in 1820 when the General Society of Mechanics and Tradesmen of the City of New York opened a library for apprentices and established a mechanics school. The second and most famous of the mechanics institutes in America was the Franklin Institute of Philadelphia, opened in 1824. In 1825, a mechanics institute began in Baltimore, and in 1827 a mechanics institute was organized in Boston. These institutes were designed to provide adult workers with an education that encompassed technical and industrial instruction. The Franklin Institute included the following purposes, which were copied by succeeding institutes throughout the country: (1) to present lectures on the arts and the application of science to them, (2) to hold exhibitions of American manufacturers and award medals to worthy workers, and (3) to establish schools to teach architecture and mechanical drawing and chemistry as applied to the arts and mechanics (Martin, 1981).

The mechanics institutes were short-lived, with a few of them developing into technical or trade schools and the vast majority of them dying as a result of ineffective teaching and the formation of the land-grant colleges, American high schools, and private trade schools. These institutes conducted classes in the evenings for workers and played a significant role in the establishment of evening programs for adults in community colleges and the technical schools of today (Martin, 1981).

American Lyceum Movement

The American Lyceum, created to serve towns in the country, was the counterpart of the mechanics institutes, which served cities and large towns. It was based on the concept that "men may improve themselves through sharing their knowledge and expertise." The lyceum was an organization in the towns of America where speeches were given to increase the knowledge of the common person. From this humble beginning a local, state, and national federation was established called the American Lyceum. The format of the lyceum was simple; it gathered the inhabitants of a town, village, or district together and called upon members of the audience to contribute something from their own stores of experience for the benefit of all. Presenters could deliver a lecture, essay, or conduct a debate. Topics varied widely and included education, common schools, political and domestic economy, morals, public improvements, agriculture, geology, chemistry, manufacturing, mechanic arts, trade, architecture, geology, meteorology, geography, and mathematics. The lyceum movement, like the mechanics institute movement, was short-lived, but it served to popularize education for all and placed an emphasis on acquiring useful information. It perpetuated the idea that education was a community affair and responsibility, an idea that was critical in establishing publicly supported elementary and secondary schools (Martin, 1981).

Manual Labor Movement

Another American educational experiment, which took place between 1830 and 1845 and was designed to impart information about manual activity and work, was the manual labor movement. Like the mechanics institute movement, manual labor education was widely practiced in Europe before being brought to America. In Europe, manual labor was combined with subject instruction in schools. It was expected that combining the two would influence the health of the mind and body and would better prepare students for the larger social interests of life, politics, economics, and religion. In America, the manual labor movement was first introduced in order to integrate regular school subjects with agriculture training. Later, manual labor was used as a means of providing physical activity, reducing the cost of education by selling student labor or the products of that labor, promoting a respect for all kinds of honest work, building individual character, promoting originality, stimulating intellectual development, and increasing the wealth of the country. One of the early manual labor schools was organized by the Methodist Church at Cokesbury College in Maryland in 1787. It featured manual labor in gardening and carpentry taught by experienced persons. Manual labor gained acceptance in a number of literary (higher education) institutions, such as Oneida Institute in Whitesboro, New York, and in manual labor schools like those established in New Harmony, Indiana. Many private schools established for African-Americans, like Hampton Institute in Virginia established in 1868 and Tuskegee Institute in Alabama established in 1881, were manual labor schools that later incorporated manual training into their instructional programs. While manual labor schools were short-lived in the North, manual labor schools for African-Americans in the South continued to operate into the 1920s and beyond. The manual labor movement lasted for 15 years and then began to decline rapidly for a variety of reasons, including insufficient financial support from the institution or philanthropic society, manual work that was not educative, and manual work consisting of odd jobs not related to the student's interest or later calling in life (Martin, 1981; Walter, 1993).

Early American Technical Schools

The most popular subject for courses and lectures in the evening school programs of mechanics institutes and American Lyceums were those dealing with science and mathematics and their applications to agriculture and mechanical and manufacturing processes. As the teaching of science became more popular, a new type of full-time institution emerged. These institutions provided a curriculum to prepare individuals with advanced scientific knowledge in agriculture, the mechanic arts, and engineering. These schools were the early technical schools of our country and many of them later became engineering schools. One of the first of these schools was the Gardiner Lyceum in Maine, which opened in 1823, and was a full-time scientific and technical school at the college level. This school and other technical schools focused on the application of mathematics and science to agriculture and the arts. The Gardiner Lyceum lasted for about 10 years but was closed because of lack of financial support from the legislature of Maine (Bennett, 1926).

The second and most famous of the early technical schools was the Rensselaer School established in 1824 at Troy, New York. It was established to give instruction in the application of science to the common purposes of life. It was organized to benefit the sons and daughters of farmers and mechanics in the application of experimental chemistry, philosophy, and natural history to agriculture, domestic economy, and manufacturing. A number of well-cultivated farms and quality workshops in the vicinity of the school were used as work sites for students to experience the practical applications of scientific principles. The technical school attracted many college graduates because of its research and development activity and was recognized as the first graduate school in America. Today, it is Rensselaer Polytechnic Institute, one of the premier engineering schools in America (Bennett, 1926).

Still another school, organized in 1868, that emphasized practical training and the application of scientific principles was the Worchester County Free Institute of Industrial Science in Massachusetts. It was organized to train engineers, designers, of machinery, factory managers, and other masters of both scientific principles and practical details. One of the departments of the institute was a commercial machine shop that produced articles for sale made by the students during lessons. Students did not receive pay for their work; therefore, shop training had a wholly educative purpose. Shopwork was to be essentially on the same educational plane as laboratory science. The school claimed that combining shopwork and science was advantageous to both. Soon after the news spread about the success of the Worchester school, other engineering schools began to introduce shopwork into their programs (Barlow, 1976).

The Land-Grant Act of 1862 was one of the most important pieces of legislation concerning vocational and higher education ever passed by Congress. It had its beginning in the realization that the best way to promote agricultural education and agricultural innovation was to bring together the professors of science in higher education institutions and the practicing farmer who learned from daily labor how to improve agricultural production. Jonathan Baldwin Turner conceived the idea of a state industrial university that would educate for all agricultural and industrial occupations in the state. He made many presentations at various professional meetings promoting his scheme for establishing these state universities through funds provided by grants of state land. These lands could then be used to raise revenue to pay for establishing and maintaining one university in each state of the country. Professor Turner teamed up with Senator Justin Morrill of Vermont to introduce a land-grant bill to congress, which passed and was signed into law by President Abraham Lincoln in 1862. Thus, the nation received its most important legislative enactment supporting higher education that prepared teachers and trained leaders for agriculture and the mechanical arts. Out of this act, with its important amendments of 1890 known as the Second Morrill Act, which included funding for land-grant universities for African-Americans, came the present day state colleges of agriculture and many of the state universities (Bennett, 1926). Examples of schools that started as Agricultural and Mechanical schools include the University of Georgia, Mississippi State University, the University of Illinois, and the Ohio State University and African-American Universities like Alcorn University in Mississippi, Hampton Institute in Virginia, and Claflin University in South Carolina.

Trade School Movement

After the Civil War, the idea of "educated labor" as opposed to just "skilled labor" gained wider acceptance. The public schools of that day resisted the inclusion of practical subjects, especially those that would prepare people for work. But the necessity of providing an education for the vast number of workers could not be overlooked. For over fifty years, private academies had included some practical subjects in the areas of business, domestic science (home economics), agriculture and mechanical arts. Evening schools had been established as a result of the mechanics institute and lyceum movements to provide related academic instruction to interested adult workers. Agricultural was promoted through a number of societies and departments of agriculture were established in academies, colleges, and universities The land-grant colleges and universities were established by the provisions of the Morrill Act of 1862 to provide instruction in agriculture, mechanical arts, and domestic science for higher education students. The manual labor movement resulted in a number of institutions that attempted to meet the needs of the farmer and mechanic. One of the most famous of these manual labor schools was Rensselaer School established in Troy, New York in 1824. Some female seminaries were organized as manual labor schools as well. Here, young women experienced academic instruction combined with several hours of domestic work each day in order to reduce the operating expenses of the institution (Barlow, 1976).

Private schools for business (business colleges) had developed after 1850, and enrollment in these schools increased greatly after the typewriter was invented in 1873. Some high schools included business education as part of the curriculum in the late 1800s. Other high schools had included drawing as part of their curriculum after 1870, but not to prepare people for employment as drafters.

The reconstruction period following the Civil War demanded a new type of school that could prepare people for employment in the rapidly expanding industrial economy. The trade school movement emerged to provide a workable system of industrial education for all Americans, regardless of the color of their skin. One of the first trade schools was Hampton Institute in Virginia, established in 1868 to provide both liberal education and trade training to African-Americans to improve character and social status. Students devoted eight hours each day to the study of a trade through organized courses lasting for a three-year period, along with academic courses that required four years. If students completed the entire four-year educational experience they could earn a diploma. Booker T. Washington was one of Hampton Institute's most famous graduates. He later became principal at Tuskegee Institute in Alabama and had a distinguished educational career until his death in 1915 (Barlow, 1976).

The trade school was designed to provide specific trade training supplemented with directly related academic subjects. While the evening schools had attempted such training, they emphasized "book learning" and did not solve the need for an understanding of the basic trade skills. Some trade schools were private tuition schools, some were free, and others were sponsored by manufacturing companies in order to train their employees. The first trade school to offer specific trade training with supplementary studies directly related to each trade for the purposes of pre-employment as well as for employed workers was the New York Trade School established in 1881. This school was founded by a wealthy industrialist and was supported through contributions as well as tuition. It was operated by a board of trustees composed of influential educators and business leaders and was guided by a counsel of trade advisory committees—one of the early references to the use of vocational advisory committees (Barlow, 1976).

Two other early trade schools were the Hebrew Technical Institute organized in New York City in 1883 to serve the large number of Jewish immigrants and the William Free School of Mechanical Trades organized in 1891 in Philadelphia by a wealthy philanthropist. The Hebrew Technical Institute was more of a technical school than a trade school because it offered a wider range of subjects of a general nature. It was organized to combine trade training with general education subject matter. The Williamson School was dedicated to producing graduates who were as good as or better than journeymen who had just completed high quality apprentice-ships. The school was very selective in admissions but was entirely free to those who could meet admission requirements. The Williamson School started with a program of manual training for students, added some general education, and finally provided specific, intensive trade training. These three different types of trade schools gave birth to a number of trade schools throughout the country in the late 1800s (Barlow, 1976).

Corporate Schools

Another type of trade school was established by large manufacturing companies in an attempt to revise the old apprenticeship method of training high quality employees. It was believed that an apprenticeship program alone could not solve social and trade problems as well as a good trade school that incorporated academic instruction. One of the first corporate trade schools was established in 1872 by R. Hoe and Company—manufacturers of printing presses. The company needed a more educated class of workers to produce improved machinery and responded to this need by establishing a school that met two evenings each week. The school was free to employees and although it was not compulsory, advancement opportunities were tied to participation. The subjects studied in this school were those directly related to work requirements and included English, mechanical drawing, arithmetic, geometry, and algebra. The school proved to be very satisfactory and produced a superior class of worker (Barlow, 1976).

In 1902, the General Electric Company established an apprenticeship system that combined the activities of shop and classroom instruction. Academic content was selected that would help apprentices develop a better understanding of machines and machine parts. Included in the studies were courses in interpretation of mechanical drawings (print reading), sketching, and design of auxiliary tools required for modern manufacturing.

The plan to provide instruction in industrial science with apprenticeship learning proved to be highly successful and was copied widely by other companies. Modern companies are still using corporation schools to train workers (Barlow, 1981).

In 1901, the Baldwin Locomotive Works of Philadelphia established a corporation school that served three classes of workers through three different programs: (1) a program for those who had completed elementary school but had not reached 16 years of age that met three evenings each week for three years and provided instruction in geometry, arithmetic, mechanical drawing, and shop practice, (2) a program for those over 18 years of age who had more advanced education that met two evenings each week for two years and provided studies in chemistry, advanced mathematics, and mechanical drawing, and (3) an educational program for graduates of colleges and other advanced institutions who did not meet in classes but used reading and reports of technical journals as the teaching medium. The view of this company and many others was that public school education could prepare people better for apprenticeships, but evening schools would be necessary to supplement daily learning on the job in a company (Barlow, 1976).

Educational Reforms in the Common School

There were a number of other experiments launched by educational reformers to introduce manual activity into the common schools of America. These experiments were based on the teachings of European educators like Pestalozzi and Froebel and overly emphasized abstract learning of subject matter. One of these was the Oswego movement that began in Oswego State Normal School in 1861.

President Edward Sheldon adopted some of the teaching methods of Pestalozzi to train teachers to change their teaching methods from (1) memorization to reasoning and individual judgment, (2) book-centered to object-centered, (3) overdependence on words in text to oral instruction using objects, (4) teachers "keeping school" to teachers teaching with skill, (5) textbook lessons to oral language lessons, (6) text-dictated lessons to teacher-planned lessons, and (7) reciting what was read to expressing ideas (Wright, 1981).

A second educational reform for the common school was popularly known as the Quincy Plan, developed by Francis Parker in 1875 in Quincy, Massachusetts. The plan reoriented the school system toward an activity-oriented curriculum based on the needs and interests of children. Parker was able to Americanize Pestalozzi's ideas and develop a model of a child-centered curriculum that changed the teaching methods and curriculum of elementary education in this country forever (Wright, 1981).

A third reform period of elementary education occurred through the development of the American kindergarten, which was and remains the best example of a truly child-centered school. The kindergartens of America were based on the work of Friedrich Froebel and emphasized natural but directed self-activity and a focus upon educational, social, and moral ends. The kindergartens was intended to be a miniature ideal society—a place where people were courteous, helpful, and involved in cooperative activity. It emphasized doing, self-activity, individual expression, directed play, song, color, the story, nature study, gardening, and motor activity. Passive lessons were replaced with object lessons stressing the use of concrete objects that were real to the students. The kindergarten had individual development as its primary aim, motor expression as its teaching method, and social cooperation as its means (Wright, 1981).

The first public school kindergarten in the United States was established in St. Louis, Missouri in 1873 for the purpose of dealing with urban poverty. This kindergarten was to be a substitute for the habits of living and moral training formerly taught by families that had disintegrated in the slums of urban areas. A major effort of this kindergarten was to teach virtues and manners believed to be essential for healthy and productive community life. Emphasis was placed on teaching moral habits, cleanliness, politeness, obedience, punctuality, and self-control. Thus the kindergarten was not only to be a substitute for dysfunctional families but also to be a form of preparation for the habits required in school. A major goal of the kindergarten movement was to teach children habits that would help reform their homes. The kindergarten was viewed as a means to compensate for the supposed loss of socialization within the slum family; a way to protect young children from the influences of the street; a means of preparing children for entry into regular elementary classes; and a means of educating parents and improving family life. The first urban kindergartens in America departed significantly from Froebel's idea of nurturing children and giving them the opportunity for creative play and self expression; instead, the early American kindergarten stressed creating order and discipline in the lives of children and preparing them for entry into regular elementary schools (Spring, 1990).

The three educational movements just presented have reshaped the elementary schools of America. With the exception of some business subjects, the academies that once included practical subjects had all but eliminated them and had become primarily academic. In 1890, high schools were highly selective and had programs mostly for young people preparing to become professionals—ministers, lawyers, doctors, teachers, and engineers. With the passage of compulsory school laws, the high schools of America had a much larger and diverse student population to serve. Students came to the high school with different social and cultural backgrounds, with low to high abilities, and with a wide variety of future job interests. The high school was no longer a transition school for those planning to enter college, it became a terminal school for the masses. Many high schools began to offer a two-tract curriculum, a practical one for terminal students and a classical one for college bound youth. The comprehensive high school that offered two parallel curriculums became the common high school model. There were, however, some special purpose high schools, such as the manual training high schools, and later, special high schools for commercial and agricultural pursuits (Smith, 1981).

The industrial revolution created a large working class that demanded new educational opportunities for their children. Industrialization was more than the growth of factories and urban areas; industrialization was the foundation of the change in the whole structure of society. It created two classes of people: a working class and a non-working class. As time passed, the gap between these two classes continued to widen. Many of the children of the working class worked beside their parents in dangerous factories instead of attending school. The illiteracy rate of the working class soon became a problem. Parents who were illiterate and had limited practical skills could not pass on much of an education to their children. Crime was the second major problem plaguing society in the 1800s. It was out of these undesirable conditions of ignorance, delinquency, and human suffering that the drive to create a system of universal, free public schools was initiated. The working class wanted schools that would provide the basic academic skills for their children and would also include instruction in practical subjects that would prepare their children for better jobs than the ones they presently endured.

Drawing—initiated by Richard Mulcaster in England a hundred years earlier— had already been included in a number of high schools (it was a required subject in Boston high schools in 1836), but there was growing public sentiment in favor of including of other types of practical subjects. Elementary schools had included more activity into their curriculum and some high schools had established programs in agriculture, general business, and domestic science (home economics) and more were being added as a result of land-grant universities. Technical schools at the college level had already experimented with combining shopwork with academic subjects in science and mathematics and found this curriculum vastly improved the preparation of their engineering graduates. America was moving from an agricultural to an industrial society, and business and industry advocated the inclusion of subjects that would give students, as part of their general education, the underlying principles and practices of industrial occupations so they would be better prepared to live in the new industry society.

A great debate arose among educational leaders of the late 1800s over the inclusion of more practical subjects into the curriculum of the public high schools of America. Proponents argued that the lack of practical education in the public schools represented a deficiency in the school system and a lack of commitment to serving the majority of the students. Opponents claimed that the introduction of practical subjects would interfere with the intellectual culture and that schools were not the place to prepare people for business and industry. From 1875 to 1900, the pages of educational literature covered the debate over what should be taught in the public schools: subjects preparing people for only culture or a mix of courses preparing people for both work and life. At the center of the debate was the new manual training movement championed by two engineering professors, Calvin Woodward, and John D. Runkle (Barlow, 1976).

Manual Training Movement

The manual training movement in America began at Washington University in St. Louis, Missouri and at the Massachusetts Institute of Technology (MIT). In 1878, Professor Calvin Woodward, dean of the Washington University Polytechnic faculty, implemented a program of shopwork for engineering students so they could become more versed in the application of engineering principles through the use of tools and machines. He became convinced that secondary students should have access to shop courses and that a combination of academics and shopwork would increase student interest in school and provide a means of supplementing the mostly liberal education of the day. In 1880, with the philanthropic support of several prominent business leaders, the first manual training high school in America was established in St. Louis. The new school was a four-year institution that provided instruction in mathematics, science, drawing, language, and literature, as well as practice in the use of tools. Students attended class six periods each day, one period for academic subjects and a double period for shopwork. The desired end of manual instruction was acquisition of skills in the use of tools and materials, not production of specific articles or direct preparation for the trades. The laboratory method of instruction was used. This consisted of graded lessons in the use (demonstrated by the instructor) of ordinary tools, with opportunities for students to ask question and take notes, followed by the students proceeding with their own work (Roberts, 1971).

In 1876, John Runkle, president of MIT, took a large party of students and faculty to the Centennial Exposition in Philadelphia where he saw the solution to one of his most pressing problems: the methodology of providing practical training to his engineering students. He and his students were fascinated with the Russian exhibit of the Imperial Technical School of Moscow under the direction of Victor Della Vos. The four instructional directives of the Russian system that impressed them the most were: (1) separate instruction shops from construction shops, (2) provide only one kind of work in each shop, (3) provide as many work stations and tools for each station as a teacher can reasonably handle in one instructional period, and (4) graduate the instruction in each shop according to the difficulty and complexity of the operation. Upon Runkle's return from the exposition, he formulated and received approval from MIT to establish an American version of the Russian manual training system for his engineering students at MIT. In addition, he established the School of Mechanic Arts, which was open to qualified grammar school students (Barlow, 1976).

Woodward and Runkle soon became advocates for introducing manual training into the public schools of America. They proposed its inclusion because training in the manual arts was desirable and advantageous for all students, regardless of their educational goals. They felt strongly that the education in the schools had been dealing too exclusively with the abstract and the remote and not enough with the concrete and the near at hand. They saw manual training as a way to improve the basic education of all youth. Woodward listed the following outcomes of manual training when combined with academic and moral training:

- longer attendance at school
- better intellectual development
- more wholesome moral education
- sound judgment of men and things
- better choice of occupation
- material success for the individual and the community
- elevation of the perception of manual occupations from brute, unintelligent labor to work requiring and rewarding both knowledge and skill
- basis for an individual career in the mechanical arts
- first step in the solution to labor problems
- basis for higher education

Woodward truly believed in manual activity as a way to enhance general education. He recognized that the overwhelming sentiment of educators was that vocational education had no place in the schools but should be the province of business and industry. He also recognized that business and industry wanted manual training to serve more of a vocational education purpose, but organized labor opposed manual training for fear it would flood the market with poorly trained workers who would be inferior to those produced through apprentice programs. He was keenly aware of the many critics that believed that anything manual could never be elevated to the same plane as the classics and made a part of the public school curriculum. Some educators supported the concept of manual training as long as it was conducted in a separate school (Wright, 1981).

The success of the manual training school in St. Louis led to the establishment of manual training high schools in other cities and towns. Like the pioneer manual training school, most were established as separate and apart from academic high schools and supported as part of a higher education institution or through donations and tuition. One of the earliest separate manual training schools was the Baltimore Manual Training High School, founded in 1884 as part of the regular public school system supported at public expense. The second manual training school, which was part of the public supported school system, was the Philadelphia Manual Training School established in 1885 (Roberts, 1971).

Special Manual Training Schools Become Technical Schools

As manual training high schools grew in popularity, their curriculum included a broader range of courses and elective opportunities. This expansion of programs and curriculum in manual training high schools later led to the formation of the combined cosmopolitan high school (comprehensive high school) and the technical school. Some manual training schools in larger cities placed more emphasis on shopwork, drawing, and science and changed their names to technical schools. Among the first of these schools was the Technical School of Springfield, Massachusetts, established in 1898. This school provided instruction in the usual high school subjects together with the fundamentals of drawing, design, and hand and machine tools. Soon other technical schools were established in New York City, Detroit, and Chicago (Barlow, 1976).

Beginning of Junior High and Comprehensive High Schools

In the early 1900s a complex set of social, economic, and educational conditions led to changes in the traditional high school, which was portrayed as an elite institution serving only a small minority of students. At first, a small number of students chose to attend high schools. They were typically students preparing for higher education and entrance into the professions. As more and more students entered high school, the one-track academic curriculum began to be challenged by students, parents, and business and industry leaders. Early high schools were dedicated to providing students with an academic and civic education along with a few opportunities to develop practical skills. Social conditions, however, forced students and parents to exert pressure on schools to provide training for success in the job market as well. It was this emphasis on education to serve economic and social needs that shaped the development of the comprehensive high schools, which featured a differentiated curriculum to serve the vocational aspirations of students. The result was establishment of a three-track curriculum: a college preparatory curriculum for those intending to enter higher education institutions, a more general curriculum for students who planned to enter employment in the community immediately following high school, and in some schools, a vocational curriculum that would prepare students for semi-skilled and skilled jobs in business and industry. The comprehensive high school was also challenged to take on more of the social development of youth through the addition of schools activities such as clubs, student government, assemblies, organized athletics, and other social events (Spring, 1990).

In the early 1900s a great debate arose between those who advocated the older academic concepts of the high school and those who embraced the concept of social efficiency. Most business and industry leaders supported the doctrine of social efficiency. Most business and industry leaders supported the doctrine of social efficiency and wanted education to produce individuals who were trained for a specific role in society and who were willing to work cooperatively in that role. First, advocates for social efficiency argued that school curricula should be organized to meet the future social needs of individual students. Second, they argued that school activities should be designed to teach cooperation as preparation for future social activities. Third, social efficiency advocates proposed a differentiated curriculum based on the future social destination of the student. In other words, social efficiency proponents wanted the high school curriculum to be based on the key concepts of cooperation, specialization, and equality of opportunity. They wanted high schools to increase their emphasis on cooperation and reduce competition. They felt that in the modern corporate society workers needed to learn to work together and not engage in battles with management in a competitive environment. They felt that in the modern corporate society workers needed to learn to work together and not engage in battles with management in a competitive environment. They wanted students trained in special areas for specialization. It was reasoned that efficiency would increase by allowing individuals to concentrate fully on a single individual task. Finally, they wanted schools to ensure equality of opportunity in the labor market by objectively selecting students for different educational programs. These doctrines of social efficiency ran counter to the traditional academic thrust of the high school embraced by many educators (Spring, 1990).

The National Education Association (NEA), founded in 1857 in Philadelphia, took up the challenge of advancing the cause of public education. Several important NEA committee reports eventually paved the way for the modern comprehensive high school. In 1892, at the beginning of the rapid expansion of high schools, the NEA formed the Committee of Ten which took up the debate over an educational system designed to provide everyone with a common education versus an educational system organized to provide everyone with a specific education based on a future social destination. This committee ruled against creating different curricula for the college-bound and non-college-bound high school students and endorsed four different courses of study, all of which would meet college admission requirements. They were afraid that a two-track system of education would perpetuate a class system of education. With increasing numbers of youth attending high schools and the recognition that the preparation of American youth was critical to the future of the nation, pressure mounted for changes in the American high school. Social-efficiency educators who wanted to shape the high school to meet the needs of the corporate state stepped up their attack on academics in the high school. Recognizing the need to address concerns about the American high school, the NEA organized the Commission on the Reorganization of Secondary Education in 1913. The report of this commission, *Cardinal Principles of Secondary Education,* established the framework for the organization of the comprehensive high school. It called for the creation of a comprehensive high school that would include a wide variety of curricula designed to meet the needs of different types of students. The commission ruled against the establishment of separate schools for special curricula and argued for the establishment of a comprehensive high school where all students could come together and experience a wide variety of contacts that would help them make intelligent choices as to the type of education and careers they wanted to pursue. The commission used the arguments of social efficiency to justify the comprehensive high school, namely the two important aspect of democracy—specialization and unification. The comprehensive high school became a mixture of planned social activities and a variety of curricula that was designed to prepare a new generation for a society based on large organizations and occupational specialization (Spring, 1990).

According to Spring (1990) vocational education, vocational guidance, and the establishment of the junior high school were key elements in the development of the comprehensive high school and its goal of developing human capital. Prior to 1900, little support existed for public education that would train students for specific occupations. However, it was becoming increasingly clear that youth would have to receive training for jobs if the United States was going to enjoy favor in world markets relative to that enjoyed by other industrialized countries. Vocational education, with its promise of providing specialized training, was viewed as an important part of the comprehensive high school that would help promote industrial efficiency through proper selection and training of manpower. Early claims as to why vocational education needed to be included in the high school curriculum were articulated by the 1914 Commission on National Aid to Vocational Education. Vocational education (1) met the individual needs of students for a meaningful curriculum, (2) provided opportunity for all students to prepare for life and work, (3) helped foster a better teaching-learning process—learning by doing, and (4) introduced the idea of utility into education. The real development and expansion of vocational education in high schools came in the form of federal support for these programs through the Smith-Hughes Act of 1917, which was passed around the time when comprehensive high schools were being established. The act provided incentive to include vocational programs as part of the comprehensive high school curriculum.

The social-efficiency movement in education in the early 1900s also led to a vocational guidance movement. This movement helped educators understand how to select students for programs that would lead to more efficient development of human capital. Vocational guidance was needed, not only to guide students toward appropriate occupations, but also away from destructive occupations. Vocational guidance was viewed as a means of changing the general pattern of industrial development. Frank Parsons, founder of the first vocational guidance bureau in Boston in 1908 (often called the father of vocational guidance), developed the guidance process that would allow efficient matching of students to constructive occupations. Educational guidance was defined as the process for helping students select educational programs that matched their interests, abilities, and expected future occupations. Ideally, the counselor would match a student to an occupation and then to a course of study that would prepare the student for a chosen vocation (Spring, 1990).

Prior to 1900, the common school model consisted of eight years of elementary school and two to four years of high school. In 1905, New York established its first seventh and eighth grades for intermediate schools, or junior high schools, and began adding the ninth grade by 1915. National attention was drawn to the

California school systems's three-year intermediate school in 1910 with its differentiation of curriculum. One of the main arguments for establishing junior high schools was that they would facilitate the guidance of students and provide a differentiated curriculum. Proponents of junior high schools advocated three major opportunities: an opportunity to offer different courses of study, an opportunity to adapt instruction to the two sexes and to the requirements of high schools and vocational schools, and an opportunity to classify students according to ability. Early junior high schools placed emphasis on guidance and soon implemented the advisory or homeroom period to fulfill this function. Socialization was another important outcome for junior high schools, and clubs began to form to deliver specific activities that would enhance instruction in selected areas. The establishment of the junior high school and comprehensive high school brought about a major change in the school's role in providing equality of opportunity. In the early days of the common school movement, education was meant to provide this opportunity by giving everyone a common or equal education. In 20th century junior and comprehensive high schools, equality of opportunity was provided through vocational guidance and a differentiated curriculum (Spring, 1990).

The comprehensive high school plan occurred in large cities at the beginning of the 20th century. This plan brought together the courses and equipment of general, commercial, and manual training education into one school with courses classified as either academic or technical—a practice carried over into today. The academic program of these early comprehensive high schools included general subjects, classical subjects, domestic science, and manual training. The technical program consisted of commercial subjects, technical cooperative subjects, art and music. The comprehensive high school offered a wider choice of curricula and courses, which reflected the growing concern that students should receive preparation for more than college; they should receive preparation for career options not requiring a college education (Roberts,1971).

Movements for Including Practical Subjects into High Schools

Between 1880 and 1920, a number of educational movements emerged in and effort to infuse practical subjects into the high schools. These movements were manual training, American sloyd, arts and crafts, manual arts, industrial arts, and vocational education. The manual training movement as envisioned by Runkle and Woodward did not last many years for a variety of reasons, one of which was the wide variety of programs that sprang up under the name of manual training. Also, manual training exercises that did not result in useful products did little to capture the interest of American youth. Then, there was the constant pressure to make manual training more vocational to prepare youth for industrial jobs.

American Sloyd

Woodward's manual training system, adapted from the Russian system, was one method of hand tool instruction that entered public schools. Another was a manual training method in Sweden called sloyd. In 1888, Gustaf Larson, a teacher of sloyd in Sweden, came to America and established sloyd instruction in Boston. Very early, Larson had to make changes in traditional sloyd methodology to make it work in America: (1) Swedish models that were first used had no appeal to American youth and had to be replaced with models of interest to students, (2) the practice of students working from models was replaced with students working from teacher-prepared drawings and later from student-developed drawings, as drawing was already an important subject of study in general education, and (3) the mostly individualized method of instruction was broadened to include more group instruction, which had become successful in American schools. These adaptations of Swedish sloyd led to the term "American sloyd" (Smith, 1981).

The major differences between manual training and American sloyd were the focus sloyd had on the development of the learner rather than the development of skill in the use of hand tools, and the use of trained teachers rather than the use of skilled craftsworkers to teach tool skills. Manual training focused on teaching the use of specific tools by completing exercises or making incomplete objects without sufficient attention directed to the individual needs and capacities of youth. Sloyd, on the other hand, placed careful attention on developing the capacities of the individual in the selection of graded models and projects that were interesting to youth and on the sequence of instructional tasks based on the capacity of each youth to create a useful object. Other advantages of sloyd over the Russian system of manual training were (1) the prominence of form study of the object, (2) the greater variety of tasks, (3) the importance of using completed models, and (4) the importance of the teacher being a trained educator (Smith, 1981). According to Kincheloe (1999), proponents of American sloyd proclaimed that the instructional system developed the student physically, mentally, and morally; its manual regimentation employed the central nervous system, thereby enhancing students' kinesthetic coordination, nurturing their neurological complexity, and developing their talents and habits. These advocates also proclaimed that participation in sloyd instruction would make school more interesting and encourage students to stay in school longer. The sloyd movement lasted only a few years, but it did change the way practical art subjects were taught. It also encouraged the use of trained teachers (Smith, 1981).

Arts and Crafts Movement

The arts and crafts movement, which began in England as a backlash against the poor quality of manufactured products, came to America after 1880 when Charles Leland introduced the plan into the schools of Philadelphia. The arts and crafts movement emphasized artistic design, practical skill development for vocational as well as for future work applications, the revival of artistic pursuits all but eliminated by industrial machinery, and the teaching of decorative arts to the abilities and interest of youngsters. Subjects in the arts and crafts included drawing, wood carving, clay modeling, mosaic work, leather carving, metal embossing, embroidery, carpentry, wood turning, wood inlaying, and ornamental wood sawing. Students were given considerable freedom in the selection and designing of projects. The arts and crafts movement had little effect on manual training in America. However, it did broaden the materials and tasks used to train student in tool usage, and it emphasized the importance of artistic design in the construction of useful projects. While the arts and crafts movement lasted into the early twentieth century, primarily through the efforts of various arts and craft societies, its application in schools declined as the public became more concerned with industrial skill development training (Smith, 1981).

Correspondence Schools

Toward the end of the 19th century, the population in America increased rapidly due to immigration (mostly from Europe) and due to the rural population's need to establish large families to help perform the many tasks of life. Correspondence schools were established to bring education and training to those who (a) did not live near enough to a school to attend classes, (b) could not attend classes because of their rigorous work schedules, (c) wished to receive additional training beyond what they had received in public schools, and (d) did not have a wide selection of courses in their local schools. Many of these correspondence schools offered courses in vocational areas as well as academic areas. One of these early schools was the American School of Correspondence.

The American School of Correspondence was founded in 1895 by R. T. Miller, Jr. in Boston, Massachusetts based on the belief that all Americans should have an opportunity to receive a high school diploma and learn the job skills required to prepare them for the working world. In 1898, Mr. Miller founded the American Technical Society (now American Technical Publishers, Inc.) to publish the books and guides for his correspondence school. Typical trade subjects offered by the American School of Correspondence included mechanical drawing, carpentry, and the electrical trades. Mr. Miller moved these companies to the University of Chicago campus in the early 1900s to take advantage of central mailing and to utilize personnel from the University to grade correspondence papers. Both of these companies continue to meet their original founding purposes today.

Manual Arts

Manual arts was primarily a name given to a revised form of manual training that placed its emphasis on applied design and constructive and decorative arts. Charles Bennett was considered the "father of manual arts" for he spoke out about the neglect of the aesthetic principle in manual training and advocated that free as well as mechanical drawings should be encouraged and that beautiful and useful objects should be produced as an outcome of the learning process. He advocated combining creative design with the teaching of tool usage to help students produce beautiful objects that would be expressions of the art produced by youth. In 1909, Bennett outlined a classification system for elementary school manual arts that included five areas: graphic arts, mechanical arts, plastic arts, textile arts, and bookmaking arts. The impact of the manual arts movement was chiefly changing the name from manual training and combining drawing and design with construction activities in mechanic arts (Smith, 1981).

Industrial Arts

In 1904 Charles Richards, editor of *Manual Training Magazine,* suggested in his editorial that it was time to change the name of manual training and manual arts to industrial arts. He concluded that manual training was nothing less than a subject field of study teaching the basics for the industries that had become fundamental to modern civilization. He spoke of the content of industrial arts being drawn from industry (Smith, 1981).

Dean James Russell of Teachers College, Columbia University expanded the idea of industrial arts in 1909. He suggested that the elementary schools (grades 1–8) of the nation had become too bookish and recommended that economics and scientific studies be included in the general education curriculum of the elementary school. He described economics as "the study of industries for the sake of a better perspective on man's achievements in controlling the production, distribution, and consumptions of the things which constitute man's natural wealth." He stated that "the chief consideration of content for courses of study should be on the ordering of the industrial processes by which raw materials are transformed into things of greater value for the satisfaction of human needs." Russell, following the philosophy of John Dewey, believed that industrial arts could be the basis for the elementary school program. He advocated that manual training, fine arts, domestic art, and domestic science be dropped from the elementary school curriculum (an unpopular idea) in favor of the elements of industry, or industrial arts (Smith, 1981).

As industrial arts programs replaced manual training in the elementary school, the terms manual training and manual arts gave way to the term industrial arts. The focus of manual training programs evolved toward the study of occupations that change the forms of materials to increase their value for human usage and of the problems of life related to these changes as proposed by Frederick Gordon Bonser in 1923. Industrial arts was to be a study with manufacturing industries as the curriculum base and an understanding of the functioning of our industrial society as the goal. Russell and Bonser advocated industrial arts at the elementary school level and vocational education at the secondary school level, but the concept of industrial arts began to replace the name of manual arts and manual training in secondary schools over a period of years (Smith, 1981).

Like manual training and manual arts, industrial arts was to be a component of general education and not of vocational education. It was a subject field that all students could take in order to understand the industrial society in which they lived. Manual arts and manual training programs had made significant changes in instructional practices prior to the advent of industrial arts. They had included drawing and design as an integral part of the curriculum; incorporated the marking of useful articles to increase the interest of youth; used field trips to expose students to industry and industrial processes; introduced flexibility into the rigid instructional methodology, allowing students to experiment and engage in problem-solving activities with a variety of tools and processes; and incorporated more individualized instruction and the assignment of work to students on the basis of their abilities and interests.

At the same time that the industrial arts movement was beginning, a strong vocational education movement was taking shape. As America became the world's foremost industrial power, competition in world trade accelerated, and business and industrial leaders were in desperate need of more skilled workers. A growing number of influential leaders began a crusade to introduce some form of vocational education into the secondary schools of America. Manual training programs came under attack by vocational education proponents as being inadequate to meet the educational needs of 90% of the people who would be involved in industrial pursuits. The constant public pressure placed on manual training programs caused some educators to introduce more of a vocational flavor to their instructional programs, which led to "vocationalizing" some manual training programs. Some manual training teachers actually organized their programs like a commercial factory in which students did production work for schools and community organizations. Instructional emphasis was placed on duplicating industrial operations and processes and developing skills that would later lead students into jobs in industry and the trades. Some proponents argued that manual training needed to be eliminated entirely and replaced with vocational education programs. Others recommended that manual training programs continue but serve a pre-vocational purpose: as a feeder for vocational programs at the secondary level (Barella, 1981).

The growing public sentiment for vocational education programs at the secondary level made it difficult for industrial arts programs, designed to be part of general education, to grow and reach their full potential as an important part of the education of all students. With the passage of federal legislation establishing vocational education programs in secondary schools, the attacks on manual training, manual arts, and industrial arts subsided, and the field was free to find its niche in the American educational system. Influenced by the progressive education movement of John Dewey, in 1947 William Warner refined the ideas of earlier leaders in industrial arts by identifying major areas, or courses of study. These were management, communications, power, transportation, and manufacturing. Out of Warner's work emerged two theories for the field of industrial arts. One suggested that the domain of industrial arts education was industry, with its products, processes, materials, management, organization, and occupations, as well as the impact of industry. The second theory for industrial arts reflected the changes that occurred in society as a result of technology and recommended that the curriculum of industrial arts programs should be based on the study of technology and its evolution, utilization, and significance. As industrial arts programs matured and developed a more consistent identity, they became an important component of practical arts education at the elementary and secondary school level until they were slowly converted into technology education programs in the late 1980s (Wright & Barella, 1981).

Agriculture Education Prior to 1917

Prior to the Civil War, agriculture was conducted using age-old techniques and crude implements. Very little scientific knowledge was applied to raising crops or animals. Following the Civil War, tremendous progress was made in mechanizing agricultural production. Many new field machines were developed, such as improved tractors, binders, planters, and harvesters. Transportation with refrigeration capacity made it possible to move produce quickly over long distances. The amount of food produced through mechanized farming exceeded the demand even in a rapidly growing America, and the prices of food fell sharply, forcing many small farms out of business and causing a flood of rural people to move to urban centers for their livelihoods. The education of youth and adults engaged in agriculture was provided through agricultural societies, lyceums, some academies, and a few private agricultural schools, manual labor schools, and public schools (Barlow, 1976).

As agriculture became more scientific, individuals engaged in this occupation needed formal education beyond what they could learn through apprenticeship on the farm or through efforts of societies and lyceums. Some early school efforts used the work-study method to offer elementary courses in agriculture and a means of acquiring general knowledge. Some academies that served students who completed grammar school offered courses in agriculture. A few high schools offered courses in agriculture, which consisted mostly of textbook study and instructor lectures. Some special agricultural schools were established to provide scientific information related to agriculture. Courses in agriculture were offered in some manual training high schools. The Country Life Movement, beginning in 1890, stimulated the development of general agriculture study in elementary schools, and by 1910 seventeen states had passed laws requiring courses in elementary agriculture (Barlow, 1976).

The Morrill Land-Grant College Act of 1862 established colleges and universities that provided programs combining practical applications of agriculture and industry with scientific knowledge. This act was established out of concern that private and public schools, agricultural societies, and mechanics institutes were not enacting needed changes in their respective occupational areas. At first, the Land-Grant Act dealt a tremendous blow to existing agricultural programs in high schools because it was assumed that colleges and universities would meet the educational needs of agriculture. However, it soon became apparent that farmers were either unwilling or could not afford to send their sons to universities. Agricultural societies began to advocate the inclusion of agriculture as a subject area in high schools. In 1881, the Storrs Agricultural School was established in Mansfield, Connecticut. This school combined practical farm studies and related academic instruction. In 1888, a secondary school of agriculture was organized as part of the Department of Agriculture of the University of Minnesota. In 1889, the state of Alabama passed legislation establishing secondary agricultural schools (Barlow, 1976).

These special agricultural schools required many students from farms to travel long distances and to reside at the school for two or more years. This made attendance at these schools too expensive for the children of farmers as well as making it impossible for them to be utilized on the farm. The solution that gained increasing support was the establishment of courses of agriculture in numerous schools that were supported with public funds and located within a reasonable distance from the farm. This allowed for students who finished the common school to further their educations (Barlow, 1976).

Congress recognized the need to provide more support for agricultural education than was being provided through existing institutions. For example, by the 1870s many state colleges like the Michigan Agricultural College and the Farmers High School (which evolved into Pennsylvania State University) had already begun experimental work, and by 1875 agricultural experiment stations were established in Connecticut and California followed by 13 additional states that established formal experiment stations by 1887. In 1887 Congress recognized the importance of agricultural experiment stations and passed the Hatch Act, which provided for the scientific study of agriculture in addition to the study already being provided in land-grant institutions. In 1890, the second Morrill Act was enacted to expand funding for land-grant institutions and to create at least one land-grant college or university in each state for African-American students. In 1914, Congress passed the Smith-Lever Cooperative Extension Act to increase the extension work of land-grant colleges and universities. This act provided for instruction and practical demonstrations in agriculture and home economics to be delivered to persons not attending the land-grant colleges through field demonstrations and publications and incorporated the county agent system of agriculture, with instructional centers located in each county and supported by federal and county funds (Barlow, 1976).

Agriculture and agricultural education were enhanced considerably by the many farm journals that began being published as early as 1810 with the first American Periodical, the *Agricultural Museum,* and by 1841 more than 30 farm journals were being circulated to over 100,000 subscribers. By the 1890s a number of secondary agricultural education programs began to appear in local areas and in states. The number of secondary agricultural education programs expanded rapidly after the passage of the Smith-Hughes Act of 1917 and by 1920, more than 31,000 students were enrolled in agriculture courses. The number of agricultural education programs continued to grow and by 1940, more than 548,000 students were enrolled. By 1970 the number reached over 853,000 students. One of the significant events that led to increased enrollment in agricultural education was the establishment of the Future Farmers of America in 1928.

The mechanization of agriculture began around 1880, but technology was already at work changing farming with the invention of the steel plow in 1837 and Cyrus McCormick's reaper at about the same time. In 1892 the first gasoline-powered tractor was introduced to the farm and by 1910 some 25,000 tractors were doing the work of the farm. New plant breeding techniques introduced plants that were more uniform and easier to pick by machines and also produced higher yields. Animal husbandry practices also became increasingly mechanized with new innovative breeding techniques, specialized feeds, and pharmaceuticals that greatly improved the growth and productivity of farm animals. Breakthroughs in the chemical industry led to chemical fertilizers that made it unnecessary to let land lie fallow so it could restore itself and increased productivity through higher yields and less plant diseases. The mechanical, biological, and chemical revolutions that began in the middle 1800s changed farming forever, reducing the number of workers required for production agriculture and expanding agriculture-related jobs significantly. Agricultural education was needed to provide individuals with the information and skills needed to implement the breakthroughs in production agriculture, and the number of students enrolled in agricultural education classes increased nationwide until the 1980s when the farm crisis began to affect enrollments (Rifkin, 1995).

Home Economics Education Prior to 1917

The establishment and growth of home economics was made unnecessarily difficult because of prejudice against the education of women. There was a general feeling in colonial America that women had little need for education for their place was in the home. Education beyond simple reading and writing was geared to producing ministers and leaders of the state, and since women were deemed ineligible for these positions, their education was of little concern. During the colonial period, girls as well as boys were taught how to read and write by their parents (if their parents were literate), by their churches, by a literate apprenticeship master if they were lucky, or, after the Massachusetts law was passed requiring towns to establish schools for their inhabitants, by a schoolteacher. Industrial schools for orphans, poor children, and the delinquent often included instruction for girls in household labor and sewing. Academies, like the Franklin Academy founded in 1751, were open to both boys and girls, and other academies and private schools copied its curriculum, which included both academic and practical subjects. Girls attending the Boston public schools were taught needlework along with academic subjects. Girls and young women of the affluent often attended private venture schools where they were taught academic subjects and leisure activities such as needlework, dancing, drawing drawing, and vocal and instrumental music. For the vast majority of girls and young women who lived in rural America on farms and on the frontier, education beyond reading and writing was very limited until after the Revolutionary War (Roberts, 1971).

Following the Revolutionary War, special schools for women began to appear. They were founded by those concerned with extending educational opportunities for women beyond the common school. Female seminaries emerged along the Atlantic seaboard with one of the earliest established in Troy, New York in 1821— Emma Willard's Troy Female Seminary. Female seminaries taught domestic or household duties and intellectual subjects. In 1820, girls were taught sewing in the primary grades of Boston schools, and in 1835 the practice was extended into the grammar schools. Girls were taught domestic responsibilities through direct application in the private manual labor schools that emerged in the first half of the nineteenth century. The first high school for girls was opened in Worcester, Massachusetts in 1824, followed by schools in Boston and New York two years later. Oberlin College in Ohio, founded in 1833, was one of the earliest coeducational institutions of higher learning. In 1837, Mary Lyon founded Mount Holyoke Female Seminary in Massachusetts. This was a college-level institution providing elementary instruction for women in cooperative living and requiring them to engage in domestic work two hours each day to help reduce the operating expenses of the institution. In 1842, the New England Female Medical College was founded, and in 1855 Elmira College in New York, which was the first women's college to grant degrees, opened its doors. This college required its young women to take courses in domestic science and general household affairs (Barlow, 1976).

The Morrill Act of 1862 resulted in the establishment of departments of domestic science in colleges and universities to provide leadership for establishing home-making in the public schools of America. Iowa State College started formal instruction in home economics in 1872, which began with instruction in housekeeping and over a period of years included the areas of cooking, house furnishing, care of children, care of the sick, management of help, dressmaking, physiology, domestic chemistry, laundry work, and sewing. These institutions were the forerunners of the movement to establish educational programs for women that paved the way for homemaking programs in the public schools after 1880 (Barlow, 1976; Roberts, 1971).

Two important women stimulated the development of home economics in the middle of the nineteenth century. Catherine Beecher published her *Treatise on Domestic Economy for the Use of Young Ladies at Home* in 1841. This scholarly work covered nearly every phase of homemaking and was adopted widely by public and private schools, setting the pattern for homemaking education. The acknowledged leader of the home economics movement, however, was Ellen Richards, a graduate of the Massachusetts Institute of Technology in the field of chemistry. She used her knowledge of chemistry for the improvement of living conditions in the home, particularly in sanitation. It was her work in the study of the family and the problems of homemaking that made her the leader of the home economics movement. She was instrumental in establishing a series of ten annual conferences to address issues related to the content and training methods of home economics in manual training schools and was a key leader in establishing the American Home Economics Association in which she served as its first president (Barlow, 1976).

After 1880, when the manual training school movement began, domestic science courses were included among the practical arts. These programs were sometimes called household science, domestic science, domestic art, or home economics. In 1872, Massachusetts authorized schools to offer courses in sewing and other industrial education subjects. The Kitchen Garden Movement, which began in 1877, utilized small toys, games, and songs to teach household arts to children. The Kitchen Garden Association, which became the Industrial Education

Association in 1884, affirmed that domestic science was an important program of manual training and began to develop subject matter and methods of instruction for home economic subjects. The Philadelphia High School for Girls offered a course in sewing in 1880 and extended this course into the elementary school in 1885 (Roberts, 1971).

Household science (the forerunner of domestic sciences and home economics) courses such as cooking, sewing, laundry, rug weaving, gardening, basket making, and child care were offered for African-American girls at Hampton Institute in 1868 and at Tuskegee Institute in 1881 (Ralston, 1992). The household science curriculums in some African-American schools were an integral part of the industrial education movement. Household science was emphasized for African-American women on the grounds that it would prepare them to become better domestic workers, as well prepare them as better prospective wives and mothers, and help them maintain moral, religious, and sanitary home environments (Ralston, 1978). Most of the manual labor schools for African-Americans included household science courses for young African-American women. According to Roberts (1971), domestic science courses began to appear in manual training schools and many public schools throughout the country at the close of the century.

The period between 1899 and 1908 was significant for the home economics movement. It was at this time that a series of ten annual conferences led by Ellen Richards were held at Lake Placid and Chautauqua, New York and another was conducted in Boston. These conferences addressed a broad range of topics concerning economics and social aspects of the home including training teachers, courses of study, evening schools, extension teaching, rural school work, home economics in women's clubs, and manual training and education for citizenship. The fourth conference produced an early definition of home economics as "the study of laws, conditions, principles, and ideals which are concerned on the one hand with man's immediate physical environment and on the other hand with his nature as a social being, and is the study especially of the relation between these two factors." In addition, the issues regarding terminology for the field were discussed, resulting in the conclusion that the term domestic science was not adequate to describe the various homemaking programs. The sixth conference brought closure to the terminology discussion with "handwork" chosen as the elementary school term, "domestic science" in the secondary school, "home economics" in normal and professional schools, and "euthenics" in colleges and universities.

In 1913, the American Home Economics Association, founded in 1909, developed the *Syllabus of Home Economics*, which offered a new definition for home economics and described what topics could properly be included under the term. Home economics was defined as "the study of the economic, sanitary, and aesthetic aspects of food, clothing, and shelter, as connected with their selection, preparation and use by the family in the home or by other groups of people." Courses in home economics could be offered as cultural, technical, or vocational in nature and could be offered in the primary and secondary school or in college. The major divisions of the subject matter were food, clothing, shelter, and household and institution management (Roberts, 1971).

Under the leadership provided by the American Home Economics Association and state and local educators, every state had some type of home economics in one or more schools prior to 1917. It was offered as part of general education in most schools with two periods per week as the typical delivery system. For the most part, home economics programs emphasized cooking and sewing, with few comprehensive programs. Such programs would be established a few years later after passage of the Smith Hughes Act of 1917 (Roberts, 1971).

African-American participation in the mainstream profession of home economics was limited because African-Americans were not always welcomed within the larger profession. According to Ralston (1992) African-American home economists were not involved in the Lake Placid Conferences and state associations of the American Home Economics Association in the South were segregated until after the passage of the Civil Rights Act of 1964. An African-American vocational student organization, the New Homemakers of America, was created to serve home economic students. Despite the barriers that prevented their full participation in the field, African-American home economists devoted considerable energy and enthusiasm to the profession. African-Americans embraced the field of home economics for its fundamental purposes, developed their own network and opportunity structure, and emphasized social purposes that served to interpret the field to those of ethnic racial diversity.

Perhaps the professional who best exemplified the contributions of African-American leaders in the field was Flemmie Kittrell, chair and subsequently dean of home economics at Howard, one of the top African-American universities. For over 30 years Dean Kittrell devoted herself to the mission of opening up the field of home economics for people of all cultural backgrounds. She became an internationally known nutritionist who developed the agenda that home economics was important to all people, regardless of nationality, creed, or color. She implemented this agenda at Howard University through advocating the requirement of home and family education for all students. Dean Kittrell's research in nutrition became the basis for such programs as Head Start in the United States and for nutrition policies in countries such as Liberia and West Africa. Dean Kittrell was a tireless leader and advocate for all home economics professionals, encouraging them to become more involved in researching, learning, and working to understand people of various ethnic or racial backgrounds for the good of the profession (Ralston, 1992).

According to Ralston (1992) African-American women embraced home economics as a viable field, even though they were excluded under the law from equality of human rights and equal employment opportunities, for three major reasons. First, as the field of home economics continued to develop, especially with the help of federal funding, marked improvements were made in the quality of curricula in predominantly African-American schools, and African-Americans assumed more control over the goals of instruction. Second, as enrollments in public high schools increased as well as in African-American colleges and universities, employment opportunities for home economists expanded. In 1945, some 23 African-American colleges offered home economic programs and extension and 4-H programs, resulting in jobs in teaching and extension that served African-American populations. Over the years, African-American home economists had developed an extensive network that provided employment opportunities. The third reason that African-American women embraced the field of home economics was that the mission and subject matter of the field included the values of strong family bonds, extended family networks, and the desire to raise children, all a part of African-American culture from the beginning and continuing through slavery and emancipation. Home economics was attractive to African-American women for it held the promise of helping African-American people improve their lives and helping families meet the basic needs for food, clothing, and shelter. Furthermore, young African-American women were often the first in their families to complete a college education and enter a profession. Because of the constant struggle of African-American families to earn a living after emancipation, from sharecropping in the South, which was eventually eliminated by agricultural machinery, to mass migration to urban areas of the North, where many families lived in poverty, no ambition seemed higher to African-American women than to carry on the tradition established by the many women who had given their lives to the development of a high standard of home life (Ralston, 1992).

In the late 1880s and early 1900s, women in general began to work in low-wage jobs in such places as clothes-making, textile, and food-processing plants. Rapid expansions in the industrial economy brought women into offices as file clerks and typists, jobs that were once held almost exclusively by men. Although most women prepared themselves for the roles of wives and mothers, industry needed women in jobs that involved tasks that were closely aligned with homemaking. As office workers, women were often called upon to do the routine tasks associated with homemaking. Jobs in clothes-making, textile, and food-processing plants were viewed as a natural extension of the female predisposition and ability. As more and more women entered work in industry, they were faced with balancing family roles with work roles, a situation that continues today. From very early on, it was recognized that home economics needed to be taught as part of the general curriculum for both boys and girls to prepare them for shared family roles and not exclusively for work preparation in the form of vocational education (Kincheloe, 1999).

General Business Education Prior to 1917

Historical records indicate that the English grammar schools and semiprivate academies offered courses in arithmetic, handwriting, and bookkeeping in the eighteenth and nineteenth centuries for the purposes of preparation for life as well as for college entrance. According to Roberts (1971), bookkeeping was included in the curriculum of the English High School of Boston in 1823. Under an 1827 Massachusetts law, bookkeeping, along with other subjects, was specified for certain schools of the state. Some high schools of the nineteenth century offered commercial courses for general education as well as for practical application. In the nineteenth century, a number of private business colleges emerged to prepare individuals for business and commerce, which reduced the emphasis on establishing business education programs at the secondary school level.

According to Kincheloe (1999), more than 90 percent of clerical workers in the nineteenth century were men, with one out of every five jobs described as clerical. By 1850, clerical workers were making very good salaries, exceeding nearly 90% of salaries made by other workers. In the late 1800s women began to enter clerical occupations, and the status of the occupation began to shift from high-skill with demanding tasks to low-skill with routine tasks. Expanding business and industrial firms needed more clerical workers, and women were willing to work for less money than men. Instead of the fully trained clerical person, many companies began to employ clerical workers to perform specialized the tasks that were created as a result of the application of Fredrick Taylor's scientific management practices, which were implemented to introduce efficiency and time management into the clerical office. Specialized job titles began to emerge such as stenographer, typist, file clerk, receptionist, and several levels of secretaries.

At the beginning of the twentieth century, a renewed interest developed in providing business education as part of the manual training high school curriculum for purposes of mental discipline, general education, and vocational usage. It was at this time that business education was introduced into the junior high school curriculum for purposes of general knowledge, exploration for careers, and to reduce the dropout rate. Business education remained an important part of the practical arts until federal legislation, in the form of the Vocational Education Act of 1963, cleared the way for vocational business education programs to receive federal funds (Roberts, 1971).

The Smith-Hughes Act of 1917 did not authorize funds for the promotion of business education programs, but it did create the Federal Board for Vocational Education, which was required to conduct studies, investigations, and reports to aid states in the establishment of vocational schools and classes and in the delivery of instruction in commerce and commercial pursuits. An executive order issued by President Franklin D. Roosevelt in 1933 changed the Federal Board for Vocational Education from an administrative to an advisory board and transferred it to the Department of the Interior, which assigned the duties of the Federal Board to the U.S. Commissioner of Education. In 1935, Commissioner Zook placed the responsibility of rendering professional services to all forms of business education, both general and vocational, to the Commercial Education Service of the Vocational Division. In 1938 the name of the Commercial Education Service, which was rendering services to commercial and business education, was changed to the Business Education Service. In the order that resulted in the name change, business education was defined as an inclusive title that included not only such courses as secretarial science, accounting, business law, business management, general business, consumer business education, and business economics, but also retailing, merchandising, salesmanship, and other distributive subjects. In 1939 by executive order, the U.S. Office of Education was transferred from the Department of the Interior to the Federal Security Agency. The U.S.

Office of Education in its several locations did provide some leadership to business education in the form of studies, investigations, and reports concerning commerce and commercial pursuits. The George Dean Act of 1936 cleared the way for federal funding for one phase of business education—that of distributive education. Other aspects of business education were considered a part of general education or educational outcomes desirable for all students. The Vocational Act of 1963 finally cleared the way for federal funds to be used to support programs serving individuals who were seeking gainful employment in business and office occupations (Zelliot, 1952).

Status of Practical Arts Programs in 1900

In the early years of the twentieth century, the programs of agriculture education, business education, home economics education, industrial education, and industrial arts had been established in manual training schools, public elementary and secondary schools, and public and private colleges and universities. For the most part, these programs were viewed as having a cultural, social, and general education purpose, with vocational usage being an unplanned natural outcome. Special schools were created to offer instruction in these occupational areas for vocational purposes, including public and private trade schools, technical schools, evening schools, colleges of engineering and technology, and corporation schools.

Practical subjects were added to school curricula to supplement the purely academic content of most schools with the hope that these subjects would hold the interests of students and help them better understand academic content through practical application. It was also hoped that this would reduce the dropout rate, which was estimated to be about 50% by the eighth grade. In addition, these subjects were believed to be important for preparation for life in an industrial economy (Barella, 1981).

The impact of industrialism was being felt in every phase of human life. Technological innovations created new industries and expanded existing ones, causing a tremendous need for semiskilled and skilled workers. The prevailing view of the day regarding business was that individuals had the right to regulate their economic affairs without government interference. This philosophy caused government to side with big business and adopt a hands-off policy concerning the regulation of business and industry. This in turn allowed big business to exploit its workers. For most people at this time in American history, the process of creating wealth seemed to be more important than religion, education, or politics. John Dewey understood the reality of corporate power and its abuses and spoke out about it. He also voiced his disdain of the inequitable distribution of wealth and the irrational system of production that placed major emphasis on making a profit and little emphasis on the human needs of workers. Most Americans accepted the belief that the individual was responsible for personal success, and this belief was reinforced in the schools of the day. Slogans like "America is the land of opportunity" revealed the belief that success was personal and not social. It was believed that economic inequality resulted from differences in an individual's ability and motivation and not his or her social circumstances. Hard work allegedly paid off and when it did not, individuals were assumed responsible for personal failures. Increasing production, employment, and income became the measures of community success and personal riches the result of hard work. Labor formed unions to protect themselves against the exploitation of workers and bitter battles occurred between management and labor over the employment of poorly trained workers, working conditions, and pay (Barella, 1981).

Kincheloe (1999) describes the plight of the worker in the early 1900s as very dismal. In the name of efficiency, scientific managers de-skilled most jobs by taking a particular activity and analyzing it to determine minute steps, then dividing the tasks into subtasks and assigning workers to do the subtask with little or no idea of the shape or form of the product being produced. Rarely were workers able to see how their everyday labor contributed to the larger goals of the business or to a better way of life. Workers were reduced to machine caretakers with little hope for advancement in jobs or society. Workers daily experienced the removal of thought and creativity from their work. What managers wanted included the following: (1) increased output without wage increases, (2) reduced labor turnover, (3) reduced conflict between labor and management, (4) more loyalty among workers, (5) workers who respected authority, and (6) workers who valued the work ethic. If workers did not fit this mold, they were fired, and few workers could afford to lose their jobs as they lacked the education and skills to obtain other jobs. Workers were forced to work in mindless jobs for long hours and low pay and often in dangerous and unhealthy conditions. Workers were not compensated for injury or death. That idea was unheard-of in the late 1880s. While employers wanted skilled workers, they were often more interested in the attitudes of individuals. They wanted to employ dependable, passive, cheerful workers who would endure simplistic work that demanded little analysis or creativity. They began to see the public high schools as a place where students could be prepared for these adult roles. They looked to the public schools and to practical arts programs in particular to provide students with good work attitudes and a strong work ethic since these programs were generally not designed to produce skilled workers.

Business and industry leaders were not particular advocates of public education as the vehicle to produce an educated citizenry; they supported education primarily to protect their economic self-interests and their need for workers with attitudes conducive to the industrial organization of labor. They were not necessarily strong supporters of manual training and later vocational education in public schools as a source of skilled workers but were motivated to gain some control over these types of educational programs in the hope that they could undermine union-controlled apprenticeship programs.

The United States had become the industrial giant of the world, and the demand for goods internally and across the seas spurred increased production and industrial activity. Even though many skilled workers were coming to this country from Europe as a result of relaxed immigration laws, American industry needed additional skilled workers and they became very vocal about the need to better prepare workers in the public schools of this country. Pressured by business and industry, a growing number of educators were ready for a new type of education that included specific skills training. They began to endorse the idea, strongly supported by industry, of vocational education programs that would produce individuals with specific skill training and good attitudes toward work. It was hoped that vocational programs would impart to students industrial values like respect for hard work, submission to authority, willingness to follow directions, and loyalty to the company and that employing workers with these values would eliminate political labor problems. No longer could educators ignore the issue of preparing students for industrial occupations. Some form of vocational education was inevitable. What was needed was a thorough study of the interest in and need for more specific vocational training than was being offered through existing practical arts programs. This study came in the form of the Douglas Commission Report of Massachusetts in 1906, and the research of the National Association for the Promotion of Industrial Education and the Commission of National Aid to Vocational Education (Barella, 1981).

Douglas Commission of Massachusetts

Massachusetts had led the way for universal public education thanks to the leadership of educators like Horace Mann. According to Kincheloe (1999), Mann endorsed the concerns of business and industry leaders when he advanced his arguments for a common school that would teach a common core of values and support and promote industrial development. Mann promised that the common school would reduce the poor's hostility toward the wealthy and that it would prepare factory workers who were productive, respectful, easily supervised, and who would avoid participation in strikes or worker violence. Massachusetts had been one of the first to introduce practical subjects into the public school; they were among the leaders in the manual training movement; and they had passed legislation opening the way for the establishment of industrial schools in 1872. Industrial progress and the education of their citizens was important to the leaders of Massachusetts, as evidenced by the re-evaluation of their education system in 1905 to see what needed to be done to better meet the needs of expanding industry. Governor Douglas, responding to a legislative mandate, appointed the Commission on Industrial and Technical Education, which consisted of nine representatives from manufacturing, agriculture, education, and labor, to investigate the need for industrial education (the term then used for vocational education), to determine the extent to which existing programs were meeting this need, and to make recommendations regarding how to modify existing programs to serve a vocational purpose (Barlow, 1976).

The commission released its report, which contained the following findings, in 1906:

1. There was widespread interest in the general subject of industrial education or special training for vocations.

2. There was a practical and specific interest among manufacturers and wage earners because of personal need. Industry wanted workers with more than skill in manual operations; they wanted workers with "industrial intelligence."
3. There was a growing feeling of the inadequacy of the existing public school system to fully meet the needs of modern industrial and social conditions. Schools were found to be too exclusively literary in their spirit, scope, and methods.
4. Their was no evidence that the people interested in industrial education had any concrete ideas as to its scope and method.
5. Their investigation had aroused the suspicion and hostility of many of the labor unions of the state.
6. There was little opposition to technical schools but significant opposition to trade schools.
7. There was general agreement that the financial support for technical education should be born wholly or in part by the state (Barlow, 1976).

The Douglas Commission Report concluded that the lack of industrial training for workers increased the cost of production. The report stated that workers with general intelligence, technical knowledge, and skill would command the world market. It emphasized that the foundation for technical success required a wider diffusion of industrial intelligence and that this foundation could only be acquired in connection with a general system of education in which it was an integral part of the curriculum from the beginning (Barlow, 1976).

The Douglas Commission Report generated considerable interest. It brought to the nation's attention the urgent need to introduce programs of vocational education into the nation's secondary schools to prepare workers for America's growing industries. The report was instrumental in starting a definite movement for the inclusion of vocational education in secondary schools, which would come some eleven years later with the passage of the Smith-Hughes Act of 1917.

National Society for the Promotion of Industrial Education

The widespread interest in industrial education discovered by the Douglas Commission prompted a group of 13 influential men to gather at a meeting of the Engineer's Club in New York City in 1906 to discuss the formation of a society to further the promotion of industrial education. Two leaders of manual training, James P. Haney and Professor Charles R. Richards, were responsible for arranging the meeting. Prior to adjournment, these men agreed on the need to establish an organization and appointed an ad hoc committee to plan a fall meeting at which organizational details would be discussed and a large group of industrialists and educators would be invited to discuss their views on industrial education. At the fall meeting, the National Society for Promotion of Industrial Education (NSPIE) was formed. Its mission was the promotion of industrial education by focusing public attention on the value of an educational system that could prepare young men and women to enter industrial pursuits. More specifically, the society wanted to unite all the forces of industrial education by providing them with opportunities for the study and discussion of mutual problems and by making them aware of experiences in industrial education both in this country and abroad (Barlow, 1976).

One of the first accomplishments of the society was to define the term industrial education. It was determined that industrial education referred to "that area of education between manual training and college engineering." Industrial education was intended to apply to vocational training of direct value to the industrial worker. While the focus of the society was originally on the development of education for trade and industrial workers, it broadened its scope to include other areas of vocational training (Barlow, 1976).

In 1908, the NSPIE formed state societies. These state societies would carry on the work of informing the citizens of their states about industrial education. The NSPIE realized that each state had different educational, industrial, and social conditions that would alter its views toward industrial education. Prior to the Smith-Hughes Act, these societies were most influential in the passage of state legislation favoring industrial education (Barlow, 1976).

The National Society for the Promotion of Industrial Education included some of the most informed and dynamic leaders in manufacturing, labor, education, business, and government. Included were James P. Haney, Charles Richards, David Sneeden, and the foremost leader in the development and promotion of vocational education in America, Charles Prosser. Prosser served as executive secretary of the NSPIE and was the person most influential in securing passage of the Smith-Hughes Act of 1917, which established the principle of federal support for vocational education in America. With passage of the Smith-Hughes Act of 1917, the NSPIE changed its name to the National Society for Vocational Education, and in 1925 it combined with the Vocational Association of the Middle West to form the American Vocational Association (AVA), which continues to this day to meet the needs of vocational educators (Barlow, 1976). The AVA is now the Association of Career and technical Education.

Commission on National Aid to Vocational Education

In 1914, President Woodrow Wilson responded to a joint resolution of Congress and appointed a special nine-member commission to study the issue of federal aid to vocational education. Senator Hoke Smith of Georgia was named as chairman, and Charles Prosser, executive director of the NSPIE was one of the members. Hearings, conferences, and reports were used to gather information to determine (1) the need for vocational education, (2) the need for federal grants, (3) the kinds of vocational education for which grants should be made, (4) the extent and conditions under which aid should be granted, and (5) the proposed legislation. Six months after its creation, the commission issued its report recommending grants for vocational education in agriculture and the trades. The report included the following important recommendations, which were included in the Smith-Hughes Act of 1917:

1. Grants should be used for training vocational teachers, paying part of teachers' salaries, and making studies and investigations helpful to vocational education.
2. Federal aid should be given to publicly supervised and controlled schools of less than college grade.
3. Instruction should be limited to youths over age 14 and designed for profitable employment in agriculture and the trades.
4. Three types of classes should be developed to provide vocational education: day school, part-time, and evening classes.
5. A federal board should be established to oversee federal grants.
6. State boards should be created to administer the grants and states should develop a state plans for administering vocational education programs.

The commission included a draft bill, which was brought before Congress in 1914 but was not acted upon until President Wilson urged its passage in 1916 Representative Dudley Hughes of Georgia introduced an important revision to the original bill that included home economics as a vocational program eligible for federal grants. With the help of the NSPIE, the American Federation of Labor (AFL), The National Association of Manufacturers (NAM), the National Education Association (NEA), the Chamber of Commerce of the United States, the Commission on Aid to Vocational Education, the Vocational Education Association of the Middle West, and the general will of the people, federal aid to vocational education became law in the form of the Smith-Hughes Act of 1917 (Barlow, 1976).

EDUCATIONAL PHILOSOPHIES OF JOHN DEWEY AND CHARLES PROSSER

In the late 1800s, industrialization had changed nearly every aspect of society, and educational theory was being challenged by emerging social and economic issues. America was a democracy that required every citizen to be literate and to be able to contribute toward the good of society. Industrialization had created great wealth for a few, but living and working conditions were deplorable for many. The gap between the wealthy and working class was widening and education was viewed then, as it is today, as the solution to economic and social problems.

Universal educational opportunities were available for most Americans up to at least the eighth grade. Maximizing each individual's chances for lifelong learning and assisting individuals to obtain the "good life" was the ultimate goal of the educational system. The school curriculum of the late 1800s, however, was focused on preparing students for higher education in colleges and universities despite the fact that only a few students would complete formal schooling and enter higher education institutions.

For most Americans, what was needed was a more practical curriculum that would prepare them for work. Manual training was introduced into schools as a form of general education with the hidden objective of elementary preparation for work. Leaders in education and in business and industry began to realize that the diverse student population enrolled in schools was not receiving the type of education needed to prepare for life and work. Many who lead the fight for the introduction of vocational education in the public schools did so because of a strong belief that schools needed to provide equality of educational opportunity. They felt that the schools' almost exclusive concentration on academics required for a few students to enter college was undemocratic and unfair to the majority of students, most of whom did not finish high school. They were also concerned with the social issues of the working class and believed that individuals who were trained for a job and became wage earners would be more likely to become contributing members of their communities and to society in general. Finally, they recognized that people who work for wages and salaries buy goods and services produced or delivered by others, which strengthens the economy and contributes to the wealth of the country. The vocational education movement, which became a reality with the passage of the Smith-Hughes Act, was based on economic, social, and philosophical factors (Calhoun & Finch, 1982).

As America entered the twentieth century, drastic changes were being made in educational practice and thought. The century old faculty psychology, which held that the mind was made up of separate, independent entities or faculties such as memory, imagination, reason, etc., was giving way to American Herbartian psychology, which emphasized the interests of the child and de-emphasized memorization and the textbook method of learning. This psychology lead to the development and presentation of carefully sequenced lessons that were of interest to the child and within the child's capacity to understand. The focus on teaching methodology did much to open the curriculum to the inclusion of practical subjects (Smith, 1981).

An equally important change that was occurring was a gradual switch from the philosophy of idealism, which had been the prevailing philosophy though most of the nineteenth century, toward pragmatism, instrumentalism, or experimentalism. Pragmatism emphasized the concrete over the abstract problems of life. It emphasized an understanding of social institutions and the evolutionary character of societies and their ideologies. The role of education was not to train the mind like it was a muscle under the mindset of faculty psychology, but to awaken and broaden the interest of the child. Pragmatic theory proposed that children and youth needed to be trained in productive thought and ethical action and given opportunities to test their ideas whenever possible. Education was to be viewed more as a science and use scientific methodology and scientific assumptions. Teachers were to use the problem-solving method, which involved students in identifying a need or problem; analyzing the problem; experimenting with various solutions; developing workable theories; selecting the most appropriate solution; and testing the chosen solution through concrete application. Under this philosophy, teachers were free to engage students more directly in concrete applications of what they were learning. Two influential psychologists-philosophers that promoted pragmatism were William James and John Dewey (Calhoun & Finch, 1982).

John Dewey was a strong advocate for vocational education. He was critical of the existing traditional liberal education of the time and felt that it did not provide the skills and attitudes that individuals needed to live in an age of science. He believed that children were inherently active beings who wanted to communicate with others, to construct things, and to investigate and create. He advocated accommodating these natural traits in schools through activities such as language, manual and household arts, nature study, dramatics, art, and music. He believed that the curriculum should include a series of situations in which students could be involved in solving problems of interest to them such as the "project method" being employed in some manual training schools that engaged students in activities that required thinking as well as doing. In his book published in 1916, *Democracy and Education*, Dewey expressed the view that education needed to have a practical outcome to be meaningful. Dewey was the undisputed leader of the progressive education movement; a movement that is still affecting education today (Smith, 1981).

At about the same time Dewey was promoting his views that education should become more democratic, another educator-philosopher was advocating the same outcome but with a different view on how to accomplish it. Charles Prosser had become an influential leader in the vocational education movement and his aggressive leadership had earned him the position of executive secretary of the National Society for the Promotion of Industrial Education in 1912. He was appointed by President Wilson to the Commission on National Aid to Vocational Education and was instrumental in developing the draft bills for federal aid to vocational education that were passed in 1917 as the Smith-Hughes Act. Undoubtedly, the leaders who were involved in the passage of the Smith-Hughes legislation were aware of the progressive education philosophy advocated by John Dewey, which centered around meeting the needs of individuals, but it was Prosser's philosophy of essentialism—a vocational education philosophy grounded in meeting the needs of industry—that permeated the vocational education act. These two philosophies continue to affect vocational education today and should be understood by teachers and leaders of vocational education (Griffin, 1994).

Griffin (1994) studied the educational philosophies of John Dewey and Charles Prosser in her dissertation and compared and contrasted the important tenets of each philosophy. Both men wanted to make education more democratic and more practical. Both supported vocational education and favored programs that mirrored real-life situations and made use of on-the-job training. However, the manner in which vocational education programs were to be infused into the curriculum differed significantly between these two men. See Figure 1.1.

Charles Prosser contended that public education in a democracy was not intended for individual fulfillment but to prepare its citizens to serve the society. He expressed the idea that the interests, needs, and aptitudes of individuals should be served in order to perpetuate society. Conversely, John Dewey's idea of the purpose of education in a democracy was to equalize individual differences for the improvement of society. Dewey recognized the rapid change that was occurring in society and maintained that individuals needed to be educated to personal initiative and adaptability so they would be better prepared to cope with the changes affecting life in the family, community, and workplace (Griffin, 1994).

The philosophy of Charles Prosser emerged in the Smith-Hughes Act and remained the dominant educational psychology guiding vocational education until the passage of the Vocational Act of 1963 and subsequent amendments. Prosser established sixteen theorems based on his philosophy, which were instrumental in the formation of vocational education programs and practiced for over 50 years. The impacts of these theorems are still felt somewhat today. Prosser's theorems, reworded, are as follows:

1. Vocational education should replicate the actual work environment and occur in the most realistic setting possible.
2. Vocational education should take place where the training jobs are carried on using the same operations, the same tools, and the same machines that are used in specific occupations.
3. Vocational education should provide students with the thinking habits (technical knowledge and scientific problem-solving skills) and the manipulative skills required in the occupation itself.
4. Vocational education should be planned and delivered in a manner that capitalizes on the student's interest, aptitudes, and intrinsic intelligence.
5. Vocational education is not for everyone. It is for those individuals who need it, desire it, and are able to profit from it.
6. Vocational education should provide opportunities for students to repeat operations of thinking and manipulative skills until habits are formed characteristic of those required for productive employment.
7. Vocational education should be taught by instructors who have had successful experiences in the application of skills and who have the required knowledge.
8. Vocational education should be comprehensive and of sufficient duration for students to master the competencies required to obtain and retain employment in a chosen occupational area.
9. Vocational education should prepare individuals primarily for the occupations as they currently exist and future labor markets should be a secondary concern.
10. Vocational education should provide opportunities for students to perform operations on actual jobs when possible and not just simulated work tasks.
11. Vocational education curricula should be based on the actual work tasks performed by experienced, competent workers and should be verified and updated frequently.
12. Vocational education curriculum should include the directly related body of content that is unique to occupational areas and emphasize the application of mathematics and scientific principles to problems of the occupation.

DIFFERENCES IN EDUCATIONAL PHILOSOPHIES: CHARLES PROSSER AND JOHN DEWEY . . .		
	Prosser	**Dewey**
Philosophical Criteria		
Teaching Styles and Methodologies	Sequential, begins with basic facts. Instructors have strong industrial experience.	Begins with problem solving–results in knowledge base. Instructors have strong educational experience.
Administrative Structure	Seeks advice from industrial leaders, planner, implementer; is cost effective.	Facilitator of personal choices, advisor.
Personal/School Philosophies	Accents the needs of industry.	Accents the needs of individuals.
Benefits of the Program	Students gain marketable skills to become productive society members.	Students gain life skills and adaptability skills.
Prosser/Dewey Dichotomy		
Transferability of Skills	Transfer occurs naturally between similar tasks. Transfer is not a focus.	Transfer is the focus of a broad education.
Training to Work Transition	Facilitated through current equipment and instructors with industrial backgrounds.	Facilitated through focus on transfer.
Development of Problem-Solving Skills	Acquisition of a base of knowledge precedes problem-solving skills.	Instruction begins with problem-solving skills.
Continuation of Prosser/ Dewey Philosophy		
Major Goal of the School	To meet the needs of industry and prepare people for work.	To meet the needs of individuals and prepare people for life.
Influencing Factors on School Success	Follow Prosser's Sixteen Theorems.	Follow guidelines in Dewey's *Democracy and Education.*

... DIFFERENCES IN EDUCATIONAL PHILOSOPHIES: CHARLES PROSSER AND JOHN DEWEY		
	Prosser	**Dewey**
Social and Economic Factors		
School Climate	Individualized differences are recognized, and all people and types of work are seen as having value.	Individual differences are equalized.
Adequate Supplies, Space, and Equipment	Schools must have adequate supplies, space, and equipment.	Schools need to have adequate supplies, space, and equipment, but students may use transfer skills to cover deficiencies.
Personal Motivations	Vocational education should be reserved for those who are motivated and can benefit from it.	Vocational education is for everyone, and everyone can benefit.

Source: Griffin, D. (1994). *North Carolina's first post-secondary technical institution: Past, present and future.* Unpublished doctoral dissertation, University of Georgia.

FIGURE 1.1   The Philosophies of Prosser and Dewey differ in terms of Practical Application

13. Vocational education should meet the needs of individuals in such a way as they can benefit from it.
14. Vocational education is more effective when its methods of instruction are best suited to each individual's interest, aptitudes, and abilities.
15. Vocational education should be implemented in a flexible manner but should be grounded on sound standards and continually evaluated in order to make adjustments in light of changing employment requirements.
16. Vocational education requires more funds to operate than general education, and the educational cost per student is higher because of the lower number of students that can be served in vocational classes. If sufficient funds are not available, vocational programs should not be attempted (Prosser & Allen, 1925).

Most vocational educators acknowledge that the prevailing philosophy guiding vocational education today is the philosophy of John Dewey. Vocational education, which is now called career and technical education, is faced with many challenges in helping students become productive, contributing members of a rapidly changing society. Many of the lower-level skilled jobs have been eliminated by advancing technology, and jobs of today require individuals who have a wide range of knowledge and skills so they can function in a variety of positions within their field. Jobs of today require skills in thinking and problem-solving, which is one of the major tenets of Dewey's philosophy. Dewey believed that individuals are capable of adapting and solving problems. The social and cultural problems facing educators today call for emphasis on human development in order to stabilize and improve American society—one of Dewey's principles. One of the goals of modern vocational education is to assist individuals to become more adaptable and self-sufficient, which will render them capable of pursuing a number of career options—another Dewey principle (Griffin, 1994).

In the late nineteenth and early twentieth century, industrialization and immigration of African-Americans and Europeans to urban areas expanded these areas and created many social problems. Crowded ghettos, inadequate housing, inadequate urban services, and a population primarily rural in origin and unprepared for life in cities contributed to unsanitary living conditions and the spread of disease and crime. In addition, many Americans held the belief that the sense of community was being lost in the growth of urban America and that this would lead to a breakdown in social values and control and increase crime and poverty. Another concern of many Americans was that the continuous flow if immigrants would destroy traditional American values and create a threat to democracy and the American way of life. The school was considered the logical institution to prevent these problems by providing social services, teaching appropriate behaviors, and providing a community center where students from different cultures could learn to appreciate each other and form a sense of unity as Americans. Schools responded to these social needs by adding nurses, health facilities and sanitary instruction, playgrounds for recess periods and after-school activities, and auditoriums and special facilities to serve the total student body during the day and to serve as meeting places and community centers for adults. All of these changes enhanced the social function of the school (Spring, 1990).

John Dewey, the great educational philosopher of the period saw the school as an agency for providing social services and serving as a community center that would solve the problems of alienation in an urban society. He saw the role of schools and education as a means of bringing people from different backgrounds with different ideas and beliefs together in such a way as to lessen friction and instability and increase sympathy and understanding. He considered the school to be a potential clearinghouse of ideas that would interpret the intellectual and social meaning of work and the worker's place in the modern world for the new urban industrial worker. He argued that work in the vocational sense connects an individual's abilities with the benefits of social service and thus transforms the world and human interaction. Dewey's methods of instruction emphasized student interests, student activity or learning by doing, group work, and cooperation. He believed that ideas, values, and social circumstances originate in the material circumstances of life and that humans should adopt the ideas, values, and institutions that work best in a particular social situation. Dewey believed that urban industrial life was not providing the social context for teaching children habits of order, industry, and cooperation and the school could and should fill this void. Dewey recognized that many workers had become mere appendages to the machines they operated because they had no opportunity to develop insight into the social and scientific values found in their work. He promoted a type of education that would help students and workers grasp the meaning of their work and that would lead to reform of the industrial system (Spring, 1990).

Today, with growing social and economic problems, the United States faces many of the same challenges that it did a century ago. The increasing pace of technological innovations is introducing a new period of history, one in which fewer and fewer workers will be needed to produce the goods and services of our global society. Business and industry still places profit margins above the good of workers and the community. Social and economic problems are very real in most communities, especially in our nation's urban areas. Schools are serving a very diverse student population and are called upon to perform many social functions similar to those required years ago. It is little wonder that the philosophy and principles of John Dewey proclaimed nearly a hundred years ago have gained favor among educators today.

GI JOE AND GI JANE GO TO COLLEGE

No one forecast the amazing success of the higher education opportunity afforded by the GI Bill. Most predictions, including that of President Roosevelt, estimated that college enrollments would increase by only 150,000 per year, with an eventual grand total of about 600,000 or 700,000 by the time the law expired in 1956. These were reasonable estimates in light of past experience.

> *"The GI Bill changed the lives of millions by replacing old roadblocks with paths of opportunity. And, in so doing, it boosted America's work force, it boosted America's economy, and really, it changed the life of our nation."*
> President George Bush (June 5, 1990)

High school graduation was a rare achievement prior to World War II. Millions of members of the armed forces had not even graduated from grammar school and many young Americans did not go beyond the tenth grade.

Prior to 1940, colleges were mostly private, small, liberal arts, elitist, white, and protestant. In 1940 about 160,000 people earned degrees.

The graduating class of 1950 numbered about 500,000, most from state universities, having pursued both liberal arts and professional degrees. Ethnically, racially, and religiously they were reflective of the American population.

Initial interest in the educational opportunities was disappointing, and in August 1945, *The Saturday Evening Post* carried an article "GIs Reject Education." But by 1947, there were 1,164,000 veterans registering for college on the GI Bill accounting for forty-nine percent of all enrollments. Catholic, Jewish, and black veterans sat in classrooms in many institutions for the first time. Many women's

Taken from Greenberg, M. (1997). *The GI Bill: The Law That Changed America.* New York: Lickle Publishing, (pp. 35–61).

colleges became coeducational. Married students, with children, went to college. Prior to the war, marriage had been cause for dismissal at many colleges and having a child while in school was unthinkable. Over time, more than 2.2 million veterans went to college, about half of whom were the first in their families to do so. About 500,000 would not have attended except for the GI Bill. Higher education had become democratized, irrevocably altered. As the twentieth century draws to a close, the descendants of GIs have made college attendance an expectation and by the mid 1990s enrollments soared to more than fourteen million students.

The GI Bill's association with higher education fails to account for the full measure of its educational impact. Actually, close to eight million veterans received education benefits. In addition to the 2.2 million in colleges, 3.5 million attended other schools such as business schools, trade schools, art and drama schools and even high school. About 1.4 million were involved in on-the-job training programs and 690,000 in farm training.

The education benefits were extraordinarily generous. Any veteran who served for ninety days was entitled to one year of full time education plus a period equal to their time in service up to a maximum of forty-eight months. The VA paid the school for tuition, fees and books. In addition a monthly stipend was sent to the veteran.

It has been estimated that for every dollar spent on GI Bill education benefits, the nation received as much as eight dollars in income taxes but the true value is incalculable. This could be attributed then, and even more so in the 1990s, to the correlation between increased earning capacity and educational achievement.

> *"The funny thing about it, these scholars were afraid that the GI would pull the average university grades down. Instead of that, they were the ones who made the best grades."*
>
> Ernest W. McFarland Former Senate Majority Leader
> (Arizona Republic, August 13, 1978)

It is the college and university educational provisions that endure as the symbol and romance of the GI Bill. Veterans on long lines, in crowded classrooms, living in makeshift quarters, and, in substantial numbers, married, many with children. The scene made for great newspaper, magazine, and film coverage.

Veterans applied to the college of their choice. Their eligibility was certified by the Veterans Administration and the necessary checks mailed to the school (tuition, fees, books, supplies, up to $500 per year) and to the ex-GI ($50 per month for a single veteran, $75 if married, and $15 for one or more children—amounts later raised).

The enormous success of the program was unforeseen, whether in terms of numbers attending, especially married students, the high quality of performance by veterans, or the implications of what a commitment to higher education would mean for the nation generally and higher education specifically.

Higher education associations were cautious at first and the presidents of Harvard University and The University of Chicago were outspoken in their opposition. James B. Conant of Harvard feared that unqualified people would flood the campuses. Robert M. Hutchins of Chicago, in a widely noted article in *Collier's* magazine, labeled the bill unworkable, a threat to education and warned that the lure of money would turn the colleges into "educational hobo jungles." The Hutchins article drew numerous responses and *Collier's* printed a lengthy response from Alfred E. Kuenzli who was medically discharged after two years with the Marines in the South Pacific and then enrolled at the University of Notre Dame under the GI Bill. He found the University of Chicago president's article to be "disillusioning and fallacious" and suggested that perhaps the colleges as well as the veterans required rehabilitation.

Both educational leaders had reason to eat their words eventually and Conant, in 1947 called the veterans "the most mature and promising students Harvard has ever had."

All over the nation, educators and non-veteran students were aware of the enormous achievements of veterans as competent and serious students. Senator, presidential candidate, and wounded veteran Robert Dole of Kansas, recalled those days when so many were in school solely because of the help of the GI Bill and said, "...we knew it was for real. If we were going to do anything in life, we had to settle down, go to work and study."

Most campuses took cognizance of the educational training taken by many GIs while in service. The American Council on Education, the umbrella organization for all sectors of higher education, developed a guide for evaluating military experiences so that suitable credits could be awarded, a practice continued to this day.

Educators were relieved by the easy adjustment made by most veterans to civilian student life. On many campuses, the adjustment problems were felt more by faculty who lacked experience with such mature, knowledgeable students ("Oh, professor, I know about that. I was there"). Nonveteran male students who sought traditional college fun and access to female students, were made to appear particularly immature compared with the GIs in their khakis and flight jackets and tales of travel and war. Veterans who had lost years to war were not interested in the fun and games of fraternity life, freshmen beanies, or pep rallies.

"I wanted to go to graduate school and I wanted to study physics, and while I was in Germany—the German, the European war had ended and it didn't look as if I was going to be sent to Japan or to the other war, and that was winding down, too. That's when I applied to graduate school knowing that there was the GI Bill, and that I could see surviving that way.

I also had a lot of savings because I was paid every month, and I didn't know—I never collected that money. Mostly I lived on poker winnings and, you know, meals were free, and you didn't really have any needs there.

I applied to the GI Bill. You had to be discharged before you could actually get it, but I did make applications and I applied to a number of graduate schools, but most intensely at Columbia University.

Some of the people I had met at MIT were professors at Columbia, so I pulled that, you know, don't you remember we pal'd around at MIT and I was there and so on and so on. And whether that helped or not, I don't know—but I did get accepted, and it was, in fact, helpful to—you got a quicker return home if you were accepted to a graduate school, and that was another incentive to get out of occupying Germany."

Leon Lederman

During the peak enrollment years, veterans accounted for close to fifty percent of all enrollments and nearly seventy percent of registered male students. About 40 percent of all GI Bill students went to just thirty-eight major colleges and universities. As *TIME* magazine asked, why go to Podunk U if you can go to Yale? Many veterans preferred the professional training which larger schools could offer, leaving many smaller liberal arts colleges with unfilled space.

"The GI Bill commanded of institutions that veterans be given opportunity... there would be no government subsidy if they didn't open their doors to GIs... for black participants, the single most important thing in our lives was a subsidy that would help us go to school. Without that subsidy there would be no other resource, as a classic fact of history."

Harry Belafonte

They became engineers, scientists, manufacturers, doctors, dentists, accountants, lawyers, teachers and scholars. At least ten Nobel Prize winners were GIs. About fifty percent of the engineers who worked for the National Aeronautics and Space Administration (NASA) and designed or managed space flight, took their degrees under the GI Bill, most of whom would not otherwise have gone to college. Spurred by wartime applications of science and technology, college educated GIs contributed to a scientific revolution in television, computers, civil engineering, medicine, chemistry, physics, space exploration, and a continuing tradition of invention. Nobel Laureate and veteran Martin Perl put it in perspective when he commented that progress in a complex universe does not come from tinkering. What the GI Bill did was to open up opportunity "and then all these fresh minds came in and all these things were invented."

Don A. Balfour of Washington, D.C. was the first applicant for educational benefits. Balfour, who now owns an insurance agency, was a government employee and a part-time student at George Washington University after leaving the service. The day after President Roosevelt signed the GI Bill, Balfour, serving as editor of the school paper, visited the Veterans Administration to get a story about the legislation, asked if he could apply and instantly received a suitable letter. He took leave from his job which paid him $2,000 a year and instead of facing years of part-time study, accelerated his studies free of charge and received $50 per month for expenses. "That was the best time of my life...I didn't have to work all day and go to school at night and then study late and not get any sleep. I could do nothing other than study and learn, and it was a great pleasure."

George Merritt, attended McAllister School of Embalming and became a licensed funeral director under the GI Bill. He lives in the legendary GI village of Levittown, New York and recalls how veterans began to accept the idea that college was not just for the rich. "I can go to school, I can get a better job, I can get an education. I can go to college, too. Not just the rich man's son."

The cover of *TIME* magazine of November 3, 1947 featured a college football star, Bob Chappius of the University of Michigan. Chappius, a radioman and gunner on a B-25 bomber was shot down over Italy, rescued by Italian partisans and hidden for several months.

The University of Michigan football team, seventy percent of whom were on the GI Bill won the Rose Bowl in 1947. Chappius was twenty-four years old at the time. He had attended the university prior to being drafted in 1942 and would likely have returned anyway. He did not win the Heisman Trophy in 1947, but it was won by another veteran, Johnny Lujak of Notre Dame, who had served three years as a naval officer.

GI educational benefits were available abroad as well. In 1950, the Veterans Administration reported that 5,800 veterans were studying in forty-five countries under the GI Bill. Art Buchwald, noted humorist and columnist, spent time as a GI Bill student in Paris after enrolling at the University of Southern California.

A permanent and vital legacy of the educational provisions of the GI Bill is a change in the very idea of who could be a university student. The sons of unemployed depression victims, the sons of immigrants, the children of sharecroppers were just as smart as the children of wealthy and successful industrial leaders or descendants of those who arrived on the Mayflower. Older people could share classrooms with recent high school graduates and adults could go to school while married, raising children, and working at a job.

The most often used phrase by World War II veterans who took advantage of educational opportunities remains: "I don't know where I would have been without the GI Bill."

CAMPUS LIVING

Few colleges and universities were prepared for the numbers of veterans who appeared to register. None were prepared for wives and children of students, a phenomenon never before experienced or even permitted.

Memories of those times unfailingly bring smiles to the faces of those who were probably not smiling then. The numbers of students on some campuses were impressive and troublesome. The University of Wisconsin grew from 9,000 to 18,000 in one year, Rutgers from 7,000 to 16,000. Registration and school cafeterias brought back memories of "hurry up and wait" in long lines. Classrooms were in short supply and were in use night and day including Saturdays. Faculty carried heavy teaching loads and text books and laboratories were not always available.

Barracks and quonset huts sprung up to house students military style. Gymnasiums and lounges were converted to lines of double decker cots. Students filled rooming houses near campus. Marietta College in Ohio anchored a surplus coast guard vessel in the Muskingum River. Four LSTs (landing ships-tanks) were moored in the Hudson River in Troy, New York for veterans attending Rennselaer Polytech Institute.

The only place that Phil could find for his wife and baby to live in Berkeley was at an incredible beehive rooming house, an old-fashioned white clapboard house that fairly sagged under the weight of nineteen families, sixteen of which were young couples with a child each. One bedroom there, with kitchen privileges, cost $10 a week plus a $2 utility fee monthly.

It was the married housing that most challenged campus leaders and attracted the most press attention. Typically called "Vetsville," the facilities usually consisted of extensive trailer camps and surplus barracks converted to small apartments. Water, lavatories, and showers were shared in central locations. Water for daily use was hauled in buckets. Children played in mud roads and the bitterly cold Wisconsin mornings did not excuse a trip to the community facilities. While many Vetsvilles occupied open spaces on campus, many were miles away. Badger Village in Wisconsin, thirty miles from Madison, developed its own stores, services and elementary school. At the University of Minnesota, veterans housing became known as "Fertile Acres" for good reason.

Many of the colleges and universities which exist today, particularly in the public sector were not established until the late 1950s and 1960s as pressure for higher education grew largely as a result of the example set by veterans. In New York State, then the most populous in the nation, public higher education was scarce and state financial aid was given to private colleges to house students. In 1946 New York established the first "GI college," Champlain College in Plattsburg and soon added others such as at the former Sampson Naval Base.

Most of the more than 3,500 colleges, universities and community colleges in the United States in the 1990s were not in existence until most World War II veterans had left the campuses. The large system known as The State University of New York, for example, with its numerous colleges and universities was not yet established and it was largely in the 1960s that many small teacher colleges

How the Grays Spend Their Money

Rent ($25 a month)	$300.00
Utilities	120.00
Food ($10 a week)	520.00
Bank loan	264.00
Payments on furniture	150.00
Clothes	60.00
Baby doctor	40.00
Recreation	50.00
Life insurance ($1000 for Phil, $500 for Gary)	67.20
	$1571.20

became universities known usually by location, such as Western Michigan University or the University of South Alabama.

Sheer necessity to make higher education responsive to unforeseen and unprecedented demand led to performance of miracles by all involved. At the University of Indiana, for example, a threefold rise in enrollment gave the campus "the general appearance of a vast shipyard in full operation," according to a campus historian. About seventy buildings were under construction in the summer of 1946 and the east side of the campus was pushed back a half mile. A trailer park and small apartment structures went up overnight and army barracks were towed in from various parts of the country. Most of the great state universities shared this experience and few campuses (and few campus towns) escaped the drama of the "energizing" of higher education in America.

VOCATIONAL EDUCATION

Higher education dominated the scene but education for life and work was in full swing everywhere, spurred on by the same generous provisions of the GI Bill of Rights. Recall that millions of men in service had very little education. The military had done an excellent job of creating techniques for teaching a wide array of subjects from reading to high technology to millions of people of varied backgrounds.

Harry Belafonte, the distinguished singer and actor, tells "I didn't hardly finish first term high school. I had no desire to read, to learn...most of the men in my outfit were unskilled black workers, unskilled laborers. And how do you then compete for jobs if you have no training....It is in this respect that I think the GI Bill became a God-send." The GI Bill enabled people to reach for the middle class, said Belafonte and "once we had access to education, to knowledge, to skill, we could upgrade ourselves."

Many veterans completed their high school education through the General Educational Development Testing Service of the American Council on Education, an exam still in use, known as the GED. Others, their interests stimulated by military training continued on in vocational training schools in electronics, medical services or business schools. Employers were encouraged to train their own workers with the help of the GI Bill, thereby facilitating movement into the working mainstream. Now-famous movie stars, Tony Curtis, Harry Belafonte, Walter Matthau and Rod Steiger used their GI Bill rights to study drama at the New School for Social Research in New York. Still others took training in agriculture and farming, changing the ways of prewar rural life to adapt scientific and technical knowledge to food production and land management.

Among the many lasting legacies of the GI Bill of Rights is the acceptance of continuing lifelong education, of the continuing upgrading of skills and the joining of government, employers and workers in making educational opportunities available. In any post high school educational program today, eighteen-year-olds barely outnumber those over twenty-five.

SCHOOLS OF PHILOSOPHY AND THEIR INFLUENCE ON EDUCATION

As philosophers attempt to answer questions, they develop answers that are clustered into different schools of thought. These schools of philosophical thought are somewhat contrived; they are merely labels developed by others who have attempted to show the similarities and differences among the many answers philosophers develop. As you examine the schools of thought described in this section, keep in mind that the philosophers who represent these schools are individual thinkers, like yourself, who do not limit their thinking to the characteristics of any one label or school of thought. Four well-known schools of thought are idealism, realism, pragmatism, and existentialism. In addition to these, we will touch on Eastern thought and Native North American thought. Technically, these two final clusters of thought are not termed *schools* because they encompass greater diversity and often extend beyond the limits of philosophy into beliefs, customs, and group values.

Idealism

Idealism is a school of philosophy that holds that ideas or concepts are the essence of all that is worth knowing. The physical world we know through our senses is only a manifestation of the spiritual world (metaphysics). Idealists believe in the power of reasoning and de-emphasize the scientific method and sense perception, which they hold suspect (epistemology). They search for universal or absolute truths that will remain constant throughout the centuries (axiology).

Educational Implications of Idealism

The educational philosophy of the idealist is idea-centered rather than subject-centered or child-centered because the ideal, or the idea, is the foundation of all things. Knowledge is directed toward self-consciousness and self-direction and is centered in the growth of rational processes about the big ideas. Some idealists note that the individual, who is created in God's image, has free will and that it is this free will that makes learning possible. The idealist believes that learning comes from within the individual rather than from without. Hence, real mental and spiritual growth do not occur until they are self-initiated.

Idealists' educational beliefs include an emphasis on the study of great leaders as examples for us to imitate. For idealists the teacher is the ideal model or example for the student. Teachers pass on the cultural heritage and the unchanging content of education, such as knowledge about great figures of the past, the

Taken from Johnson, J.A., Musial, D., Hall, G.E., Gollnick, D.M., & Dupuis, V.L. (2008) *Foundations of American Education: Perspectives on Education in a Changing World* (14th ed.). Boston, MA: Allyn & Bacon. pp. 302–315.

humanities, and a rigorous curriculum. Idealists emphasize the methods of lecture, discussion, and imitation. Finally, they believe in the importance of the doctrine of ideas.

No one philosopher is an idealist. Rather, philosophers answer questions, and some of their answers are similar. These similarities are what make up the different schools of philosophy. To describe adequately any one school of philosophy, such as idealism, one needs to go beyond these general similarities to examine the subtle differences posed by individual thinkers. Plato and Socrates, Immanuel Kant, and Jane Roland Martin represent different aspects of the idealist tradition.

Plato and Socrates

According to Plato (c. 427–c. 347 BCE), truth is the central reality. Truth is perfect; it cannot, therefore, be found in the world of matter because the material world is both imperfect and constantly changing. Plato did not think that people create knowledge; rather, they discover it. In one of his dialogues, he conjectures that humanity once had true knowledge but lost it by being placed in a material body that distorts and corrupts that knowledge. Thus, humans have the arduous task of trying to remember what they once knew.

The modern world knows the philosophy of Socrates only through Plato, who wrote about him in a series of texts called "dialogues." Socrates

Although the Socratic method dates back to 400 BCE, the art of asking probing questions and using dialogue to enhance learning is still widely used today.

(c. 470–399 BCE) spoke of himself as a midwife who found humans pregnant with knowledge—knowledge that had not been born or realized. This Socratic "Doctrine of Reminiscence" speaks directly to the role of the educator. Teachers need to question students in such a way as to help them remember what they have forgotten. In the dialogue *Meno*, Plato describes Socrates' meeting a slave boy and through skillful questions leading the boy to realize that he knows the Pythagorean theorem, even though he does not know that he knows it. This emphasis on bringing forth knowledge from students through artful questioning is sometimes called the Socratic method.

Immanuel Kant

German philosopher Immanuel Kant (1724–1804) believed in freedom, the immortality of the soul, and the existence of God.

The German philosopher Immanuel Kant (1724–1804), in the *Metaphysics of Morals* and the *Critique of Practical Reason*, spelled out his idealistic philosophy. Kant believed in freedom, the immortality of the soul, and the existence of God. He wrote extensively on human reason and noted that the only way humankind can know things is through the process of reason. Hence, reality is not a thing unto itself but the interaction of reason and external sensations. Reason fits perceived objects into classes or categories according to similarities and differences. It is only through reason that we acquire knowledge of the world. Once again, it is the idea or the way that the mind works that precedes the understanding of reality.

Jane Roland Martin

Often labeled a feminist scholar, Jane Roland Martin (1929–) is a contemporary disciple of Plato's dialogues. In "Reclaiming a Conversation," Martin describes how women have historically been excluded from the "conversation" that constitutes Western educational thought. Martin advocates a return to Plato's approach. Dialogues such as the *Apology*, the *Crito*, and the *Phaedo* illustrate educated persons—well-meaning people of good faith, people who trust and like one another, people who might even be called friends—getting together and trying to talk ideas through to a reasonable conclusion. They engage in conversation, learning something from one another and from the conversation itself.

For Martin, to be educated is to engage in a conversation that stretches back in time. Education is not simply something that occurs in a specific building at a specific time. Nor is it simply training or preparation for the next stage in life. Education is the development of the intellectual and moral habits, through the give-and-take of the conversation, that ultimately give "place and character to every human activity and utterance." Education—the conversation—is the place where one comes to learn what it is to be a person.

RELEVANT RESEARCH

Using Socratic Dialogue to Enhance Reflective Learning

STUDY PURPOSE/QUESTION: The ancient philosophers Socrates and Plato believed that learning is best achieved through dialogue. Both philosophers contended that a teacher's main task is to ask good questions. By so doing the learner would reason to new knowledge. Socratic dialogue has been the topic of research studies in contemporary education and is now described as a dual-way communication between a teacher or tutor and a learner. The teacher does not teach a subject by direct exposition. Instead, learners' beliefs are challenged by the teacher through a series of questions that lead learners to reflect on their beliefs, induce general principles, and discover gaps and contradictions in their beliefs.

Using this type of questioning strategy is difficult when attempting to teach precise mathematical, scientific relationships. Researchers have proposed a Pictorial Socratic Dialogue coined to refer to a Socratic dialogue involving only graphics (e.g., drawings of objects or Cartesian graphs).

STUDY DESIGN: All student participants were asked to investigate a Spring Balance System on their own. The Spring Balance System models an experimental apparatus employed for the verification of Archimedes' Principle in a physics laboratory. Students were randomly assigned to three different learning conditions. Prior to beginning the experiment, all students were pretested on the mathematical and physics principles surrounding Archimedes' Principle. One group of students investigated the Spring Balance System with the help of a teacher who assumed the role of a Socratic tutor and who prescribed immediate and intelligent feedback based on the Socratic questioning method. A second group of students investigated the Spring Balance System with the help of a Socratic tutor as well as the assistance of an articulation tool. The articulation tool offers different problems that have similar solutions (DPSS) and similar problems with different solutions (SPDS). The Socratic tutor not only provided questions but also used the different DPSS and SPDS problems to guide the learning of the students.

STUDY FINDINGS: After both groups of students investigated the Spring Balance System, students were post-tested. Results showed that all students improved their understanding of Archimedes' Principle. However, students who only received the help of Socratic Dialogue improved their understanding on a surface level and did not achieve a more abstract understanding of critical attributes. Students who were assisted by both Socratic Dialogue and the DPSS and SPDS problems significantly improved both surface level and abstract understanding concerning Archimedes' Principle.

IMPLICATIONS: Socratic dialogue is an effective teaching tool. When teachers guide the development of students' understandings, learning occurs. However, when teachers wish to help students understand technical, abstract principles, Socratic dialogue needs to be enhanced by carefully structured, supporting problems that are designed to make explicit to the learner underlying critical entities that might be missed.

Source: Ah-Lian Kor, John Self, and Ken Tait, "Pictorial Socratic Dialogue and Conceptual Change," 2001 International Conference on Computers in Education, AACE-APC (Association for the Advancement of Computing in Education-Asia Pacific Chapter) Computer-Based Learning Unit, University of Leeds, Woodhouse Lane, Leeds LS29JT, UK, www.icce2001.org/cd/pdf/P02/UK002.pdf.

oots lie in the thinking of Aristotle. **Realism** is a school of philosophy that reality, knowledge, and value exist independent of the human physics). In other words, realism rejects the idealist notion that ideas are the ultimate reality. Refer to Figure 1.2, which illustrates the dualistic position of idealism and realism.

Educational Implications of Realism

Realists place considerable importance on the role of the teacher in the educational process. The teacher should be a person who presents content in a systematic and organized way and should promote the idea that there are clearly defined criteria one can use in making judgments (axiology). Contemporary realists emphasize the importance of scientific research and development. Curriculum has reflected the impact of these realist thinkers through the appearance of standardized tests, serialized textbooks, and a specialized curriculum in which the disciplines are seen as separate areas of investigation.

Realists contend that the ultimate goal of education is advancement of human rationality. Schools can promote rationality by requiring students to study organized bodies of knowledge, by teaching methods of arriving at this knowledge, and by assisting students to reason critically through observation and experimentation (epistemology). Teachers must have specific knowledge about a subject so that they can order it in such a way as to teach it rationally. They must also have a broad background to show relationships that exist among all fields of knowledge.

Thus, the realist curriculum would be a subject-centered curriculum and would include natural science, social science, humanities, and instrumental subjects such as logic and inductive reasoning. Realists employ experimental and observational

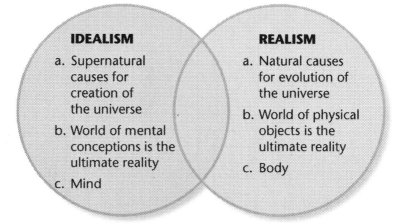

FIGURE 1.2   Dualistic Position of Idealism and Realism

techniques. In the school setting, they would promote testing and logical, clear content. To understand the complexity of the realist philosophy, we must once again turn to the ideas of individual thinkers: Aristotle, Locke, and Whitehead.

Aristotle

Aristotle (384–322 BCE) thought that ideas (forms) are found through the study of the world of matter. He believed that one could acquire knowledge of ideas or forms by investigating matter. To understand an object, one must understand its absolute form, which is unchanging. To the realist, the trees of the forest exist whether or not there is a human mind to perceive them. This is an example of an independent reality. Although the idea of a flower can exist without matter, matter cannot exist without form. Hence, each tulip shares universal properties with every other tulip and every other flower. However, the particular properties of a tulip differentiate it from all other flowers.

Aristotle's writings are known for their analytic approach. In contrast to Plato, whose writings are in the form of a conversation, Aristotle took great care to write with precision.

Ancient Greek philosopher Aristotle (384–322 BCE) believed that one could acquire knowledge of ideas or forms through an investigation of matter.

John Locke

John Locke (1632–1704) believed in the tabula rasa (blank tablet) view of the mind. Locke stated that the mind of a person is blank at birth and that the person's sensory experiences make impressions on this blank tablet. Locke distinguished between sense data and the objects they represent. The objects, or things people know, are independent of the mind or the knower insofar as thought refers to them and not merely to sense data. Ideas (round, square, tall) represent objects. Locke claimed that primary qualities (such as shapes) represent the world, whereas secondary qualities (such as colors) have a basis in the world but do not represent it.

The little or almost insensible impressions on our tender infancies have very important and lasting consequences: and there it is, as in the fountains of some rivers, where a gentle application of the hand turns the flexible waters into channels, that make them at first, in the source, they receive different tendencies, and arrive at last at very remote and distant places.

I imagine the minds of children as easily turned, this or that way, as water itself; and though this be the principal part and our main care should be about the inside yet the clay cottage is not to be neglected.

John Locke (1632–1704) believed that a person's mind is like a blank tablet at birth and that a person's sensory experiences make impressions on this tablet.

Alfred North Whitehead

Philosopher and mathematician Alfred North Whitehead (1861–1947) attempted to reconcile idealism and realism.

Alfred North Whitehead (1861–1947), a philosopher and mathematician, attempted to reconcile some aspects of idealism and realism. He proposed "process" to be the central aspect of realism. Unlike Locke, Whitehead did not see objective reality and subjective mind as separate. He saw them as an organic unity that operates by its own principles. The universe is characterized by patterns, and these patterns can be verified and analyzed through mathematics.

Culture is activity of thought and receptiveness to beauty and humane feelings. Scraps of information have nothing to do with it. . . . In training a child to activity of thought, above all things we must beware of what I will call "inert ideas"—that is to say, ideas that are merely received into the mind without being used, or tested, or thrown into fresh combinations.

In the history of education, the most striking phenomenon is the schools of learning, which at one epoch are alive with a ferment of genius, in a succeeding generation exhibit merely pedantry and routine. The reason is that they are overladen with inert ideas. Education with inert ideas is not only useless: it is, above all things, harmful—Corruptio optimi, pessima.

Pragmatism

Pragmatism is a late-nineteenth-century U.S. philosophy that affected educational and social thought. It differs from most forms of idealism and realism by a belief in an open universe that is dynamic, evolving, and in a state of becoming (metaphysics). It is a process philosophy, which stresses becoming rather than being. Wedded as they are to change and adaptation, pragmatists do not believe in absolute and unchanging truth. For pragmatists, truth is what works. Truth is relative because what works for one person might not work for another, just as what works at one time or in one place or in one society might not work in another (axiology).

Educational Implications of Pragmatism

Like the realist, the pragmatist believes that we learn best through experience, but pragmatists are more willing to put that belief into practice. Whereas realists are concerned with passing organized bodies of knowledge from one generation to the next, pragmatists stress applying knowledge—using ideas as instruments for problem solving (epistemology). Realists and idealists call for a curriculum centered on academic disciplines, but pragmatists prefer a curriculum that draws the disciplines together to solve problems—an interdisciplinary approach. Refer to Figure 1.3,

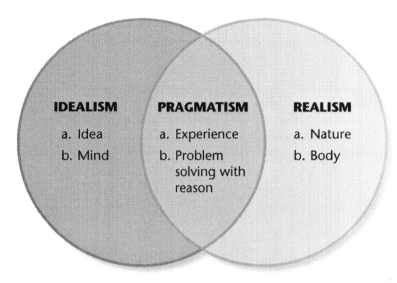

FIGURE 1.3   **Relationship of Realism, Idealism, and Pragmatism**

Charles Sanders Peirce (1839–1914) believed that the purpose of thought is to produce action.

which illustrates the relationships among realism, idealism, and pragmatism.

Charles Sanders Peirce

Charles Sanders Peirce (1839–1914) is considered the founder of pragmatism. He introduced the principle that belief is a habit of action undertaken to overcome indecisiveness. He believed that the purpose of thought is to produce action and that the meaning of a thought is the collection of results of actions. For example, to say that steel is "hard" is to mean that when the operation of scratch testing is performed on steel, it will not be scratched by most substances. The aim of Peirce's pragmatic method is to supply a procedure for constructing and clarifying meanings and to facilitate communication.

John Dewey

Early in his philosophical development, John Dewey (1859–1952) related pragmatism to evolution by explaining that human beings are creatures who have to adapt to one another and to their environments. Dewey viewed life as a series of overlapping and interpenetrating experiences and situations, each of which has its own complete identity. The primary unit of life is the individual experience.

Dewey wrote the following passage early in his career. In it he shows his zeal for education as a social force in human affairs.

> I believe that all education proceeds by the participation of the individual in the social consciousness of the race. This process begins unconsciously almost at birth, and is continually shaping the individual's powers, saturating his consciousness, forming his habits, training his ideas, and arousing his feelings and emotions.
>
> In sum, I believe that the individual is a social individual and that society is an organic union of individuals. If we eliminate the social factor from the child we are left only with an abstraction; if we eliminate the individual factor from society, we are left only with an inert and lifeless mass.

Richard Rorty

Richard Rorty (1931–) is a contemporary pragmatist philosopher who has spent much of his life reinventing the work of John Dewey in light of the chaotic, ever-changing view of the world. Rorty contends that reality is not fixed, and it is the task of thinkers to come up with a procedure for correctly describing the nature of the real. He argues that reality is the outcome of inquiry, and as human inquiry shifts so too will shift the nature of what we call real. Rorty contends that different disciplines have different avenues for studying the world and therefore these avenues of inquiry create different realities. The way an artist looks at the world and creates a work of art and the way a chemist looks at the world and develops a new way of looking at molecules both affect the very nature of what is. Essential to this point of view is the understanding that disciplines such as science, mathematics, art, and history are not rooted in a fixed reality but are constructed by groups of people who are trying to make sense of the world. Hence, disciplines are arbitrary contrivances and one discipline is as good as another. Also, because disciplines are created by persons, they are subject to all the foibles, limitations, and prejudices of any human convention.

Although Rorty has not spoken directly to the field of education, his work provides a significant challenge to teachers. No longer can teachers represent expert knowledge as accurate or as true. Rather, expert knowledge is the current agreement of scholars at this point in time. Expert knowledge is simply a set of ideas and procedures that have been found to be useful. Rorty contends that a thinker should no longer be represented as a discoverer; rather, a thinker is more of a maker or cobbler who crafts meaning. People come together, agree on certain things, and then try to talk or reason their way to a sensible conclusion. Expertise is more a matter of "usefulness" than truth.

Existentialism

In **existentialism,** reality is lived existence, and the final reality resides within the individual (metaphysics). Existentialists believe that we live an alien, meaningless existence on a small planet in an unimportant galaxy in an indifferent universe. There is no ultimate meaning. Whereas some people might be paralyzed by this view, existentialists find the definition of their lives in the quest for meaning (episte-mology). The very meaninglessness of life compels them to instill life with meaning.

The only certainty for the existentialist is that we are free. However, this freedom is wrapped up in a search for meaning. We define ourselves; that is, we make meaning in our world by the choices we make. In effect we are what we choose (axiology).

Educational Implications of Existentialism

The existentialist believes that most schools, like other corporate symbols, de-emphasize the individual and the relationship between the teacher and the student. Existentialists claim that when educators attempt to predict the behavior of students, they turn individuals into objects to be measured, quan-tified, and processed. Existentialists tend to feel that tracking, measurement, and standardization militate against the creation of opportunities for self-direction and personal choice. According to the existentialist, education ought to be a process of developing a free, self-actualizing person—a process cen-tered on the feelings of the student. Therefore, proper education does not start with the nature of the world and with humankind, but with the human indi-vidual or self.

The existentialist educator would be a free personality engaged in projects that treat students as free personalities. The highest educational goal is to search for oneself. Teachers and students experience existential crises; each such crisis involves an examination of oneself and one's life purposes. Education helps to fill in the gaps with understanding that the student needs in order to fulfill those purposes; it is not a mold to which the student must be fitted. Students define themselves by their choices.

The existentialist student would have a questioning attitude and would be involved in a continuing search for self and for the reasons for existence. The existentialist teacher would help students become what they themselves want to become, not what outside forces such as society, other teachers, or parents want them to become.

Existentialist thinkers are as varied as the notions of individual thought and self-defined meaning would suggest. There are atheistic existentialists as represented by Jean-Paul Sartre, critical existentialists as exemplified by Friedrich Nietzsche, and humanistic existentialists such as Maxine Greene.

Jean-Paul Sartre

Modern existentialism was born amidst the pain and disillusionment of World War II. Jean-Paul Sartre (1905–1980) broke with previous philosophers and asserted that existence (being) comes before essence (meaning).

Sartre saw no difference between being free and being human. This view opens great possibilities; yet it also creates feelings of dread and nausea as one recognizes the reality of nonbeing and death as well as the great responsibilities that accompany such radical freedom to shape oneself out of one's choices. The process of answering the question "Who are we?" begins at a crucial event in the lives of young people called the existential moment—that point somewhere toward the end of youth when individuals realize for the first time that they exist as independent agents.

Friedrich Nietzsche

Friedrich Nietzsche (1844–1900) is an existential philosopher who stresses the importance of the individuality of persons. Throughout his writings, Nietzsche indicts the supremacy of herd values in modern democratic social systems. He criticizes the way social systems such as modern educational institutions foster a spirit of capitalistic greed. When Nietzsche turns his attention primarily to social systems, human beings are portrayed much more as victims of social dynamics than as inferior or superior beings.

In Nietzsche's texts there is a strategy to liberate people from the oppression of feeling inferior within themselves, a teaching of how not to judge what one is in relation to what one should be. Although Nietzsche did not author a comprehensive teaching methodology, he teaches how to cultivate a healthy love of self-care, a taste for solitude, a perspective on perspective, literacy as a vital capacity, and an overall gratitude for one's existence.

Nietzsche observed that most teachers and parents

hammer even into children that what matters is something quite different: the salvation of the soul, the service of the state, the advancement of science, or the accumulation of reputation and possessions, all as the means of doing service to mankind as a whole; while the requirements of the individual, his great and small needs within the twenty-four hours of the day, are to be regarded as something contemptible or a matter of indifference.

Maxine Greene

A theme that permeates most of Maxine Greene's work is her unyielding faith in human beings' willingness to build and transcend their lived worlds. To Greene (1917–) philosophy is a deeply personal and aesthetic experience. Her writing blurs the distinction between philosophy and literature. This is appropriate because Greene contends that living is philosophy. Greene asserts that schools must be places that offer "an authentic public space where diverse human beings can appear before one another as best they know to be."

Philosopher Maxine Greene (1917–) contends that living is philosophy and that freedom means overcoming obstacles that obstruct our attempts to find ourselves and fulfill our potential.

TEACHER PERSPECTIVES

Does Prepping for High-Stakes Tests Interfere with Teaching?

More and more states require students to pass tests in order to graduate or to receive a diploma. Some states offer different types of diplomas based on how well a student performs on a test. This type of testing is called high-stakes testing and it poses several philosophical questions. What do high-stakes tests say about the nature of knowledge? What does it mean to be educated in a high-stakes testing environment? What behaviors do high-stakes testing encourage? How do high-stakes tests influence teaching? The following debate raises these types of questions.

YES

Nancy Buell teaches fourth grade at the Lincoln School in Brookline, Massachusetts. She has taught for thirty-two years and serves on the state Board of Education's Advisory Council for Mathematics and Science.

As I watch my students debate how much taller fourth graders are than first graders, I am struck by their intuitive use of significant features of the data. As in:

Lee: Fourth graders are 10" taller because the tallest fourth grader is 64" and the tallest first grader is 54".

Tamara: A first grader is about 5" shorter. I found the middle height for each and just subtracted. The middle for the fourth graders is 57" and the middle for the first graders is between 51" and 52".

Dana: 5" or 4", because the most common height for first graders is 53" and the most common height for fourth graders is 58" or 57".

These students are exploring ideas involving maximum, median, and mode. They are considering what features to use to tell what is typical of the two groups so they can be compared. Students support their ideas with information in the data itself. They are developing ways to think about data that will lead to deep understanding of more formal statistics.

NO

Charlotte Crawford teaches fourth grade at Coteau-Bayou Blue School in Houma, Louisiana. A twenty-seven-year teaching veteran, she helped set the cut scores for her state's high-stakes fourth-grade test and now serves on a state panel for staff development.

Preparing students to take high-stakes tests does not interfere with teaching. It enhances teaching. When used properly, high-stakes tests can focus attention on weaknesses in the curriculum and in the teaching of it, as well as furnish an assessment of student progress. Once identified, student weak areas can be strengthened.

When the new high-stakes tests and revised curriculum were introduced in Louisiana, along with new accountability standards, many teachers were bewildered at the prospect of being held accountable for teaching a new curriculum without being told how to teach it.

Yet many of these teachers were also open to the new ideas and began working to find ways to implement them. They were aided by funding from the state for additional reading materials and in-service training.

Teachers often feel overwhelmed by the changes involved in our state's rigorous new standards, but many Louisiana educators are beginning to take ownership of their new

(continued)

TEACHER PERSPECTIVES

(continued)

YES   NO

The rich mathematical discussions in my class are an outgrowth of my participation in professional development that focused on inquiry-based teaching and the big ideas we should be teaching.

But since high-stakes testing arrived, professional development meetings often focus on how to improve test scores, not on how to improve learning.

Teaching that concentrates on improving test scores is very limited—by the nature of both testing and teaching. Testing involves sampling student knowledge. It is fragmented and only examines learning outcomes. It seldom looks at how well a student understands complex ideas.

A typical test item might give students a set of data and ask for the median. Students would not be asked to select the appropriate statistic to address a question and justify their choice. Yet knowing how to find the median, without knowing when to use it, is useless, except on tests.

If we teach facts and procedures likely to be on the test, without the deeper understanding behind them, we shortchange our students. We must not limit what we teach to what will be tested.

Many teachers feel pressured to choose teaching techniques that help with testing more than learning. They're urged to spend more time on information that mimics test items.

Students should, of course, know how to answer multiple choice, short answer, and open response questions, but teaching these test-taking skills should not be confused with teaching a subject. Some teachers spend a day a week using test-like items, not to

curriculum. They're growing confident when making scope and sequence decisions. They're consistently reevaluating what they have taught, and how they have taught it, so they can do better next time.

These educators are revamping their classroom activities and their teacher-made tests to match them more closely to the format and tone of the state-mandated tests.

Helping students become familiar with the state-mandated test formats, by using them in the classroom, prevents having to spend valuable class time to "practice" for the high-stakes tests.

Learners, meanwhile, are reaping the benefits of having teachers who are determined that their students will be as prepared as possible to relate the skills they learn in school to real-life situations. They're becoming lifelong learners, besides performing well on standardized tests.

Some educators complain that they must "teach to the test."

But others consider this to be a weak objection since the state tests focus on information and skills students are expected to know at certain points in their schooling.

These educators say the curriculum objectives covered by the state tests should be taught before the tests are given, with the remaining objectives covered afterwards. This is a very workable arrangement when high-stakes tests are given early in the spring.

To be sure, some Louisiana educators are still resisting the changes that come with the state tests.

But most realize this is an idea whose time has come.

(continued)

TEACHER PERSPECTIVES

(continued)

YES

sample what children know, but to try to teach the content.

Teaching should build on what students already know and help them develop a rich web of interconnected ideas. Real learning involves inquiry, hypothesis testing, exploration, and reflection.

Teaching to the test will not help my students think about how to use features of data sets to answer real questions. Teaching to the test is not teaching.

NO

In 1998, my school helped pilot the fourth-grade language arts test. I was nervous about how my students would fare. When they finished, I asked for reactions.

Much to my surprise, students calmly informed me that the state test was "kind of hard, kind of easy, kind of fun."

That day, my students unwittingly reassured me that learners who are prepared for high-stakes tests need not fear them.

Source: "Does Prepping for High-Stakes Tests Interfere with Teaching?" *NEA Today* (January 2001), p. 11. Reprinted by permission of the National Education Association.

Eastern Ways of Knowing

Most studies of Western philosophy typically begin with the Greek philosophers. Yet there is evidence that Platonic philosophy owed much of its development to Eastern thinkers who emphasized the illusory quality of the physical world. Although there are many different philosophical writings among the Far Eastern and Near Eastern philosophers, **Eastern ways of knowing** as a group stress inner peace, tranquility, attitudinal development, and mysticism. Western philosophy has tended to emphasize logic and materialism; on the other hand, Eastern ways of knowing, in general, stress the inner rather than the outer world, intuition rather than sense, and mysticism rather than scientific discoveries. This has differed from school to school, but overall Eastern ways of knowing begin with the inner world and then reach to the outer world of phenomena. Eastern ways of knowing emphasize order, regularity, and patience that is proportional to and in harmony with the laws of nature.

Eastern thinkers have always concerned themselves with education, which they view as a way of achieving wisdom, maintaining family structure, establishing law, and providing for social and economic concerns. Instruction includes the things that one must do to achieve the good life, and education is viewed as necessary not only for this life but also for achievement of the good life hereafter.

One good reason to study Eastern ways of knowing is that they offer vantage points from which to examine Western thought. Eastern ideas encourage one to question seriously the Western world's most basic commitments to science, materialism, and reason.

Indian Thought

Far Eastern Indian thought has a long, complex history and is permeated by opposites. To Western philosophers, opposites need to be reconciled, but to the Eastern mind, this need for consistency is unimportant. For example, great emphasis is placed on a search for wisdom, but this does not mean a rejection of worldly pleasures. Though speculation is emphasized, it has a practical character. Far Eastern Indian thinkers insist that knowledge be used to improve both social and communal life and that people should live according to their ideals. In Far Eastern Indian thought, there is a prevailing sense of universal moral justice, according to which individuals are responsible for what they are and what they become.

Ancient Chinese philosopher Confucius (551–479 BCE) believed that people need standards for all of life so he developed rules for a wide range of activities.

Chinese Thought

The emphasis of Far Eastern Chinese philosophy is on harmony; correct thinking should help one achieve harmony with life. This harmony of government, business, and family should then lead toward a higher synthesis. Confucianism and Taoism provide two major contexts for Chinese thought.

For more than two thousand years, Confucian thought has influenced education, government, and culture in China. Confucius (551–479 BCE) believed that people need standards for all of life, so rules were developed for a wide range of activities. Confucian thought gives education a high place but stresses building moral character more than merely teaching skills or imparting information. This moral approach has a practical component. Children should obey and defer to parents and respect the wisdom adults have gained in their journey through life. Following these principles enables children to become *chun-tzu*, persons distinguished by faithfulness, diligence, and modesty.

The central concept of Taoism is that of the "Tao," the Way or Path. The Tao is the way the universe moves, the way of perfection and harmony. It is conformity with nature. Perhaps the most significant aspect of the Tao is letting things alone, not forcing personal desires onto the natural course of events. It is a noncompetitive approach to life. Taoists believe that conflict and war represent basic failures in society, for they bring ruin to states and a disrespect for life.

GLOBAL PERSPECTIVES

The Fabric of Eastern Ways of Knowing

As you can see, Eastern thought is like a rich fabric of diverse ideas. It emphasizes sets of views that are quite different from the neat categorizations of Western thought. Eastern thought suggests that cohesive views can be achieved without the necessity of neat, hierarchically distinct categories. Although they are quite difficult to summarize, the philosophy and thought of the East suggest new ways of looking at long-accepted meanings and assumptions. As such, the study of Eastern thought is an important part of all future educators' preparation in an increasingly multicultural society.

Questions for Reflection

1. In what ways do Eastern ways of knowing affect character education programs?
2. What values would receive greater or lesser emphasis?

Japanese Thought

Japanese thought is rooted in Shinto, a way of thinking that recognizes the significance of the natural world. This respect for all nature permeates Japanese thought and life. Shinto accepts the phenomenal world (the world people apprehend through their senses) as absolute; this acceptance leads to a disposition to lay greater emphasis on intuitive, sensible, concrete events rather than on universal ideas. On the social level, Japanese express this focus on the natural world through many artifacts, including the patterns of traditional kimonos. Within the house, flowers are arranged in vases and dwarf trees placed in alcoves, flowers and birds are engraved on lintels, and nature scenes are painted on sliding screens.

Educational Implications of Eastern Ways of Knowing

Eastern educational thought places great emphasis on the teacher–student relationship. Change springs from this relationship; that is, the student is changed as a result of contact with the guru, master, or prophet. Eastern educational thought emphasizes transformation: The individual must be transformed to face life. Attitude shaping is important because the attitude a person holds toward life will determine the individual's levels of goodness and wisdom.

A recurring educational aim in Eastern ways of knowing is to put humanity in tune with nature. There is great emphasis on observing nature and learning through wanderings and pilgrimages. The importance of achieving wisdom, satori, enlightenment, or nirvana is supreme. All paths must lead to this, and from this wisdom spring virtue, right living, and correct behavior.

Native North American Ways of Knowing

Just as the rich past and diverse cultures make it difficult to summarize Eastern thought, Native North American ways of knowing are equally difficult to synthesize. **Native North American ways of knowing** include a varied set of beliefs, positions, and customs that span different tribes in North America. These beliefs, positions, and customs center on the relationship of humans to all of nature, including the earth, the sun, the sky, and beyond. Because Native North American ways of knowing center on the relationship of humans to all of nature, it is sometimes difficult to separate knowing from a way of life. In fact, to understand is to live and to develop an ever closer, more profound human-to-nature relationship. The types of relationships and the symbols that inform these human-to-nature relationships differ widely among tribes.

Although Native North American ways of knowing are as different as the four hundred–plus tribes in North America, these ways of knowing do have similar elements. They all include traditional stories and beliefs that dictate a way of knowing and living. All include a reverence for nature and a sense of humans' responsibility to nature. And all groups make reference to a supreme being—although the names are different, the relationships vary, and the expectations of some supreme beings are interpreted through natural elements. Thus, the Black Hills are sacred to the Lakota, the turtle is revered as Mother Earth by the Ojibwa, and so on. Native North American ways of knowing are orally developed rather than written. Hence, they change slightly from age to age. Additionally, the ways of knowing are subject to interpretation by the shaman, or holy one.

Native North American ways of knowing provide a perspective that connects knowledge to the earth that surrounds us and of which we are a part.

Navajo Thought

The Navajo nation is the largest tribe in the United States. The Navajos' early history was nomadic, and their thoughts and customs are known for their unique ability to assimilate with and adapt to the thought and customs of other tribes. As with most Native North American cultures, the Navajo universe is an all-inclusive unity viewed as an orderly system of interrelated elements. At the basis of Navajo teachings and traditions is the value of a life lived in harmony with the natural world. Such a view enables one to "walk in beauty." To understand the Navajo worldview, one must note the teachings of the "inner forms" of things. These inner forms were set in place by First Man and First Woman. The concept of inner form is similar to the concept of a spirit or soul; without it, the Navajos say, the outer forms would be dead.

Lakota Thought

The Native American culture of the Great Plains, of which the Lakota form part, is based on mystical participation with the environment. All aspects of this ecosystem, including earth, sky, night, day, sun, and moon, are elements of the oneness within which life was undertaken. The Lakota celebrate the "sacred hoop of life" and observe seven sacred rites toward the goal of ultimate communion with Wakan-Tanka, the great Spirit.

Hopi Thought

The Hopi follow the path of peace, which they believe is a pure and perfect pattern of humankind's evolutionary journey. The Road of Life of the Hopi is represented as a journey through seven universes created at the beginning. At death the conduct of a person in accordance with the Creator's plan determines when and where the next step on the road will be taken. Each of the Hopi clans has a unique role to play, and each role is an essential part of the whole. Hopis must live in harmony with one another, with nature, and with the plan. Out of this complex interplay, then, the plan is both created and allowed to unfold.

> *We feel that the world is good. We are grateful to be alive. We are conscious that all men are brothers. We sense that we are related to other creatures. Life is to be valued and preserved. If you see a grain of corn on the ground, pick it up and take care of it, because it has life inside. When you go out of your house in the morning and see the sun rising, pause a moment to think about it. When you take water from a spring, be aware that it is a gift of nature. (Albert Yava, Big Falling Snow, Hopi)*

Educational Implications of Native North American Ways of Knowing

Native North American educational thought emphasizes the importance of nature. The pursuit of knowledge and happiness must be subordinate to a respect for the whole universe. To know is to understand one's place in the natural order of things. To be is to celebrate through ritual and stories the spirit that informs all reality. These principles encourage educators to study the physical and social world by examining the natural relationships that exist among things, animals, and humans.

Studying ideas in the abstract or as independent entities is not as important as understanding the relationships among ideas and the physical reality. Hands-on learning, making connections, holding discussions, and celebrating the moment are essential components of an educational experience.

SUMMARY

Structure and Methodology of Philosophy

The study of philosophy permeates every aspect of the teacher's role and provides the underpinning for every decision. This unit describes how philosophy is related to daily teaching decisions and actions, and it clarifies some of the major ideas that different philosophers have developed in their private quest for wisdom.

Philosophy revolves around three major types of questions: those that deal with the nature of reality (metaphysics), those that deal with knowledge and truth (epistemology), and those that deal with values (axiology). Successful teachers are those who are dedicated to and thoroughly understand their preferred beliefs. Decisions about the nature of the subject matter emphasized in the curriculum are metaphysical commitments to reality—what is real? Questions related to what is true and how we know are epistemological. Classroom methods are practices that aim to assist learners in acquiring knowledge and truth in the subject area. Classroom activities that deal with ethics (what is right or wrong), beauty, and character are in the realm of axiology (values). The task of the teacher is to identify a preferred style, understand that style as thoroughly as possible, and use that style with each unique group of learners.

Analytic and prophetic thinking provide two approaches to the process of philosophy. Analytic thinking provides clarity and precision, whereas prophetic thinking fosters breadth and sensitivity. Both thinking approaches are valuable and help educators understand the essential and critical features of situations or problems.

Schools of Philosophy and their Influence on Education

Four classical Western schools of philosophical thought (realism, idealism, pragmatism, and existentialism) were introduced. For each school of philosophy, representative philosophers and their ideas were provided to give prospective teachers a sense of how they might develop their own educational philosophy.

The unit concluded with overviews of Eastern and Native North American ways of knowing. The Eastern and Native North American ways of knowing are varied and diverse. Despite such diversity, many of these ways of knowing share an underlying sensitivity to nature and an emphasis on wisdom, virtue, spirituality, and harmony within the larger universe. The educational implications of these ways of knowing include the importance of teaching respect for the earth and awareness of the interrelationships among all things.

PROFESSIONALISM AND ETHICS

Workforce education is a professional endeavor. As argued by Thomas Green (1987), professions "are practices related to the central life-giving, life-sustaining, life-fulfilling events of human existence." Clearly, having an occupation either provides a life-sustaining and life-fulfilling event, or provides the freedom to pursue one's avocation. Although an individual's life calling or vocation may or may not be his or her occupation, having an occupation is often a necessary evil in order have the money to follow one's "calling."

Those involved in workforce education perform a practice that is essential to human existence and so engage in a professional activity. They, therefore, are viewed as professionals and should act accordingly. But what does "act as professionals" mean? Clearly, it means something more than dressing appropriately, joining professional organizations, and reading professional journals. Obviously, it includes preparing oneself and keeping current with the knowledge base and skills of the profession and using these skills to the best of one's ability. But something more is involved. We could envision, for example, an individual who is technically competent, dresses correctly, belongs to professional organizations, and reads professional journals but does not act professionally. Why? Because one important ingredient of professionalism may be missing—ethics. Only when individuals act ethically are we willing to embrace them with the highest of all accolades—namely, calling them professionals.

Implicit in a professional endeavor is the requirement that practitioners "do the right thing." As Green (1987) points out, professionalism implies "sacrifice." To do the right thing may require sacrifice, but to do so is to act ethically. The key question, therefore, is what are the standards for "doing the right thing," or acting ethically. Thomas Green calls these standards the "points of the profession." In medicine, for example, the point of the profession is to do whatever possible to improve health, short of doing harm. This simple point is a powerful guide to doctors and should be a hint as to the practical importance of knowing what is the point of the profession.

FOUR ETHICAL OBLIGATIONS

Simply being technically competent is insufficient to be called a professional workforce educator. What is required is using the skills and practices in accordance with professional ethical standards. Only when one practices the skill of workforce education and development in accordance with the ethical obligations of the profession, will one be acting both competently and ethically. Thus,

Taken from Gray, K.C., & Herr, E.L. (1998) *Workforce Education: The Basics.* Boston, MA: Allyn & Bacon. pp. 5–39.

**TABLE 1.1   The Four Ethical Obligations of a
                      Workforce Education Professional**

- Promote learning
- Ensure health and safety
- Protect the public or private trust
- Promote the transfer of learning

a fundamental foundation of workforce education and development professionals is to know the ethical obligations of the profession.

To be considered a professional, an individual must conduct the practice of
workforce education in accordance with four ethical obligations (see Table 1.1).
Each is discussed below.

Promote Learning.   As implied by the title of the profession "workforce education," promoting learning among clients (students, employees, welfare recipients,
and so forth) is clearly one point of the profession. More important, the reader is
reminded that learning is not synonymous with time in training or even teaching;
simply providing instruction in no way means that learning is taking place. Only
effective instruction will lead to learning, when learning is defined as the act of
acquiring knowledge or skill.

Ensure Health and Safety.   Conducting workforce education in a manner that
promotes learning but also ensures the health and safety of the learner is another
obvious point or obligation of the profession. One could imagine, for example,
developing an instructional design that promoted a high degree of learning by
making physical harm a consequence of failure. Clearly this is unethical behavior
and is also called negligence in a court of law, a hint that professional ethics and
legal liability are closely related.

Protect the Public or Private Trust.   Workforce education professionals are bound
by a certain trust placed in them by their clients, their employers, and others, such
as parents and the public. Some types of public trust are universal. For example,
being a professional implies the need for sacrificing personal gain when it conflicts
with a professional duty, such as promoting learning. It is a matter of public trust
that individuals will not use their position for personal gain, be it outright stealing,
or more covert methods such as kickbacks, conducting private for-profit business
on employers' time, coercing subordinates for personal gain, and so forth.

Other public trusts are specific to the workforce education setting. In private
industry, upper management supports training efforts based partly on a trust that
the professionals involved will conduct training that is consistent with the mission of the organization, namely, to make a profit. Parents of teens, for example,
allow their children to participate in high school occupational/technical education because of a public trust that those in charge will not abuse them and will

ensure their safety in potentially dangerous instructional labs. Violating these "trusts" is unethical and therefore unprofessional.

Promote the Transfer of Learning.   Unlike more general education, workforce education and development has a final more focused purpose, namely, that the learning that occurs effectively transfers to the workplace and thereby results in students or clients making the transition from one state of employment or occupational effectiveness to a more advanced state. This transition can take two forms. In the private sector, in HRD activities for example, an essential point of the profession is that the learning that takes place transfers back to the work site and results in improved performance of the learner on the job. In the military, this transfer to the real world can be a matter of life and death for the learner. In the public sector, workforce education clients typically are seeking knowledge that leads to labor market advantage in competing for limited high-skills/high-wage work. In other cases, the goal is simple employment in the primary job market. The ethical, thus professional, obligation for the workforce education practitioners is to do everything possible to ensure that this transition occurs. Conducting a postsecondary technical education program of study that has few ties with employers or the labor market and does not result in clear labor market advantage to the learner is unethical, and therefore unprofessional.

Ethics That Guides Practice

Beginning practitioners are likely to dismiss this discussion of professional obligation as having no practical use. They are wrong. As one indication, the courts consider these ethical standards as the benchmarks for deciding questions of negligence. Thus, professional codes of ethics, such as the American Society for Training and Development's (ASTD) codes of ethics for trainers and the American Vocational Association's (AVA) code of ethics for vocational educators have legal weight in a court of law, and civil suits alleging willful negligence are often centered on the accepted code of ethics of the profession.

A clear understanding of the points of the profession has, however, a much more important practical use than defending against legal challenges, namely, its usefulness in making the hundreds of professional decisions workforce education and development professionals are called on daily to make. Take a fairly common decision that faces secondary occupational/technical educators—deciding whether to conduct or approve a field trip. Is this a junket or something of value? How does one decide? By asking oneself how it relates to the points of the profession: Will it promote learning? Will it be safe? Will it violate the public trust? Will it promote transfer? A trip to a local manufacturing facility may not promote the learning of additional skills but probably is safe and will promote transfer by increasing student awareness of the workplace. On the other hand, a trip to the local amusement park may not.

Ethical Conflicts

Invariably, workforce education professionals will encounter ethical conflicts in their careers. These conflicts occur when they are faced with having to make decisions that conflict with the points or obligations of the profession. For example, in an administrative role, workforce educators may find themselves under pressure to reduce the budget, knowing that to do so will reduce learning. In this case the conflict results both from a public or an employer's directive to spend less and from the ethical obligation to promote learning. The best advice is to always try to make decisions that are consistent with professional obligations, recognizing that compromises may be inevitable. But one should never compromise on the issue of health and safety; to do so is career threatening.

ECONOMIC AND LABOR FOUNDATIONS

Studying the World of Work

Tinker, tailor, soldier, sailor,
rich man, poor man, beggar man, thief,
doctor, lawyer, merchant, chief.

This counting rhyme reminds us that children are aware of only a few occupations, usually through exposure to their parents' work and to workers whom they have met in education, medicine, and other social services. But as you saw in modern industrial economies are specialized. Even adults may know relatively little about the world of work beyond their own jobs. Because of evolving technologies, new jobs are rapidly being created while old jobs become obsolete. Studying the rapid changes in the workplace poses a challenge for social scientists just as it does for all workers.

This unit examines how sociologists study the world of work, especially when that world is expanding and changing. The unit will explain some concepts and techniques used to gather information about work and workers. Finally, it will look at problems that researchers encounter when studying work. Anthropologists, economists, psychologists, and other social scientists use some of the same methods to study work. The techniques and tools discussed may also help students or workers changing jobs to find useful information about the labor market.

Taken from Hodson, R. and Sullivan, T.A. (2008) *The Social Organization of Work,* Fourth Edition. Belmont, CA: Thomson Wadsworth. pp. 35–52.

TECHNIQUES OF ANALYSIS

Work is so varied and important an aspect of human life that sociologists need many methods to study it. Any social science method should be both **valid** and **reliable**. A valid method yields accurate information about the phenomenon being studied. A reliable method produces the same results if it is used repeatedly or if different investigators use it. The strong emphasis on valid and reliable methods is one important distinction between social scientific studies of work and journalistic accounts in newspapers or magazines.

This section presents three major techniques that sociologists use to study work and workers: ethnographies, case studies, and sample surveys. These techniques do not exhaust the available methods. For example, some sociologists may study work or workers using experiments (Valian, 1999), historical approaches (Bernstein, 1997), or comparative studies of societies (DiPrete, 2002). But the three methods described here are among the most important.

Ethnographies

One way to learn what workers actually do on the job and how they interact with their fellow workers is through an **ethnography**, a careful analysis of a work situation written by a knowledgeable observer after many months or years of observation. The observer seeks not only to explain the work from the worker's perspective but also to describe and explain larger patterns that may be invisible to individual workers. This narrative account of work seems familiar because it superficially resembles friends' or relatives' accounts of life on the job. It is different, however, because the trained observer is sensitive to subtle features of the job and interactions among the workers. Their observations are also more detached. Each ethnography helps social scientists understand a work role or work settings. Evidence cumulated from many ethnographies provides an even stronger basis for conclusions (Hodson, 2001).

There are several types of ethnography. In **participant observation** the observer actually becomes a worker for a period of time. This technique gives the observer an intimate, everyday familiarity with the job content and the actual interactions among the workers. Sociologist Everett C. Hughes and his students at the University of Chicago in the 1950s and 1960s popularized participant observation with provocative studies of medical students, janitors, and dancers, among other occupations. Box 2.1 provides a participant observer's account of work at a fast-food restaurant. These studies are valuable for their rich detail about working and about interactions among workers and between workers and supervisors.

The validity and reliability of participant observation have limitations. Participant observers can typically study only a limited range of jobs. It is unlikely that the sociologist observer would have the skills or access necessary to participate, even for a short time, in highly technical jobs or in top-level management positions. In addition, the participant observer may inadvertently choose an atypical work site or join a work group that is atypical. Different observers of the same work situation might also interpret aspects of the job quite differently because of their different backgrounds, predispositions, or experiences.

In **nonparticipant observation** the trained observer does not actually become a part of the work group. One famous example of nonparticipant observation is the study of the Bank Wiring Room in the Western Electric Company plant in Hawthorne, Illinois (Roethlisberger and Dickson, 1939:379–408). Fourteen men worked in this room, wiring, soldering, and inspecting electrical boards. An overt

---

BOX 2.1   An Ethnography of Hamburgers

Ester Reiter conducted participant observation at a Burger King in Toronto. Fast food is popular in Canada, but the industry is dominated by multinational companies headquartered in the United States. The Toronto Burger King outlet where she worked opened in 1979, and by 1980 it was the highest-volume Burger King in Canada.

Fast-food establishments standardize their products in part by standardizing the way in which workers do their jobs. One objective of Reiter's participant observation was to learn the impact of this standardization on the workers. Making hamburgers, she found, was one of the most enjoyable jobs.

The store had two conveyors that could broil up to 835 patties per hour. Near the meat conveyor were two bun chains that toasted the buns and dropped them into a chute near the cooked patties, a process that took about thirty seconds.

A worker keeps the freezer near the broiler filled by hauling boxes stored in the walk-in freezer located on the other side of the kitchen. During busy times, one worker keeps the chains of the conveyor belt broiler filled with meat and buns, while another worker stands at the other end. The worker at the "steamer" end of the belt uses tongs to pick up the cooked patties as they fall off the belt, and places them on the "heel" of a bun (the bottom half). The bun is then "crowned" with the top half and

the ungarnished hamburger is placed in a steamer, where, according to Burger King policy, it can remain for up to ten minutes. Jobs at the broiler-steamer are often assigned to new workers as they can be quickly learned.

The burger board, where the large and small hamburgers are assembled, is made of stainless steel and can be worked from both sides. When the store is busy, the larger hamburgers, called "[W]hoppers," are produced on one side, and the smaller hamburgers on the other. . . .

First the [W]hopper cartons are placed printed side down on the table, and the patty removed from the steamer. The bottom half, or the bun heel, is placed in the carton, and the pickle slices spread evenly over the meat or cheese. Overlapping the pickles is forbidden. Then the ketchup is applied by spreading it evenly in a spiral circular motion over the pickles, starting near the outside edge. The onions (1/2 oz.) are distributed over the ketchup. Mayonnaise is applied to the top of the bun in one single stroke and 3/4 oz. of shredded lettuce placed on the mayonnaise, holding the bun top over the lettuce pan. Then the two slices of tomato are placed side by side on top of the lettuce. If the tomatoes are unusually small, the manager will decide whether or not three tomato slices should be used that day.

Source: Excerpt from Ester Reiter, 1991, Making Fast Food: From the Frying Pan and into the Fryer. Montreal: McGill-Queen's University Press, pp. 99–100.

nonparticipant observer sat with them for a number of days, watching their work and interactions. Initially, the observer noticed how the workers joked with and teased one another, or occasionally helped one another with their work.

The observer also noticed that the group's productivity was basically constant, despite company efforts to increase it. The observer eventually learned that the small work group had developed an informal norm defining an appropriate level of productivity. A norm is a rule that a group develops for thinking, feeling, or behaving. Laws are examples of formal norms, but most norms are informal. A worker who could not reach the normatively defined productivity level would be helped by others, but a worker who produced too much would be teased, called a "speed king," or eventually be subjected to "binging" (a thump on the upper arm). The observer reasoned that the workers, concerned about job security as many workers were during the Great Depression, feared that increased productivity would become an excuse for laying off workers.

Nonparticipant observation is useful to sociologists who cannot study a job as participant observers. It would be difficult, for example, to be admitted to medical school to do a participant observation of medical students. Box 2.2 describes a study of young physicians who were learning to become surgeons. The sociologist who studied them was allowed into operating rooms and conferences but was not himself a physician. Nonparticipant observation has disadvantages, too. The nonparticipant observer may have a more difficult time than the participant observer in winning the confidence of the workers being observed, and workers who appear to be acting naturally may nevertheless be quite conscious of the observer.

Workers may also change their behavior to please the observer, a phenomenon similar to **experimental bias**. An example of experimental bias may have occurred in early research at the Hawthorne plant. The researchers had designed experiments to test the relationship between levels of lighting and worker efficiency. Workers maintained their productivity even under conditions of very low light (Roethlisberger and Dickson. 1939: 14–18; Schwartzman. 1993). One interpretation is that the factory workers were trying to please the experimenters, regardless of the lighting conditions. The phrase **"Hawthorne Effect"** has come to refer to an experiment in which participants try to do what the experimenters want. Experimental bias is difficult to detect, and there is dispute over whether it really occurred at the Hawthorne plant (Jones, 1992: Gillespie, 1991). In principle, however, if workers change their behavior because of the observer, both the validity and the reliability of the observations are endangered.

Regardless of whether the researcher is a participant or a nonparticipant observer, the observation may be either overt or covert. If the observation is overt, the other workers may know the observer's true "cover story." Which is often that the observer is writing a book. The workers may initially feel uneasy or suspicious at the presence of an overt observer, but many researchers find that after a few days their presence is no longer noted.

In covert studies the workers do not know that their fellow workers is an observer. Alternatively, the covert observer may be disguised as a customer, an inspector, or some other stranger with a right to be in the workplace. Covert

---

BOX 2.2   Putting on the Hair Shirt: A Nonparticipant Observation of Surgery Residents

Sociologist Charles Bosk is now a professor of sociology and medical ethics at the University of Pennsylvania. As a graduate student, he conducted an eighteen-month nonparticipant observation in a hospital he identifies only as "Pacific Hospital." He was studying how recently graduated physicians learn to become surgeons in the course of their surgical residency. Although not medically trained himself, he was allowed to be present at surgical interviews and rounds with patients, and he observed the interactions between the "attendings" (the fully accredited surgeons who ran the surgical residency) and the house staff (residents).

An important feature of the surgeons' work is the weekly Mortality and Morbidity conference at which any mistakes or complications from the previous week's operations are discussed. Particularly high-risk surgeries that had bad results were "expected failures," but the conferences focused on the "unexpected failures," when a patient was expected to recover without complication and something went wrong. Surgeons were expected to admit their mistakes and accept the criticism of their peers, a ritual called "putting on the hair shirt." In the conference reported below, a resident tried to

suggest that an unexpected failure was in fact an expected failure.

Andrew, a resident, had just explained that the death of an elderly lady following a gallbladder removal was caused by her old age and general physical weakness. He was immediately challenged by an attending. "That's not what I would call thinking real hard. I mean, you didn't exactly scratch your head until it bled on that one, did you, Andrew? You can't stand there and tell us this lady died from old age. If she was going to die from old age, why operate on her to begin with?" Dr. White, the attending on the case, rose to his resident's defense: "You're not exactly being fair. You know well enough that things like this can happen any time. It was just one of those unpredictable catastrophes." The other attending answered, "That's bullshit. It doesn't sound like the treatment of this lady was very well thought out." White replied, "C'mon now, you have your share of cases like this. She was a very strange old woman."

Source: Charles L. Bosk, 2003, *Forgive and Remember: Managing Medical Failure,* 2nd edition. Chicago: University of Chicago Press, pp. 134–135.

---

observers may avoid experimental bias, but this enhancement of the validity of the study is counterbalanced by the ethical issues raised by subterfuge and pretense. Covert observers may not be able to ask clarifying questions, and so their interpretations may be superficial or incorrect.

Case Studies

Ethnographic studies are usually limited to fairly small work groups during a specific period. The reader of an ethnography typically learns the point of view of one group of actors in a workplace. A **case study** attempts to bring several perspectives to understanding a workplace issue, such as the views of supervisors, customers, suppliers, and union leaders, in addition to the workers. Thus a case study is usually larger in scope and uses more types of data. Case studies may also use various methods. A case study typically examines a work site using combinations of personal interviews, analyses of written documents, and observations. Both official documents and personal records of workers may be consulted. Case studies frequently analyze entire companies or large divisions within companies. The findings and conclusions emerge from all the materials and people that the researcher consults.

Ethnographies typically present a work group at a particular point of time—the time frame in which the observer was there. By using written documents, the case study can provide information about the history of a work site and how existing arrangements came about (Feagin, Orum, and Sjoberg, 1991). Case studies may illustrate how an organization solves a problem, or they may identify new problems faced by workers. Case studies are often used to examine the effects of recent job changes. For example, a case study might examine a work site before and after the introduction of computerized workstations. Because different management teams implement innovations in different ways, a researcher might develop case studies to compare the effects of the innovation in different work settings.

Sociologist Rosabeth Moss Kanter presents a case study of gender roles in a large company in her book *Men and Women of the Corporation* (1977). Box 2.3 is a brief selection from her work illustrating the types of conclusions that can be drawn from a case study. Because case studies use several kinds of information, the researcher can search for agreement and disagreement among the various sources. This cross-checking tends to improve both the validity and the reliability of the evidence. Many case studies are based upon interviews of informants along with studies of documents. The semi-structured interview consists not only of questions covering certain specified content but also allows the interview subject to address the issues in multiple ways or to introduce new content. Such interviews may last an hour or longer.

A good case study nearly always requires the cooperation of the employer. The researcher is unlikely to receive access to written records in any other way. Some companies are so eager to have the research conducted that they will commission and pay for it. Even these companies, however, often insist that published research refer to the company using a disguised name. For example, Kanter refers to the company she studied as "Indsco."

Some workplaces, however, do not welcome research. They may place certain documents off-limits to the researcher or allow access only if their documents are not quoted. Case studies are especially threatening to companies that are in fiercely competitive economic situations, are closely regulated by the government, have a record of hostile labor relations, or are suspected of wrongdoing by citizen's watch groups, environmentalists, or others (Cornfield and Sullivan, 1983). These, of course, may be the very companies that are of greatest interest to the sociologist.

Multiple Methods

Researchers may seek to enhance the validity and reliability of their studies by using multiple methods. Historical methods look at specific data or at case studies from several different time periods. Comparative methods look at specific data or case studies that have been completed in different countries or different workplaces. Box 2.4 discusses "rape work," which refers to a set of jobs whose members interact with rape victims. This study drew its conclusions after comparing information from a large number of interviews at a large number of sites.

BOX 2.3   Gender: Praise-Addiction Among Secretaries at Indsco:
An Example of a Case Study

Rosabeth Moss Kanter served as an outside consultant for several years to the company she calls the Industrial Supply Corporation (Indsco). During this period she collected materials and developed a network among employees. Convinced that a case study of a large corporation was needed, she began to analyze many sources of information, including group discussions, conversations, and documents. She also used participant observations of meetings, and she analyzed data from employee surveys (Kanter, 1977:293–298). She could then check each source of information against the information available from other sources. Specific incidents were reported to illustrate the more general principles that she developed.

She uses the term praise-addiction *to describe a condition she observed and heard others use to describe secretaries. Kanter's identification of praise-addiction is one sort of finding that can result from a case study.*

The emotional-symbolic nature of rewards in the secretarial job; the concern of some bosses to keep secretaries content through "love" and flattery; and the continual flow of praise and thanks exchanged for compliance with a continual flow of orders—all of these elements of the position tended to make some secretaries addicted to praise. Praise-addiction was reinforced by the insulation of most secretaries from responsibility or criticism; their power was only reflected, the skills they most exercised were minimal, and authority and discretion were retained by bosses. Thus, many years in a secretarial job, especially as private secretary to an executive, tended to make secretaries incapable of functioning without their dose of

praise. And it tended to make some wish to avoid situations where they would have to take steps that would result in criticism rather than appreciation. Their principal work orientation involved trying to please and being praised in return.

One older executive secretary with long tenure at Indsco was a victim of praise-addiction. Though happy as a secretary, and well-respected for competence, she accepted a promotion to an exempt staff job because she thought she should try it. After a year and a half, it was clear to her and to those around her that she could not take the pressures of the new job. Her nervousness resulted in an ulcer, and she asked to return to the secretarial function. In the exempt job she had supervisory responsibilities and had to make decisions for people—sometimes unpleasant ones, such as terminations. Her manager thought she spent much too long making such decisions, "moaning" afterwards even if she knew she had made the right decision. But she felt herself to be in an intolerable position. She had a feeling she was not appreciated. No one said "thank you" for her work in the new job. As the manager put it, "She was used to lots of goodies from her boss—'Hey, that's a good job.' Here we have to be of service to managers as well as subordinates. The managers feel we're one of them, so they don't go out of their way to thank us. And subordinates don't thank managers. So she was missing something she had been used to."

Source: Excerpt from Rosabeth Moss Kanter, *Men and Women of the Corporation.* Copyright © 1977 by Rosabeth Moss Kanter. Reprinted by permission of Basic Books, Inc., Publishers.

Sample Surveys

The **sample survey** is widely used to study many social phenomena, including work. A survey is conducted by asking a uniform set of questions of a systematic sample of people. The people who answer the survey are called *respondents*. They are selected according to the principles of a branch of mathematical statistics known as sampling theory, so that they will be representative of the population, the larger group from which they were selected. The **sample** may be selected to represent all workers in the United States, all employers, the workers in a particular workplace, or any other population of interest.

The set of questions, or questionnaire, may include questions of fact ("How long have you worked at your current job?") and questions of opinion ("How satisfied

---

BOX 2.4   Learning about Rape Work: An Example of Multiple Methods

Patricia Yancey Martin, a sociologist at Florida State University, set out with several colleagues to learn about the service needs of rape victims in the state of Florida. As part of this work, she visited twenty-eight Florida communities and interviewed and observed 124 different settings, including police offices and sheriff's offices, hospitals, prosecutor's offices, and rape crisis centers. Her research required interviewing 145 people, as well as observing rape trials, collecting financial reports and statistics, and reading technical reports and policies from other researchers and state agencies. Rape victims encounter a number of workers whose jobs range from providing medical assistance and consolation, to collecting evidence and conducting criminal trials. Her findings about this type of work are summarized in a book-length study (Martin, 2005:4–5).

Rape is a violent act that arouses strong emotions, including in the people who come into contact with the victim. One of Martin's findings was that different workers must manage their emotional reactions in different ways. Some of the workers, such as the rape crisis center workers and victim witness advocates, are expected to develop emotional closeness with victims. Other workers, such as the prosecutor, are expected to maintain emotional distance. One of her informants explained the concept:

[(Interviewer)Do prosecutors become emotionally involved with the victims?] No . . . they don't. They can't afford to. They are supposed to stay objective and concentrate on the victim so we can help [her]. They don't become personally that involved. It's not really their job. And they wouldn't be very good at their job if they did. [(Interviewer): so you people, the victim advocates, help them?] In a way. They tell us to tell the victim something or find out something. So we're the ones always in touch. Their job is to look at the facts and see what they have and prosecute. (prosecution victim advocate, white woman, age forty-six) (Martin, 2005:187)

Perhaps not surprisingly, the rape crisis center workers are more likely to feel distress, powerlessness, and sadness, whereas the prosecutors are more likely to feel skepticism and anger. To understand the services that rape victims receive, Martin could not study just one occupation, nor just one workplace. Instead, she interviewed a number of people in different workplace settings and also studied other information about the organizations to reach her conclusions.

Source: Patricia, Yancey Martin, *Rape Work: Victims, Gender, and Emotions in Organization and Community Context* (New York: Routledge, 2005).

would you say you are with your current job—very satisfied, somewhat satisfied, or not at all satisfied?"). Unlike the semi-structured interview, however, the sample survey places great emphasis on asking the respondents the same questions in the same ways, with relatively little opportunity for the respondents to introduce new topics. In addition, only a brief time is typically required to complete the questionnaire. Researchers administer questionnaires in three basic ways: (1) personal interviews are conducted face-to-face by a trained interviewer; (2) telephone interviews take place over the respondent's home telephone, again with a trained interviewer asking the questions; (3) self-administered questionnaires are handed, mailed, or e-mailed to respondents who answer the questions at a convenient time.

A cross-sectional survey is administered once to a sample of respondents. The same questionnaire might be administered again to a different sample of respondents. The repeated use of cross sections is useful for detecting trends in job satisfaction, work commitment, and so on. In a longitudinal or panel study, the researchers return several times to survey the *same* sample of respondents. Longitudinal studies are useful for such things as studying job changes that occur during the work life of the sample of workers.

Sample surveys are extensively used in many countries to study work. Every month, the U.S. Bureau of the Census and Bureau of Labor Statistics conduct the Current Population Survey (CPS) (http://www.bls.census.gov/cps/). This survey of about fifty thousand households asks various questions about whether its members who are over the age of sixteen are looking for work or have jobs. Those with jobs are asked additional questions about hours of work, type of work, and earnings. This is a cross-sectional survey, but some of the respondents are reinterviewed eight months after their first interview, so it also has a longitudinal component.

The Bureau of the Census also conducts the American Community Survey (www.census.gov/acs/www/index.html). This annual cross-sectional survey of three million households collects information about individuals and households, including information about age, race, education, commuting time to work, and some information about individuals' jobs. It is designed to provide information for local labor market areas and for states as well as for the nation.

The National Longitudinal Surveys (NLS), supported by the Department of Labor, contain interviews of the same samples of workers several times over a period of years to examine changes in employment, earnings, and work-related attitudes (www.bls.gov/nls/).

Various **establishment surveys** sample employers to ask questions concerning the characteristics of their companies and employees. An **establishment** is the location of an employer; it is also the work place to which an individual worker reports. The Bureau of Labor Statistics conducts the Current Employment Statistics Survey, which is used to develop estimates of earnings. The National Organizations Survey (http://webapp.icpsr.umich.edu/cocoon/ICPSR-STUDY/04074.xml) is conducted by asking half the respondents to a large annual survey (called the General Social Survey) for the names and addresses of their employers. The employers are then asked for information on topics such as company structure, employment policies, the effects of workplace stress on worker productivity, and health insurance.

Sample surveys may be designed to represent certain groups of workers or certain regions or states. Professional associations or unions survey their members on workplace issues. Trade associations survey employers or owners who are members. Many businesses survey their customers to evaluate customer satisfaction. Innovations based on the use of laptop computers, e-mail, and web-based surveys are extending the range of contemporary survey practices.

Compared with ethnographies or case studies, surveys have the advantage of being more easily generalized to the population they were designed to represent. Sampling theory allows the researcher to estimate by how much the survey results are likely to vary from the "true" answer, which is the answer that would have resulted from interviewing the entire population. By directly questioning workers, a survey can measure subjective indicators, such as job satisfaction. Changes in facts and attitudes can be traced and studied if the same question is asked in repeated surveys.

Potential disadvantages also arise from the use of survey methods. One problem is selection bias in which only certain types of people respond to a survey. Respondents may mistrust the interviewer or fear what use might be made of their replies. Some respondents refuse to cooperate at all with surveys. If such refusals cluster within an important subgroup, the resulting sample is no longer representative of the population. For example, if rich people refuse to answer questions about their income, estimates of overall income will be too low.

Another common problem is **response error**, resulting from a respondent's misunderstanding a question or intentionally giving a false answer. Response error may happen if the questionnaire contains ambiguous or double-barreled questions. A double-barreled question includes more than one issue so that the answer cannot be clearly interpreted: "Have your hours of work or your working conditions recently changed?" A "yes" answer might mean that either hours of work or working conditions or both had changed. Selection bias and response error may also result if the questions pry into areas that respondents consider sensitive or confidential. Response error is difficult to detect, and it threatens the validity and reliability of the information gathered.

The collection and analysis of survey information forms a specialized area within the social sciences. Sociologists, political scientists, and economists all make use of survey data.

UNITS OF ANALYSIS

Ethnographies, case studies, and sample surveys are examples of how sociologists study work; specific units of analysis are what and whom they study. The unit of analysis may be the individual worker or groups of workers. Or the unit of analysis may not be individuals at all—it may be groups or organizations. For example, the sociologist may study unions, businesses, factories, or corporate networks. The world of work may look quite different from one perspective—say, that of an individual worker—than it does from the perspective of the managers of a large corporation.

Individual workers are quite concrete units for the analyst. Other units are more abstract and highly aggregated. One important unit of analysis is the **labor force**, a collective term for all the workers within a country. Outside the United States an equivalent term is the *economically active population* (Sullivan, 2005).

The Worker and the Labor Force

The most straightforward unit of analysis is the individual worker. Workers can be analyzed in terms of their background, or demographic characteristics, which consist of **ascribed characteristics** and **achieved characteristics.** The worker does not control ascribed characteristics, such as sex, race, or age, although employers and coworkers may react strongly to them. The worker does have some control over achieved characteristics, such as educational background, work experience, and skills.

The U.S. Bureau of Labor Statistics reports the size and composition of the labor force every month by using information from the CPS. Anyone is eligible to be counted in the labor force who is aged sixteen or older, who is not on active duty in the Armed Forces, and who is not institutionalized (for example, in a prison or a residential hospital). Members of the labor force can be either employed or unemployed.

According to the government's definition of employment, employed people in the labor force are those who in the week preceding the survey (1) worked at least one hour for pay or profit, or (2) worked at least fifteen hours without pay in a family business, or (3) were temporarily not working because of illness, vacation, or similar reasons. The unemployed are not merely those without jobs; rather, they are people who are not employed but who actively sought work during the four weeks preceding the survey and were currently available to take a suitable job. In addition, people are counted as unemployed if they are temporarily laid off or are waiting to report to a new job in the near future (U.S. Bureau of Labor Statistics [BLS], 2001b). An eligible person who does not fall into either of these categories is termed **NILF** (not in the labor force). Most NILF people in the United States are students without jobs, retirees, people who are chronically ill or have disabilities, or people who are keeping house.

Using these concepts, the Bureau of Labor Statistics publishes every month two rates to describe the status of the labor force. The first rate, the civilian **labor force participation rate**, is the number of persons in the labor force divided by the number of persons eligible to be in it, multiplied by 100 to convert to a percentage. This can be expressed as:

$$\text{LFPR} = \left(\frac{\text{labour force}}{\begin{array}{c} \text{all noninstitutionalized} \\ \text{persons aged 16 +} \end{array}} \right) \times 100$$

The labor force participation rate indicates what proportion of the eligible population is economically active. In August 2006 the U.S. participation rate was 66.2 percent (BLS, 2006b). Trends in the rates for certain groups, such as women, teenagers, and elderly people, indicate their levels of incorporation into the economy. Nearly every industrialized country has experienced a phenomenal increase in women's labor force participation rates since World War II. In August 2006 the rate for U.S. women aged twenty years or more was 60.4 percent, compared with 76.2 percent for men (BLS, 2006b).

BOX 2.5   How to Read a Table

Sociologists frequently present their data in tables, which condense a great deal of information within a small space. Because of their concentrated information, however, tables can be difficult to read and understand. We will be presenting many tables in this text, and this box is designed to provide a method of reading tables to glean the maximum information.

Table A presents some information about unemployment rates in the United States and other countries from North and South America. The table has also been marked to indicate the principal parts of a table. Reading the table in the order of the numbered parts will convey efficiently and accurately the information in the table.

① **TABLE A   Unemployment Rates for Selected North and South American Countries, by sex, 2003**

② (annual data, except as noted)

③

Country	Total	Male	Female
Argentina	16.4%[a]	NA	NA
Brazil	12.3	10.1	15.2
Canada	7.6	7.9	7.2
Colombia	14.2	11.0	18.5
Chile	8.5	7.9	9.7
Mexico	2.4	2.3	2.6
USA.	6.0	6.3	5.7
Venezuela	18.0	16.0	21.1

Unemployment Rates ③ · Column headings ④ · Entries ⑦

⑤ [a]Monthly data for April, 2003
NA Not available

⑥ SOURCE: International Labour Office, http://laborsta.ilo.org

Parts of a Table:

1. Headline
2. Headnote
3. Stub
4. Column headings
5. Footnote
6. Source note
7. Entries

The **unemployment rate** is the number of unemployed people divided by the number of people in the labor force, multiplied by one hundred. This may be expressed as:

$$UR = \left| \frac{\text{unemployed}}{\text{labour force}} \right| \times 100$$

Box 2.5 presents recent data on labor market indicators, and it includes important information on how to read statistical tables. These data indicate

1. The *headline* tells the reader which data are presented in the table, for which groups. The headline in Table A indicates that the table contains unemployment rates, and data will be provided separately for men and women. Sometimes a headline specifies the time and place in which the data were collected. This headline notes that the data are for 2003 and for selected countries.

2. The *headnote* is a parenthetical expression that contains information important in interpreting the table. The headnote in Table A indicates that the data in the table are annual averages, unless otherwise noted.

3. The *stub* is the left-hand column of a table. The categories indicate which data appear in the horizontal rows of material in the table. In this case, the stub contains the names of the countries for which data will be presented.

4. The *column headings* indicate which data are given in the vertical columns in the table. In Table A, the first column presents the unemployment rate for the total national labor force, and the next columns present separate rates for males and females, respectively.

5. A *footnote* contains information that is important for interpreting some, but not all,

of the entries of the table. Not every table has a footnote. In Table A, the footnote indicates that for Argentina, the data represent a single month and not an annual average. The notation NA, not available, also applies to the row of data for Argentina; in 2003, the source did not have unemployment rates by sex available.

6. The *source* note is important because it tells the reader where the data were obtained. The reader can refer to the original source for additional information or to check the accuracy of the data.

7. The *entries* of the table should be read last. The reader draws conclusions by carefully reading the entries and comparing them across rows and down columns. Notice, for example, that the unemployment rates differ a great deal among these countries. Also notice the difference by sex. In many countries, such as Brazil and Colombia, the unemployment rate for women is much higher than the rate for men. But in Canada and the United States, men have higher unemployment rates that women.

What other conclusions can you draw from the data in Table A?

overall economic activity as well as the differing labor market experiences of workers from various demographic groups.

A rise in the unemployment rate often indicates that the business cycle is about to enter a downturn; conversely, a decline often indicates economic improvement. The unemployment rate is high in economically depressed areas and lower in prosperous ones, so unemployment rates indicate local labor market conditions. Historically, the unemployment rate for black workers has been at least twice the rate for whites, and the Hispanic unemployment rate has been intermediate between the rates for white workers and the rate for black workers.

As useful as labor force statistics are, the definitions used by the government trouble some observers (National Commission on Employment and Unemployment Statistics, 1979). The definition of the labor force parallels in some ways the measurement of the gross national product (GNP). The gross national product is the value of all the goods and services produced for the market during a year. People who produce goods or services for sale in the market are included in the labor force. The labor force definition excludes many people who perform useful services outside the market economy. For example, homemakers and volunteers perform needed services but not for pay or profit. If there were no homemakers or volunteer workers, then families, churches, and hospitals would have to hire workers to perform those duties or leave then undone. Although the newly hired workers would be in the labor force, homemakers and volunteer workers doing the same work are not in the labor force.

The measurement of unemployment is also controversial. The Bureau of Labor Statistics considers about 1.6 million persons to be marginally attached to the labor force; these people wanted and were available for work and had looked for a job sometime during the year prior to the survey. In the four weeks prior to the survey, however, they had not actively searched for work and so they were not counted as unemployed. Among the marginally attached workers, there are about a half million **discouraged workers**, who were not currently looking for work specifically because they believed no jobs were available. By excluding the marginally attached workers, the measured unemployment rate is arguably too low.

Others argue that many unemployed people conduct only halfhearted searches for work, perhaps because they are required to look for work to continue unemployment compensation benefits. Others may reject available jobs and prolong their search looking for more ideal work. In the view of such critics the measured unemployment rate is too high, for it includes people who could hold jobs if they changed their behavior.

One might wonder why data on unemployment insurance benefits are not used to estimate unemployment (Bureau of Labor Statistics, 2001b). The principal reason is that not every worker is covered by unemployment compensation. In 2006 the number of people receiving unemployment benefits amounted to only about 34 percent of the number of unemployed people. Some types of work, such as agricultural labor, are not covered. Unemployment insurance laws require that a worker have been employed in a covered occupation for a specified length of time, and some workers have not worked long enough to qualify. For example, young people seeking their first jobs are unemployed, but they are not eligible for unemployment compensation. Other workers continue to seek work after exhausting their unemployment compensation benefits. Consequently, unemployment benefit records seriously underestimate total unemployment.

Industry

Industry provides another unit of analysis. **Industry** refers to a branch of economic activity devoted to the production of a particular good or service. The good or service may be quite specific; thus, we might speak of the fast-food industry, but it, in turn, can be considered part of the restaurant industry or part of the even larger personal service industry.

Knowing a worker's industry is important for several reasons. First, conditions of economic competition tend to be quite specific to industries. Some industries experience heavy pressure from foreign competition, for example, while others do not. Some industries are closely regulated by the government, and others are unregulated. Second, the nature of production varies by industry. An industry with an electronically automated production process differs substantially from and industry that still requires large inputs of hand labor. The industrial process determines which specific jobs will be available and what the working conditions will be—specifically, what hazards workers may face on the job, what skills are needed for employment, how much training is needed, and so on.

Finally, workers experience economic consequences from their industries (Sullivan, 1990). Declining industries are often less productive and provide sporadic, lower-paid work. Growing industries are more likely to be productive and to provide better wages, benefits, promotion opportunities, and job security. In 2006 the earnings in industries varied from $27.54 an hour in utilities to $9.50 in leisure and hospitality (BLS, 2006a).

Industrial codes enable researchers to contrast the characteristics of workers in different industries. The North American Industry Classification System (NAICS), which was jointly developed by the governments of Canada, Mexico, and the United States, classifies 1,170 industries based on the activity in which they are primarily engaged. NAICS attempts to ensure that the same code will be used for establishments using similar raw material inputs, similar capital equipment, and similar labor. The code consists of six digits that classify all economic activity into twenty industry sectors. The first two digits indicate the sector. Five sectors are mainly goods-producing sectors and fifteen are entirely services-producing sectors. Each sector is then divided into subsectors by the use of the third, fourth, and fifth digits. For example, the "information sector" consists of communications, publishing, motion picture and sound recording, and online services. Each sector can be subdivided into subsectors, such as the computers and electronics subsection of manufacturing. (BLS, 2004a). Respondents in a sample survey can be assigned an industrial code based upon their responses to questions about what good or service they produce at their worksite; these codes can then be used to compare information about workers in different industries.

A company's sales, profits, or production can be expressed as a proportion of all the sales, profits, or production within its industrial code. The larger a proportion attributable to a single company, the more dominant or concentrated that company is within its industry. The *four-firm concentration ratio* is the proportion of all production, sales, or receipts accounted for by the largest four firms within an industry, and it can be calculated for large industry groupings or much finer groupings, depending upon the industry code. For example, in 2002 the food manufacturing industry (NAICS code 311) was a $458 billion industry, with a four-firm concentration ratio of 16.8 for the value of shipments. That is, the top four food manufacturing firms accounted for nearly 17 percent of the value of all shipments. But within this large industry, the four-firm ratios for specific industries varied a great deal: 64.2 for dog and cat food manufacturing (code 311111), 53.6 for flour milling (code 311211), 78.4 for breakfast cereal (code 311230), and 69 for chocolate and confectionery manufacturing (code 311320) (U.S. Bureau of the Census [Census], 2006, Table 2, pp. 3–4).

Table 2.1 presents information on the employment changes projected to 2014 for rapidly growing industries, with the NAICS codes provided for reference.

TABLE 2.1   Industries with the Fastest Growth in the Number of Employees, 2004–14

Industry description	2002 NAICS[a]	Thousands of jobs		Change, 2004–14	Average annual rate of change, 2004–14
		2004	2014		
Home health care services	6216	773.2	1,310.3	537.1	5.4
Software publishers	5112	238.7	400.0	161.3	5.3
Management, scientific, and technical consulting services	5416	779.0	1,250.2	471.2	4.8
Residential care facilities	6232,6233,6239	1,239.6	1,840.3	600.7	4.0
Facilities support services	5612	115.6	170.0	54.4	3.9
Employment services	5613	3,470.3	5,050.2	1,579.9	3.8
Independent artists, writers, and performers	7115	41.9	60.8	18.9	3.8
Office administrative services	5611	319.4	449.9	130.5	3.5
Computer systems design and related services	5415	1,147.4	1,600.3	452.9	3.4
Outpatient, laboratory, and other ambulatory care services	6214,6215,6219	836.1	1,160.4	324.3	3.3

Source: U.S. Bureau of Labor Statistics, available at *http://www.bls.gov/emplempfastestind.htm*
[a]North American industry Classification System

Occupation

Industry differs importantly from occupation. Industry identifies what a worker helps to produce, but occupation identifies the specific kind of work a worker does. More formally, an **occupation** is a cluster of job-related activities constituting a single economic role that is usually directed toward making a living. Because the distinction between occupation and industry is sometimes difficult to understand, it is helpful to see how they are related to each other. Some occupations are found in every industry. Nearly every industry, for example, requires administrative service workers, maintenance workers, and managers. Other occupations are heavily concentrated within a single industry—for example, nurses within the health-care industry or lawyers within the legal services industry. Even these examples have their exceptions, however; some nurses work in factories, camps, or schools; and many lawyers work as house counsel for firms in manufacturing or service industries. A few occupations work only in a single industry; an example would be taxi drivers in the transportation industry. As a rule, however, we must consider both occupation and industry for a full understanding of working life.

Some workers have several occupations because they have more than one job or are able to do more than one kind of work. Occupations are also an important unit of analysis.

White-Collar/Blue-Collar

Perhaps the simplest occupational classification is the white-collar/blue-collar division. This classification is simple but it is also increasingly outdated and misleading. Blue-collar workers—mostly factory and craft workers—once did only manual labor. White-collar workers—office workers and most professionals—had clean working conditions that made it possible for them to wear white shirts. Traditionally they earned more than blue-collar workers, but today a factory or craft worker may earn more than a clerical or sales worker.

The white-collar/blue-collar classification is less useful today for several other reasons. First, there are now many service workers, some of whose work resembles blue-collar jobs and some of whose work is more like white-collar jobs. For example, the cook in a fast-food restaurant and the elite chief of police in a large city are both service industry workers. The fast-food cook may experience factory-like conditions reminiscent of blue-collar work. The police chief has job training and autonomy on a par with other white-collar management jobs.

Second, some jobs presently classified as either blue-collar or white-collar may seem misclassified when the actual work conditions are considered. Technicians, for example, are considered white-collar workers. Many of them are highly educated, like other white-collar workers, but they spend most of their day working with machinery, as do blue-collar workers. Some factory operatives, on the other hand, work in industrial laboratories that are not just clean, but sterile. Their day-to-day job responsibilities may look very much like those of the technicians, but they are classified as blue-collar workers.

Finally, the white-collar/blue-collar distinction ignores the so-called pink-collar workers. These workers labor in occupations traditionally filled by women, such as nurse, secretary, or child-care worker. Pink-collar jobs are usually characterized by relatively low pay given their specialized skills. Elementary school teachers, for example, are classified with professional workers, but their pay may not be as high as that of other upper-level white-collar workers. Such jobs are difficult to classify as either white collar or blue collar.

Standard Occupational Classification

A more precise and detailed classification for analyzing occupations was released in 2000 by the U.S. Government. The Standard Occupational Classification (SOC) System provides comparable information for many users of occupational data, such as government program managers, students considering career training, job seekers, vocational training schools, and employers wishing to set salary scales or locate a new plant. The SOC is designed to cover all occupations in which work is performed for pay or profit, reflecting the current occupational structure in the United States.

The 2000 SOC classifies workers at four levels; (1) 23 major groups, which are subdivided into (2) 96 minor groups, which in turn are subdivided into (3) 449 broad occupations, which in turn are further classified into (4) 821 detailed occupations. Each detailed occupation is designated by a six-digit code. The first two digits of the SOC code represent the major group; the third digit represents the minor group; the fourth and fifth digits represent the broad occupation: and the detailed occupation is represented by the sixth digit (BLS, 2004b).

For example, your college professors would be classified within major group 25–0000. "education, training, and library occupations," and within minor group 25–1000, "postsecondary teachers." Your social science professors would be classified within the broad occupation 25–1060, "social sciences teachers, postsecondary," and the authors of this book, who teach sociology, would be in the detailed occupation 25–1067, "sociology teachers, postsecondary." Because of the dynamic shifts in the American workplace, the SOC is revised every ten years.

Detailed occupational information is valuable for analyses of workplaces and worker skills. Occupation, however, has many social ramifications beyond its instrumental and economic consequences. Sociologists often consider occupation as a proxy for one's position in the social class structure. People of similar occupation, besides having similar incomes and work experiences, often pursue similar patterns of leisure and consumption, share distinctive lifestyles, and are perceived in similar fashion by other members of the society (Trice, 1993). It is for this latter charactertic—how occupations are perceived by others—that sociologists have developed measures of **occupational prestige**.

One of the earliest prestige scales was developed using survey techniques, and it is often called the NORC scale because the National Opinion Research

Center carried out the research (North and Hatt, 1947: Hodge, Siegel, and Rossi, 1964). Numerous survey respondents were asked to rate occupations in terms of how much standing members of that occupation have in the community. The ratings were combined and transformed into a ranking of the occupations on a one hundred-point scale. Supreme Court justice received the highest ranking (89), and shoe shiner the lowest (27). Similar prestige scales have been developed in many countries, and the findings in one country tend to approximate closely those in other countries (Treiman, 1977). Studies in both the United States (Nakao and Treas, 1994) and Canada (Goyder, 2005) indicate that over time an individual occupation may shift up or down, but the overall standing of occupation tends to be stable.

Occupational prestige, education, and income tend to be closely related, but there are exceptions. For example, members of the clergy may receive relatively low incomes despite their extensive education and considerable prestige within the community. Nevertheless, occupation, prestige, and income are so closely related that we can often predict the general status of an occupation by the knowing the average education and earnings of its members. Such predictions are called *socioeconomic status (SES) scores.* Data on occupation, education, and income collected from censuses or in periodic surveys are combined statistically to develop the SES scores (Duncan, 1961; Stevens and Cho, 1985).

Occupation is an important concept for sociologists, for studying both work life and life off the job. For this reason there are several ways to study occupations, ranging from simple dichotomies (blue-collar/white-collar) to the complex SOC scores, prestige scales, and SES indicators. Industry and occupation intersect in a specific job, and jobs are found in specific workplaces.

Workplaces

Many workers go to work each day for enormous corporations. Some of them may not even know from day to day just which corporate entity is their employer because of reorganizations, acquisitions, or mergers, but workers have a good idea of approximately how many people work at their particular work site. Sociologists are interested in both the local work site and its position within the larger organizational context, often using the workplace as a unit of analysis.

Some employing organizations have only one **establishment**; others may have many. For most workers the establishment is important, because it is where they perform their daily tasks and interact with other workers. Even for workers whose jobs require travel, the establishment serves as a base of operations. The establishment can be distinguished from the **firm**, which is the employing organization. Sometimes the firm may have only one establishment, but other firms may have many establishments.

Firms may be organized as corporations, partnerships, professional practices, or sole proprietorships. A number of firms may be bought or controlled by a **parent company**, which is a firm that owns other firms. The firms that are owned are called **subsidiary** companies. Burger King, the company described in Box 2.1, was at the time of the study a subsidiary of Pillsbury. Pillsbury's traditional products—flour, baking mixes, and other convenience foods—were in industries somewhat related to the fast-food industry. If the subsidiary firms are in unrelated industries, the parent company can be called a **conglomerate**. If the establishments or firms are located in different countries, as Burger King is, the parent company is called a **multinational company** or MNC.

Firms are often linked to one another through complex networks of suppliers and customers, subcontracts, credit lines and other financing agreements, and "tie-ins" of one product line with another. A new movie, for example, may have "tie-ins" with a toy company, various magazines, television network, recording studio, Internet provider, and other organizations in addition to the customary movie theaters. An additional source of links is **interlocking directorates**, which occur when a director of one corporation is also a director or officer of another corporation.

Sociologists collect information on workplaces directly from workers or employers, and information on many firms is available from annual reports, government regulatory agencies, and other sources. Social scientists analyze data on firms to provide information on conditions that affect workers. In a later unit, we will be discussing the effects of work organizations on workers and their jobs.

Other Units of Analysis

Sociologists also analyze other social units that affect work. Examples include unions and professional associations representing groups of workers. **Trade associations**, which are organizations of firms within the same industry, are significant in understanding the economic conditions and technological considerations affecting and industry. Government agencies, especially those with local, state, or federal regulatory power, are also important units for sociologists to study. The web sites for some of these government agencies appear in the resources.

PROBLEMS IN STUDYING WORK

Work is a complex human phenomenon with far-reaching effects. Although researchers continue to refine their techniques and expand their studies, there remain many aspects of work life about which we have little information. This section examines some of the problems researchers encounter in studying work.

Lack of Information

Even with the many sources of information we have already discussed, sociologists have many gaps in their knowledge and understanding of the world of work. Partly because of the definition of the labor force used by most of the world's governments, we have only begun to examine nonmarket work such as homemakers (Bose, Bereano, and Malloy, 1984; Davies, 2005), volunteer workers (Kendall, 2002), neighbors who exchange labor, and so forth. In addition, we have little useful information on the production of illegal goods and services—such as prostitution, gambling, or illegal drugs, to mention just a few.

The employment generated by other legal goods and services is sometimes hidden to avoid taxation. For example, some workers are paid cash to avoid income tax withholding and the payment of employer's and employee's social security tax. Illegal aliens are sometimes employed in this fashion. Smuggling goods or bartering goods and services also constitute unmeasured economic activity and employment. These uninspected aspects of employment, which are not captured in official labor force statistics.

Hard-to-Measure Characteristics

Some characteristics of work are important but difficult to measure. Social scientists are very interested in issues such as job commitment and underemployment, but there is little agreement about how they should be measured (Sullivan, 1978; Hodson, 1991). One reason such characteristics are hard to measure is that they have both objective and subjective elements. For example, workers who are subjectively bored with their jobs may consider themselves uncommitted to their jobs and underemployed. A researcher might reach the same or a different conclusion for these workers by looking at indicators such as rates of absenteeism (for job commitment) or hours and wages (for underemployment).

Even productivity, a relatively easy concept to measure in manufacturing industries, is difficult to measure in service industries. Is a service worker more productive because more customers have been served, or because fewer customers have been served but have greater feelings of satisfaction about the service they received? Developing methods to measure and study such characteristics is an important frontier for research on the sociology of work.

SUMMARY

Sociology and the other social sciences seek to develop valid and reliable information on the world of work. In advanced industrial societies, work is complex and heterogeneous, and the study of work involves subjective elements. For these reasons, sociologists have devised different ways to examine the world of work. Although each method has its limits, each also illuminates certain aspects of work situations.

Three important ways to examine the world of work are ethnographies, case studies, and sample surveys. Using different methods, sociologists study individual workers or collective groups of workers such as the labor force. Labor force studies include the study of the demographic characteristics of workers and their rates of labor force participation and unemployment. Social scientists also study occupations, industries, firms and other workplace units, unions, and government regulatory agencies. Although some aspects of work are not yet being adequately studied, the existing methods have yielded important and substantial findings about the complex modern world of work. In subsequent units the authors will present some of these results.

INTRODUCTION

Courses in economics abound at universities and colleges, along with an ample supply of texts focusing on the many facets of this discipline. These courses and books increasingly recognize that women play an important role in the economy as workers and consumers and that in many ways their behavior and their problems differ from those of men. However, male patterns often receive the major emphasis, just as patterns of the majority racial and ethnic groups do, while gender differences are, at best, just one of many topics covered. For example, workers are often assumed to enter the labor market after completing their education and to remain until their retirement. Similarly, institutions studied are mainly those involved in traditional labor markets, from businesses to labor unions and relevant government agencies. Although women in growing numbers are spending an increasing proportion of their time working for pay, their lives and their world continue to be significantly different from those of men, and more of their time continues to be spent in nonmarket activities.

In recent years, much attention has been focused on the rising labor force participation rates of women and particularly on the changing economic roles of married women. Much has been made, especially in the popular media, of the often large percentage increases in the number of women in nontraditional occupations, not to mention the publicity received by "the first woman" in a given field, whether it be stockbroker, jockey, or prime minister. All this focus tends to obscure both the continued responsibility of most women for the bulk of nonmarket work and the large occupational differences between men and women that remain, despite considerable progress. As long as this situation persists, there is a need to address these issues in depth.

Although economic behavior is clearly not isolated from the remainder of human existence, the primary focus of this unit is on the economic behavior of women and men, on economic institutions, and on economic outcomes. To refresh the memory of students who have some acquaintance with economics, and to provide a minimal background for those who do not, the authors begin with a brief introduction to the tools of this discipline. Neoclassical or mainstream economic theory provides the major emphasis of this unit. However, students need to be aware that the authors endeavor to constantly stretch and challenge the existing theories to shed light on issues related to gender and work. So, in addition to

Taken from Blau, F. D., Ferber, M. A., & Winkler, A. E. (2006) *The Economics of Women, Men, and Work* (5th ed.). Upper Saddle River, NJ: Pearson Prentice Hall. Chapter 1, pp. 1–12.

presenting conventional analyses, the authors sometimes offer critiques of existing approaches. Further, the authors tend to emphasize the importance and implications of gender inequities in the labor market and in the household to a greater extent than some of our colleagues might and also take more note of diversity by race and ethnicity. In addition, the authors point to the increasingly divergent outcomes for individuals and families by level of educational attainment. Finally, the authors attempt to take account of institutional factors, alternative perspectives, and the insights of other disciplines where relevant.

Throughout this unit, but especially in those segments where the authors deal with policy, they are confronted by a dilemma common to the social sciences. On the one hand, much of what the authors present is positive, rather than normative, in the sense that they present facts and research results as they find them. Furthermore, the authors try to avoid value judgments and prescriptive attitudes; personal values should not be permitted to intrude upon objective analysis. On the other hand, it is unrealistic to claim that the choice of topics, the emphasis in discussions, and the references provided are, or even can be, entirely value free. A reasonable solution is to try to present various sides of controversial questions, while making clear that different premises will lead to different conclusions and that the policies one should adopt depend on the goals one wants to reach. The authors attempt to follow this approach.

At the same time, the tenor of this unit is undoubtedly colored to some extent by the authors' feminist perspective. Thus, they recognize, for instance, the extent to which persons of the same sex may differ, and persons of the opposite sex may be similar. And, like other feminists, in considering gender differences, the authors are increasingly aware of how these differences vary by race and ethnicity. Our feminist perspective also means the authors believe that, as much as possible, individuals should have the opportunity to live up to their potential, rather than be forced to conform to stereotypical roles. Most of all, it means that, while recognizing differences between women and men, some possibly caused by biological factors and others by the way girls and boys are reared in our society, the authors are less inclined to emphasize the differences between them than the common humanity that unites them.

WHAT ECONOMICS IS ABOUT

Neoclassical economics is concerned with decision making under conditions of **scarcity**, which means not enough resources are available to satisfy everyone's wants, and choices have to be made about their use. Given this constraint, it is crucial to recognize that using labor, capital, and land to produce one good means that fewer of these inputs will be available for producing other goods. Hence, the real cost of having more of one good is forgoing the opportunity of having more of another.

This concept of **opportunity cost** is fundamental to an understanding of the central economic problem—how to allocate scarce resources so as to maximize well-being. In order to make a rational decision whether to spend money to buy a new coat or whether to spend time going for a hike, it is not sufficient to know how much utility or satisfaction will be derived from each. Because the amount of money and time is limited, and we cannot buy and do everything, it is crucial also to be aware of how much satisfaction is lost by giving up desirable alternatives. **Rationality**, as economists use the term, involves some knowledge of available opportunities and the terms on which they are available. Only on the basis of such information is it possible to weigh the alternatives and choose those that provide more utility than any others.

One of the most fundamental assumptions in traditional economics is that people may be expected to behave rationally in this sense. It does not mean, as critics have occasionally suggested, that only monetary costs and benefits are considered. It is entirely rational to take into account nonpecuniary factors because *satisfaction*, not, say, money income, is to be maximized. This definition is so broad that almost everyone might be expected to behave this way. Nonetheless, rationality cannot be taken for granted. It is not satisfactory simply to argue that whatever a person does must provide more satisfaction than any alternative course of action because he or she would otherwise have made a different choice. Such an argument amounts to a mere tautology. An individual who blindly follows the traditional course of action without considering costs and benefits, or who fails to consider long-run implications or indirect effects is not necessarily rational. Nor is it uncommon to find persons who, with surprising regularity, make choices that they presently appear to regret. Most of us have probably known someone whose behavior fits one or more of these patterns.

These facts should be kept in mind, lest we accept too readily that whatever people do must be for the best. On the other hand, as a first approximation it is probably more realistic to assume that people tend to try to maximize their well-being rather than that they are indifferent to it. We shall, for the most part, accept this as a reasonable generalization, while recognizing that it is not necessarily appropriate in every instance. Specifically, it must be kept in mind that the knowledge needed to make optimal decisions is often difficult and costly to obtain. When this cost is likely to exceed the gain derived, it is rational to *satisfice* rather than to insist on maximization. By the same token, however, when additional information can be provided relatively cheaply and easily, it is likely to be useful in improving decision making.

Uses of Economic Theory

Assuming that individuals are rational is only one of the many simplifying assumptions economists tend to make in formulating **theories** and building **models**. The justification for making such assumptions is that, much like laboratory experiments in the biological and physical sciences, these abstractions help to focus attention on the particular issue we are attempting to clarify and on the main relationships we want to understand.

In many instances, the approach is to examine the effects of changes in a single variable, such as price or income, while assuming that all else remains the same. This approach does not suggest that economists believe the real world actually works in such a simple way. An aerospace engineer finds it useful to test a plane in a tunnel where everything except wind speed is artificially stabilized, even though the vehicle will later have to fly in an environment where temperature, atmospheric pressure, and humidity vary. Similarly, the social scientist finds it helpful to begin by abstracting from numerous complications.

A theory is not intended to be a full description of the underlying reality. A description is like a photograph, which shows reality in all its details. A theory may be likened to a modern painting, which at most shows the broad outlines of its subject but may provide deeper insight than a more realistic picture would. Hence, a theory or model should not be judged primarily on its detailed resemblance to reality, but rather in terms of the extent to which it enables us to grasp the salient features of that reality. Thus, economic theory, at its best, can help us to understand the present and to correctly predict the future.

Economists should not, therefore, be faulted for making simplifying assumptions or using abstractions, as long as they are aware of what they are doing and test their conclusions against empirical evidence, which is drawn from the real world with all its complexities. Unfortunately, such testing is not always easy to do. Computers now enable us to process vast amounts of information, and econometricians have made substantial progress in developing better methods for doing so. The availability, timeliness, and quality of the data, however, often still leave much to be desired.

Collecting data is a slow, expensive, and generally unglamorous undertaking. The U.S. government does more and better work in this respect than governments of many other countries. Even so, collecting, compiling, and publishing the information may take quite some time. Some data are, in any case, collected only intermittently, other data not at all. For a variety of reasons, including the government's appropriate reluctance to invade certain areas, as well as lack of interest in pursuing topics with no strong political constituency, some substantial gaps occur in official data collection. Private research organizations endeavor to fill these holes to a degree, but they are even more likely to be constrained by lack of necessary funds. The data from such special surveys are particularly likely to be collected sporadically or at lengthy intervals. Despite these difficulties, the possibilities for empirical work have improved beyond the wildest dreams of economists of even one or two generations ago.

When suitable data are available, evidence for some relationships can be obtained using such simple devices as averages and cross-tabulations. In other instances, however, sophisticated statistical methods are required to analyze the data. Such studies are time consuming, and rarely are conclusions from any one study regarded as final. At times ambiguities occur, with different sets of data or various approaches producing inconsistent results. Even so, such studies enhance the progress of science and help us to identify important areas for future research.

Because of these difficulties of data collection and analysis, timely and definitive answers are simply not available for every question. We have, however, done our best to summarize existing knowledge on each topic considered in this unit.

THE SCOPE OF ECONOMICS

Traditionally, and for the most part even today, economics has focused on the market and on the government. In the market, goods and services are sold. Government is itself a major buyer and seller of goods and services and is also an agent that regulates and otherwise influences the economy. Only in recent decades have mainstream economists devoted any significant attention to the allocation of time within the household itself, and even now such material is not always included in general economics courses. Also, for the most part, the value of nonmarket household production is ignored when aggregate indicators of economic welfare, such as gross domestic product (GDP), are computed. This exclusion is a matter for concern, in part because women play the dominant role in the nonmarket sector. The U.S. government, following the lead of many other countries, has recently initiated a national survey that collects data on time spent in nonmarket activities that could be used in the future for this purpose. It also promises to provide greater insight into a number of issues related to how people allocate their nonmarket time.

In its microeconomics section, the typical introductory economics course puts primary emphasis on the analysis of product market transactions with the firm as seller, concerned with maximizing profits, and the household as buyer, concerned with maximizing satisfaction or utility. Later it introduces markets for factors of production, specifically labor, in which the household is generally the supplier and the firm the purchaser. As a rule, however, this discussion is a brief portion in the section on factors of production, and most students may well come away with a view of the market as chiefly an institution where goods and services are supplied by businesses, and the demand for them comes from the household.

In this unit, our interest is most specifically in women and men, their work in the labor market and in the household, and the interdependence among individuals within the household. Therefore, we briefly review supply and demand in this context in the appendix.

In a market economy, the forces of supply and demand for labor determine both the jobs that will be available and how much workers will be paid for doing them. Much of the authors' analysis throughout this unit will be concerned with the determinants of the supply of labor. We shall examine how individuals and their families decide to allocate their time between housework and market work and how women's changing roles in this regard are affecting their own well-being and that of their families.

Demand is essentially determined by the behavior of employers, who are in turn influenced by the business climate in which they operate. In the simplest case, their goal is to maximize profits, and their demand for labor is related to its productivity in making the goods or producing the services sold by the firm. Thus, the firm's demand for labor is *derived* from the demand of consumers for its final product. It is, however, possible that employers depart from the dictates of profit maximization and consider aspects of workers that are not directly related to their productivity. Discrimination is one such aspect. In this text, discrimination against women in the labor market and its role in producing wage and occupational differences between women and men is another topic that we shall explore in some depth. In doing so, we also take note of the fact that differences exist within each of these groups, most notably by race and ethnicity.

On the supply side, workers may influence their productivity by attending school or getting training on the job. We shall also consider the determinants of such human capital investment decisions and their role in producing gender differences in labor market outcomes.

INDIVIDUALS, FAMILIES, AND HOUSEHOLDS

Throughout this unit, we shall at times focus on the behavior of families and, at other times, on that of individuals. A **family** is officially defined as consisting of two or more persons, related by blood, marriage, or adoption, living in the same household. It is, of course, the individual who, in the last analysis, consumes commodities and supplies labor. Nonetheless, it is often appropriate to treat the family as the relevant economic unit because decisions of various members within a family are interdependent, much of their consumption is joint, and it is common for them to pool income. At the same time, it is important not to lose sight of the fact that the composition of families changes as individuals move in and out and that the interests of family members may diverge to a greater or lesser extent. We shall return to these issues throughout this unit as we discuss the status of women and men within the family and in the labor market.

The broader concept of the **household** is also relevant to economic decision making and is becoming increasingly more so. A household consists of one or more persons living in one dwelling unit and sharing living expenses. Thus, all families are households, but one-person households, or those composed of unrelated individuals, are not families. The term *household* is more general than *family* and does greater justice to the increasing prevalence of alternative living arrangements; however, because families still constitute a substantial majority of households that include more than one person, and because the term *family* is more familiar and connotes a more uniform set of relationships, in this unit we choose to use it primarily.

A NOTE ON TERMINOLOGY

Traditionally the terms *sex* and *gender* were used interchangeably to refer to the biological and social differences between women and men. More recently, it has become increasingly common to use the term *sex* to refer to the biological differences between males and females, and *gender* to encompass the distinctions society has erected on this biological base. Thus, *gender* connotes a cultural or social construct, including distinctions in roles and behaviors as well as mental and emotional characteristics. We see enough merit in this distinction between *sex* and *gender* that we have generally observed it in writing this unit.

The question of appropriate language also arises with respect to racial and ethnic groups. Historically, people of African origin in the United States were generally called Negroes. Several decades ago the term *black* came into use, followed more recently by *African American.* For purposes of this unit, we generally use *black,* mainly because *black* is the term that continues to be used in the official government statistics on which we frequently rely. For the same reason, and to keep terminology consistent in the text, we use the term *Hispanic* rather than other alternatives such as *Latino.*

APPENDIX 1A

A REVIEW OF SUPPLY AND DEMAND IN THE LABOR MARKET

As we explained in this unit, supply and demand provide economists with a framework for analyzing labor markets. We briefly review these concepts here in the context of a particular type of labor, clerical workers.

Curve *DD* in Figure 2.1 shows the typical downward-sloping **demand curve**. Wage rate (price) is on the vertical axis, and quantity (number of workers) is on the horizontal axis. The demand curve represents the various amounts of labor that would be hired at various prices by firms in this labor market over a given period of time. If all else remains the same, including methods of production and prices of other inputs, changes in the wage rate cause movements along this curve. In this case, a change occurs in the *quantity demanded,* but demand (i.e., the demand curve) remains the same. If, on the other hand, other factors do not remain the same, the entire demand curve may shift.

Demand curves are normally expected to slope downward to the right, which means that the firm will hire more workers at a lower wage rate and fewer at a higher wage rate. There are several reasons for this. The first is that in the short run there is **diminishing marginal productivity** of labor, meaning that additional units of labor provide progressively less additional output when combined with fixed amounts of capital (plant and equipment). Capital can only be expanded or contracted over a longer period of time, which means that the only way to immediately increase output is to hire additional workers or have workers put in longer hours. The second is the **substitution effect**. When the price of a particular input changes, while prices of potential substitutes remain the same, the tendency is for profit-maximizing employers to use more of the input that is now relatively cheaper and less of the input that is now relatively more expensive. In the short run, for example, less-skilled labor may be substituted for more-skilled workers. In the long run, it may be possible to substitute capital for labor. Last, the **scale effect** can operate in both the short and long run. As wages increase, the price of the product will go up, less of it will be purchased, and fewer workers will be employed. The scale effect is likely to be especially large when wages constitute a substantial part of the costs of

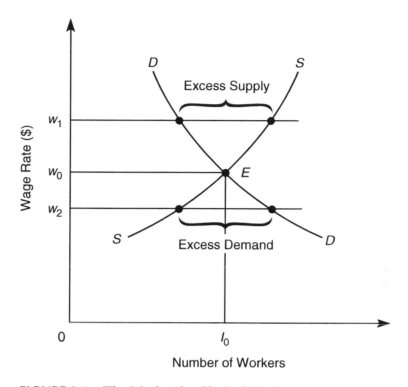

FIGURE 2.1   The Market for Clerical Workers

production, as is usually the case for services. These factors cause the quantity of labor hired to decrease as the wage rate increases, but the movements are along the given demand curve and do not involve a shift of the demand curve.

The **supply curve**, shown by SS in Figure 2.1, slopes upward and to the right. It shows the number of workers who would be willing to do clerical work at all possible prices. The supply curve is upward sloping because, if rewards for one type of job increase while those for all others remain the same, additional workers will be attracted from related occupations. So, for example, an increase in the wages of clerical workers may induce individuals who are currently employed in other jobs to improve their clerical skills and compete for clerical positions. Similarly, if pay for clerical work declines relative to others, the quantity of labor supplied to clerical jobs is expected to decline as workers move to other sectors.

It is important to emphasize that the supply curve depicted in Figure 2.1 represents the number of individuals available for a particular line of work. The number of hours supplied to the market by any particular individual may not increase when wages rise. This situation may happen because, at a higher wage rate, an individual who participates in the labor market may choose to allocate more of his or her time to nonmarket activities and the satisfactions they bring.

The intersection of the supply and demand curves shown in Figure 2.1 represents a **stable equilibrium**. An equilibrium exists when all persons willing to work at the going rate are able to find employment and all employers willing to hire someone at the going rate are able to find workers. In other words, the quantity demanded and the quantity supplied are equal at E, and no forces are causing the wage to move from its present level as long as no external shocks take place. In this case, the equilibrium wage is w_0, and the equilibrium quantity of labor employed is l_0. To illustrate why point E represents a *stable* equilibrium, let us assume that, for whatever reason, the wage rate is initially set higher than w_0, say at w_1. At this point, the quantity of labor supplied would exceed the quantity of labor demanded and push wages down toward E. Conversely, if wages were initially set at w_2, the opposite would be true. In short, we have a stable equilibrium when there is no tendency to move away from E. If an external shock were to cause a deviation, the tendency would be to return to E.

External shocks may, of course, also cause shifts in demand, supply, or both, leading to a new equilibrium. Such shocks may come from changes in markets for goods, for nonlabor inputs, or for other types of labor, and they are extremely common. Therefore, a stable equilibrium is not necessarily one that remains fixed for any length of time. It merely means that at any given time the tendency is toward convergence at the point where the quantity of labor supplied equals the quantity of labor demanded, until conditions cause this point to shift.

It may be instructive to consider a couple of examples of shifts in the supply or demand curves. These sample situations can help to clarify the difference between factors that cause a movement along an existing supply or demand curve and those that cause a shift in the entire curve. We shall also be able to see how the new equilibrium position is established.

Suppose that the government issues a report on the dangers of credit spending and that it is effective enough to cause a reduction in the demand for such services provided by the banking industry. That is, at any given price of these services, consumers demand less of them. Because this industry employs a substantial number of clerical workers, such a change would cause a marked inward shift in the marketwide demand curve for clerical workers, from DD to $D'D'$ in Figure 2.2a. At any given wage rate, then, firms are willing to hire fewer clerical workers. This example illustrates that the demand for labor is a *derived* demand: It is derived from consumer demand for the goods and services that the workers produce. A new equilibrium will occur at E_1, where the quantity of labor supplied again equals the (new) quantity of labor demanded. At E_1, fewer individuals are employed as clerical workers and a lower wage rate is determined for that occupation.

Shifts in supply curves can also alter the market equilibrium, as shown in Figure 2.2b. For instance, suppose that the government's antidiscrimination policies increase opportunities for women in managerial jobs, raising their wages and making it easier for them to obtain such employment. This change will result in a reduction in the supply (inward shift in the supply curve) of clerical workers, an occupation staffed primarily by women. At any given wage, fewer women would be available to work in clerical jobs than previously. At the new equilibrium (E_1), the wages are higher, and the number of workers employed is lower than in the

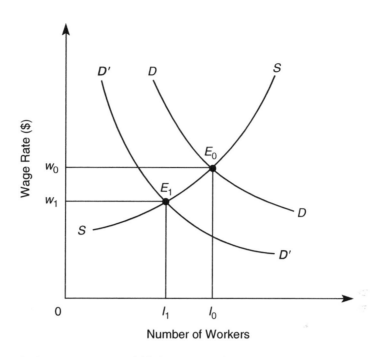

FIGURE 2.2a   A Shift in Demand

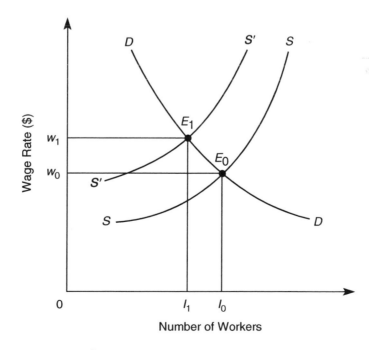

FIGURE 2.2b   A Shift in Supply

initial situation (E_0). This example illustrates that improved opportunities for women in traditionally male jobs can potentially improve the economic welfare even of those women who remain in traditionally female pursuits.

TRENDS IN THE LABOR MARKET AND THE FACTORS THAT SHAPE THEM

The workplace in this country has always been in a state of flux, primarily because of technological advances. The first industry to experience rapid and dramatic job change was agriculture and that change continues to this day. Millions of people were displaced. Technology will continue to change the nature and type of work that people do, but today another major force is reshaping the occupational structure. This force is the global economy. However, this unit is not about understanding the global economy or the nuances of how technology influences job growth and decline. It is about understanding that change in the labor market is inevitable. As a career development professional, you will need to help your clients understand that, during their working lives, they need to monitor their jobs and anticipate changes that may occur. Survival in the modern workplace requires a certain degree of prescience. Unless workers in many industries develop a sense of the changes that are to come, they will be out of work as surely as the coal miners in West Virginia were in the middle of the twentieth century and the textile workers are today.

The occupational structure is in a perpetual state of change. Some of the changes that occur are quite sudden and dramatic, which was the case in 2001 when terrorists crashed two Boeing 767s into the World Trade Center and when hurricane Katrina hit New Orleans in 2005. The jobs of tens of thousands of people were temporarily displaced because of disrupted communications systems, people's reluctance to travel, and reduction in oil consumption resulting from a sharp decrease in travel. Most change occurs far more gradually as a result of economic cycles, the impact of wage differentials on business decisions in various parts of the world, the impact of technology that eliminates jobs, and business consolidations. Even given the likelihood that many of the changes that occur within the occupational structure cannot be anticipated even by the most savvy prognosticator, predictions about the future of jobs in the U.S. workforce abound. One set of these predictions is considered in this unit.

Predicting the future is hazardous business, and even the best estimates often leave many factors unaccounted for. The risk of error increases with the need for precision and the distance projected into the future. Even though we cannot build a formula that weights all factors accurately, we can usually identify those factors that are most likely to be influential. Then we can either proceed on the basis of

Taken from Brown, D. (2007) *Career Information, Career Counseling, and Career Development,* Ninth Edition. Boston, MA: Allyn and Bacon. Chapter 13, pp. 347–360.

all other things being equal or, as the Bureau of Labor Statistics does, with a best-case and worst-case approach that identifies the range within which real change is likely to occur.

In this unit four broad topics that relate to anticipated change and the present structure in the world of work are discussed:

Causes of long-term trends
Causes of short-term trends
The occupational world through 2012
Sources of information on change and structure

Three issues are addressed in the discussion that follows. One of these is where the jobs are located, now and in the future, that is, the occupational groups. These occupational groups can be divided into two sectors: service providing and manufacturing. Alcoa produces aluminum by converting raw materials into finished products. The construction industry converts raw materials into houses, buildings, roads, and so forth. Service-providing groups produce no products. Rather, they offer medical, educational, financial, and custodial services, to name a few. For the most part job growth in this country is occurring in the service sectors. The second issue addressed is the matter of the jobs that are available now and in the future. It is this second issue that is of greatest concern to careers counselors and other career development professionals. The third issue taken up in this unit is the *who* of the labor force, that is, the people who fill the jobs that are available in the economy.

CAUSES OF LONG-TERM TRENDS

Technology

In the author's introduction to this unit the impact of technology on agriculture was mentioned. The result of mechanization in farming changed the landscape of America forever as people left the farm to find jobs in cities. Technology continues to have an impact. Just as technology has eliminated jobs in the past it is currently eliminating jobs and changing the face of others. Table 2.2 lists occupations that are declining in number of workers because of technological changes. Meter readers are among the occupations listed. In 2005, Progress Energy of North Carolina announced it was installing new meters that could be read with scanners operated from moving vehicles. This innovation will allow meter readers to read approximately 10 times as many meters in the same time frame as they could do when walking. The number of jobs in the manufacturing segment of the labor market has been declining proportionately in this country since the middle of the twentieth century for a number of reasons, but technology has been a major factor in the decline of manufacturing positions. Clerical jobs of all types are another group of occupations that is being impacted by technology as is shown in Table 2.2. Voice-activated computers, user-friendly software packages that allow

TABLE 2.2   Occupations with Greatest Job Loss by Numbers (thousands) and Percentages, 2002–2012

Job Title	Employment		Change	
	2002	2012	Number	Percentage
Jobs loss most likely the result of occupational restructuring—outsourcing and placing jobs offshore				
Textile Workers	531	179	–352	–66
Team Assemblers	1,174	1,155	–19	–2
Electrical Assemblers	281	230	–51	–18
Prepress Operators	91	81	–10	–11
Job loss most likely the result of advances in technology				
Secretaries Except Medical/Legal	1,975	1,918	–59	–3
Word Processors	241	148	–93	–39
Computer Operators	182	151	–32	–17
Meter Readers	54	46	–8	–14
Telephone Operators	50	22	–28	–56
Data Entry Keyers	392	371	–21	–5
Postal Workers	253	226	–26	–10
Brokerage Clerks	78	67	–11	–15

workers to do much of their own clerical work, and high-speed scanners are only a few of the reasons these jobs are declining in numbers.

The Global Economy

Many decades ago the goods and services produced in this country were consumed in this country. Today, as documented by the U.S. trade deficit with countries such as China which exceeded $160 billion in 2005, many of the goods consumed in this country are produced abroad. For example, most of the oil consumed in this country is imported from Saudi Arabia, Venezuela, Mexico, and elsewhere. Similarly, agricultural products, manufactured goods, and other products produced in this country are sold abroad.

However, the nature of the global economy goes far beyond exports and imports. Most corporations in this country are multinational, which means not only do they do business with other countries but they have investments and operations abroad as well. For example, Ford Motor Company owns all or part of Volvo, Jaguar, and Mazda, which are located in Sweden, England, and Japan, respectively. Many companies have relocated their customer service operations offshore, and software development and production operations for U.S. companies can be found in places such as Ireland and India. For the most part the decision to place production and service-providing operations abroad is based on economics. Wages for textile workers in China and Mexico are much less than those paid to workers in this country, and as can be seen in Table 2.2, thousands of textile workers have been the big losers. Also, environmental regulations in many countries are far less stringent than those in this country; this is one reason why the manufacturing giant Alcoa is exploring building production plants in China.

The United States has also been the beneficiary of foreign business decisions to locate a portion of their businesses in this country. These decisions have largely been driven by the fact that the United States has the world's largest and most robust economy and that we use the money that we earn to buy products such as automobiles, electronics, furniture, and so forth. Toyota, Hyundai, BMW, and Mercedes Benz have all located major manufacturing facilities in this country, which have produced thousands of jobs. Electronic companies headquarted in Japan and South Korea, such as Sony and Hitachi, have also invested heavily in manufacturing and assembly facilities in this country.

The future portends the continuation of fierce rivalries among companies and by countries to create climates that will attract business investments. These cross currents impacts the type of work available and the geographic location of that work. Moreover, it impacts the wages paid to workers, the fringe benefits available to them, and the quality of their workplaces.

Finally, as is perhaps clear from the discussion to this point, the economies of the world are linked. A weak economy in a country that purchases goods and services from the United States hurts businesses and, thus, workers. Similarly, because of the sheer magnitude of our economy, a recession in this country reverberates through the economies and, thus, the labor markets of the world.

Other Economic Factors

The global economy is an economic factor that is shaping the labor force in the United States in the future and may be the major one at this juncture. However, there are other economic factors that have profound impacts on the availability of work. For example, we are now in a long-term housing boom that has been fueled by the availability of funds at historically low interest rates. The availability of these funds has prompted nonhomeowners to buy houses; existing homeowners to buy larger, more expensive homes; and many others to purchase second homes. This boom has created a great demand for construction workers and has stimulated growth among businesses that produce building supplies, appliances, furniture, and so forth. When this boom slows as it seems to be doing, these industries will be adversely affected, as will the people who work in them. Low interest rates have also stimulated automobile sales and consumer spending generally.

Low interest rates stimulate growth in the business sector, which in turn influences the number of jobs available. If a business borrows $50 million at 4 percent to expand an existing operation, the annual cost in interest is approximately $2 million per year. If the rate is 8 percent, the cost is $4 million per year. In order to pay off the debt, the business must earn $2 million more and that in itself makes the expansion riskier. The downside of low interest rates is that it makes it harder for the U.S. government to finance its considerable debt because foreign investors may find more lucrative investments elsewhere.

The national debt, which passed the $8 trillion mark in 2005, also has an impact on the labor force in direct and indirect ways. In order to pay off the national debt, the government must either stimulate the economy, which increases personal income and thus tax revenue, or raise the tax rate. Increasing taxes to pay down the debt or to fund the government diminishes the amount of money that people have to save or spend on goods and services. It also decreases the ability of the government to provide services because money must be diverted to pay the interest on the national debt. Therefore, a high level of national debt is typically a drag on the economy and reduces economic growth and job creation. The argument in this area is what constitutes a high level of debt.

The value of the dollar in the currency exchange market is another economic factor that influences job growth. For example, when the value of the dollar is low versus the Japanese yen, businesses in this country that compete with the Japanese have an advantage. Japanese businesses sell goods in the United States and get dollars in return. They then must use the dollars they receive, which are worth relatively less than the yen, to buy yen to pay for goods and services in Japan. Because this exchange buys less yen than would be the case if the dollar was worth more than the yen, costs in Japan are driven up and this increases the competitive advantage of U.S. businesses.

Population Factors

In earlier editions of the source book, population factors, such as the baby boomers, birth rates, and the influx of minority workers into the labor market, were at the center of the discussion. As can be seen in Table 2.3, the trends of the past are expected to continue into the future with increases in labor force participation by Hispanics, African Americans, and others. What is not certain is whether these projections account for the 700,000 to 900,000 legal immigrants that enter this country each year (Center for Legal Immigration Studies, undated). Also, what is unaccounted for in Table 2.3 is the impact of the approximately 11 million illegal workers who work at a variety of jobs. An illegal worker is one who did not enter this country via legal immigration and thus does not possess a work permit, often referred to as a green card because of its color. The "coyotes" who are involved in arranging illegal passage to this country through Mexico often provide directions for securing illegal work permits.

The types of jobs held by illegal workers are typically low-paying jobs in agriculture and construction. Others find jobs as domestic workers, maids and custodians, wait staff workers, retail salespeople, and other similar types of jobs. The issues involving illegal workers are varied. Some people want to close the

TABLE 2.3 Civilian Labor Force by Age, Sex, Race, and Origin, 1992, 2002, and Projected to 2012

Group	Level 1992	Level 2002(2)	Level 2002(3)	Level 2012	Percentage Distribution 1992	Percentage Distribution 2002	Percentage Distribution 2002	Percentage Distribution 2012
Total, 16 years and older	128,105	142,534	144,863	162,269	100.0	100.0	100.0	100.0
16–24	21,616	22,425	22,366	24,377	16.9	15.7	15.4	15.0
25–54	91,429	99,865	101,720	106,866	71.4	70.1	70.2	65.9
55 and older	15,060	20,244	20,777	31,026	11.8	14.2	14.3	19.1
Men	69,964	76,052	77,500	85,252	54.6	53.4	53.5	52.5
Women	58,141	66,481	67,363	77,017	45.4	46.6	46.5	47.5
White	108,837	118,569	120,150	130,358	85.0	83.2	82.9	80.3
African American	14,167	16,834	16,564	19,765	11.1	11.8	11.4	12.2
Asian	5,106	7,130	5,949	8,971	4.0	5.0	4.1	5.5
All other groups	n/a	n/a	2,200	3,175	n/a	n/a	1.5	2.0
Hispanic or Latino	11,338	16,200	17,942	23,785	8.9	11.4	12.4	14.7
Other than Hispanic origin	116,767	126,334	126,921	138,484	91.1	88.6	87.6	85.3
White (only) Non-Hispanic	98,724	103,360	103,348	106,237	77.1	73.5	71.3	65.5

Source: Bureau of Labor Statistics. (2005). Available at http://stats.bls.gov/news.release/ecopro.t06.htm, accessed 12/18/05.

borders and deport all illegal workers. Others wish to establish a procedure by which these people can become legitimate workers. It seems likely that this country will be unable to mount a program to deport 11 million people, although it seems certain that some will be expelled from this country. It is more likely that some type of program will be put into place that allows workers to legitimize their standing in this country because, although they are illegal entrants to this country, they fill a legitimate need for workers in a segment of our labor force. Once they become legitimate parts of the labor force, people who are now illegal will be in a better position to demand appropriate pay and working conditions, which they rarely receive at this time.

The presence of illegal workers' children in schools has created other issues for school counselors and career development professionals generally. Some of these children wish to continue their education after high school and the matter of in-state versus out-of-state tuition fees for these students has been debated in state legislators across the country. Children born in this country are citizens, but most of the children of illegal immigrant were born in other countries and are not citizens. Other chil-dren of illegal workers do not pursue postsecondary educa-tion because they are afraid that their parents' status will be jeopardized. The future of the children as workers is also tentative because they are not citizens.

Birth rate, legal and illegal immigration, longevity, and retirement rates are but a few of the long-term population trends that influence the availability of workers in the labor market. The demographics of the labor force are projected to shift in a few categories as is shown in Table 2.3. For example the percentage of the labor force of Latino heritage is expected to reach 14.7 percent of the work-force in 2012, up from approximately 11 percent in 2002. The percentage of Asian Americans in the workforce is expected to reach 5.5 percent in 2012 as compared to 5 percent in 2002. However, the increase in workers of Asian descent is more dramatic than this figure suggests. The projections are for Asian Americans only. In 2002, Asian Americans were included in a category that included other groups, such as Pacific Islanders. The proportion of African Americans is expected to increase only slightly in this period.

The presence of 16- to 24-year-old workers in the labor force is expected to remain relatively stable until 2012. However, the percentage of the labor force in the 55 and over age category is expected to reach 19 percent as opposed to about 14 per-cent in 2002. Also, in keeping with a long-term tend, the proportion of the workforce made up of white workers is expected to decline by 2012. White workers are expected to make up about two-thirds of the labor force in the United States by 2012.

The overall implications of these statistics is difficult to assess. However, given the increase in the oldest group of workers it can be expected that retire-ments will influence the availability of jobs for younger workers. But, as has been noted from time to time throughout this unit, older workers are electing to con-tinue their careers on full- and part-time bases to maintain their incomes and because the enjoy their work. These decisions may make it more difficult for younger workers to move up in their occupations. Certainly, the workplace will be increasingly diverse. The increase of minorities in the workplace heightens the need to develop an appreciation for cultural differences among the current labor force and among future workers. This may well be the major challenge con-fronting career development professionals in public schools, postsecondary edu-cational institutions, and in the workplace itself as we look ahead. Advocacy on behalf of minority workers, women, and illegal workers is also needed as we look ahead. Also, it seems likely that workers who speak a second language will be at an advantage because of the nature of the labor force, the presence of a global economy, and the diversity of the clientele served by most businesses.

The Size of Government

Local, state, and national governmental agencies employ millions of people. Arguments for and against downsizing government at all levels abound.

Generally speaking, conservatives favor smaller government and liberals favor larger government, but these lines have been blurred in recent years. Government agencies are operated at taxpayers' expense and are seen as a burden on the economy by some for that reason. This issue is likely to be debated at length for some time, but should there be a decision to downsize government at all levels, the result would be dramatic.

CAUSES OF SHORT-TERM TRENDS

Several examples of factors producing short-term trends can be identified. Viewed objectively, these usually have less effect than do long-term trends. Nevertheless, to individuals who are caught in the crunch produced by transitory factors, the impact can be devastating. Some influences have a generalized effect across almost the entire economy; others may be more specific.

One of the most obvious causes of short-term trends is various types of calamities, either humanly caused or natural. Natural disasters such as earthquakes, hurricanes, floods, and volcanic eruptions can disrupt and change occupational patterns in the area for extended periods of time. Unexpected freezes in citrus-growing areas may not only destroy the current crop but also, if trees are seriously damaged, require new plantings that need several years to become productive.

Human disasters can be just as disruptive. War or the threat of war diverts large numbers of workers from civilian occupations to military assignments. It further affects others by switching manufacturing and other sectors to the production of military goods. It may create serious shortages of workers in fields that are considered less essential to the national welfare.

New directions in fashion, recreation, and other activities can also alter the occupational structure by creating new demands or reducing old ones. For example, unisex salons have largely replaced barbershops. Similarly, changes in lapel width and hemline height can make clothing obsolete long before it wears out. Imitation of movie idols, popular athletes, or television stars can create demands where none previously existed. Some technological developments occasionally start as fads (e.g., iPods) and quickly become the basis for large-scale job creation.

Seasonal variations are also influential. Summers tend to increase demand for goods and services in mountain and seaside resorts; winters have the same effect on resorts located in warm areas. The back-to-school season includes buying in retail stores, for which manufacturers have been preparing. Planting time and harvest time change typical patterns in agricultural areas. The annual holiday shopping season creates demand for temporary sales workers, letter carriers, transportation workers, and other workers.

Short-term economic factors also exert an influence. Although the general business trend over long periods is either upward or downward, small segments of that larger trend show considerable variation. Factors that create these short-term zigzags include strikes, unexpected surpluses or shortages of raw materials or processed goods, temporary market disruptions, fluctuations in access to short-term capital caused by changes in interest rates, inflationary pressures, changing tax laws, and sometimes even the anticipation of possible events.

THE OCCUPATIONAL WORLD THROUGH 2012

Having identified some of the factors most likely to create occupational change, the world of work as it is today and as it may be in the near future is examined briefly. The previous discussion pointed out the sudden changes that can occur. Major changes usually take some time to transpire; thus, a projection based on recent trends is usually the safest estimate of what the near future is likely to hold. Most of the attention in this discussion focuses on the period between 2002 and 2012, for which Bureau of Labor Statistics estimates are available.

Projections for the Future

The Bureau of Labor Statistics (2004) regularly issues forecasts regarding the various aspects of the labor force. Table 2.2 was one of those tables. In this section the 2004 projections for jobs and industries are considered.

Tables 2.4 and 2.5 contain two types of information. Table 2.4 lists the fastest-growing occupations based on percentage increase in jobs. Table 2.5 contains information about the occupations that will experience the largest job growth based on the number of new jobs. Both tables include information about the education needed to enter the occupations listed.

Look first at Table 2.4, which contains the information about job growth based on the percentage of new jobs created. Not one of the jobs listed in that table had more than half a million workers in 2002 and three, home health aids, medical assistants, and preschool teachers, are projected to have more than half a million workers in 2012. The 10 fastest-growing occupations based on proportions will add approximately 1.5 million jobs in the 2002–2012 time period. However, the 10 occupations that will produce the greatest job growth based on numbers will expand by approximately 4.7 million workers. The news media often reports growth based on percentages, which may be misleading to workers.

It is also important to note that 7 of the 10 occupations that will add the most jobs listed in Table 2.5 require only short-term and moderate-term on-the-job training (OJT). Three of the 2 jobs listed in Table 2.4 that are expected to grow the fastest based on percentage of new jobs also require relatively short-term preparation. The others require some form of postsecondary preparation. There are two implications of these observations. First, the jobs that pay the most require some form of education after high school. Second, there will continue to be jobs for people with relatively little education, albeit low-paying jobs, in spite of the often-stated myth that those jobs are disappearing.

It is interesting to note that half of the occupations listed in Tables 2.4 and 2.5 are in the health care arena. This is related to the fact that people are living longer, but as they age, people require higher levels and more intensive health care. Also,

TABLE 2.4   Jobs with the Highest Percentage Growth 2002 Projected to 2012 (in thousands of jobs)

Job Title	2002 Employment	2012 Employment	Number Change	Percentage Change	Education Required
Medical Assistants	365	579	215	59	Moderate term on-the-job training
Systems and Communication Analysts	186	292	105	57	Bachelors degree
Social and Human Service Assistants	305	454	149	49	Bachelors degree
Physicians Assistants	63	94	31	49	Bachelors degree
Home Health Aids	580	859	279	48	Moderate term on-the-job training
Medical Records and Health Information Technicians	147	216	69	47	Associates degree
Physical Therapist Aides	37	54	17	46	Short-term on-the-job training
Preschool Teachers Except Special Education	424	577	153	36	Postsecondary vocational award
Computer and Information Systems Managers	284	387	103	36	Bachelors degree or higher
Physical Therapists	137	185	48	35	Masters degree
Occupational Therapists	82	110	28	35	Bachelors degree
Respiratory Therapists	86	116	30	35	Associates degree

Source: Bureau of Labor Statistics. (2004, February). Table 3 Fastest growing occupations, 2002–2012. *Monthly Labor Review,* p. 15.

only two of the twenty-two occupations listed deal with technology, which will also be a surprise to many. In a sense, jobs in the future will be where they were in the past, with one major exception. Table 2.6 contains the projections by major occupational group for the 2002–2012 period. As can be seen in that table, production work is expected to grow very little in the 10-year period from 2002 to 2012. Only the group titled farming, fishery, and forestry is expected to produce less jobs. Three categories, management, business, and financial; professional and related; and service occupations are expected to produce the largest number of new jobs according to BLS projections. Service occupations include customer service representatives, wait staff, janitors and cleaners, retail salespeople, cashiers, and food preparation workers. Professional and related include, among others,

TABLE 2.5   The 10 Occupations with the Largest Projected Job Growth, 2002–2012 (in thousands of jobs)

Job Title	2002 Employment	2012 Employment	Number Change	Percentage Change	Education Required
Registered Nurses	2,284	2,908	623	27	Associate degree
Postsecondary Teachers	1,581	2,184	603	38	Doctorate
Retail Salesperson	4,076	4,672	596	15	Short-term on-the-job training
Customer Service Representative	1,894	2,354	460	24	Moderate on-the-job training
Food Preparation Workers, Including Fast Food	1,990	2,444	454	23	Short-term on-the-job training
Cashiers, Except Gaming	3,432	3,886	454	13	Short-term on-the-job training
Janitors/Cleaners, Except Maids and Housekeeping Cleaners	2,267	2,681	414	18	Short-term on-the-job training
General and Operations Managers	2,049	2,425	376	18	Bachelor's or higher degree, plus work experience
Wait Staff	2,097	2,464	367	18	Short-term on-the-job training
Nursing Aides, Orderlies, and Attendants	1,375	1,718	343	25	Short-term on-the-job training

Source: Bureau of Labor Statistics. (2002, January). Occupational Data, 2002 and Projected 2012. In Occupational Projections and Training Data, Bulletin 2542, pp. 18–19.

teachers, nurses, doctors, lawyers, social workers, physical and occupational therapists, and the workers who assist them. The management, business, and financial workers include stock brokers, bankers, and general managers, to name a few occupations.

Following is a summary of the BLS projections for 2002–2012.

- The number of workers in the labor force is expected to increase by 21.3 million.
- Job growth will concentrate in the service industry.
- Construction is the only goods-producing occupational group that is expected to grow relative to the growth of the labor force.
- Six of the 10 fastest-growing jobs based on percentage will require postsecondary education.

TABLE 2.6   Employment by Major Occupational Group in 2002 and Projected to 2012 (in thousands of jobs)

Occupational Group	Number in 2002	Number in 2012	Number Change	Percentage Change
Management, Business, and Financial	15,501	17,853	2,382	15.4
Professional and Related	27,687	34,147	6,459	23.3
Service	26,569	31,905	5,336	20.1
Sales and Related	15,260	17,231	1,971	12.9
Office and Administrative Support	23,851	25,464	1,613	6.8
Farming, Fishery, and Forestry	1,072	1,107	35	3.3
Construction and Extraction	7,292	8,388	1,096	15.0
Installation, Maintenance, and Repair	5,696	6,472	776	13.6
Production Occupations	11,258	11,612	354	3.1
Transportation and Material Moving	9,828	11,111	1,282	13.0

Source: Bureau of Labor Statistics. (2004, February). Occupational employment projections to 2012. *Monthly Labor Review,* p. 14.

- The rate of growth in the participation of women in the labor force is expected to be 14.3 percent women versus 10 percent of men.
- White non-Hispanics will decrease to 66 percent of the labor force by 2012.
- The number of Hispanic workers will increase to 23.8 million. African Americans will comprise approximately 12 percent of the labor force in 2012.
- Asian Americans will be the fastest-growing group of the four labor force groups during the 2002–2012 period.
- Professional and related occupations and service occupations, which are at opposite ends of the earnings range, are projected to increase the fastest and to add the most jobs.

Practical Implications

Career development professional must understand the implications of the changes in the labor market if they are to provide accurate career information to their clients. With the exceptions of Asian Americans, these groups are overrepresented in the low-paying occupations. At the point they are making occupational decisions, students need to be aware of the long-term economic implications of their choices. Moreover, because of the relationship between education and the availability of jobs, great effort must be expended to ensure that there is equity in the educational arena as well.

Finally, people who are actively considering a manufacturing occupation need to be aware of its declining status in the U.S. labor force. Manufacturing workers are competing with individuals who are willing to work for far less, accept fewer fringe benefits, and, in many instances, try to be more productive than their U.S. counterparts.

SOURCES OF INFORMATION ON CHANGE AND STRUCTURE

Whether one is assisting sixth graders to become more familiar with occupations generally, high school graduates to initiate job searches, workers with disabilities to move to compatible jobs, or structurally unemployed workers to find new directions, both helper and client need information about the present and future structure of the world of work as well as about likely change in the near and distant future. Current, useful information is available in a variety of publications.

Information about the current and projected national occupational structure is as close as the Internet. The Bureau of Labor Statistics website (http://bls.gov) provides up-to-date information in both of these areas. Two other important websites at the federal level are

Occupational Outlook Handbook	www.bls.gov/oco
U.S. Department of Labor	www.dol.gov

However, many individuals are more interested in state-level information, which is also available on the Internet at America's Job Bank (www.ajb.dni.us). Simply go to this site, click on labor market information and follow the prompts to the state of interest.

State Employment Security Commission (SESC) reports on the Internet and in print form are also sources of information about local and regional occupations. Analysts within these offices are responsible for the collection and collation of statewide occupational information. Their reports, which are disseminated within each state, become the basis for many of the regional and national publications regarding the occupational structure, as well as for the information located on websites.

Print materials regarding the occupational structure are also available from the Bureau of Labor Statistics and the Bureau of Industrial Economics in the Department of Commerce. A sample of these materials—national as well as state and local—-follows. These publications can often be found in the local library. Some, such as the *Occupational Outlook Handbook*, are available in career resource centers of high schools, community colleges, and universities.

National Sources

Occupational Outlook Handbook: Published biennially by the Bureau of Labor Statistics (BLS), this publication covers about 185 occupations, including data on job outlook.

Occupational Outlook Quarterly: Published quarterly, also by the Bureau of Labor Statistics, this journal provides updated information related to the *Handbook* and other relevant outlook data. (Online subscription is available.)

Occupational Projections and Training Data: Published annually, again by the Bureau of Labor Statistics, this publication provides data on employment prospects and on training requirements so one can see not only the likely number of vacancies in an occupation but also the supply of trained individuals who can enter those positions.

U.S. Industrial Outlook: Published annually by the Bureau of Industrial Economics in the Department of Commerce, this publication provides a survey picture of current developments in each industry as well as long-range forecasts of what can be expected over the next decade.

State and Local Sources

Occupational Employment Survey Statistics: Published on a three-year cycle (and available online) by each State Employment Security Agency, the survey collects current data on wage and salary employment by industry on a sample basis, covering about 2,000 occupations.

OES Employment Outlook: Published irregularly and updated as needed by the State Employment Security Agency, this material (also available online) includes long-term projections on both occupations and industries and is produced through a federal–state cooperative arrangement.

Covered Employment, Wages, and Contributions: Published quarterly (and available online) by the State Employment Security Agency, this report provides a detailed summary of employment and wage information for workers covered by state unemployment insurance laws.

Labor Market Information Newsletter: Published monthly by the State Employment Security Agency, this monthly summary shows significant changes in the labor force during the month and the year.

SUMMARY

One objective in this unit was to make readers aware that the occupational structure and labor force are dynamic in nature. Some of the major forces that have far-reaching consequences for the occupational structure, including technological, economic, and population variables, were identified. A brief discussion of the factors that have short-term effects on the labor market was also presented. Familiarity with the current and future status of the labor market can be of great value to practitioners who hope to maximize their client's potential in the world of work.

REFERENCES

Bureau of Labor Statistics. (2004). BLS releases 2002–2004 employment projections. Available at www.bls.gov/release/ecopro.nr0.htm, accessed 11/20/05.

Bureau of Labor Statistics. (2004). Occupational data 2002 and projected 2012. In Occupational Projections and Training Data, Bulletin 2542, pp. 18–19.

Bureau of Labor Statistics. (2004, February). Fastest growing occupations: 2002–2012. *Monthly Labor Review,* p. 15.

Bureau of Labor Statistics. (2004, February). Occupational employment projections to 2012. *Monthly Labor Review,* p. 14.

Bureau of Labor Statistics. (2005). Civilian labor force by age, sex, race, and Hispanic origin, 1992, 2002, and projected to 2012. Available at http://stats.bls.gov/news.release/ecopro.106.htm.

Center for Legal Immigration Studies. (Undated). Available at www.cis.org/topics/legalimmigration.html, accessed 11/18/05.

UNIT 3

SOCIOLOGICAL FOUNDATIONS

Examining the foundations or knowledge base of workforce education is important because such a process emphasizes that work and preparation for it can be viewed through multiple lenses: historical, philosophical, economic, psychological, and, particularly, in this unit, sociological. Each of these disciplines provides insights on how workforce education has been and is organized; the assumptions about human nature that underlie different approaches to workforce education; the market value of such preparation; individual action related to the choice and implementation of workforce education; and how workforce education is organized, who chooses it, and the network of roles that make up the occupational structure for which such students are preparing.

In the preceding units a number of concepts about the historical and philosophical foundations of workforce education were discussed (e.g., Taylorism, social Darwinism). Such concepts suggest that the philosophical perspectives that are accented in a given historical period and the political and economic trends comprising the external environment that exist during such periods are extremely influential in shaping how workforce education is conceived and implemented. Sociological perspectives advance such views by further focusing on contexts, organizations, and groupings of workers into which workforce education must be integrated and to which such education must be directed. These views are particularly vital to those persons preparing for or engaged in human resource development or management.

Taken from Gray, K.C., & Herr, E.L. (1998) *Workforce Education: The Basics.* Boston, MA: Allyn & Bacon. Chapter 6, pp. 91–111.

SOCIOLOGICAL PERSPECTIVES OF WORK

In broad terms sociological foundations emphasize several major themes. One is that sociological perspectives tend to accent the environmental factors that facilitate or constrain individual action. For example, as Hotchkiss and Borow (1990) suggest,

> *Psychologists are interested in how constellations of personal attributes, including aspirations, aptitudes, interests, and personality traits, shape subsequent job performance and satisfaction. Sociologists, by contrast, generally are more interested than psychologists in how institutional factors such as formal rules, informal norms, and supply and demand factors shape the settings in which individuals work. Sociologists have generally viewed paid employment and occupational choice as embedded in a broad system of social stratification. (p. 263)*

Thus, among other emphases, a sociological view is concerned with the structural factors that condition individual choices and their consequences, about the network of roles in which work takes place, and who plays what roles and why. Sociological perspectives also articulate the characteristics of the social environments in which work takes place, the normative culture that prevails in different workplaces, and how these affect individual behavior.

Implicit in sociological views of work is that work is a social institution, work is social behavior, and workers perform their roles within a network of social roles. In other words, a given worker interacts with other people: coworkers, supervisors, customers, managers, and more indirectly, stockholders and other investors. To accent this point and how various disciplines view work differently, Super and Bohn (1970) have contrasted sociological, economic, and psychological views of an occupation as follows:

> *Viewed* sociologically, *an occupation is a role with certain socially defined expectations, played in a network of related roles that constitute the systems of production, distribution, and service, for certain generally expected material and psychic rewards. Viewed* psychologically, *an occupation is a set of tasks and role expectations, the performance of which requires certain skills, knowledge, aptitudes, and interests and brings certain rewards. Viewed* economically, *an occupation is a means of assuring the performance of necessary work and therefore, also of securing a steady flow of income to individuals. (p. 113)*

A fundamental concept in the sociology of work is that work is performed by individuals who operate within a network of role relationships. As such, worker behavior is affected both by role perceptions held by the worker of how his or her job should be performed and by role expectations of what the worker should do as seen by those with whom the worker interacts or for whom he works. In some instances role perceptions by the worker and role expectations by others are in conflict. Such role constructs emphasize that work performance does not take place in a vacuum but occurs within an organizational culture, an environment in which job hierarchies, power and authority relationships, the division of labor, and related role dynamics between people, are played out (Hodson & Sullivan, 1990). These role dynamics organize the performance and organization of work and translate the work structure into rules, policies, and beliefs about how individual work should be done and why. These role dynamics indicate, clearly or less clearly, the relationship of each worker to the group.

Such role dynamics also provide possible responses to some of the major goals people hope to attain from work. In this case, their needs may include social affiliation, friendship, identity with something larger than themselves, a sense of contribution to a shared, organizational mission, and a feeling of being valued or needed by others to get the job done or to achieve mutual goals. Although not necessarily sought directly, work also confers social status on workers and their families. The money one is paid and the responsibility and title conferred on the individual in the workplace is, in many ways, the source of one's socioeconomic status, with all of its related aspects to be discussed later.

As suggested above, sociological perspectives describe work as complex and not confined to either its technical content or its economic implications. Landy (1989) has suggested that

> *work is something that happens to an individual. It is a treatment of sorts. People go to a work setting and are exposed to various elements. These elements include things such as heat, light, and noise. In addition, there are such elements as pay and supervisory style and coworkers. Even the duties and responsibilities that make up the job are treatments. Workers are exposed to a work pace, a certain demand for productivity, and accountability. (p. 600)*

Landy's view can be extended to suggest that when an individual chooses a job, a whole series of other choices are made with virtually no intent or information. In addition to the work content or technical tasks to be performed, one's choice of a job typically brings with it the choice of a work group of which one will be a part with all its support or hostility, its role expectations for each worker, and its definitions of the values and merits of an individual's work performance. Indeed, in most instances, the work role is not a solitary one. Workers perform in combination with others on whom they rely or who rely on them, in teams, in departments, or in other forms of collectives. Therefore, when a job is chosen, one also chooses the persons with whom one will work, the role expectations of others, the social status ascribed to the job, the types of leisure in which one will likely engage and with whom one will likely engage in leisure, how much vacation time will be taken and when vacations will occur, the types of continuing education or training required, the style of supervision, whether one's use of time is rigidly prescribed or discretionary, and the "work culture," the beliefs and traditions, in which the work group will function and work tasks will be performed.

Although sociologists are less concerned than psychologists and other specialists about how individuals make the choice of a job or why, they are concerned about most of the contextual dimensions named above as aspects of the work environment, how they vary across work settings and organizations, their implications for the organization of work, and the nature of the role relationships that support work as a goal-directed group activity. Industrial and organizational sociologists are also concerned with the factors and social forces that combine to alter the sociology of work or how the sociology of work differs cross-nationally or cross-culturally.

SOCIOLOGICAL CLASSIFICATION OF LABOR MARKETS

A final area of particular concern to those engaged in workforce education and development is a vocabulary of the workplace and the interaction of access and mobility within it with issues of race and gender. Sociologists have introduced a variety of interesting and important ways to classify both the nature of firms and the types of jobs that exist within these firms. It is, then, a short step to classify the types of persons who hold jobs within different types of firms and at different levels within them.

At a basic level sociologists concerned with structuralist approaches to resources available and their relationship to the distribution of the rewards of work have advanced notions that have been technically described as *dual economy theory* and *dual labor market theory*. In dual economy theory, firms have been classified by economic sector as core or periphery (Hotchkiss & Borow, 1990) or by the more familiar notions of a *primary labor market* and a *secondary labor market* (Doeringer & Piore, 1971). Core or primary labor markets typically refer to large firms that hold major power in the markets in which they operate, are typically engaged at national or international levels, usually are technology intensive in their application of advanced technology, provide high income and excellent fringe benefits (e.g., health care, education) for their employees, and have extensive career ladders that provide multiple opportunities for advancement, movement to supervisory and management opportunities, and security for workers. Periphery firms tend to be smaller, with lower wages and fewer benefits, less security, shorter career ladders, and fewer opportunities for advancement, and less opportunity for training or for educational benefits than firms in the core or primary labor market. It might be noted here that periphery firms may be divided into those that are essentially "start up," or young firms that may be highly technological, creative and innovative, well on their way to becoming part of the primary or core economic sector, or those firms that are more likely to be described as part of a secondary labor market. These are often described as the world of fast-food restaurants with minimal career ladders, a transient work force, often minimum wages, few health or other benefits, and work content that is designed to be achieved by workers who are primarily part-time and with limited education or technical training. Often this subset of periphery firms is a place for young persons to establish their credibility as workers and obtain spending money or some income to apply to education.

In essence core firms and primary labor markets not only differ in terms of the economic sectors they occupy, but they also differ in terms of the internal labor markets, entry ports, and who is likely to be hired. Firms in the core or primary labor markets are likely to be larger and with greater resources to train workers. The salaries, promotional opportunities they provide, and job security are likely to attract persons with good education, experience, and training. Core or primary labor market firms also can afford to train those they employ and, indeed, repeat training as often as their industrial processes or equipment change and require work relearning. Often because of size, attractiveness to experienced and educated workers, and resources that allow training to be done in-house and by experienced workers, these firms have not historically required or supported workforce education. In contrast, many of the periphery firms, because they are small and frequently cannot afford in-house training departments or the loss of production that occurs when master workers train neophyte workers, have relied on workforce education to provide persons who have sufficient skills that reduce their need for training. These workers are less expensive to train and experience a shorter period of time to become productive than those with no technical skills and those who need extensive training before they can be productive.

As has been suggested, the characteristics of internal labor markets and career ladders are not independent of the description of firms as core or periphery or as in the primary or secondary labor markets. Internal labor markets are shaped and developed within these different work organizations as symbolic and as de facto mechanisms for advancement, in which earnings are related to the level of the job, its responsibilities, and technical skill requirements. Internal labor markets in firms in various economic sectors have, for example, different entry ports for persons employed in different occupations important to the firm and reflected in the career ladders detailing experience and skills or training prerequisites.

Although frequently cast as a dual labor market or dual economy, in fact it would be more realistic to speak of the occupational structure as comprising a continuum or range of firms that differ in size, command of resources, internal labor market characteristics, training requirements and availability, and other variables discussed earlier. But whether one thinks of more and less desirable employment organizations, a dual classification or a continuum of firms, a primary or a secondary labor market, who works in which of these firms and sectors differs by race and gender. Access to these firms, and to desirable positions within them has to do with institutionalized formal and informal rules, organizational culture, and often institutionalized beliefs about which classes of individuals are suited for specific jobs. For example, unionized core firms in urban areas tend to be dominated by white males in the internal labor force. Indeed, much of the empirical research on the subject suggests that minority group members are concentrated in low status occupations and earn substantially less than whites (Farley & Allen, 1987) and that women remain employed in a narrow band of occupations and consistently earn less than men (England & McCreary, 1987). Gender segregation by occupation is more apparent than racial segregation by occupation, although there have been declines in the gender composition and segregation of jobs and occupations (England &

Farkas, 1986). However, sociologists have pointed out that there is a difference between job and occupational segregation in which it is possible for occupations to show less gender segregation, even though some jobs within occupational groupings remain segregated (Bielby & Baron, 1986). In the main, racial and gender differences cannot be accounted for by human capital variables such as training and ability but are primarily a function of structural barriers of stereotype, prejudice, and discrimination. Discrimination against women and minority group members is not confined to access to occupations or mobility within them. It is also reflected in income differences, which is a proxy for the quality of jobs available to minority persons and women and promotions attained and which suggests that the median family income for African American families is about 60 percent of that for white families and that full-time female workers make about 65 percent of the earning of full-time male workers (Hodson & Sullivan, 1990).

SOCIOLOGICAL PERSPECTIVES OF CONTEMPORARY WORK TRENDS

As sociological perspectives are applied to characteristics of contemporary work forces and work organizations, many factors arise from the emerging global economy and the resulting changes in the national economy that are affecting the sociology of work in the United States. Examples of these factors include the following:

The Downsizing and Reorganization of Work Organizations

Among the trends associated with downsizing are reductions in middle-level management and the reconfiguring of many jobs in order to use advanced technology in the workplace to its fullest advantage as a source of increased productivity. Such changes have affected the organizational structures of work, changing many from a pyramidal, centralized, and hierarchical structure to a more flattened and decentralized structure. In such circumstances traditional patterns of upward mobility are being modified to accommodate horizontal or lateral mobility as managers and skilled workers are frequently assigned to work teams, solving different types of organizational or production problems rather than specializing in one type of problem or process. In such cases, the sociology of work shifts its foci from the hierarchical structure of power relations to the diffusion of power through the organization, work-team consensus building, team building, quality circles, and other forms of shared decision making that include all workers who have relevance to a given production or organizational decision.

Just-in-Time Procedures

The search for efficiency in the workplace has led to such processes as "just-in-time inventories," which reduce the space and personnel necessary to warehouse and distribute parts, materials, and other elements important to particular work goals or processing. Just-in-time inventory procedures ensure that necessary parts and raw materials arrive at the production site just in time to be used, thereby dramatically reducing the costs of storage. Monitoring these production needs by advanced technology and tracking their convergence from suppliers at just the right time increase the importance of timing and the complexity of logistical planning, but they reduce the number of permanent workers required to manage inventory, keep it secure, or engage in related jobs.

Just-in-time inventory control is, in some ways, related to just-in-time workers. Although not described in those terms, corporations and industrial sociologists increasingly talk about the use of a "contingency workforce," which really means a part-time or temporary workforce, to augment a core, permanent workforce. The basic point of such an approach to personnel management is to reduce the permanent overhead costs of maintaining a large core workforce by supplementing the core workforce with temporary or part-time workers who do not receive permanent pension or health-care benefits and are less costly than permanent workers. In such situations part-time or temporary workers can be added at seasonal work peaks or when needs for labor surge for short periods of time. In some cases particular functions (e.g., data entry and other administrative tasks, recruitment of employees, employee assistance programs, and social services) can be outsourced to firms that provide such services under contract without adding to the corporation's permanent costs for functions that would otherwise require core employees and the long-term costs of housing them and providing them with individual benefits.

As these changes in work organization and personnel management unfold, they pose new challenges to the application of the sociology of work. Among them are concerns about the meaning of work for thousands, perhaps millions, of workers who may no longer anticipate having a lifelong career identity with a particular firm or the assurance of stable employment during their work life. They pose such sociological questions as, How will such potential instability affect work preparation patterns or work choice? How will economic uncertainty affect long-term spending patterns of persons who become part-time or temporary employees on an essentially permanent basis? What are the distinctions in characteristics, ability, and skills between those who become core, permanent employees and those who do not? Are temporary or reserve employees disproportionately members of minority groups or women? What are the effects for society of having large numbers of persons experience underemployment (e.g., part-time employment, jobs that do not fully use one's skills)? How do part-time and temporary workers satisfy their needs from work for social relations, affiliations, and personal identity?

The Global Economy

The rise of a global economy and the international economic competition that it spurs among nations have accented the fundamental importance of advanced technology as the element that makes such world economic structures possible.

Satellite transmissions, computers, telecommunications, electronic mail, Picture Tel, and facsimile transmissions (faxes) are only part of the enormous array of mechanisms that permit work units for the same corporation to be located throughout the world and coordinated by electronic means. Such technologies allow huge sums of capital to be moved electronically overnight without respect to political boundaries. Advanced technologies permit industrial parks to arise in the Caribbean nations, in Ireland, or in India, to download from satellites electronically communicated work tasks involving information processing, data entry, and related activities and then upload the finished work to satellites and return it to the corporate location in the United States, Western Europe, or Japan where it originated. Computer software development and information processing by electronic means are only examples of the many ways advanced technology has contributed to the globalization of the workforce, to the creation of what anthropologists are now calling the global factory (Blim, 1992: 1) in which industrial production for the capitalist world market is now found on every continent and in most regions of the world, incorporating "vast new populations of workers—peasants, artisans, industrial workers—in novel production or labor processes" and contributing as well to a global labor surplus and to global unemployment. All of these possibilities are present at the same time; they allow corporations in any developed nation to reach out across the globe to find talented and willing workers, and typically less expensive workers than exist in the United States, and to engage in what might be described as transnational outsourcing.

In such circumstances the sociology of work becomes increasingly internationalized as it examines the impacts of the economic and political events that have caused a restructuring of the world's economy. Among contemporary concerns are the shifts in the nature of the labor market in one nation or another as specific industries are moved from nation to nation. An example are the effects that result as multinational corporations acquire industries recently privatized in countries shifting from a communist form of economy to a market-driven, capitalist economy and as these corporations introduce a variety of new management and organizational dynamics to make the previously communist economies more dynamic, productive, and interactive with the rest of the world's economy. In such circumstances, sociologists have important concerns about how such major introductions of technology and knowledge affect the social rhetoric about work in countries where the work ethic had been stable and advanced technology was not a major part of the workplace. They are concerned with how various cultures embrace work identity, become innovative or marginal in the world economy (Hodson & Sullivan, 1990), make assumptions about workers and how work should be organized, and describe patterns of work meaning and outcomes in different nations. England (1990), for example, has demonstrated in his research that patterns of work meaning and related work outcomes are differently distributed among the workforces of Japan, Germany, and the United States. England has reported some eight patterns of work meaning in which work is more or less valued and more or less central to individual identity. The eight patterns are arrayed in Table 3.1

TABLE 3.1   Cultural Patterns of Work Meaning

Pattern A—nonwork-centered, nonduty-oriented workers
Pattern B—nonwork-centered, high duty-oriented workers
Pattern C—economic worker pattern
Pattern D—high rights and duties economic workers
Pattern E—low rights and duties noneconomic workers
Pattern F—moderately work-centered, noneconomic, duty-oriented workers
Pattern G—work-centered and balanced work values workers
Pattern H—work-centered expressive workers

Each of these patterns represents different combinations of work centrality, economic values, levels of obligation and commitment, and entitlement. England's research showed that the labor forces of the United States, Germany, and Japan were represented differently by the proportions of workers in each of these patterns.

Although each of the three countries has workers in each of these patterns, they vary in the percentage or concentration of workers in particular patterns. For example, patterns E, F, G, and H are the most work-centered patterns and those in which workers define working in terms of "contributing to society," "something which adds value," "being accountable for one's work," and "basically interesting and satisfying." According to data presented by England (1990), Japan has 63.9 percent, the United States has 49.8 percent, and Germany has 30.6 percent of its workers in the four most work-centered patterns identified (E, F, G, and H). These are the patterns in which job satisfaction, company orientation, contributing to society, being accountable, and adding value have been found to be the highest in the definitions of work.

Such cross-national or cross-cultural views on work, meaning how work is perceived by workers and how central work is to individual worker identity, provide sociologists of work important insights into how workers in a particular nation are likely to incorporate perspectives about work into their personal psyche and the work behavior they manifest. Sociologists of work also study how the values and perspectives about human resources or individual behavior that predominate in a given society are likely to be accommodated in work organizations and, indeed, in national policies.

The classic work in this area has often contrasted the United States and Japan in their expectations of worker behavior, their organization of work, and in their related governmental policies. As has become axiomatic in discussions of social values and individual traits that are dominant in the United States, freedom, justice, liberty, and unfettered individual achievement tend to be frequently cited. In such perspectives the burden of achievement rests with individual action, aspirations, and skills; individual advancement is an individual responsibility, not a corporate one. Work organizations are organized around such assumptions about the primacy of individual responsibility to remain employable and to gain skills that allow one to be competitive for advancement and occupational mobility. These social values are not those that predominate in Japan. In that nation loyalty, conformity, hierarchy, duty, and obedience are dominant social values. To accommodate and reinforce these social values, work organizations and policies toward workers are different in Japan than in the United States. Japan's economic and political system related to work has increasingly been referred to as a "developmental model" rather than as a "regulatory model," the term that often tends to be used to refer to the United States and to the United Kingdom (Dore, 1987).

Developmental models of work organization are more prone than regulatory models to clearly define strategic economic goals, ensure that workers are constantly prepared to manage and implement the processes required to meet the economic goals of the work organization, and to reinforce worker identification with these goals and the personal contributions necessary to achieve such outcomes. It is within such contexts that Japanese work policies emphasize harnessing the tacit or latent skills of every worker from the factory floor to the executive office, to encourage all workers—whether custodian, machine operator, or manager—to diagnose problems they encounter and organize information and actions that will improve productivity and corporate knowledge. It has been suggested (Wood, 1990) that in a developmental model every worker is expected to "figuratively" think as an industrial engineer in order to find ways to seek continuous improvement in one's personal job and in an aggregate sense throughout the organization. It is within such a perspective that notions emerge of a corporate family in which everyone, whatever the job, has an important contribution to the whole. It is also why workers in Japan are trained in teamwork, multifunctional or cross-trained approaches, interpersonal skills, and problem-solving capabilities. It is assumed that such skills are critical to creating conditions that encourage cooperation rather than competition among workers, collective identity and commitment relevant to the organizational mission, and a personal sense of being responsible for and diagnosing the ways by which the organization can become more productive and effective (Wood, 1990).

A regulatory model, in contrast to the developmental model just described, is seen as being more concerned with the processes and rules of competition rather than the substance. Issues about antitrust regulations, antimonopolistic power in the marketplace, and the separation of government functions and influences from those of the private, corporate sector are addressed with intensity, legislation, and punishment, if breached. Certainly this is not so in the same ways in Japan. In the perspective of some observers the regulatory model assumes that individuals or organizations will constantly try to "beat the system," to abuse power, and, therefore, they must be regulated in order to promote equity, access, and fairness in competition (Fallows, 1989). But, somewhat paradoxically, in the United States and in a regulatory model, considerable expenditures occur in legal services and in the creation of bureaucratic structures by which to monitor, interpret, and implement regulations while at the same time developing mechanisms by which to stimulate a constant search for short-term profits in which individual workers are expected to be aggressive risk takers and to manifest relative autonomy as they pursue individual achievement and as they apply their personal ability to cope with market forces and the competition from other firms.

It would be inaccurate to argue that a developmental model and a regulatory model are extreme points of a dichotomy and as such they describe perfectly the differences that characterize the sociology of work in the United States and Japan. They are not. They are rather on a continuum of difference that emanates from historical, political, and cultural differences in beliefs about work and work organizations. Indeed, Hodson and Sullivan (1990) have examined in a comprehensive fashion work practices across the global economy. In doing so they distinguish industrial relations in the least developed nations and in the more advanced developing nations. Within these emphases they compare sociological perspectives in the developed economies through a variety of lenses: state-regulated capitalism, macroplanning, codetermination, autonomous work groups, state-planned economies, and worker self-management. Discovering and applying these differences in the work culture, in work groups, and in work outcomes, as these constitute the sociology of work in specific nations or cultures, are important foundational content for workforce education. This is true for many reasons but, perhaps significantly, because the sociology of work differs not only in selected cross-national comparisons but also across industries in the United States. The models of work organization, expected individual work behavior, and the network of roles in which workers perform is not the same in the construction industry, the transportation industry, the health care industry, or in retailing and financial services. Each of these industries manifests a somewhat different sociology of work that persons engaged in workforce education and development need to anticipate and study as relevant.

Technology, Information, and Power

A further example of a major emphasis in the sociology of work is how advanced technology has changed the distributions of power and information in organizations as well as how it has changed the preparation for work. For example, as more work activity is information-based and more workers are using computers and other forms of advanced technology to implement the work processes for which they are accountable, more persons in a plant or firm are sharing larger quantities of information. Because, in the past, power has frequently rested on possessing restricted information that was held only in the hands of managers or other executives, as information is more widely held by workers at lower levels in the work organization, there is a diffusion of power. In essence, the implementation of computers has redefined the social role of workers, modified the work environment, changed the social relationships among workers in organizations, and changed the flow and exchange of communications and information within organizations. For some workers the installation of computers in the workplace has engendered more autonomy, but for others it has placed them within new forms of monitored worker productivity, surveillance of worker behavior, social or organizational control, and an altering of employee and management relationships.

The inclusion of computers and other advanced technology in the workplace has changed the mix of jobs available in the American occupational structure and blurred boundaries, not only between management and employers but also between different occupational classifications of workers. For example, by the year 2000, the automotive assembly plant and the tasks performed by workers on the assembly line will be dramatically different from what was true in the 1980s or even early 1990s. In the latter period, workers on the automotive assembly line were still installing automotive parts manually as a total car was assembled on the line. In the year 2000 much, if not all, of the fabrication, assembly, and finishing of an automobile will be done by robots, monitored and directed by computers. In most instances during these processes humans will rarely, if ever, touch an automobile as it is being assembled. Rather they will program and maintain the computers and robots that perform these tasks. In such contexts, even though the worker is still classified as engaged in manufacturing and automotive assembly, what that person is actually doing is akin to that of a service industry, to applying information and knowledge to program, operate, and service computers and other forms of advanced technology.

Stress in the Workplace

At a minimum, then, the intensity of the implementation of advanced technology has altered the work environment, the language of the workplace, communications among workers and management, the nature of the work organization itself, and the mix of jobs available in the United States and in other countries as the reach of advanced technology becomes worldwide. It has also introduced new forms of stress to the workplace and it has, in general, been responsible for a rise in educational requirements expected of workers in many occupations.

The Office of Technology Assessment (1988) has asserted that stress resulting from working conditions has become a major health hazard, resulting in stress-related absenteeism and medical expenses. In addition, alcoholism and drug abuse may be related to job-induced stress. Although uncertainty in the American economy has often been greater, pressures can increase in periods of rapid change. Rapid change in working environments and management practices can lead to stress. Many new office jobs result in increased responsibility without increased authority—a combination that easily leads to stress.

Another factor likely to increase stress in contemporary workers is the rise in educational requirements associated with emerging occupations and with those occupations being redesigned to become more technologically intensive. For more than a decade in the United States, the average education or skill level required for employment has steadily increased. This phenomenon has occurred, at least partially, because many unskilled and semiskilled jobs have been eliminated by the use of technology in the United States or they have been exported to overseas locations, thereby pushing up the levels of education required by the jobs that remain.

Another factor is that, although there will remain many jobs requiring a minimum education, particularly in the service sectors, new jobs being created require functional competence in reading, writing, communications, and frequently in computer literacy. In these emerging jobs, knowledge is replacing experience as the basic requisite for employment throughout the workforce (Drucker, 1989; Toffler, 1990). Technical skills learned at a postsecondary level, not necessarily college, are becoming the expectation for high-skills/high-wage employment in many occupations, including skilled workers and technicians. These rises in educational requirements are occurring throughout the world as it has become increasingly accepted that the primary asset of a nation hoping to be a central player in the global economy is not its raw materials or even its capital resources but rather the literacy, numeracy, teachability, and flexibility of its workforce.

The modifications in the workplace, in communications, and in information flow among workers and among workers and managers in the amount and types of stress in changing work environments, in the shifting classifications and availability of jobs, and in the rising educational requirements in the workplace lend themselves to sociological study and explanation. Although each of these shifts ultimately has direct effects on individual workers and their family members, sociologists, by definition, are more likely to be concerned about the nature of these changing work contexts, the effects of social forces on the organization of work, and the social relations and communications among workers. Clearly, the new factors that have emerged as preeminent sociological problems in work as a social institution are the pervasive impact of advanced technology and a changing international and political environment to which domestic work organizations and workers must accommodate.

SOCIAL CLASS, WORKFORCE EDUCATION STUDENTS, AND WORK

However important sociological perspectives are on the organization of work and the contemporary forces affecting such organization, there are other important applications of such perspectives as well. For much of the history of workforce education, particularly as it has appeared in the secondary school in vocational education curricula, there have been concerns that vocational education was a dumping ground for students of low achievement (Aring, 1993) or that it tended to recruit students of low socioeconomic background into vocational education and thereby limit their opportunities for social mobility. Such views tend to be borne out when one views selected profiles of students who take academic or college preparatory curricula in high school in contrast with those students who major in vocational education. For example, Berryman (1982) reported that these contrasts showed the following for vocational students:

- They demonstrate substantially lower school performance and measured ability than academic students.

- They derive from families of much lower socioeconomic status than those of academic students.
- They show more self-esteem than academic students but have less sense of control over events that affect them.
- They value occupational security and family happiness more than academic students.
- They value occupational contacts and steady progress in work more than the academic group.
- They participate in extracurricular activities less than academic students.
- Their postsecondary plans differ substantially from academic students.

Berryman (1982) summarized her findings by stating that,

When we look at this array of variables, we see a group that, relative to one or both of the other curricula groups, comes from the economically lower-status families in the community; does not do well at what schools tend to define as their highest status mission—cognitive development. This group is not part of the high school's extracurricular structure except for that part directly related to the vocational curriculum, it rates the quality of the school positively, is not alienated from the high school, does not regard itself as having been channeled into its curriculum, wants money, steady work, and a happy family life, prefers to work after high school, selects practical (technical/vocational) postsecondary education, has higher postsecondary employment rates and a higher number of hours worked per week and is more satisfied with jobs as a whole and with their specific dimensions. (p.184)

Other studies of vocational education students show some greater heterogeneity among such students than does the research of Berryman. For example, Dayton and Feldhauser (1989) have reported on the presence of gifted students in vocational education as defined by their high level of academic talent and ability, vocational talent, high level of motivation, persistence, study skills, and leadership. The National Center for Educational Statistics has reported that,

The vocational curriculum appeals to a diverse group of students. Individuals from all racial-ethnic backgrounds and all levels of academic ability and socioeconomic status take vocational "education courses." But, these data also show that participation in most vocational areas decreases as students, socioeconomic status, academic ability, and high school grades increase, Graduates in the highest socioeconomic, academic quartile, or those who mostly earn As in high school, are less likely than students with lower socioeconomic status, academic ability, and grades to participate in vocational education. (p. xxii)

A sociologist who looks at these data may interpret them in a number of ways. One would be to characterize students in vocational education as being predominantly from low socioeconomic environments, carrying out the implications of family influence to pursue blue-collar jobs in the trades and technical areas. This could possibly be because their fathers are engaged in such an occupation or because there are no role models in the students' environment that demonstrate how to pursue other occupations of a managerial or professional nature. Sociologists might suggest that these students lack information about possibilities other than vocational education or that employers, because of ageism or other prejudices against lower socioeconomic youth, have deliberately or inadvertently created obstacles to their mobility and further education. Such hypotheses would each be accurate for some students. Certainly, information about a spectrum of educational and occupational possibilities through role models in one's immediate environment, positive counselor contact, or systematic exploration opportunities has been shown to be less available for most students in vocational curricula than for students in college preparatory programs (e.g., Herr, Weitz, Good & McCloskey, 1981; the Business Advisory Committee, the Education Commission of the States, 1985; the Research Policy Committee, the Committee for Economic Development, 1985).

FAMILY INFLUENCES OF WORK AND STATUS ATTAINMENT

In such contexts, existing research findings suggest that family socioeconomic status is comprehensively related to the career development, socialization, and career choices of children. This basic sociological postulate, called the status attainment model, contends that "the social status of one's parents affects the level of schooling one achieves, which in turn, affects the occupational level that one achieves" (Hotchkiss & Borow, 1990: 267). More recent studies have expanded this fundamental concept to include greater attention to socio/psychological processes and mental ability as parts of this model of family status and occupational attainment (Sewell & Houser, 1975; Alexander & Palla, 1984). In addition, there are a number of perspectives that relate the influence of parents' socioeconomic status to the assignment of the student to an ability group in elementary school and subsequently to placement within a curriculum track in high school. In turn, the track a student pursues in the secondary school has a great deal to do with the type of academic learning to which one is exposed, whether or not one is likely to drop out or persist to high school graduation, and the total amount of education one ultimately completes. These curriculum choices in the secondary school tend to be proxies by which parents' socioeconomic status is linked to students' learning and aspirations in elementary and secondary schools and ultimately to their adult attainments (Vanfossen, Jones & Spade, 1987; Gamoran & Mare, 1989; Lee & Bryk, 1988; Garet & DeLany, 1988). Embedded in the socioeconomic status of families are many other issues and possibilities. Socioeconomic differences are associated with differences in information one acquires about work, the types of work experience one has access to, and the development of occupational stereotypes that, in turn, affect the development of vocational interests.

*Question becomes What shapes
the clientel? ·ILC-government influenced not neutral
of education

These exploratory experiences and the attitudes toward types of work available and for which one is "worthy," start early and differ in the educational experiences and content pursued. For example, McKay and Miller (1982) found in their research that elementary school children from middle and upper socioeconomic backgrounds choose white-collar and professional occupations as goals more often than children from lower socioeconomic backgrounds; that these attitudes are firmly established by the time a child is in grade 3, and that there is a positive relationship between socioeconomic level and the complexity of the data used to make occupational choices.

Friesen (1986) has contended that in trying to understand the positive effects between socioeconomic status in families and the vocational attainment of children, it is necessary to consider both opportunity and process issues. In the first instance the higher the socioeconomic status (SES) of the family, the more likely parents are to have the resources to finance educational opportunities that lead to higher status occupations. In addition, different socialization patterns exist among SES groups. As examples, middle-class parents tend to value self-direction in their children, and lower SES parents tend to value conformity. Other research has shown that parents reinforce behaviors or goals differently in sons and daughters, which leads to differences in career development (e.g., Schulenberg, Vondracek & Crouter, 1984; Bloch, 1983). The family's influence, both in SES terms and in other ways, has shown that familial dynamics and the process of career decision making are intertwined and can be related to difficulty by their children in making decisions about their careers and to career indecision (Kinnier, Brigman & Noble, 1990) and that occupational preference is socially constructed and is highly influenced by the career decision maker's expectations of approval from significant others for making certain occupational choices (Rockwell, 1987). Obviously, depending on the family's vision of the acceptability of the choice of vocational or other forms of workforce education, that choice may or may not be reinforced by a particular family or, indeed, even allowed into consideration by the student as a viable possibility.

Implicit in such views of family influence on choices of occupations and educational pathways is the reality that socioeconomic classes, however defined, differ in their values and behavior. Persons whose social class backgrounds can be described as lower, middle, or upper class or some combination thereof (e.g., lower middle) are distributed differently across occupational types and levels. For example, Evans and Herr (1978: 120) observe that, "Managers and professionals tend to be upper class or upper middle class. Skilled workers, semiprofessionals, small proprietors, and white collar workers most frequently are lower middle class. Semiskilled workers are frequently upper lower class, and those people who work only when they choose to do so are usually lower lower class." Although they are not precise or without exceptions, such a relationship of social class to occupation has at least two dimensions. One, what is the social class of origin when a child or adolescent is making occupational and other career choices? Two, what is the likelihood that one can change one's social class through occupational mobility? Taking the second question first, it is clear that persons can exceed their parents' social class through substantial education, hard work, self-discipline, chance, and other factors related to occupational mobility. Opportunity for such occupational mobility and the higher income, material possessions, and status that accompany it have long been a professed article of faith in the historical and political metaphors that are used to describe the United States. Certainly, in comparison with nations in which class boundaries are more rigid or virtually impenetrable, the United States does allow for occupational and status mobility, even though it is not easy. The other issue has to do with the social class of parents or a family household at the point of an educational or occupational decision. Whether the parents have been born and remained in a particular occupational class or risen in social class through the factors described, the attained social class is related to what parents are likely to advocate for choice among their children or other family members. Thus, middle- and upper-class parents tend to desire that their children obtain white-collar, managerial, and professional occupations and to do so by attending college and graduate school. Within such perspectives vocational education, as a subset of workforce education, has historically been focused on occupations that lead people to lower middle-class status or, for adults, to provide the skills necessary to cope with technological change or other factors that, if such education and skills were not obtained, could reduce the occupational and socioeconomic status of the worker. Indeed, one of the unclaimed outcomes of vocational education has been its demonstrated ability to increase a student's social class (particularly from lower class to lower middle class) by providing the technical skills required of skilled workers, semiprofessionals, technicians, small proprietors, and many white-collar occupations (Evans & Herr, 1978).

From a sociological perspective, the family is a facilitator, and particular family members may be role models of experience that limits or expands the knowledge and support of family member choices of educational and occupational options. The family is also the locus of reinforcements, contingencies, and expectations that subtly or directly shape work choice and behavior, and the family is a conduit for the attribution of socioeconomic status to children. In addition, the home is a workplace, a center in which social and occupational roles are modeled and given validity by the members of the nuclear family or by the network of relatives, friends, and acquaintances with which this unit interacts (Herr & Lear, 1984).

From a sociological perspective, as suggested above, the breadth and the specific substance of the individual's family, culture, or social class boundaries have much to do with the choices that can be considered, made, and implemented. The specific factors that operate in the lives of an individual are likely to include some combination of social class membership; home influences; school achievement, values, and faculty or peer influences; community opportunities available and values; range and characteristics of exploratory opportunities and role models available; and role perceptions of the individual relative to leadership and technical self-efficacy. Although these operate with different intensity and content in the lives of individuals, a consistent finding is that social class factors create barriers or open possibilities that tend to overarch the other sociological factors identified. Members of lower social classes, and particularly those from a culture of poverty, experience more undesirable life events; are more vulnerable to life stressors;

receive different information about the world of work and pathways to it; receive less education, training, and counseling; and have a more fragile sense of control than their more economically advantaged contemporaries. As a result social class and racial differences are found in the amount of unemployment, resources available, and in the transition from school to work. Strong and comprehensive programs of workforce education have the promise of neutralizing the types of deficits that many persons from lower socioeconomic backgrounds experience as they consider educational possibilities and occupational options.

WORK ATTAINMENT

Hotchkiss and Borow (1990: 262) have described the work of sociologists as investigating the characteristics and behavior of people in organized groups, for example, in the family and in economic groups, including the workplace, and in identifying "the principles that govern the beliefs and conduct of group members in each of these institutional settings."

With particular attention to how the sociology of work differs from the psychology of career development, Hotchkiss and Borow discuss three major dissimilarities. One is that sociologists, unlike most psychologists, are particularly concerned with power and authority as well as with how these are reflected in the status hierarchy in the workplace, how the work-socialization process occurs, the role of such mechanisms as labor unions and collective bargaining, how the labor market operates, and the related issues of job satisfaction, work alienation, and occupational mobility and career patterns.

A second difference between sociologists studying work and psychologists is where the major emphasis should be placed on the influences that affect individual choice making about work. Typically, psychological theories related to career development assign major importance to individual action and motivation in which individuals have at least some control over the choices they make in spite of the external obstacles that may prevail in given circumstances. Sociological theories, in contrast, would give much greater weight to the role of institutional factors, market forces, and the availability and timeliness of opportunity than to the power of individual action. It is in this context that some sociologists would argue that the developmental and psychological notions of individual choice that undergird some approaches to career guidance are unrealistic. Perhaps the classic sociological view of this matter has been captured by British sociologist Kenneth Roberts.

In Roberts's view (1977) most people do not choose, in any precise sense of that term. Instead, they are chosen or act when opportunities arise. He summarizes the point as follows:

> The notion that young people possess freedom of choice and that they can select careers for themselves upon the basis of their own preference is pure myth. It is not choice but opportunity that governs the manner in which many young people make their entry into employment. (p. 145)

Roberts goes on to contend that the factors that are of major consequence in implementing his opportunity model are mechanisms of educational selection, the patterns of recruitment into different types of employment, home background, and other social culture factors. Although he does not address these explicitly, his model would incorporate the importance of socioeconomic class and family characteristics discussed previously as major influences on who finds access to, and mobility in, work. Thus, Roberts's view, although of particular importance at the point of entrance to the workplace or the labor force, also has implications for human resource management at various transitions in the employee's working life as institutional or work organization shifts occur (e.g., downsizing and the use of contingency or temporary workers to replace core, long-term workers) and change the opportunity structure. In Roberts's terms these factors also affect who will be chosen to continue to work, to advance, or to be unemployed.

Whether one embraces the sociological perspective advocated by Roberts and others who share his view about the importance of social structure factors in work attainment, there are corollary perspectives. One is that social structure factors found in a complex socioeconomic stratification system, such as that of the contemporary United States, is also a complex generator, filter, and dispenser of information. In essence, one's position in the SES strata of the nation has much to do with the kind of information one gets; the alternative opportunities one knows about and can consider; the overt or subtle barriers that one will face in seeking access to, or mobility in, work; and the kind of encouragement for certain actions one is likely to receive from family members, schools, peer groups, or communities. Thus, persons are often, if not generally, selectively informed, reinforced, or rewarded for certain types of behavior, depending on the SES, gender, racial or ethnic, religious, or ability group to which they belong.

A third major difference has to do with how sociologists and psychologists view the cause and effect relationships that shape work attainment, job performance, and job satisfaction. Again, psychologists tend to focus on how individual differences in attitudes, aptitudes, values, and interests affect choice of success in training, work performance, satisfaction, and job. Sociologists take a more contextual view that gives emphasis to how supply and demand, formal rules, and informal and other institutional policies and actions shape what work is available for individuals and how they attain and perform it.

WORK AND SOCIAL STRATIFICATION

One of the major characteristics of the sociology of work is the emphasis it places on paid employment and occupational choice as functioning within, and interacting with, a broad system of social stratification. Such views are additional ways to emphasize the importance of structural factors that influence individual choices and that relate to status attainment in the labor force or a particular workplace.

Sociological research in social stratification, status attainment, and structural approaches has different emphases. An important one is the attempt to examine how occupational fields differ in the social structure, structural factors, and job structures that comprise them. For example, what are the rules of access or the educational prerequisites to entering one occupation as compared to another (e.g., becoming a physician versus becoming a construction superintendent)? What is the social status ascribed to each? Who gains access and typifies the characteristics of workers in the occupation? What are the barriers, real or covert, to minority member access or access by persons described in other ways? What are the structural steps in an occupational career that relate to social stratification (e.g., apprentice/intern, journey person/resident, master/fully licensed, supervisor/department head)? Some of these structures facilitate or impede individual status attainment. Some of these structures affect access to an occupation and performance of the work, whereas others affect one's sense of well-being or job satisfaction in work. The latter include the type of career ladder that is available, the chances of advancement, the intensity of continuing education required to do the job and the availability of opportunities to acquire it, the clarity of requirements needed to become a supervisor or manager, the sense of fit with and contribution made to an organizational mission, the prospects for future earnings and how they are achieved, benefits provided for oneself and one's family, job security, and the presence or absence of discrimination.

In some theoretical perspectives, sociological theory and economic theory interact, although with some tension because of the different emphases on structural barriers and influences on social stratification each represents. One of these conceptual examples is human capital theory, which essentially contends that individuals invest in their own productivity in order to maximize their lifetime earnings. Typically included are individual expenditures for education and delayed or foregone earnings during a period of investment, for example, while going to a postsecondary trade school or to college. Sometimes expenditures on health care and travel costs to another location to improve earning power are included as investments in human capital theory. But the primary investment of interest to theorists is education, its form and substance and its relation to subsequent earnings and other forms of productivity.

Sociologists both criticize and incorporate elements of human capital theory. In the first instance, they argue that human capital theory places too much emphasis on the ability of individuals to choose jobs, to choose in ways to optimize their work attainment and to make rational decisions by which to match their personal profile of attributes (e.g., interests, aptitudes) to those required by jobs and occupations. In such perspectives, economic approaches to human capital theory, as just described, have more similarity to many of the psychological concepts of career development that are major theoretical assumptions on which career counseling and career guidance rest than they do to sociological perspectives about contextual and structural factors in choice. But the utility of human capital theory to sociologists is that inherent in its depiction of individual investments in education and other costs to improve occupational attainment and productivity is the likelihood that certain structural barriers and attitudes will nullify the effects of such investments on the attainments sought. For example, women or minority males may invest in schooling that they expect will prepare them for entrance into occupations that allow them to acquire earnings that they desire. While this rationale is economically and psychologically viable, sociologists may say that such a view does not attend sufficiently to the likelihood that many desired occupations will impose barriers on the ease of women or minority male access or on their occupational mobility beyond a particular level of attainment. As an example of such phenomena there is the possibility that, for persons investing in workforce education rather than in some other form of education investment as their way to maximize their earnings and to acquire access to a desirable occupation, societal stereotypes about the value of workforce education or incorrect information about its clear and positive relationship to future earnings will nullify the potential benefits of such a decision for an individual or be used as information by policy makers to make decisions to limit the workforce options available.

SUMMARY AND IMPLICATIONS FOR PRACTITIONERS

This unit has focused on examining some of the major constructs and theories that comprise the sociological foundations of workforce education. Although deserving of a more exhaustive analysis of many of the sociological concepts that are important to workforce education, several major points are of particular relevance here. One is that sociological foundations emphasize that neither workforce education nor the types of work available, the stability of jobs, and who obtains access to, and mobility in, the workplace occur in a vacuum. Such processes and institutions occur within a complex set of social forces and structural elements. If workforce education is to be successful, it must be attentive to the social policies as well as to the social stereotypes that affect its function and substance.

Sociological foundations also describe work as occurring within a network of roles and social relations. Again, if workforce education, or human resource management, is to be effective, it must teach students that work preparation cannot be confined to technical content alone but must also attend to the interpersonal skills and understanding of organizational mission and context that are essential to the worker's ability to cooperate with coworkers, customers, and supervisors and to adapt to the organizational culture in which work takes place.

Sociological perspectives provide insight into the importance of parent and family characteristics, socioeconomic status, race, and gender in predicting how occupational preferences and interests are formed and how these factors operate in facilitating or impairing entrance to, and mobility within, the occupational structure. Workforce education can provide information and skills that can help workers to neutralize SES and other structural barriers to work attainment and advancement.

Sociological research about the characteristics of the occupational structure provides insights into its divisions into core and periphery firms, primary and secondary labor markets, and the different requirements each has for workforce education. Such occupational classifications carry implications for the different types of work performed, structural elements of income and fringe benefits, comprehensiveness of career ladders and mobility, and who is likely to be employed in each of these sectors.

Finally, sociological perspectives demonstrate that workforce education must be a dynamic, not a static, process. Analyses of the changes in the occupational opportunity structure, the requirements of workers, the nature of work organizations, the implications of integrating advanced technology into the workplace, and related processes accent the reality that workforce educators in their planning and implementation of instruction must be willing to respond to a world economic structure in significant flux.

THE FUTURE OF WORK

> The media provide mounting evidence of "time poverty," overwork, and a squeeze on time. Nationwide, people report their leisure time has declined by as much as one third since the early 1970s. Predictably, they are spending less time on the basics, like sleeping and eating. Parents are devoting less attention to their children. Stress is on the rise, partly owing to the "balancing act" of reconciling the demands of work and family life.
>
> The experts were unable to predict or even see these trends. I suspect they were blinded by the power of technology—seduced by futuristic visions of automated factories effortlessly churning out products. . . . To understand why forty years of increasing productivity have failed to liberate us from work, [it is necessary] to abandon a naive faith in technological potential and analyze the social, economic, and political context in which technology is put to use.
>
> (SCHOR, 1992:5–6)

Changes of great significance are occurring in the nature and organization of work. For the first time in history we can meaningfully speak of a global workplace. Telecommunication networks link distant work sites. Night shifts in North America communicate instantaneously with morning shifts in Europe and with afternoon shifts in Asia. Multinational corporations link production sites around the world with little regard for geographic or political boundaries.

It is tempting to view these transformations in terms of technological change alone. But each aspect of change—new products, new technology, and new work organizations—has its own unique dynamics. Innovations in the organization of work, such as the assembly line, have historically contributed at least as much to productivity as have mechanical inventions.

It is also tempting to view these changes as beyond the control of the average worker. Even chief executives may feel helpless in the face of "world competition"

Taken from Hodson, R. and Sullivan, T.A. (2008) *The Social Organization of Work*, Fourth Edition. Belmont, CA: Thomson Wadsworth. pp. 414–433.

or "the system." The welfare of workers and of all of us depends on who controls the nature and direction of change. Workers around the world are deeply involved in this process and are far from powerless. **Workers' power** is based on their knowledge of the technology and the product and on their collective organizations, such as unions and professional associations.

The difficulty, for workers and analysts alike, is to anticipate the consequences of these changes in the nature of work. All changes have multiple effects. Some are likely to be benign, others not so benign. In this chapter we examine three master trends that will be of crucial importance in determining the nature of work in the twenty-first century. We project, based on these trends, the possibility of a future society in which there is an increasing divide between a highly innovative and productive sector and a marginal sector. The emergence of such a divided society is a possibility but not a certainty. Therefore, we also discuss mechanisms for increasing innovation and reducing marginality.

PIVOTAL WORK TRENDS

The beginning decades of the twenty-first century are witnessing many important changes in the nature of work. Three trends are particularly important: (1) the spread of electronic technology throughout the workplace, (2) increased competition in the world economy, and (3) the increased movement of women into paid labor. In this section we review each of these trends and discuss how they are shaping the nature of work in the twenty-first century.

Computer Technology

During the twentieth century advances in technology and organization greatly increased productivity in manufacturing. Initially, these advances involved a finer division of labor into more and more minute tasks and the organization of jobs along moving assembly lines. New manufacturing technologies in the twenty-first century involve the use of automated machines and computer-controlled robotics. These electronic technologies are having an even greater impact on a broader range of industries and occupations than did the mass-production technologies of the twentieth century.

On the positive side, computer technologies have increased productivity and created skilled jobs. They have also shortened the time needed to develop new products. Thus, the pace of change has increased, giving rise to potentially faster economic growth. Microprocessor technologies have also encouraged greater worker participation, which is required to ensure the successful use of sophisticated technologies. On the negative side, new technologies have created new stresses because of the deskilling of some workers, the displacement of others, and the electronic monitoring of many others.

In sum, an acceleration in the pace of technological change associated with the extensive use of microprocessors has created a period of rapid change in the workplace and in workplace relations. These changes have destabilized older patterns of work and relationships among workers and between workers and managers. Technological change has created a period of tremendous flux in the workplace. Technology by itself, however, does not determine the direction of these changes. Other factors are equally important for determining changes in the nature of work.

An Integrated World Economy

Starting in the 1950s, an integrated world economy emerged following the devastation of World War II. Today, this integrated world economy includes tremendous diversity among nations. Countries vary in their level of industrialization and in how they are integrated into the global economy. Some are dependent suppliers of raw materials or partially finished components to more industrialized nations; others are autonomous producers of finished goods and services.

Recent developments in the world economy have greatly increased competition. After World War II, Japan and the European nations rebuilt with newer, more modern factories and reentered the world market. Many developing nations have also industrialized and have become important producers of manufactured goods. For example, South Korea now sells cars in the American market, something undreamed of twenty years ago. In addition, much of the work in low-wage, labor-intensive industries is now performed in less-developed nations, further intensifying the competitive pressure on workers in the industrialized countries.

Thus, changes in the world economy have also contributed to a period of change and flux in the workplace. Increased international competition has heightened threats to the jobs of workers in the industrialized nations. Greater competitive pressures require organizational change and innovation for economic survival.

Similar technological, organizational, and market forces have caused a convergence between capitalist and socialist nations. Formerly socialist nations today incorporate market forces in significant parts of their economies. And the most successful capitalist nations have moved toward greater economic planning. Such planning includes targeting specific industries for expansion, identifying the training needs of the labor force for these industries, and developing programs to meet these needs. The next stage of industrial society will transcend the distinction between capitalism and socialism. Other distinctions, such as those between more innovative and less innovative industrial systems and those between developed and less developed nations, however, are becoming more salient. Both capitalist states and the former communist states of China, Eastern Europe, and the Soviet Union are likely to face problems of high unemployment and may need to encourage greater worker participation to facilitate technological change.

Female and Minority Workers

Women have always worked; however, the transformation of their work into paid labor outside the home occurred somewhat later for women that it did for men, and it is still continuing today. The decline of high fertility and the reduction of child-rearing duties have been crucial in this process. In addition, employment opportunities have expanded in areas that have traditionally employed female workers, especially in clerical and service occupations. In combination, these factors have resulted in a rapid increase in the proportion of female workers in the labor force. This process has had tremendous consequences for the family. It can no longer be assumed that women will remain at home for child-care and home-tending duties. It would be incorrect, however, to assume that women's and men's paid jobs are similar. Women are still segregated by occupation and industry, and they are much more likely than men to be part-time and part-year workers.

Since the passage of the Civil Rights Act of 1964 and related legislation, female and minority workers in the United States have made important strides in the workplace, as well as in other spheres of society. Opportunities for female and minority workers have increased significantly. Full equality, however, is still far away. For minority workers, centuries of oppression have become embedded in class inequalities that make it difficult for many to take advantage of increased opportunities. Similarly, continuing assumptions on the part of both men and women that home and child-care duties should fall more on women's shoulders make it difficult for many women to take advantage of increased opportunities. In addition, for both female and minority workers, blatant and subtle forms of prejudice and discrimination continue to create barriers. Thus, in spite of improved conditions, women continue to suffer segregation into lower-status and lower-paying jobs, and blacks and other minorities still differentially occupy the lowest positions in society.

THE FACE OF WORK IN THE TWENTY-FIRST CENTURY

Technological change, increased world market competition, and the increased proportion of women and minority workers in the labor force are major changes that will determine the nature of work in the future. What will work be like in the twenty-first century? It appears likely that the economy will be typified by two very different employment sectors. In one, which we call the **innovative sector**, the response to heightened international competition and technological change will be the development of technological and organizational innovations leading to increased productivity. In the innovative sector, technological innovation will be continuous, jobs will be reasonably secure, pay will be adequate, job conditions will be more or less pleasant, and, perhaps most importantly, workers will have an increased say in determining the conditions of their work.

In the other sector, which we call the **marginal sector**, employers will respond to heightened international competition and technological change by reducing labor costs through lowered wages and benefits. In the marginal sector, innovation will be slow, jobs will be insecure, pay will be low, and conditions will be unpleasant and even hazardous. The organizing principle of the marginal sector will be to achieve economic viability by driving down wages rather than by promoting technical and organizational innovation. Workers will have little say in determining the conditions of their employment or the policies of their organizations. It is likely that female and minority workers will be disproportionately employed in the marginal sector. Thus, we do not believe as some have proposed that work will disappear in the high-technology future (Rifkin, 1995). Rather, work is here to stay, but the nature of work appears to be diverging between two increasingly distinct sectors of employment.

In this section we discuss the reasons for a divergence between these two distinct ways of organizing work and the characteristics of work in each sector. Figure 3.1 depicts the three trends in work that we have described and possible future scenarios to which these trends may lead.

The Innovative Sector

What factors encourage the growth of an innovative sector? On what basis do we project its continued and increasing importance? The growth of innovation results from the development of microprocessor technologies that facilitate such innovation and from increased international competition and worker pressure that demand it in order to protect profits and jobs (Bluestone and Harrison, 2000). Many recent workplace innovations can be seen as attempts to use new technologies to adapt to increased competition in the world economy while maintaining high-wage employment. Another impetus toward workplace innovations has been the desire to reduce the inefficiencies of bureaucratic and hierarchical arrangements of work (Vallas, 2001). In this sense, workplace relations in the innovative sector can be better described as **postbureaucratic** than as postindustrial. Because human beings are central to the process of production, innovations in the organization of work will continue to be at least as important for the success of this sector as technological innovations.

The defining characteristics of work in the innovative sector are increased **worker education** and **participation.** Increased worker education and participation create the conditions for **continuous learning** and continual **job redesign** (Appelbaum et al., 2000). Continual job redesign will be necessary because of the pace of technological change and the highly competitive and rapidly changing global economy. The specific ways in which jobs will be redesigned are impossible to predict in great detail because they will be unique to each setting and each technology. However, some general principles are relatively clear (Szell, 1992).

The Centrality of Participation

Workers hold the power to make organizational and technological advances succeed or fail. Some observations by industrial sociologist Robert Guest provide a good example. Guest was a visitor at a steel mill in the process of making a major technological change. A new steel process was delayed for six months because of differences between the company and the union on the incentive plan that would distribute part of the benefits of the new technology to the workers. After the incentive question was finally settled, Guest got a call from a worker and was told that he would see something interesting if he came down to the mill at the start of the midnight shift. Guest reports the following events:

> *At precisely midnight a loud klaxon sounded. The lead man raised his arm and in a loud voice called out, "Let 'er roll!" The red hot billets spit out of the helical rolls at a speed I have never seen before. There were no delays or breakdowns on the shift and within a month capacity had gone up over twenty percent. (Guest, 1987:5)*

The moral of the story is that workers hold the key to the success of programs of technological and organizational redesign. To engage workers' fullest abilities requires that they have a piece of the action—not just a share of profits but a share in decision making. The sectors of the economy that succeed in introducing competitive innovations will be the sectors that include a leading role for worker participation at every stage of innovation.

Work Groups

One important form of worker participation occurs through small work groups of eight to twelve workers who are given collective responsibility for a task. Work groups offer an important role for worker participation, though they often limit the topic of discussion to product quality or to minor aspects of the work environment. Many college students work in settings that involve some aspects of team organization, or at least claim team organization by calling employees "associates" or "partners." Work groups can be an important source of innovation (Pfeffer, 1998). They can also be important for improving the **quality of work life.** However, as we will see, they can also be used to intensify work and heighten pressures on the job.

Team systems of production based on significant degrees of self-management by work groups have become increasingly important in contemporary organizations. Team-based production systems, however, actually have a long history in the workplace. Miners, seafarers, and other skilled trades have long relied on teams to coordinate work in situations involving complex and difficult tasks.

The increased importance of teams in the modern workplace reflects many forces, including increased skill demands associated with sophisticated technologies, new management theories about how best to organize production, and worker demands for increased voice at the workplace (Ortiz, 1998).

Japanese companies and their affiliates around the world have lead the way toward increased utilization of team-based production systems. Under Japanese team production systems, employees organized in *Quality Control Circles* are expected to be ever vigilant for opportunities to work more effectively by identifying and eliminating underutilization of time and resources.

An important underpinning of Japanese Quality Control Circles and other initiatives to improve productivity and increase quality has been the tying of the worker to the company through lifetime employment and through finely

---

BOX 3.1   A Crystal Cube of the Workplace

Social scientists do not have crystal balls and cannot predict the future. They can, however, examine trends and describe what might happen if certain trends continue. Throughout this unit we have tried to identify trends that may affect the workplace of the future. Three master trends that we have discussed are the role of technology and organization in the workplace, the competitive climate, and the changing composition of the labor force. These three trends may combine in many ways to produce many possible outcomes.

The cube in Figure 3.1 shows how the three master trends might interact. Imagine North American jobs right now as centered somewhere in the middle. A choice to use organization and technology in a way that increases the utilization of workers' skills would represent a shift to the left; a choice to use organization and technology to simplify or eliminate jobs would represent a shift to the right. Similarly, if increased productivity alleviates the competitive threat to North American industry, jobs would shift downward in the cube. As we have noted, women and members of minority groups will come to be a larger proportion of the labor force, but whether their labor power is adequately utilized depends on the types of jobs available to them. A "nearer" point in the three-dimensional space represents greater equality for female and minority workers. This would imply more access for female and minority workers to full-time, year-round jobs in occupations and industries comparable with those of white men. It is possible that women and minorities could be less adequately utilized than they are today; this is the "farther" end of the third dimension.

These options could, of course, be combined in many, many ways, but there are two points in our hypothetical space that we wish to discuss further. One is Point I on the figure; at this point technology and organization are used to complement workers' skills, competitive threats are lessened by productivity increases, and women and minorities move closer to equality. Even if most jobs in North America fail to move toward this point, some jobs will probably approach point I. In this unit, we refer to such jobs as comprising the innovative sector.

On the other hand, organization and technology may be used to deskill or to eliminate jobs, especially in response to competitive pressure. Under such conditions, pressures will persist to use women and members of minority groups as reserve workers, calling them up for part-time or seasonal work as needed or paying them low wages to undercut the wage demands of higher-paid workers. These conditions are represented schematically as point II in the diagram. Even if most jobs do not move toward point II, some jobs will. In this unit we refer to such jobs as representing the marginal sector.

It is difficult to predict with any accuracy the relative size of the marginal sector and the innovative sector. Most jobs will probably still lie somewhere between these extremes. But there are reasons to think that these two sectors will represent significant numbers of jobs in the twenty-first century. It is useful to discuss these possibilities as "best-case" and "worst-case" scenarios representing endpoints in the master trends we have identified.

---

graded systems of seniority-based pay (Dore and Sako, 1998). The tying of the employee and the firm together in a lifelong partnership encourages workers to use their skills to improve productivity and thus ensure the firm's future (Delbridge, 1998).

Other researchers note, however, that Japanese workers are not necessarily enthusiastic about involvement in team-based production (Lillrank and Kano, 1989).

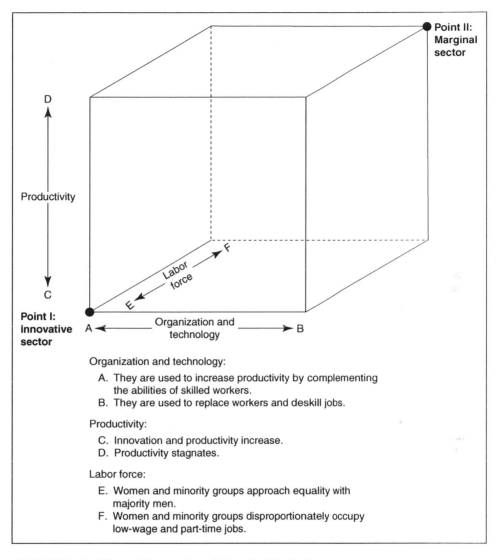

Organization and technology:

    A. They are used to increase productivity by complementing
       the abilities of skilled workers.
    B. They are used to replace workers and deskill jobs.

Productivity:

    C. Innovation and productivity increase.
    D. Productivity stagnates.

Labor force:

    E. Women and minority groups approach equality with
       majority men.
    F. Women and minority groups disproportionately occupy
       low-wage and part-time jobs.

FIGURE 3.1   Three Master Trends in the Workplace

Rather, they see participation in Quality Control Circles and related team activities as a requirement for the economic success of their enterprise. Japanese workers thus participate in problem-solving activities with honesty and candor, but not generally with great enthusiasm or a sense of personal gratification.

    In many workplaces, Japanese-style teams have been associated with work intensification (Endo, 1994), increased pressures for production (Rinehart et al., 1997:27, 78), employee monitoring of peers (Roberson, 1998:78), and antiunion campaigns (Grenier, 1988:47, 132). It is also a mistake to assume that managers and supervisors disappear in team production settings. Under Japanese teambased systems, frontline supervisors continue to play an active role in controlling and evaluating workers. In many ways, workers are more tightly controlled in team settings than in traditional supervisory settings. The power of the supervisor is not removed; rather, it is extended through allocating additional supervisory functions to the team as a whole (Rinehart et al., 1997:86).

In summary, team organizations of work are an important potential source of innovation, creativity, and heightened productivity (Smith, 1996). However, when used as the sole form of participation, they can force employees to ever greater efforts with no compensating gains for employees.

Codetermination and Joint Union–Management Programs

Worker participation can also occur through formal consultation with workers at every level of the organization, from the shop floor to the boardroom. In Western Europe, various forms of worker participation are widespread. These forms include the workers' councils in Germany, which act as an autonomous board to review management policy, and technology stewards in Norway, who review and advise on technological change. Additional forms of participation occur through joint union–management initiated programs.

Joint union–management programs Are based on explicit collectively negotiated agreements between unions and management to jointly sponsor programs that include employee involvement. In the United Kingdom, such programs are relatively commonplace across a wide range of industries (Marks et al., 1998). In North America such programs are concentrated in the automobile and telecommunications industries (Cooke, 1990). Other well-established programs exist in steel, construction, and the public sector. The key focus of many of these programs is on improved worker training to meet the challenges of automation and global competition (Milkman, 1997:160).

In joint union–management programs, the issues to be discussed are not necessarily restricted to management defined agendas. Workers in the automobile industry have successfully bargained for various forms of accelerated training under joint union–management programs and voice a great deal of satisfaction with these programs (Ferman et al., 1990). In these programs, workers receive additional training as part of an exchange for their greater involvement in the workplace and their increased contributions to productivity. The programs often involve supplemental training both on and off company time.

Increased communication and direct consultation with workers are also hallmarks of joint union–management programs. A joint program at an American car manufacturer includes the following principles:

- establish effective lines of communication among all employees,
- encourage participation of all employees who desire to become involved,
- strive for expeditious resolution of mutual problems,
- treat all employees with dignity and respect, and
- recognize the contributions of each individual (Milkman, 1997:161).

Note that these principles include a focus on employees and their rights and contributions rather than focusing solely on production-related issues as is typical of Japanese Quality Control Circles.

Workers in joint union–management programs are also increasingly allowed to go on purchasing and sales trips previously reserved for management and sales personnel. Workers provide valuable hands-on information in negotiations to secure the best components and new technologies. They also work directly with customers to learn how to improve quality and meet customer needs. The new knowledge and flexibility that such programs generate provide workers with opportunities to develop better relationships with their co-workers and with workers up and down the production chain. The opportunities provided by joint programs thus encourage employees to construct their organizational roles more actively. This active orientation generates new roles and new ideas that are often missing when work roles are unilaterally prescribed by management. In general, workers have been very enthusiastic about joint union–management programs and about participating in decision-making processes historically reserved for management (Milkman, 1997; Pfeffer, 1998).

The bilateral nature of joint initiatives provides a legitimacy to these programs that is sometimes missing when programs are initiated unilaterally by management. This legitimacy has been identified as a significant foundation for the success of joint union–management programs in stimulating productivity and improving working conditions. The initiatives emerging from joint union–management programs are also often more complementary with the public purpose than unilateral management initiatives because they include a focus on the preservation of employment and on the quality of employment as well as on increased productivity (Ferman et al., 1990:187).

Joint union–management programs are widely acknowledged to have played a leading role in stabilizing employment in the U.S. automobile industry and improving its competitive position in world markets. The resurrection of the Gary Works steel plant as a result of a worker participation program is described in Box 3.2.

Worker Ownership

An additional type of worker participation is based on **worker ownership.** Worker ownership can be either total or partial through **employee stock ownership plans (ESOPs).** In 2000, 13 million U.S. workers, or about 10% of the labor force, participated in ESOPs (Census, 2000).

Employee ownership generally results in improved productivity and improved employee satisfaction (Pendleton et al., 1998). A core underlying reason for these improvements is that worker-owned enterprises are simply more concerned with the well-being of their employees than organizations owned by outside shareholders (Tucker, 1999). They are able to solicit high levels of worker involvement and participation because of the genuine overlap between the goals of the enterprise and those of the employees (Bradley, Estrin, and Taylor, 1990). Improved communication, teamwork, and participation are important underpinnings for the relative success of worker-owned enterprises.

The greatest participation occurs in worker-owned cooperatives in which workers not only own the firm but also actively manage its day-to-day affairs (Logue and Yates, 1999). Worker buyouts have provided an important counterbalance to the tendency of conglomerate companies to shut down or reduce their labor forces in the search for profitability. For instance, in 1994, the 78,500 unionized employees of United Airlines purchased the company, making it the largest employee-owned company in the United States (Moberg, 1994).

Worker buyouts of existing companies have often been initiated in an effort to preserve jobs. Worker-owner enterprises thus often face precarious circumstances because of external factors. Worker ownership often results from an employee buyout of a plant in a last-ditch effort to save the plant and the jobs it represents. In such situations, market forces may already be working against the enterprise. The market niche it serves may be shrinking or its technology and equipment may be outdated. Employee buyouts thus often face a precarious future because of the circumstances of their birth (Keef, 1998).

Worker ownership offers no necessary panacea to troubled firms, but even tested in this harsh environment, it has had a good record of success. In the Boston Harbor area, for example, about ninety boats make a living off lobsters. However, these boats were being priced off the docks by condominiums, office complexes, and yacht marinas. With the help of the Boston archdiocese, these fishing families leased their own dock and established a cooperative enterprise that is flourishing today (McManus, 1987).

Job Security

An essential foundation for all forms of heightened worker participation is **job security.** Without job guarantees, both on paper and in a history of commitment, workers are reluctant to give their best efforts to increasing productivity. This reluctance is especially strong in areas of active technological change, where the possibility of displacement for large numbers of workers is very real. Only when there is a strong commitment by the organization to maintain employment levels will workers give their full support to overcoming the inevitable problems associated with technological and organizational innovations. Loyalty by the company to its workers is thus an essential precondition for the realization of the full benefits of worker participation.

Training

Training programs for employees are essential if they are to have the knowledge necessary to take a leading role in a more innovative workplace. Such programs have grown dramatically in the 2000s in community colleges and training institutions around the country. Community colleges provide flexible course sequences tailored to the needs of local industry. In addition, there has been increased interest in expanding traditional apprenticeship programs for the skilled trades. This

BOX 3.2   Competitiveness through Participation

U.S. Steel's Gary Works was all but banished from General Motor's supplier rolls. Ford was threatening the same. "Find a new way of doing your business," was the blunt mandate. . . .

Not only was the steel bad, it arrived late. "And we were arrogant," recalls [manager] Robert Pheanis. Gary Works—the biggest mill in the steel company—was alienating customers. It was also losing more than $100 million a year. The heart of Big Steel was about to stop beating.

Revival came from a small team of gritty union hardhats in the dreary 6-mile-long steel mill. . . . First one, than another—eventually five steelworkers were freed from mill jobs to visit automotive customers' plants and see problems for themselves. . . . The union crew was generally fre0e to change how steel was made, stored and shipped so that the 50-ton rolls and quarter-ton sheets arrived at customers' plants in better shape.

They demanded rubber pads on flatbed trucks to cushion the steel. They created plastic rings to protect the rolls from crane damage. They persuaded workers who package and load each roll or stack to take responsibility for its condition by signing a tag attached to the shipment.

The result: automotive customers, who buy almost half of Gary Works' steel, now reject just 0.6%, down from an industry worst 2.6%. . . .

Says [consultant] Thomas Johnson, "The average guy working in most American companies today is a hell of a lot smarter than top management is willing to give him credit for." . . .

Gary Works' quality-improvement program differs from many because it was created from, and continues to be built on, the experience and intuition of hourly workers battling to save their plant, their jobs, their way of life. . . . But neither is it a by-guess and by-gosh effort. In the best tradition of statistical process control, computers measure every variation and tolerance at the plant so workers know when something is too hot, too thick, or too slow.

Ford [which nearly canceled its contract the previous year with Gary Works] gave it the Q1 award as a high-quality supplier. "We'd had instances of breakage where we'd get the managers, the engineers, the metallurgists working on it. Then the hourly guys come in and get their heads together, and the problem would go away," says a manager at Ford's nearby Chicago Heights stamping plant. . . .

[In one instance] hourly worker Bill Barath was pulled from his galvanizing job applying anti-corrosion coating at the end of the Gary steel line and was sent to Ford's Chicago Heights plant to eyeball the steel.

He found a galvanizer's nightmare: flaking zinc. Steel he so carefully coated at Gary was shedding its anti-corrosion skin like a snake when Ford formed it into fenders and doors.

Barath knew instantly: too much zinc buildup on the edges of the steel. The rods that trimmed it off at the mill were out of whack. Barath took that intelligence back to the mill, and an amazing thing happened. The problem got fixed. Right now. No tangled bureaucracy, no scapegoating.

Word spread, and other auto plants demanded Gary Works' liaisons. Even GM came around and has increased Gary Works purchases fivefold.

"These are line workers in the steel industry, supplying the auto industry. I can't think of two more battered industries. They've really pushed this idea of empowerment down to the workers where it belongs," says [plant manager] Goodwin. "That's the spirit of American industry that's coming back, and people don't know it. To have hourly people with that kind of power is not typical in this industry or this country, but it has to be."

SOURCE: James R. Healey, 1992, "U.S. Steel Learns from Experience," *U.S.A. Today* (April 10):B1–B2. Copyright 1992. *USA Today*. Reprinted with permission.

interest has been sparked by unfavorable comparisons between the U.S. system of apprenticeship and the more developed German system, which many observers credit with making German products world renowned for their quality (Streeck, 1996). In-house training programs have also been expanding as employers and unions seek to expand the skills of workers as a means of increasing productivity, saving jobs, and increasing profits.

Distributing Profits

A final key to successful job redesign is the development of mechanisms for distributing some of the profits of innovation back to workers (McHugh, Cutcher-Gershenfeld, and Polzin, 1999). The redistribution of profits is important for maintaining worker enthusiasm and commitment. The most innovative organizations are aware of this and have developed a variety of means to redistribute increased earnings to workers. These include higher pay, production bonuses, and profit sharing. The Ford-UAW bonus plan provides a good example of one such plan.

Many innovative organizations also seek to tailor their compensation schemes to the needs of workers. One strategy is called the **cafeteria approach**. In this approach, workers are offered a variety of benefits and are free to choose the ones best suited to their own needs. Such packages may include supplemental retirement savings, supplemental life insurance, child-care vouchers, supplemental medical or dental coverage, or other benefits that appeal to specific workers.

The spread of such cafeteria-style benefit packages has also gained momentum from the increased presence of women in the labor force. Female workers bring different needs to the workplace than male workers. Because many men and women expect women to take greater responsibility for children, female workers often take a greater interest in workplace provisions for child care.

The increased attention to workers' needs in innovative organizations may result in an improvement in women's relative position in this sector. Because of reduced discrimination and less traditional career choices on the part of women, female workers may move increasingly into traditionally male-typed jobs, which are more likely to be in the innovative sector. The greater flexibility of women in their career choices as a result of lessened child-rearing duties may further facilitate these trends (England and Folbre, 1999).

Barriers to Innovative Job Redesign

Job redesign also faces certain barriers that may limit its effectiveness. Chief among these is the problem of limited commitment by large corporations to their workers. Worker participation programs in the United States have often been superficial and have been accused of being more window dressing than substance (Parker and Slaughter, 1994). U.S. corporations have often acted as if *proclaiming* their allegiance to worker participation somehow constitutes an adequate solution to lagging productivity and to lack of management loyalty and commitment to their workers. Developing programs that actually incorporate workers in active roles at all levels of decision making and becoming committed to the long-term interests of employees requires more than just a public relations announcement of commitment to such goals (Graham, 1995). In addition, large organizations may experiment with job redesign in one plant with great success only to cancel the experiment because of changes in organizational strategy initiated from the top (Rothschild, 2000).

A second potential point of conflict can arise because increased worker participation often reduces the need for managers by incorporating managerial and supervisory activities within shop-floor groups. Employees may even be asked to evaluate their manager's performance. These changes may threaten the jobs of supervisors and middle-level managers and may stimulate resistance on their part (Smith, 1990). Middle-level managers are in a strong position either to facilitate job redesign programs or to sabotage them through subtle noncompliance and other tactics that workers themselves occasionally use with great effectiveness. When combined with agendas of corporate restructuring and theories of "lean production" that stress downsizing, job redesign programs put middle managers at significant risk of being laid off.

The ways in which worker participation can be incorporated into job redesign and technological innovation are extremely diverse. In this unit we have described some of the forms of worker participation. The major forms of worker participation are enumerated in Figure 3.2, with the corresponding issues that are open to negotiation at the various levels of worker participation. At one extreme, workers are involved only in decisions about how to improve product quality and efficiency. At the other extreme they are involved in investment decisions about when and where to build new factories and what new lines of endeavor to pursue. Workers have shown themselves able to participate effectively in decisions about their own working conditions, in decisions about the production process, and in decisions about investment (Gittleman, Horrigan, and Joyce, 1998). All of these forms of worker participation are important, all have been proven to be effective in some circumstances, and all have problems. No one form or level of participation is right for all circumstances. In industries with rapidly changing technologies, worker participation in job design may be most important. In industries with rapidly changing market situations, worker participation in investment decisions may be essential for continued economic viability.

The persistence of enthusiasm for worker participation and job redesign demonstrates that these programs are here to stay. Greater worker participation can make important contributions to productivity and competitiveness. Such programs are precursors to new systems of industrial relations that will increasingly characterize a significant share of employment positions in the twenty-first century.

The Marginal Sector

In the economy of the twenty-first century, it is also likely that a large sector of marginal employment will exist. The existence of such a sector alongside a highly innovative sector with increased worker participation suggests a more divergent economic structure in the next century. Why might a marginal sector grow in the future? Driving down wages is one possible response of organizations to competition. By cutting wages, enterprises can remain competitive, at least for a time. In sectors where technological change is slow, such as services, such a strategy may appear more attractive than strategies for increasing productivity.

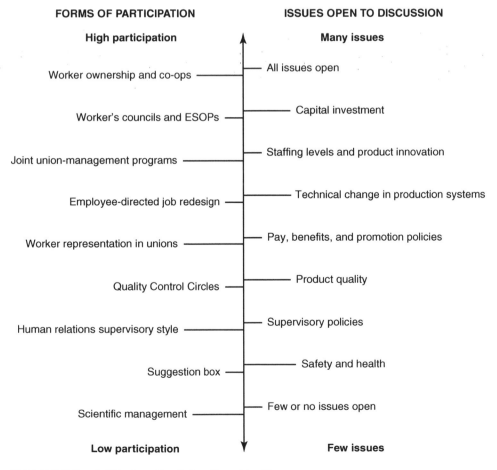

FIGURE 3.2   A Worker Participation Continuum

Low Pay and Few Benefits

An increase in the marginal sector would cause an intensification of current social problems. Workers in this sector would have reduced buying power, thus limiting the demand for the goods produced by other workers and slowing the growth of the economy as whole. Without a national health care plan, workers and families would lose health insurance and other benefits, thus putting additional pressure on already pinched social services and welfare programs. The growth of marginalized jobs is deeply implicated in increasing inequality in the United States over recent decades. It has been estimated that the highest earning 1% of U.S. families (those with incomes above $500,000) received 60% of the growth in after-tax income during the 1990s (Braun, 1997). Meanwhile, joblessness and poverty remained at high levels. Continued expansion of the marginal sector would further increase poverty and homelessness.

What will work be like in the marginal sector of the future? Based on the characteristics of the current marginal sector, we can anticipate that many aspects of long-term, stable employment will be missing. Pay will be low, and part-time and temporary work will be common. This sector will be typified by extensive subcontracting and frequent use of temporary workers (Tilly, 1996). Employers will have little interest in or commitment to employees. Probationary periods of employment with reduced rights will also be common. Two-tier pay scales with lower pay for newer employees might be used to bring in lower wage levels, with senior employees on the higher scale being rapidly phased out. Workers in the informal economy of unreported (and untaxed) work will also be part of this expanded marginal sector. While some informal work can be quite lucrative, basic benefits and employment security are largely missing from this employment sector.

Modern Sweatshops

Some aspects of work in the marginal sector of the twenty-first century will replicate those of preindustrial work and the factories of the early nineteenth-century Industrial Revolution—but with some new twists. There will be fewer safeguards against hazardous working conditions than in the innovative sector. Enthusiastic commitment to work will be rare. Discontent, subtle forms of non-compliance, and even sabotage will be relatively common. Many workers in this sector will be underemployed, and many others will experience periodic unemployment as temporary jobs come and go. Young people will have a particularly hard time locating permanent jobs. Similarly, disregard of minimum wage restrictions and fair time and hours standards will be all too common. Mandatory drug testing, electronic surveillance, and other forms of monitoring may be widespread. Workers in the marginal sector will represent a transient **underclass.** It is an unfortunate but realistic projection that such an underclass may be a sizable component of the North American workforce in the twenty-first century (Wilson, 1997).

An Absence of Employer Commitment

In what parts of the economy will marginal employment grow? According to sociologist Dan Cornfield, marginal jobs with unilateral managerial control and without formal worker participation will be most likely to occur in situations:

> with little unionization and/or with favorable macroeconomic conditions. In these industries, management encounters little organized worker resistance to technological innovation, either because, in the absence of unionization, workers have low attachment to their employers and lack sufficient bargaining strength to demand participation in managerial decision making; or because favorable macroeconomic conditions lessen the threat of technological displacement for workers. (Cornfield, 1987:332)

The marginal sector is thus likely to grow in the absence of organized worker power and of competition based on technological change or foreign producers. Service industries, such as restaurants, and retail trade provide examples of such situations. It is also possible that the marginal sector will grow where advanced technology is used to reduce the need for skilled workers.

Without technologically or market-based competition there is little reason to initiate job redesign and worker participation. Without organized worker power there is often inadequate reason for managers to respond to heightened competition with workplace innovation rather than with lower wages and reduced **employer commitment** to workers. In situations where either condition is absent, it is likely that marginal jobs will increase. Such situations may represent a sizable or even majority share of new employment positions in the economy of the twenty-first century. Indeed, if the trend continues for new areas of job growth to be outside traditional union strongholds, elements of marginality may typify many areas of new employment. In areas of growing employment, such as services and microprocessor manufacturing, marginality can be expected to increase. Box 3.3 describes a hypothetical marginal job of the future.

Continuing Disadvantages for Female and Minority Workers

How will female and minority workers fare in the economy of the twenty-first century? This question is difficult to answer. The recent past has seen improvements in employment conditions for female worker but the situation for minority workers has been more mixed. If women's earnings continue to advance against men's earnings, due to reduced discrimination in hiring and promotion and less traditional occupational choices by women, the prognosis for the future of women's employment is relatively good (England, 1992). If minority workers continue to make occupational advances into fields previously dominated by whites, the prognosis for minority employment is reasonably good. However, any remaining prejudices and discrimination against women and minority workers will result in their disproportionate representation in the marginal work sector of the twenty-first century. If the burden for child care continues to fall disproportionately on

BOX 3.3   A Marginal-Employment Scenario

It had snowed all night, but the snow-jets had not yet cleared the lot. No matter, thought Debra as she braked her bike. Like most other parking lots built in the 1990s, this one was too big. Way too big, she thought, for my bike. If today was typical, hers would be the only vehicle parked there through the ten-hour shift. Marge Henry's little van was there now, but it was nearly shift-change time. Debra eased her right leg over the bike and into the ankle-deep snow. This was no time to slip and break something: the company had already cut back the health benefits to the government-required minimum, and Debra had nothing extra for the 50% coinsurance.

The snow muffled all sounds; it was almost as quiet here in the parking lot as it would be inside. The winter sun was nearly up over the horizon, and Debra looked over her shoulder at the lightening gray clouds in the east. In the winter she saw the sun only on Sunday. Her suntan, like her marriage, was a casualty of the company's shift policy. Ten hours a day, six days a week, take it or leave it. Many, many would take it if she left it. Certainly poor Jim. It was hard having an unemployed husband. It *had been* hard, she corrected herself. She pulled off a mitten and pushed her thumb against the glass for print recognition.

As the glass doors rolled back, she stepped across the laser beam on the threshold. It was easier than punching a clock but unrelenting in its accounting of her time. All personal areas of the shop had been fenced in with laser beams, so any "nonproductive" time was deducted from your paycheck. No tolerance, she thought wryly, if you had morning sickness, a touch of the "bug," or just too much spicy food last night. That was one reason for showing up a little early—it gave you a cushion of time if you needed an extra stop in the personal room. She crossed the corridor to the control room and pressed her thumb against another print-reader. Marge, she knew, would be locked inside. The company kept tight security, mainly for the sake of the robots (which were expensive).

"Any problems, Marge?" Debra asked.

"Number thirty-two is acting up again. Quiet night otherwise."

Marge crossed the laser beam to the dressing room and sat down to pull on her snow boots. She resented Debra. Both women worked ten hours a day, but Marge worked the night shift, and so she received only minimum wage. Debra made ten cents an hour more. Education had nothing to do with it; both jobs required a degree in robotics. The difference, the company claimed, was in the volume of work. This warehouse filled orders for toys—or rather, its forty-five robots did. The orders came in on the electronic LINCOM, and the robots located the proper storage bin, selected the proper number of boxes, issued address tags, and loaded the boxes into huge shipping containers. Twice a day, trucks came to pick up these containers. During the day shift, orders came in from across the United States and Canada, a few from Mexico. During the night shift, most of the orders came from Europe, Japan, and Africa. Although the toy market was growing there (in inverse proportion, it seemed, to declining birthrates), the volume of night business was much lower. Ample reason, according to the company, for Marge's paycheck to be a dollar less everyday than Debra's even though the same forty-five robots needed routine and preventive maintenance and there were still occasional foul-ups.

Then there was the matter of the swing shift. Between 6 P.M. and 10 P.M. a young college graduate came in to work the short evening shift. It was so hard for new graduates to find jobs these days that some companies viewed these little part-time jobs as favors they did the worker, not as jobs that required a paycheck. This company paid an honorarium—half of minimum wage—for the decided advantage of gaining work experience. The evening shift wasn't all that easy, either, what with the boom in the Pacific Basin.

Marge was ready to leave. Debra saw her out, then checked the security system. The

(Continued)

BOX 3.3   A Marginal-Employment Scenario (Continued)

LINCOM was already humming, and she saw two more robots move off to fetch toys. Thirty-two was idle and would bear watching. As she punched up the maintenance record on thirty-two, she saw the reflection of a blue light blinking overhead. The blue light was the "spy in the sky," the electronic monitoring device that ensured that employees did not alleviate their boredom with transistor videos, personal message units, or other distractions. She was glad that someone, somewhere,

knew she was here, even if only to check up on her. The workday had begun, but except for the humming of the LINCOM and the soft whir of the robots' wheels, you might never have known.

SOURCE: Adapted from Teresa A. Sullivan, 1989, "Women and Minority Workers in the New Economy: Optimistic, Pessimistic, and Mixed Scenarios." *Work and Occupations* 16,4 (November):393–395. Used by permission of Sage Publications, Inc.

---

women and if the divorce rate continues at a high level or even increases, then poverty associated with family dissolution will continue to plague many women and will seriously constrain their employment options. Similarly, the reemergence and growth black underclass reminds us that, even if some minority workers have made progress in recent decades, many other have been left behind (Wilson, 1997).

We have predicted the emergence of a divided economy with large innovative and marginal sectors. Social and political forces, some of which are outside the scope of this unit, however, will influence the relative size of these two employment sectors. Similarly, the relative representation of minority groups and women in each sector will be contingent on the ability of these groups to further reduce discrimination through mass movements and legislative agendas. Nevertheless, there are many relevant factors that will influence the relative development of these two sectors that we can consider.

ACHIEVING A BRIGHTER FUTURE

The emergence of an economy divided between innovative and marginal sectors is not inevitable. The problem before society is how to increase the size of the innovative sector and how to decrease the size and diminish the negative consequences of the marginal sector. How might these goals be achieved?

Increasing Innovation

What conditions foster innovative job redesign and worker participation? Workers in industrially advanced nations today are more highly educated than ever before in history. They are also more interested in safety and health issues and in improving the conditions of their employment. They have come to have high expectations about the satisfactions and rewards that work can provide. These expectations are perhaps the most important precondition for the growth of a highly innovative sector based on heightened participation and continuous learning.

Organizational and Market Imperatives

Not all industries, however, are equally likely to pursue a strategy of workplace innovation. Innovation has tended to emerge when "both labor and management perceive a necessity for technological innovation; . . . and workers have the bargaining strength to demand participation in managerial decision making" (Cornfield, 1987:333). When these conditions are missing, innovation is unlikely to occur, and work practices will more closely resemble those of the mass-production industries of the past or those of the marginal sector.

Intensified competition also provides an impetus to workplace innovation. Labor and management do not typically cooperate unless competitive pressures force them to do so. Without these pressures they will be more likely to pursue their separate goals by engaging in adversarial bargaining over their respective shares of the economic pie.

Increased Worker Power

An important precondition for innovation is that workers have sufficient power to demand participation and innovation. When workers are unable to demand participation, managers may favor a strategy of reducing wages, benefits, and job security in order remain competitive rather than following the more uncertain, complex, and demanding route of workplace innovation. In the long run, however, the option of remaining competitive by reducing wages may be unrealistic in many industries (even ignoring ethical hazards involved in such a strategy). As a result there is reason to hope that a substantial portion of organizations in industrially advanced societies will opt for workplace innovation.

The Role of Unions

Worker participation is most likely to take place in unionized firms. The concepts of direct worker participation and worker cooperation with management, however, are to some extent antithetical to traditional union approaches to industrial relations. On topics ranging from work rules to grievance procedures, unions have increased workers' rights by negotiating explicit rules and ensuring their enforcement. This approach has often translated into a formalistic and legalistic approach to workplace issues, exactly the sort of approach that can be stifling to innovation (Freeman and Rogers, 1999).

Unions have also been cautious in advocating innovative workplace changes because they fear that altering the status quo may undermine their ability to deliver the package of benefits and protections that have been their traditional offering to workers. To survive in innovative settings, however, unions will have to stop *reacting* to changing circumstances and begin to take an *active role* in developing proposals for increasing productivity. In the past, union leaders have often dismissed worker participation as "a ruse to increase worker productivity" (Parker and Slaughter, 1994). Continuing to dismiss worker participation in this manner will undermine the role of unions in the workplace of the future. The emergence of joint labor–management groups at various levels of the organization is necessary to increase productivity in rapidly changing and highly competitive industries. If the innovative sector is to grow and prosper, it will have to include the unionized industries, but unions will have to change to accommodate and promote innovation. These changes are threatening to established union practices in many ways. Unions in the industrially advanced European nations, however, have taken a leading role in promoting increased worker participation. Unions and worker participation are not inherently antithetical; indeed, they may be dependent on each other.

Education and Training

Educating the work-force for innovation will require an increased commitment not only to college education but also to **vocational education** and to ongoing **retaining** for workers already in the labor force. Many European nations have instituted programs for mid-career retraining. Observers credit a substantial part of these countries' economic vitality to such programs. North Americans must move beyond retaining programs designed to remedy the plight of the currently unemployable. Such programs include the Comprehensive Employment Training Act and Job Training Partnership Act. Although these programs are an important safeguard for workers otherwise condemned to work in the marginal sector, they are largely inadequate for training the highly skilled labor force necessary for the innovative sector (Slessarev, 1997). Besides providing college for the middle classes and job training for marginal workers, North Americans must provide skilled workers with the education and continuing training necessary to compete effectively in the global economy.

Workplace Experimentation

Increased **workplace experimentation** is also needed to stimulate the growth of an innovative sector. Successful job redesign comes only from experimentation. It cannot be fully specified in abstract formuleas—it requires a constant process of review and change. Unfortunately, sustained programs of experimentation in job redesign and worker participation are not widespread in the United States and Canada.

To increase the innovative sector, the preconditions for its existence must be broadened. These preconditions include workplace experimentation, increased worker power, and technological innovation. Greater worker power can come about either on an individual basis, through increased education, training, and professional development, or on a collective basis, through increased representation in unions and professional associations. Encouraging education and unions fosters the growth of an innovative sector and decreases the prevalence of marginality. The impetus for these changes must come from workers, unions, and professional associations. Reforms of this sort will not occur unless workers and their organizations demand them (Freeman and Rogers, 1999).

Reducing Marginal Employment

Besides underwriting workers' abilities to demand technological innovation and competitiveness and providing a labor force educated to meet the challenge of innovation, society can also set up roadblocks against encroaching marginality. These roadblocks could include an increased minimum wage, restrictions on mergers and plant closings, and standardization of tax, labor, and environmental laws across the country so that states are not forced to compete with one another to offer companies the most minimal employment standards (Phelps, 1997). In many cases higher minimum wages have been shown to have significant positive effects on workers stability and the acquisition of additional training without substantial negative effects on new hiring (Card and Krueger, 1995). Roadblocks to capital flight would keep capital at home and in place where it can be used to foster innovation and increased productivity as preferred responses to competitive pressures. Programs encouraging worker buyouts, ESOPs, and cooperatives might also reduce marginality. Banks could be encouraged to lessen their resistance to extending needed credit to worker-owned enterprises. Such forms of collective ownership, though they do not necessarily eliminate marginality, at least reduce some of its worst consequences (Cornforth, 1992).

Expanded worker training programs are important, not only for facilitating the spread of innovation, but also for reducing marginal employment. The need for such programs is increased by the heightened pace of technological change. Fewer and fewer workers can expect to work at just one job throughout their careers. With more rapid job changes, improved job placement and matching services also become increasingly important if jobs are to be filled by qualified applicants, if workers' abilities are to be used effectively, and if workers are to avoid periods of marginality. Employment of the labor force at nearer its full potential would increase productivity and reduce welfare expenses immensely.

Reducing the marginal aspects of available jobs would help lessen underemployment, unstable employment, and blocked mobility. In conjunction with education and training programs and the expansion of the innovative sector, a reduction of marginal employment positions would facilitate the incorporation of all Americans in the mainstream of society. The success of such agendas will also depend on the vigorous enforcement of laws protecting the rights of workers.

Expanding Leisure

Expanded leisure hours could also make an important contribution to improving the quality of work life and distributing available employment. The average hours worked per week dropped from near seventy in 1850 to about forty by the 1930s. Starting in the 1970s, however, this trend began to be reversed. Fully employed U.S. workers found that their workweek increased by about 5% during the 1970 to 2000 period. Simultaneously paid holidays and vacation days fell by 15% (Schor, 1992). This change occurred simultaneously with rising unemployment. In the 2000s, full-time work has become harder to get, and it is often highly demanding when it is finally secured. Reducing the hours of work would be an effective way to distribute available employment in a period of rapidly increasing productivity and technological change. Reduced hours of work would also help prevent polarization of society between those with too much work and those with inadequate work or no work at all (Hunnicutt, 1996).

A related possibility is that people will combine work, leisure, and education throughout their lives rather than completing education before starting work and saving their leisure years for retirement. Such a pattern would deviate from the so-called normative career pattern. A career pattern with greater integration of work, education, and leisure would include periodic breaks for retraining and renewal, breaks that would be extremely important for sustaining the innovative spirit in workers. Lifestyles that allow for a greater integration of work, education, and leisure across the life cycle would also help resolve the dilemma of fewer workers being needed as technologically based advances in productivity continue to accumulate.

Expanding Public Goods

Over the history of industrial society the provision of "public goods" has increased. **Public goods** are products or services to which the citizens or residents of a society are entitled without direct payment or at a nominal fee. Such public goods include education, clean air, public parks, retirement income, and increasingly, health care. If the provision of public goods expands, workers who remain in the marginal sector of employment will at least be spared some of the most debilitating consequences of poverty and marginality. The provision of public goods can thus be an important preventive against the reproduction of a marginal sector. The provision of public goods also creates jobs, providing additional escape routes from marginality. Alternatively, if such services are provided only privately as parts of benefit packages restricted to the innovative sector, many in society will have to do without them. The provision of public goods and the training of workers for employment in the innovative sector are among the most important strategies for avoiding a deeply class-divided society in the twenty-first century. Whether we pursue such agendas as a society depends on the importance that we attach to equality and the creation of a just society (Kuttner, 1996).

SUMMARY

The rapidly changing economic, technological, and organizational realities of today's global economy are setting the stage for the world of work in the twenty-first century. Alternatives are available, but these depend on the political and social actions we take today. The dilemmas described in this unit can be resolved in a positive manner. Workers and other members of society can pressure organizations to respond to competition by increasing innovation rather than by cutting wages and fostering marginality. They can also pressure labor unions and other workers' associations to adapt to the new conditions of a competitive environment and to provide leadership in the areas of technology, organizational innovation, and worker training. Finally, they can pressure the government to enact laws and programs that will foster innovation, job creation, worker involvement, expanded leisure, and a better quality of life for all.

Industrial societies have the capacity to constantly increase productivity through technological and organizational innovation. This capacity has never been greater than it is today. However, this very capacity creates the dilemma of how to distribute available work when more and more goods and services can be produced by fewer and fewer workers. These, then, are the central challenges of contemporary industrial society: How do we increase productivity? How do we distribute available work? And how do we distribute the goods and services produced? The manner in which we resolve these dilemmas will determine the political, social, and economic landscape of the twenty-first century.

UNIT 4

PSYCHOLOGICAL FOUNDATIONS

Trait-and-Factor and Developmental Theories of Career
Choice and Development and Their Applications

Buford Stefflre, a counselor educator at Michigan State University for many years, is reputed to have coined the phrase, "There is nothing as practical as a good theory." When this statement is conveyed to students, they are at best skeptical. Isn't using *theory* and *practical* in the same sentence oxymoronic? Theories are obviously not fact, and what most students want are proven practices that they can use to help their clients. The problem is that many of our practices have not been investigated to the degree that will allow us to say unequivocally that they work. A good theory provides a framework for designing practices. The author believes Stefflre was right!

The author has tried to accomplish two tasks in this unit. The first is to present some of the theories that have been generated to explain career choice and development. Second, I have tried to illustrate how these theories can be put into practice and to indicate the groups into which the theories fit best. The implication of this last phrase is that not all theories apply to all groups; thus, caution is necessary when designing practices based on the theorist's assumptions. The author believes it will be helpful before you read this unit to consider your own personal theory about human behavior and career choice and development. Yes, you have your biases and perceptions about why people choose careers, although you may not have given them much thought previously. By identifying your own thoughts in this area, you take the first step toward the construction of a sophisticated theory of your own.

Taken from Brown, D. (2007) *Career Information, Career Counseling, and Career Development*, Ninth Edition. Boston, MA: Allyn & Bacon. Chapter 2, pp. 27–64.

One objective of this unit is to provide an overview of the history of theorizing about career choice and development. It is generally recognized that the forerunner of modern theories of career development appeared in 1909 in *Choosing Your Vocation* by Frank Parsons. Parsons's tripartite model—understanding one's self, understanding the requirements of the jobs available, and choosing one based on true logic—underpinned career counseling and career development practice into the middle of the twentieth century. However, in the 1950s and 1960s a period of intense theorizing about career development occurred. The result was eight new theories of career choice and development, many of which are still viable today. From 1970 to 1984 five new theories of career choice and development were advanced, three of which focused largely on women's career development. Another intense period of theorizing began in 1991, and since 1991 five new theories of career choice and development have been presented. A chronological account of these events can be found in Table 4.1.

The second objective of this unit is to discuss the trait-and-factor and developmental theories and their applications, that is, the theories that have stood the test of time. However, prior to embarking on discussions of the established, influential theories or the new, emerging theories, a more general discussion of the purpose and evaluation of theories of career choice and development is provided.

THE PURPOSES AND EVALUATION OF THEORY

Career development was defined as a lifelong process involving psychological, sociological, educational, economic, physical, and cultural factors that influence individuals' selection of, adjustment to, and advancement in the occupations that collectively make up their careers. Career development is, to say the least, a complex process. Theories provide us with simplified pictures, or as Krumboltz (1994) prefers, road maps to the career development process.

There are "good" theories and "bad" theories. As Krumboltz (1994) states, "Our psychological theories are as good as we know how to make them so far, but in all probability they are far short of being accurate" (p. 11). However, good theories have distinct characteristics, such as well-defined terms and constructs, that can easily be interpreted by practitioners and researchers. Just as importantly, the relationships among the constructs in the theory are clearly articulated. If the terms are clearly defined and logically interrelated, practitioners can use them as guides to practice, and researchers can generate research to test the assumptions of the theory. Moreover, good theories are comprehensive in that they explain the career development process for all groups, including men and women, people from various cultures, and individuals from various socioeconomic strata.

Well-constructed theories serve other purposes. For example, they help us understand why people choose careers and become dissatisfied with them. They also allow us to interpret data about career development that have been

TABLE 4.1   A History of Career Development Theorizing

Year	Event
1909	Parsons's book, *Choosing Your Vocation,* is published posthumously.
1951	Eli Ginzberg and associates publish *Occupational Choice: An Approach to a General Theory,* which outlines a developmental theory of career development.
1953	Donald Super publishes "A Theory of Vocational Development" in the *American Psychologist,* which outlines a second developmental theory of career development.
1956	Ann Roe publishes *The Psychology of Occupations,* which contains her personality-based theory of career development.
1959	John Holland publishes "A Theory of Vocational Choice" in the *Journal of Counseling Psychology,* which sets forth some of the propositions of his theory of vocational choice.
1963	David Tiedeman and Robert O'Hara publish *Career Development: Choice and Adjustment,* which contains a theory rooted in the idea that careers satisfy needs.
1963	Edward Bordin and associates publish "An Articulated Framework for Vocational Development" in the *Journal of Counseling Psychology,* which sets forth a psychodynamic framework for career development.
1967	Blau and Duncan publish *The American Occupational Structure,* which sets forth the premises of status attainment theory, a sociological theory of career development.
1969	Lloyd Lofquist and René Dawis publish *Adjustment to Work,* which outlines the premises of a trait-factor model of occupational selection and adjustment.
1976	John Krumboltz and associates publish "A Social Learning Theory of Career Selection" in *The Counseling Psychologist.*
1981	Linda Gottfredson publishes "Circumscription and Compromise: A Developmental Theory of Occupational Aspirations" in the *Journal of Counseling Psychology,* which focuses on how sex role identification limits occupational aspirations.
1981	Gail Hackett and Nancy Betz publish "A Self-Efficacy Approach to the Career-Development of Women" in the *Journal of Vocational Behavior,* which uses Bandura's self-efficacy construct to explain important aspects of the career decision–making process.
1984	Helen Astin publishes "The Meaning of Work in Women's Lives: A Sociopsychological Model of Career Choice and Work Behavior" in *The Counseling Psychologist,* which outlines a general theory of the career development of women.
1984	Tiedeman and Miller-Tiedeman publish "Career Decision Making: An Individualistic Perspective," which is one of the early attempts at framing a theory based on constructivist philosophy.
1991	Gary Peterson and associates publish *Career Development and Services: A Cognitive Approach,* which contains their cognitive information-processing model of career choice and development.
1994	Robert Lent and associates publish "Toward a Unifying Social Cognitive Theory of Career and Academic Interest, Choice and Performance" in the *Journal of Vocational Psychology,* which is based on Albert Bandura's (1986) sociocognitive theory. This theory was revised in 2002 to focus on the role of cultural and work values in occupational choice, success, and satisfaction.
1996	Duane Brown's "Values-Based Model of Career and Life-Role Choices and Satisfaction" is published in the *Career Development Quarterly* and *Career Choice and Development.* This theory was revised in 2002 to focus on the role of cultural and work values in occupational choice, success, and satisfaction.
1996	Richard Young and associates publish "A Contextual Explanation of Career," which is based on constructivist philosophy.
2005	Deborah Bloch and Jim E. H. Bright and Robert G. L. Pryor publish two independent versions of chaos theories of careers.

generated in the past, are being generated in the present, and will be generated in the future. Researchers and practitioners have long been aware that women and men choose sex-typed careers. Gottfredson's theory (1981, 2002) helps us understand why this occurs. Well-developed theories also help us account for all internal and external factors that influence career development, including cognitions about careers and affective responses to various career-related events (Brown & Brooks, 1996; Krumboltz, 1994). Finally, well-constructed theories are parsimonious, which means they are set forth in the simplest, most succinct fashion necessary to describe the phenomena involved. To summarize, theories of career choice and development are needed to

1. Facilitate the understanding of the forces that influence career choice and development
2. Stimulate research that will help us better clarify the career choice and development process
3. Provide a guide to practice in the absence of empirical guidelines

A History of Career Development Theorizing

The 19 publications listed in Table 4.1 are by no means the only attempts at developing theories of career choice and development, and as shown later, most of these theories have been revised numerous times. Today the theories of Holland (1997), Super (1990), Lofquist and Dawis (Dawis, 1996; Lofquist & Dawis, 1991), Lent, Brown, and Hackett (1995, 1996, 2002), and Gottfredson (1981, 1996) are making a major impact on research or practice. These theories are discussed in some detail in the developmental theories section and the socioeconomic theories section under the first subsection, Status Attainment Theory (Blau & Duncan, 1967; Hotchkiss & Borow, 1996). These theories have become influential because they possess the characteristics of a "good" theory (described previously), although each of them has shortcomings.

It is difficult to say why some theories become influential whereas others do not. Bordin's psychodynamic theory (1984) was well constructed, but it may not have become popular because it was built on psychodynamic theory, which has never been widely accepted by counselors or counseling psychologists. Roe's theory (Roe, 1956, 1984; Roe & Lunneborg, 1990) gradually lost favor because researchers were unable to verify her basic propositions that early childhood environments give rise to personality types that in turn result in career selection. No perfect theory of career choice has yet to emerge and it is unlikely that this will occur. However, to return to Krumboltz's (1994) map metaphor, some theory builders do a better job than others of providing maps to the vast array of phenomena that influence career development.

Some relatively new theories of career choice and development may become influential in the future. For example, constructivist theories (e.g., Young, Valach, & Collin, 2002) are receiving a great deal of attention from scientists and practitioners alike. Some theories are so new that they have not had an opportunity to attract large numbers of adherents. The career information–processing model (Peterson, Sampson, & Reardon, 1991; Peterson, Sampson, Reardon, & Lenz, 1996) and the values-based theory of Brown (Brown, 1996, 2002a; Brown & Crace, 1995) are included in this group.

Theories for Special Groups

Some writers (e.g., Astin, 1984; Hackett & Betz, 1981) have proposed that, because many early theories (e.g., Super, 1953) were oriented primarily to white males, they are inappropriate explanations of the career development of women and of males and females from other-than-European backgrounds. Theorists such as Holland (1997) and Super (1990) contend that these criticisms are unwarranted, although Super made some changes in his theory over time to accommodate the changing career patterns of women. Efforts to develop alternative theories that focus on specific subgroups have not been met with much enthusiasm. For example, Astin's (1997) psychosociological model of career choice and work behavior has attracted few supporters. Moreover, Gail Hackett, who, in collaboration with Nancy Betz, addressed the role of self-efficacy in women's career choice making, is now a co-author of a more comprehensive theory that focuses on the social cognitive factors that influence the career development of both men and women (Lent, Brown, & Hackett, 1995, 1996, 2002). Interestingly, Betz, along with Fitzgerald (Fitzgerald & Betz, 1994) have argued forcefully that current theories have limited applicability to minority groups, persons with gay or lesbian sexual orientation, and women.

Is Career Development Theory Unintentionally Racist?

Sue and Sue (2000) and Pedersen (1991) have proposed that most of the theories included in training programs for professional counselors, psychologists, and others are culturally oppressive because they are rooted in Eurocentric beliefs. The Western European worldview is that people should act independently when they make career decisions, a belief that arises from the cultural belief that the individual is the most important social unit (Carter, 1991). However, many Native Americans, Asian Americans, and Hispanics believe that the welfare of the group should be placed ahead of the concerns of individuals. They hold a collateral, or collective, social value and thus may reject the ideas that independence and competition are acceptable. Leong (1991) found that the Asian American students in his sample had a dependent decision-making style, not the independent style that would flow from Eurocentric values. One implication of this finding is that some Asian American students may find it perfectly appropriate to allow their parents to play a major role in the selection of their occupations. Unfortunately, most of the theories included in this unit (e.g., Dawis, 1996; Gottfredson, 1996; Holland, 1997; Super, 1990) make this assumption, along with the assumption that job satisfaction is the result of the individual's interaction with his or her work environment. It seems entirely likely that job satisfaction and factors such as achievement in one's career are related to a much more complex set of variables, including family or group approval of the career choice and the individual's performance in it. Hartung (2002) joined the chorus of criticisms of career development based on cultural validity by reviewing some of the criticisms, which more or less echo those previously discussed. He, like the others mentioned here, suggests that there is a need to move from a monocultural approach to a multicultural perspective. However, Hartung (2002) admits that not all theory produced to date does not have a monocultural perspective. He cites Lent, Brown, and Hackett (1996) and Brown (1996) as examples of theories that have abandoned a monocultural perspective. Hartung (2002) also suggests that research literature is becoming available that supports the use of some of the traditional theories with cultural minorities. Monocultural theories are flawed because they often lack cultural validity. However, they provide a valid basis for practice for people who hold a Western European worldview. Further, it is a mistake to assume that they are inappropriate for use with cultural minorities based on phenotypic characteristics of individuals. Many cultural minorities have adopted a Western European worldview and function primarily in cultural contexts that reinforce these values. It is an ethical error to apply theories of any type without assessing the cultural perspective of the individual first.

A different set of criticism of traditional theories have been advanced by Peterson and Gonzalez (2005), Bloch (2005), and Bright and Pryor (2005). These authors suggest that the modern philosophy that underpins most traditional theories is inappropriate based on advances in thinking and suggest that it be replaced with a postmodern perspective. The differences in these two philosophies are summarized as follows.

INTRODUCTION TO THE THEORIES

The theories that follow fall into several categories—trait-and-factor theories, developmental theories, learning theories, socioeconomic theories, and recent theoretical statements. Trait-and-factor theories stress that individuals need to develop their traits, which include their interests, values, personalities, and aptitudes, as well as select environments that are congruent with them. Developmental theories are based to some degree on the assumption that the factors that influence career choice and development are related to stages of personal and psychological development. The tenets of various learning theories have been used to describe both the process by which the individual develops and the choice-making process itself. Socioeconomic theories pay less attention to psychological traits, although they typically address the matter of intellect as a factor in career choice. However, these theories focus on the socioeconomic status of the decision maker and/or the influence of sociological and economic factors on occupational choice making. In the section on recent theoretical statements, two theories based on learning theory, one trait-and-factor theory and one constructivist theory, are presented.

All theories are based on certain philosophical assumptions that usually fall into two categories: positivist and postmodern. Trait-and-factor theories, developmental theories, and theories rooted in learning theory are based on modernist or positivist philosophical thinking. The assumptions of this position are

1. Human behavior can be measured objectively if reliable, valid instruments are utilized.
2. Human behavior can be studied outside the context in which it occurs.
3. Research processes should be value free. If the researcher's values enter into the process, the results are likely to be flawed.
4. Cause and effect relationships occur and can be measured.
5. If certain conditions are met, such as random sampling, the use of reliable, valid instruments, and lack of contamination of results by the researcher's values, results can be generalized to other people in similar settings.
6. As much as possible career counselors should maintain their objectivity, use instruments that are reliable and valid, and base their practice on well-designed empirical research.

Postmodern theories, often referred to as phenomenological or constructivist theories, are a relatively new addition to the theories of career choice and development. These theories depart radically from the assumptions of the theories based on positivist philosophy. The assumptions underpinning these theories are

1. Human behavior is nonlinear and thus cannot be studied objectively.
2. Cause and effect relationships cannot be determined.
3. Individuals cannot be studied outside the context in which they function.
4. Research data cannot be generalized.
5. Research is not a value-free process. The researcher's values should in fact guide the research process.
6. The stories (narratives) that students tell are legitimate sources of data.
7. Research is goal free: It is a search for actual effects based on demonstrated needs. Random samples are replaced with purposeful sampling, that is, studying individuals who can respond to the research in a meaningful manner. For example, to understand sex-role stereotyping of occupational choice, a researcher might select subjects who knowingly chose careers because of stereotypes rather than selecting a random sample that included people who made decisions based on other variables.
8. Career counselors focus on the stories (narratives) of their clients, use qualitative assessment procedures, and help clients construct career goals based on their perceptions of the context in which they function.

These assumptions should be kept in mind as the theories are reviewed.

TRAIT-AND-FACTOR THEORIES

Holland's Theory of Vocational Choice

Holland developed a theoretical position gradually revealed in a series of published theoretical and research studies (Holland, 1959, 1962, 1963a, 1963b, 1963c, 1963d, 1966a, 1966b, 1968, 1972, 1973, 1985, 1987, 1997; Holland & Gottfredson, 1976; Holland & Lutz, 1968; Holland & Nichols, 1964). Holland's theory of vocational choice is based on several assumptions:

1. An individual's personality is the primary factor in vocational choice.
2. Interest inventories are in fact personality inventories.
3. Individuals develop stereotypical views of occupations that have psychological relevance. These stereotypes play a major role in occupational choice.
4. Daydreams about occupations are often precursors to occupational choices.
5. Identity—the clarity of an individual's perceptions of his or her goals and personal characteristics—is related to having a small number of rather focused vocational goals.
6. To be successful and satisfied in one's career it is necessary to choose an occupation that is congruent with one's personality. A congruent occupation is one in which other people in the work environment have the same or similar characteristics as one's own.

Personality develops as a result of the interaction of inherited characteristics, the activities to which the individual is exposed, and the interests and competencies that grow out of the activities (Holland, 1997). Holland believes that to some degree "types beget types" but recognizes that children shape their own environments to an extent, and they are exposed to a number of people in addition to their parents who provide experiences and reinforce certain types of performance. The combination of these influences produces "a person who is predisposed to exhibit a characteristic self-concept and outlook and to acquire a characteristic disposition" (Holland, 1997, p. 19). Ultimately, the personality emerges. Holland posits six pure personality types, which occur rarely if at all in their pure form. These "pure" types are realistic, investigative, artistic, social, enterprising, and conventional. Descriptions of these types follow.

Realistic people deal with the environment in an objective, concrete, and physically manipulative manner. They avoid goals and tasks that demand subjectivity, intellectual or artistic expressions, or social abilities. They are described as masculine, unsociable, emotionally stable, and materialistic. They prefer agricultural, technical, skilled-trade, and engineering vocations. They like activities that involve motor skills, equipment, machines, tools, and structure, such as athletics, scouting, crafts, and shop work.

Investigative people deal with the environment by using intellect—manipulating ideas, words, and symbols. They prefer scientific vocations, theoretical tasks, reading, collecting, algebra, foreign languages, and such creative activities as art, music, and sculpture. They avoid social situations and see themselves as unsociable, masculine, persistent, scholarly, and introverted. They achieve primarily in academic and scientific areas and usually do poorly as leaders.

Artistic individuals deal with the environment by creating art forms and products. They rely on subjective impressions and fantasies in seeking solutions to problems. They prefer musical, artistic, literary, and dramatic vocations and activities that are creative in nature. They dislike masculine activities and roles, such as auto repair and athletics. They see themselves as unsociable, feminine, submissive, introspective, sensitive, impulsive, and flexible.

Social people deal with the environment by using skills to interact with and relate to others. They are typified by social skills and the need for social interaction. They prefer educational, therapeutic, and religious vocations and activities, such as church, government, community services, music, reading, and dramatics. They see themselves as sociable, nurturant, cheerful, conservative, responsible, achieving, and self-accepting.

Enterprising people cope with the environment by expressing adventurous, dominant, enthusiastic, and impulsive qualities. Characterized as persuasive, verbal, extroverted, self-accepting, self-confident, aggressive, and exhibitionistic, they prefer sales, supervisory, and leadership vocations and activities that satisfy needs for dominance, verbal expression, recognition, and power.

Conventional people deal with the environment by choosing goals and activities that carry social approval. Their approach to problems is stereotypical, correct, and unoriginal. They create a neat, sociable, conservative impression. They prefer clerical and computational tasks, identify with business, and put a high value on economic matters. They see themselves as masculine, shrewd, dominant, controlled, rigid, and stable and have more mathematical than verbal aptitude.

According to Holland, a person can be typed into one of these categories by expressed or demonstrated vocational or educational interests, by employment, or by scores obtained on such instruments as the Vocational Preference Inventory, the Strong Interest Inventory, or the Self-Directed Search. The last, an instrument developed by Holland, consists of occupational titles and activities that can be divided equally among the six type areas. Each method of determining personality type yields a score. Although Holland (1997) believes that all six types are descriptive of personality, he suggests that the top three scores are the most telling factors. Thus the result of the assessment of type is a three-letter code (e.g., SAE), known as a *Holland code*. If the three-letter code is consistent and differentiated, the primary (first type) is expected to be the most influential, the second type the second most influential, and the tertiary or third type the third most influential in describing vocational decisions and aspirations and academic achievement. The consistency of a personality profile can be determined by use of the hexagon shown in Figure 4.1. If the personality types are adjacent (e.g., realistic and investigative), they are said to be consistent. Inconsistent types are located opposite each other on the hexagon (e.g., investigative and enterprising). A personality profile is well differentiated if the scores on the primary type of the

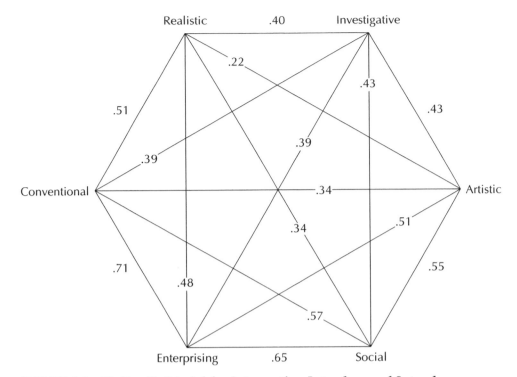

FIGURE 4.1   **Holland's Model for Interpreting Interclass and Intraclass Relationships**

Source: Reproduced by special permission of the publisher, Psychological Assessment Resources, Inc., Odessa, FL 33556. From the *Self-Directed Search Technical Manual* by J. L. Holland, Ph.D. Copyright 1994, by PAR, Inc. Further reproduction is prohibited without permission from PAR, Inc.

profile are significantly higher than the lowest score. Holland (1997) believes that consistency and differentiation are indirect estimates of identity, which he defines as the clarity of an individual's goals and self-perceptions. Identity can be measured directly by the My Vocational Situation instrument (Holland, Daiger, & Powers, 1980).

Holland (1985, 1997) also proposes six work environments (realistic, investigative, artistic, social, enterprising, and conventional) analogous to the pure personality types just described. As already noted, individuals must select vocational environments congruent with their personalities to maximize their job satisfaction and achievements. These environments are described in the following sections.

The *realistic* environment involves concrete, physical tasks requiring mechanical skill, persistence, and physical movement. Only minimal interpersonal skills are needed. Typical realistic settings include a filling station, a machine shop, a farm, a construction site, and a barber shop.

The *investigative* environment requires the use of abstract and creative abilities rather than personal perceptiveness. Satisfactory performance demands imagination and intelligence; achievement usually requires a considerable time span. Problems encountered may vary in level of difficulty, but they are usually solved by applying intellectual skills and tools. The work revolves around ideas and things rather than people. Typical settings include a research laboratory; a diagnostic case conference; a library; and a work group of scientists, mathematicians, or research engineers.

The *artistic* environment demands the creative and interpretive use of artistic forms. One must be able to draw on knowledge, intuition, and emotional life in solving typical problems. Information is judged against personal, subjective criteria. The work usually requires intense involvement for prolonged periods. Typical settings include a play rehearsal, a concert hall, a dance studio, a study, a library, and an art or music studio.

The *social* environment demands the ability to interpret and modify human behavior and an interest in caring for and interacting with people. The work requires frequent and prolonged personal relationships. The work hazards are primarily emotional. Typical work situations include school and college classrooms, counseling offices, mental hospitals, churches, educational offices, and recreational centers.

The *enterprising* environment requires verbal skill in directing or persuading people. The work requires directing, controlling, or planning activities of others, and a more superficial interest in people than in the social environment, most of that interest centered on what can be had from people. Typical settings include a car lot, a real estate office, a political rally, and an advertising agency.

The *conventional* environment involves systematic, concrete, routine processing of verbal and mathematical information. The tasks frequently call for repetitive, short-cycle operations according to an established procedure. Minimal skill in interpersonal relations is required because the work mostly involves office equipment and materials. Typical settings include a bank, an accounting firm, a post office, a file room, and a business office.

Holland suggests that each of these model environments is sought by individuals whose personality type is similar to those controlling the environment. It is assumed that they will be comfortable and happy in a compatible environment and un-easy in an environment suited to a different personality type. A congruent person–environment match presumably results in a more stable vocational choice, greater vocational achievement, higher academic achievement, better maintenance of personal stability, and greater satisfaction.

Finally, Holland developed an occupational classification system based on the model environment construct. Occupations are categorized according to the extent to which they involve activities representing the different points on the hexagon. An occupation that is mainly realistic in nature but involves some investigative activities and a lesser amount of conventional characteristics would be labeled RIC. This code would be considered consistent because the types are adjacent on the hexagon. A code of RSC, however, would be inconsistent because it involves opposites.

Status and Use of Holland's Theory

Holland's theory is the most influential of all of the extant theories. Instruments based on the theory, including his own Self-Directed Search (Holland, 1994a, 1994b) and Find Your Interests (DOD, 2005), which is used by the Department of Defense along with the Armed Services Vocational Aptitude Battery in its military recruitment program of high school students throughout the country, are best sellers. His theory has stimulated hundreds of research studies as well (Holland, 1997; Holland & Gottfredson, 1990). Moreover, Holland's conceptual scheme is used exclusively in O*NET, the major occupational classification system in the United States. However, his theory rightly has been criticized on the basis of its cultural validity and must be applied cautiously if at all with persons whose worldviews vary from that of the dominant culture.

The goal of career exploration and counseling using Holland's (1997) theory is to help client groups identify occupations that include workers in them with the same personality characteristics as their own (congruence). This process, in all likelihood, begins with an assessment of a client's Holland type using one of the following instruments:

> The Self-Directed Search (4th ed.)
> The Strong Interest Inventory
> The Harrington–O'Shea Career Decision-Making System, Revised
> Find Your Interests (part of the Armed Services Vocational Aptitude Battery [ASVAB] Career Exploration Program)
> The Career Key (online)
> Interest Profiler (embedded in O*NET)
> Wide Range Interest and Occupation Test (2nd ed.) (nonverbal inventory for special populations)

Although these instruments most often are used to measure Holland's constructs, they are by no means the only ones available for this purpose. All of the leading interest inventories produce Holland profiles.

Research generally supports the use of Holland's instruments with males and females as well as with people from diverse cultural backgrounds. Men generally score higher on realistic, investigative, and enterprising scales, whereas women tend to score higher on social, artistic, and conventional scales (Holland, 1997), and instruments tend to predict entry into occupations equally well for men and women. The newest version of Find Your Interests (DOD, 2005), which is scheduled for publication in late 2005 or early 2006, includes norms for men and women. Much of the research regarding Holland's theory has focused on whether his conceptualization fits different groups. Typically, the answer is yes (e.g., Day, Rounds, & Swaney, 1998). However, research that suggests the interest patterns of cultural minorities approximates that of white persons begs the question of appropriateness of the theory to these groups because it does little to address the issue of the decision-making process. Arnold (2004) suggests that the congruence concept also needs a great deal more exploration as it pertains to minority and white persons.

Theory of Work Adjustment (TWA)

The theory of work adjustment (TWA) has been set forth in a series of publications (Dawis, 1996; Dawis, England, & Lofquist, 1964; Dawis & Lofquist, 1984; Dawis, Lofquist, & Weiss, 1968; Lofquist & Dawis, 1991). In each of these publications the theory has been changed somewhat, but with few exceptions the assumptions underpinning the theory have not changed. The basic assumption of TWA is that people have two types of needs: biological (or survival) needs, such as the need for food, and psychological needs, such as social acceptance. These needs give rise to drive states, which in turn lead to volitional behavior. Whenever the behavior results in the needs being satisfied, reinforcement occurs and the behavior is strengthened. A second assumption is that work environments have "requirements" that are analogous to the needs of individuals. Both individuals and environments develop mechanisms for satisfying their needs. When the needs of individuals in an environment (work) and those of the environment are satisfied, correspondence exists. Workers select jobs because of their perception that the job will satisfy their needs, and workers are selected because of the perceptions that their skills will meet the needs of the workplace. If the reinforcer pattern of the workplace matches the need pattern of the worker, satisfaction and satisfactoriness occur. Satisfaction results when the worker is reinforced. Workers are judged to be satisfactory when they reinforce the need pattern of the work environment. The tenure, or time spent in a job by workers, is the result of their satisfaction with the job and satisfactoriness in performance.

Three variables—skills, aptitudes, and personality structure—can be used to predict the success of the worker if the reinforcement pattern of the work environment is known. The skills referred to in this predictive equation are the job-related skills the individual can offer to a work environment. Aptitude is the potential an individual has to develop the skills needed by the work environment, and the personality structure of the individual is determined by a combination of aptitudes and values. Values are determined by the importance attached to classes of reinforcement (e.g., pay, independence of functioning, etc.). Gender and minority group status are assumed to be critical variables in the development of personality structure within TWA.

Figure 4.2 is a graphic description of the occupational choice–making process in TWA terms. As can be seen, decision making begins with an analysis of values and abilities, followed by an analysis of the ability patterns and value patterns of the several occupations. Ultimately individuals compare all occupations being considered in terms of the extent to which they can perform the job satisfactorily and the degree to which the occupation will satisfy their needs.

To understand work adjustment, the structure of the work environment and the characteristics of the worker must be known. Predictions of success depend on the celerity, pace, endurance, and rhythm of both the worker and the

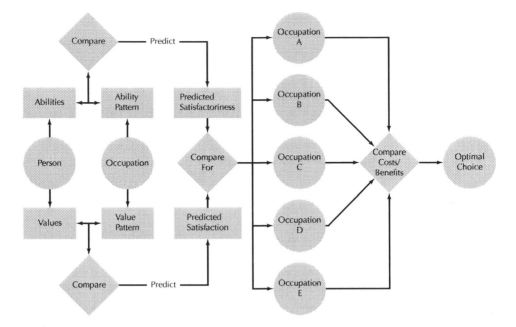

FIGURE 4.2   TWA's Graphic Explanation of Career Choice Correspondence

Source: From "The Theory of Work Adjustment and Person–Environment–Counseling," by
R. V. Dawis, 1996, in D. Brown, L. Brooks, & Associates, *Career Choice and Development* (3rd ed.,
pp. 75–120), San Francisco: Jossey-Bass. Reprinted by permission.

work environment. *Celerity* is the quickness with which workers engage their
work environment to satisfy their needs. Successful workers quickly and vigorously try to satisfy their needs prior to leaving a job. Moreover, work environments respond with varying degrees of speed when a worker is unsatisfactory.
The vigor with which individuals and work environments try to satisfy their
needs denotes *pace*. *Endurance* is used in TWA to indicate the tolerance of the individual or the work environment for dealing with unsatisfactory work conditions
or workers in the case of the work environment. *Rhythm* denotes the pattern of
attempts (e.g., steady, erratic) by individuals and work environments to satisfy
their needs.

Another factor that must be considered in the adjustment to work process is
whether individuals take an active or reactive approach. Active attempts are
those direct attempts to make the work environment more responsive to the
needs of the worker. When workers respond reactively, they change themselves
to respond to the perceived demands of the workplace. For example, reactive
workers might reconsider the needs they deem important and substitute security
for high pay. Some people have more tolerance (endurance) than others for unsat-
isfying situations and may make a series of reactive and active attempts to make
the environment respond to their needs before ending their tenure in the job.

Similarly, work environments may have greater or lesser tolerance for unsatisfactory efforts by workers. The development of work adjustment styles, including reactive and active approaches, celerity, endurance, pace, and rhythm is influenced by a variety of factors, including inherited characteristics, gender, and cultural background.

Counselors who want to apply TWA in their work will find that inventories and tests are available to measure the theoretical constructs of the theory (Dawis, 1996). Two scales, the Minnesota Satisfaction Questionnaire and the Minnesota Satisfactoriness Scales, can be used to measure satisfaction and satisfactoriness, respectively. The Minnesota Importance Questionnaire can be used to measure need preferences, and the Minnesota Ability Test Battery can be used to measure aptitudes. Occupational Reinforcer Patterns is an inventory that can be used to measure preferences for patterns of reinforcers.

Status and Use of TWA

TWA is not a widely practiced theory, probably because of its complexity. However, it has many similarities with Holland's theory in that the objective of the helping process is to help client groups match their aptitudes and values to occupations with jobs that provide appropriate occupational ability patterns and occupational reinforcer patterns. Holland (1997) uses the term *congruence* to indicate when an individual selects an occupation that matches his or her personality type. In TWA, the term is *correspondence*. The career counseling process would be as follows:

- Assess ability patterns using the General Aptitude Test Battery (GATB). The U.S. Department of Labor has compiled a list of minimum requirements for jobs, as measured by the GATB, for success on the job.
- Assess needs and values using the Minnesota Importance Questionnaire (MIQ). The results of the MIQ provide clients with a list of up to 180 occupations that match their needs.
- Counselors can also assist individuals to compare their occupational ability patterns, needs, and values to values in the Minnesota Occupational Classification System.
- The outcome of this process is expected to benefit both the worker via increased job satisfaction and the employer by increased satisfactoriness in job performance.

It seems likely that the TWA could be used with both men and women, although there are no empirical data to support this observation. As Sharf (2002) notes, one drawback to using the TWA is that the testing process may involve many hours if the GATB is included. He suggests that estimates of aptitudes may suffice as a substitute for the actual administration of the GATB. Estimates would have to be substituted for actual test results if this model were used for adults. Reading issues and the predictive validity of the tests and inventories for cultural and racial minorities are unresolved at this point. Additionally, the developers of the theory have not considered cultural values and how they may interact with work values and needs in their work on the theory. It may, therefore, be best for practitioners to consider TWA as a work in progress that may prove useful in the future.

A VALUES-BASED THEORY OF OCCUPATIONAL CHOICE

Brown (1996, 2002a; Brown & Crace, 1995) built on the work of Rokeach (1973), Super (1980, 1990), Beck (1976), and others to formulate a holistic model of career and life-role choice making. However, as he noted, the theory was aimed primarily at people with traditional Eurocentric values, including individualism, future time orientation, moderate need for self-control, emphasis on activity, and a core belief that humans should dominate nature.

Cultural values have been identified as important variables in career development and vocational behaviors (e.g., Fouad, 1995; Super & Sverko, 1995), but because these values vary across cultures, a comprehensive theory of career choice and development must take into account this variation. What is presented in this section is a major revision of Brown's (1996) theory that focuses for the most part on the values in a single life role: career.

However, cultural values are not the only variables that influence the career choice–making process or the resulting satisfaction and/or success. Contextual variables, such as socioeconomic status (SES) (e.g., Hotchkiss & Borow, 1996); family or group influence (e.g., Leong & Serifica, 1995); and discrimination (e.g., Melamed, 1996) are also considered in this revision, along with factors such as gender (e.g., Gottfredson, 1996; Melamed, 1995) and aptitudes (e.g., Jencks, Crouse, & Mueser, 1983; Phillips & Imhoff, 1997) because they have been linked empirically to career decision making and occupational attainment.

Variables that Influence Career Choice and Satisfaction

Values

Values are beliefs that are experienced by the individual as standards regarding how he or she should function. They are cognitive structures, but they have behavioral and affective dimensions. Values develop so that individuals can meet their needs in socially acceptable ways (Rokeach, 1973), and thus the behavioral aspect of values is shaped by the cultural context in which they develop. An individual's values are the basis for his or her self-evaluation and the evaluation of others, and they play a major role in the establishment of personal goals (Rokeach, 1973).

Work values are the values that individuals believe should be satisfied as a result of their participation in the work role. Values also play the central role in the decision-making process because they are the basis of goal setting. Goals, if properly constructed, move the individual toward desired end states (e.g., social acceptance). Financial prosperity, altruism, achievement, and responsibility are examples of work values. In addition to work values, individuals develop a number of other values that they expect to be satisfied in life roles other than work, such as family (Brown, 1996). The major underlying assumption of this theory that is advanced in this article is that cultural and work values are the primary variables that influence the occupational choice–making process, the occupation chosen, and the resulting satisfaction with and success in the chosen occupation.

Research (e.g., Carter, 1991; Kluckhorn & Strodtbeck, 1961) has indicated that some values seem to be more prevalent in certain cultural groups than others, although it is not uncommon for various cultural groups to hold some of the same values (Carter, 1991). Numerous efforts have been aimed at developing a taxonomy of cultural values that illustrates the similarities and differences among the values held by various cultural groups in this country (e.g., M. Ho, 1987; Ibrahim, 1985; Sue & Sue, 2000). These taxonomies draw on the pioneering research of Kluckhorn and Strodtbeck (1961), and typically they include categories for values regarding the following:

Human nature. Human beings are good, bad, or neither.

Person–nature relationship. Nature dominates people; people dominate nature; living in harmony with nature is important.

Time orientation. Time is experienced as past, past-future, present, or circular—an orientation to changes that recur in nature as opposed to time being measured by watches and calendars.

Activity. Being, that is, spontaneous self-expression, is important; being-in—becoming, that is, controlled self-expression, is important; doing, that is, action-oriented self-expression, is important.

Self-control. It is either highly or moderately important to control one's thoughts and emotions.

Social relationships. Individualism is valued and the individual is the most important social unit.

Collateral. Also referred to as filial piety, collateral lifestyle is highly or moderately valued (Lee, 1991).

Allocentrism. It is important to put the group's concerns ahead of the concerns of the individual (Marin & Marin, 1991).

How Values Develop

Enculturation is the process by which individuals incorporate the beliefs and values of their cultural group and form a values system (D. Ho, 1995; Rokeach, 1973). Although the process of enculturation is not fully understood, it seems likely that it occurs initially as a result of a complex process of modeling, reinforcement, and experience (Bandura, 1986; Rokeach, 1973). Cultural values and the work values that develop later may be vaguely perceived or crystallized. When values are crystallized, individuals can label them (I value competition) and apply them to their own behaviors (and that is why I try to work harder than other people). Values are relatively stable, but they may change throughout the life span as a result of conflict or contemplation (Rokeach, 1973).

The result of enculturation for most individuals is monoculturalism; that is, they incorporate the values and beliefs of one culture. Bienculturation or multi—enculturation occurs when the beliefs of two or more cultures are internalized. Biculturalism or multiculturalism may be the result of involvement in a bicultural or multicultural family (D. Ho, 1995) or acculturation resulting from sustained contact with other cultural groups.

Although the concept of biculturalism is often discussed in the context of multicultural literature (e.g., Leong & Gim-Chung, 1995), it is unlikely that an individual can adopt the values of two or more cultures because often these values conflict. However, this should not be interpreted to mean that individuals cannot understand and appreciate the cultural values of more than one cultural group and adapt some of their behaviors to match various cultural contexts. The enculturation process is influenced by the cultural group membership (M. Ho, 1987), gender (e.g., Brenner, Blazini, & Greenhaus, 1988; M. Brown, 1995), SES (Arbona, 1995; Blau & Duncan, 1967), and family membership (D. Ho, 1995; M. Ho, 1987).

Acculturation may or may not influence the cultural values that individuals incorporate into their values systems. Acculturation involves the enculturation of beliefs from a culture different from one's own (Berry, 1990). It may also involve adopting the language, customs, and traditions of the other culture. Individuals who are in contact with another culture often receive "messages" that conflict with their own beliefs. For example, an Asian American student who believes that it is important to make a career choice that is in keeping with his family's wishes may be "told" by members of his peer group and his counselor that the "appropriate" way to make a career choice is to act independently. The result of these conflicting messages is acculturative stress (Chan & Ostheimer, 1983; Smart & Smart, 1995). Acculturative stress can be resolved in several ways, including adopting the values of the dominant culture. However, as Rokeach (1973) noted, although values may change as a reaction to conflict, they may also change as a result of contemplation. Therefore, acculturation probably does not occur solely as a reaction to conflicts.

Members of minority groups are continuously exposed to the values of the dominant culture, values that are often at odds with those they have acquired from their own culture (e.g., McWhirter & Ryan, 1991; Smart & Smart, 1995). Acceptance and inclusion of Eurocentric values in the values system and the behavioral norms and traditions accompanying them result in acculturation. One of the outcomes of acculturation may be the rejection of one's cultural beliefs. If the conflicting images and messages that are transmitted from the different culture are rejected, no acculturation occurs (LaFromboise, Trimble, & Mohatt, 1990). Two additional points should be made at this time. First, acculturation is not necessarily a one-way process: It is reversible. Second, acculturation is a process that may affect individuals from all cultural groups, including members of the dominant culture who interact with cultural groups with different values (Berry, 1990). Because of the dynamic nature of the enculturation process in a multicultural society, it is a mistake to make assumptions based solely on cultural group membership.

Cultural Group Membership versus Internalized Culture

Cultural group membership, which is a demographic designation, has typically been used in lieu of internalized culture (D. Ho, 1995). Ho recommends that the psychological characteristic—internalized culture—be substituted for demographic designations. Internalized culture consists of the beliefs and values of the individual. Research has consistently supported the idea that values systems differ among major cultural groups as well as *within* group variation (e.g., Carter, 1991), and, thus, assuming that an individual has a particular set of cultural values is likely to lead to erroneous conclusions.

Factors that Retard Motivation to Act on Values

As noted previously, values are the major force in the goal-setting process (Feather, 1988; Rokeach, 1973). However, five factors may lead individuals to lower their expectations of success if they act on their values: mental health problems (Casserly, 1982; Pietromonaco & Rock, 1987), history of personal/cultural group discrimination (M. Brown, 1995; Leong & Serifica, 1995; Melamed, 1996), lack of information (Brown, 1996), poverty (Hotchkiss & Borow, 1996), and self-efficacy (e.g., Lent, Brown, & Hackett, 1996, 2002). These variables are all incorporated into the statements that follow.

Propositions of Brown's Values-Based Theory

1. Highly prioritized work values are the most important determinants of career choice for people who value individualism (i.e., the individual is the most important unit) if their work values are crystallized and prioritized. Such individuals feel unconstrained to act on their work values; at least one occupational option is available that will satisfy the values held; values-based information about occupational options is available; the difficulty level of implementing the options is approximately the same; and the financial resources available are sufficient to support the implementation of the preferred option.

1.a. Factors that limit the number of occupational options considered for people who value individualism include low SES, minority status, mental health problems, physical disabilities, gender (Gottfredson, 1996), low scholastic aptitude, perception that they will be discriminated against in the occupation, and lack of values-based information. Women, minorities, people from lower-SES levels, and people with mental or physical limitations who value individualism choose occupations consistent with their work values, but they are likely to choose from a more restricted range of occupations than white European American males.

1.b. Self-efficacy becomes a constraining factor in the occupational decision–making process of individuals who value individualism when the options being considered require widely divergent skills and abilities.

2. Individuals who hold collective social values and come from families and/or groups who hold the same social values either defer to the wishes of the group or family members or are heavily influenced by them in the occupational decision–making process. The result is that the occupations chosen correlate less with the individual's work values than is the case with individuals who value individualism and make their own occupational choices.

2.a. Gender is a major factor in the occupations entered by individuals who value collectivism because of decision makers' sex-stereotyped perceptions of occupations. The result is that occupational choices are more likely to be stereotypically male or female. Women who value collectivism enter a more restricted range of occupations than men who value collectivism.

2.b. Perceptions that discrimination may occur if an occupation is chosen is a deterrent to choosing that occupation by decision makers who value collectivism.

2.c. Perceptions regarding resources available to implement an occupational choice are a major limiting factor in the occupational decision–making process of individuals who value collectivism.

2.d. The outcome of the occupational decision–making process for people who value collectivism is less influenced by the availability of the values-based occupational information than it is by the work values of their families or groups.

3. When taken individually, cultural values regarding activity (doing, being, being-in-becoming) do not constrain the occupational decision–making process. People who value individualism and have both a future/past-future time value and a doing/activity value are more likely to make decisions at important transition points, such as graduation from high school, and act on those choices than people who value either collectivism or individualism and being or being-in-becoming.

4. Because of differing values systems, males and females and people from differing cultural groups enter occupations at varying rates.

5. The process of choosing an occupation value involves a series of "estimates." These include estimates of (a) one's abilities and values, (b) the skills and abilities required to be successful in an occupation, and (c) the work values that the occupational alternatives being considered satisfy. For people who value individualism, the ability to make accurate estimates is a critical factor in their occupational success and satisfaction. For individuals who value collateral relationships, estimates made by the decision makers are the key factors in their occupational success and satisfaction.

5.a. Individuals who value individualism and who come from backgrounds where little emphasis is placed on feedback about individual strengths, weaknesses, and personal traits and who make their own occupational decisions make more errors in the process as defined by mismatches between their values and those values satisfied by the job. The result is lowered job satisfaction, lower levels of success, and shorter job tenure. In the case of people who value collateral, satisfaction, success, and tenure are based on the ability of the decision maker to make these estimates.

6. Occupational success is related to job-related skills acquired in formal and informal educational settings, job-related aptitudes and skills, SES, participation in the work role, and the extent to which discrimination is experienced regardless of which social relationship value is held.

6.a. Because success in the occupational role requires an awareness of future events and the ability to accommodate the dynamic changes that occur in the workplace, success in the occupational role is related to time and activity values, with individuals with future or past/future values paired with doing/activity values being the most successful.

7. Occupational tenure is partially the result of the match between the cultural and work values of the worker, supervisors, and colleagues.

Status and Use of Brown's Values-Based Theory

Brown's first attempt at developing a values-based theory appeared in 1996. That theory attempted to account for the complexity of all life roles, admittedly a difficult task. His latest theory is a more modest attempt to account for occupational choice, satisfaction, and success and is thus more in line with the other theories in this section. Because of the newness of the theory (it was first published in 2002), it is difficult to anticipate what its impact might be. Hopefully the theory will stimulate more thinking about the importance of cultural values and the need to consider cultural differences when examining the occupational choice–making process.

DEVELOPMENTAL THEORIES

Developmental theories focus on the biological, psychological, sociological, and cultural factors that influence career choice, adjustments to and changes in careers, and withdrawal from careers. These theories focus on stages of development (e.g., childhood and adolescence). The first developmental theory was presented in 1951 by Ginzberg, Ginzburg, Axelrad, and Herma, but their theory has been overshadowed by Super's life span, life space theory, presented next. A second developmental theory is also presented, Gottfredson's (1981, 1996) theory of circumscription and compromise. Although her theory is not as comprehensive as Super's theory, it focuses on an extremely important aspect of the career development process—the impact that sex-typing occupations have on career choice.

Super's Life Span, Life Space Theory

Probably no one has written as extensively about career development or influenced the study of the topic as much as Donald Super. His writing on career development is so extensive that even the highly motivated student faces a major challenge in reviewing all of it. The references cited here provide considerable depth but are not intended to be all-inclusive: Super, 1951, 1953, 1954, 1955, 1957,

1960, 1964a, 1964b, 1969, 1972, 1974, 1977, 1980, 1981, 1983, 1984, 1990; Super and colleagues, 1957; and Super, Starishevsky, Matlin, and Jordaan, 1963.

Super's earliest theoretical statements were influenced by researchers in differential psychology, developmental psychology, sociology, and personality theory. Super has often stated that his view is a "segmented" theory consisting of several related propositions, out of which he hopes an integrated theory ultimately emerges. He has, from time to time, restated these segments, broadening slightly earlier statements and on two occasions adding more segments. His 1953 article presented the initial 10 postulates. He added two more in the 1957 book written with Bachrach. The 1990 article expands the list to 14 propositions, and these 14 propositions are the basis for the following consideration of Super's life span theory. In this sequence, the original 10 propositions fall under items 1–6 and 9–12, and the additional propositions are identified by items 7, 8, 13, and 14. Super's 1990 statements are italicized, followed, where appropriate, with a brief discussion of the proposition.

1. *People differ in their abilities and personalities, needs, values, interests, traits, and self-concepts.* The concept of individual differences is so widely recognized and accepted that no one seriously challenges it. The range of personal characteristics varies widely both within each individual and among individuals. Within each person are traits or abilities so pronounced that often they seem to caricature the individual. At the same time, in other areas each person is relatively weak or inept. Although most of us are more or less like other people in many traits, the uniqueness of each person is apparent in the individualized combination of strengths and weaknesses.

2. *People are qualified, by virtue of these characteristics, each for a number of occupations.* The range of abilities, personality characteristics, and other traits is so wide that every person has within his or her makeup the requisites for success in many occupations. Research in the field of rehabilitation has demonstrated that even individuals with severe disabilities have the choice of many occupations in which they can perform satisfactorily. For people without serious physical or emotional impairment, the gamut of possibilities is wide indeed.

Few occupations require special abilities, skills, or traits in excessive quantity. Just as most athletic activities involve only certain muscles or muscle groups, so too most jobs require only a few specific characteristics. A person, then, can perform successfully in any occupation for which he has the qualifying characteristics. The lack of a certain skill, or its presence in minute quantities, excludes the person from an occupation only if that skill is important in meeting the demands of that occupation.

3. *Each occupation requires a characteristic pattern of abilities and personality traits—with tolerances wide enough to allow both some variety of occupations for each individual and some variety of individuals in each occupation.* For each ability or trait required in the performance of a particular occupation, one might expect to find a modal quantity that best fits the nature of the work. On either side of this amount, however, is a band or range of this characteristic that satisfactorily meets the demands of the work. For example, picture an extremely simple task that requires, hypothetically, only a single characteristic. In studying this task, we might ascertain the quantity of this trait that would best meet the requirements of the job. We would also expect that a person could perform satisfactorily even though he or she possessed less than the ideal amount of the trait, as long as the person surpassed the minimum demanded by the job. However, we could also expect satisfactory performance even if the worker possessed more of the trait than was required for optimum performance.

Because the patterns of abilities required in various occupations is rarely unique, one can expect to find considerable overlap. Thus, a number of occupations exist in which a particular distribution of assets can result in satisfactory performance, just as a number of patterns of ability exist that can result in satisfactory performance in a given occupation.

4. *Vocational preferences and competencies, the situations in which people live and work, and, hence, their self-concepts change with time and experience, although self-concepts, as products of social learning, are increasingly stable from late adolescence until late maturity, providing some continuity in choice and adjustment.* As individuals exercise certain skills or proficiencies, they may increase or expand them to a higher level. As these higher-level skills develop, workers may be drawn to occupational outlets that provide opportunities to use them. Similarly, as workers perform successfully in given work situations, they may realize that participating in more rewarding or more responsible positions may result in even more satisfaction. However, work situations may be so demanding on workers that they may look for positions that do not tax the pattern of abilities so heavily.

Because the pattern of skills and preferences, as well as the work situation, undergoes constant change, it is likely that a job a worker once found entirely satisfactory is no longer viewed that way. The individual whose self-concept changes may also find that a once-satisfactory job is no longer so. Either of these changes may result in the worker seeking a new work situation or attempting to adjust the current position in some way so it again becomes comfortable and satisfying. Because neither the worker nor the job is static, either change or adjustment is necessary to keep the two in balance.

Super (1984, 1990) emphasizes that self-concept should be defined broadly to include not only an internalized personal view of self, but also the individual's view of the situation or condition in which he or she exists. This is a significant factor because the situation surrounding the individual always bears on the person's behavior and self-understanding. Super suggests that *personal-construct* might be a more useful term than *self-concept* because it permits this broader definition.

5. *This process of change may be summed up in a series of life stages (a "maxi-cycle") characterized as a sequence of growth, exploration, establishment, maintenance, and decline, and these stages may in turn be subdivided into (a) the fantasy, tentative, and realistic phases of the exploratory stage and (b) the trial and stable phases of the establishment stage. A small (mini) cycle takes place in transitions from one stage to the next or each time an individual is destabilized by a reduction in force, changes in type of personnel needs, illness or injury, or other socioeconomic or personal events. Such unstable or multiple-trial careers involve new growth, reexploration, and reestablishment (recycling).*

The *growth* stage refers to physical and psychological growth. During this time the individual forms attitudes and behavior mechanisms that become important components of the self-concept for much of life. Simultaneously, experiences provide a background of knowledge of the world of work that is ultimately used in tentative choices and in final selections.

The *exploratory* stage begins with the individual's awareness that an occupation is an aspect of life. During the early or fantasy phase of this stage, the expressed choices are frequently unrealistic and often closely related to the play life of the individual. Examples can be seen in young children's choices of such careers as cowboy, movie star, pilot, and astronaut. These choices are nebulous and temporary and usually have little, if any, long-term significance for the individual. Some adolescents and even some adults, of course, have not advanced beyond the fantasy phase. Often, the understanding of themselves or of the world of work needed to make more effective choices is either missing or disregarded.

In the tentative phase of the exploratory stage, individuals narrow choices to a few possibilities. Because of uncertainty about ability, availability of training, or employment opportunity, the list may contain choices that later disappear. The final phase of the exploratory stage, still prior to actual entrance into the world of work, narrows the list to those occupations that individuals feel are within reach and provide the opportunities they feel are most important.

The *establishment* stage, as the name implies, relates to early encounters within actual work experiences. During this period the individual, at first perhaps by trial and error, attempts to ascertain whether choices and decisions made during the exploratory period have validity. Some of these attempts are simply tryouts. The individual may accept a job with the definite feeling that he or she will change jobs if this one does not fit. As he or she gains experience and proficiency, the individual becomes stabilized; that is, aspects of this occupation are brought into the self-concept, and the occupation is accepted as one that offers the best chance to obtain those satisfactions that are important.

During the *maintenance* stage, the individual attempts to continue or improve the occupational situation. Because both the occupation and the individual's self-concept have some fluidity, this involves a continual process of change or adjustment. Essentially, the person is concerned with continuing the satisfying parts of the work situation and revising or changing those unpleasant aspects that are annoying but not so disagreeable that they drive the individual from the field.

The *decline* stage includes the preretirement period, during which the individual's emphasis in work is focused on keeping the job and meeting the minimum standards of output. The worker is now more concerned with retaining the position than with enhancing it. This period terminates with the individual's withdrawal from the world of work.

Research by Levinson and others (1978) and by Gould (1972) on postadolescent male development appears to support Super's life stages approach. Both report patterns of adult male development consisting of relatively stable, structure-building periods separated by transitional, structure-changing periods. The Levinson group found that their subjects made occupational choices between ages 17 and 29 and often made different choices later. This age period is somewhat later than Super theorized. They also report that the preparatory phase of occupational development is completed in the 28–33 age period, also later than previously assumed. The discrepancy in ages may be because data for the Levinson subjects were obtained by interviewing adult men who were recalling earlier events in their lives.

Murphy and Burck (1976), using Super's life stages concept, suggest that the increasing frequency of midlife career changes may indicate that an additional stage, the renewal stage, be inserted between the establishment stage and the maintenance stage. During this period, approximately between ages 35 and 45, individuals reconsider earlier goals and plans, and then either rededicate themselves to pursuing those goals or decide to move in other directions with a midlife career change.

6. *The nature of the career pattern—that is, the occupational level attained and the sequence, frequency, and duration of trial and stable jobs—is determined by the individual's parental socioeconomic level, mental ability, education, skills, personality characteristics (needs, values, interests, traits, and self-concepts), and career maturity and by the opportunities to which he or she is exposed.*

All factors in the individual's experiential background contribute to attitudes and behavior. Some factors obviously contribute more significantly than others. The socioeconomic level of the individual's parents may be one of these because the individual's early contact with the world of work is largely brought about through parents, family, and friends. Hearing parents and their friends discuss experiences at work; observing the impact of occupational success, failure, or frustration within the family; and obtaining or losing chances at education, travel, or other experiences because of family circumstances all greatly influence the individual's later work history. The individual's mental ability is an important factor in academic success that can open or close doors to many occupations. Ability to deal with others is important in most work situations. "Being in the right place at the right time" or "getting the breaks" is also important because the individual must first have an opportunity to demonstrate competency before becoming established in a job.

We often think that, in the Horatio Alger tradition, anyone can attain any goal if he or she only tries hard enough. In reality, however, factors over which we often have no control set limits that can be surpassed or extended only by Herculean effort, if at all.

7. *Success in coping with the demands of the environment and of the organism in that context at any given life-career stage depends on the readiness of the individual to cope with these demands (that is, on his or her career maturity).* Super identifies career maturity as a group of physical, psychological, and social characteristics that represent the individual's readiness and ability to face and deal with developmental problems and challenges. These personal aspects have both emotional and intellectual components that produce the individual's response to the situation. The person whose maturity is equal to the problem probably resolves it with minimal difficulty or concern; when the maturity is not sufficient for the task, inadequate responses of procrastination, ineptness, or failure are likely to occur.

8. *Career maturity is a hypothetical construct. Its operational definition is perhaps as difficult to formulate as is that of intelligence, but its history is much briefer and its achievements even less definite.* Super's early research (e.g., the 25-year longitudinal study called the Career Pattern Study) addressed the concept of maturity as related to career or vocational development problems. He and co-workers searched for ways to define and assess this concept. Out of these efforts emerged Super's Career Development Inventory.

9. *Development through the life stages can be guided partly by facilitating the maturing of abilities and interests and partly by aiding in reality testing and in the development of self-concepts.* Individuals can be helped to move toward a satisfying vocational choice in two ways: (a) by helping them to develop abilities and interests and (b) by helping them to acquire an understanding of their strengths and weaknesses so they can make satisfying choices.

Both aspects of this postulate emphasize the role of the school and its guidance program in assisting the individual to maximize development as a person. The teacher, having frequent contacts with a young person, has the best opportunity to observe latent or underdeveloped abilities in the classroom. The teacher has numerous chances to challenge the individual to push toward higher, but nevertheless reachable, goals. The counselor, similarly, through data obtained from tests or other guidance techniques may encounter undeveloped potential. Out-of-school adults may need similar types of help.

Three questions have occasionally been found useful in the counseling relationship by providing some indication of the extent to which the counselee has already engaged in some reality testing of vocational aspirations. The first question—What would you like to be if you could do anything you wanted?—frequently evokes a fantasy response, which the individual usually soon labels as such. The second question—What do you expect to be 10 years from now?—often elicits a reply that still includes considerable fantasy but may also include a sizable display of self—evaluation and insight. The third question—What is the least you would settle for 10 years from now?—requires the client to discard fantasy entirely and to cope with strengths, weaknesses, and potential as the client sees them.

10. *The process of career development is essentially that of developing and implementing occupational self-concepts. It is a synthesizing and compromising process in which the self-concept is a product of the interaction of inherited aptitudes, physical makeup, opportunity to observe and play various roles, and evaluations of the extent to which the results of role playing meet the approval of superiors and fellows (interactive learning).*

As the individual develops and matures, he or she acquires a mental picture of self—a self-concept. Because one's position in the world of work is important in U.S. culture, this becomes a major influence on the individual's self-concept. During the educational period, before actual entrance into work, one's anticipated occupational role plays a part in the development of self-concept. Each person attempts to maintain or enhance a favorable self-concept and thus is led toward those activities that permit him or her to keep or improve the desired self-image. As the inner drive toward this ideal self-concept pushes the individual strongly, he or she encounters restricting factors, which may come from personal limitations or from the external environment. These factors interfere with attainment of the ideal self-concept and result in the individual compromising or accepting somewhat less than the ideal.

Also influential is the extent to which individuals can gain insight into a variety of occupations and see to what extent each occupation permits them to be the kind of persons they want to be in their own eyes and in the eyes of family, teachers, peer group, and others whose opinions they value.

Super's (1980) description of a Life-Career Rainbow (see Figure 4.3) emphasizes the different roles played by each individual during his or her lifetime and the influence these roles have on lifestyle and career. Typical roles for most people include child, student, citizen, worker, spouse, homemaker, parent, and pensioner. These roles emphasize the lifelong aspect of career development.

11. *The process of synthesis of or compromise between individual and social factors, between self-concepts and reality, is one of role playing and of learning from feedback, whether the role is played in fantasy, in the counseling interview, or in such real-life activities as classes, clubs, part-time work, and entry jobs.*

Modifications of the vocational aspects of the self-concept may occur in many ways. Because the world of work is so complex and entrance requirements in many areas so difficult, it is not feasible to experiment with actual participation in more than a few actual work situations. This leaves the necessity of matching the

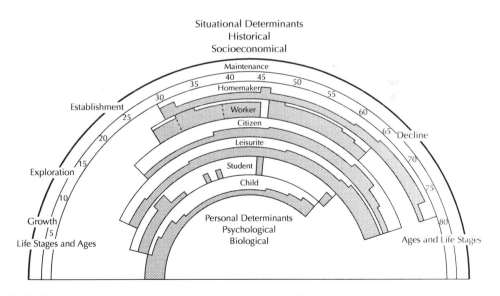

FIGURE 4.3   Super's Life-Career Rainbow: Six Life Roles in Schematic Life Space

Source: From "A Life-Span, Life-Space Approach to Career Development" by D. E. Super in the *Journal of Vocational Behavior,* Volume 16, 282–298, copyright © 1980 by Academic Press. Reprinted by permission.

self-concept and its demands against what occupations have to offer in a situation that is essentially abstract. This may be a daydream or reverie, it may involve seeking professional assistance through counseling, or it may mean seeking related experiences that help the individual evaluate the suitability of the occupation in terms of self-concept.

12. *Work satisfactions and life satisfactions depend on the extent to which the individual finds adequate outlets for abilities, needs, values, interests, personality traits, and self-concepts. They depend on establishment in a type of work, a work situation, and a way of life in which one can play the kind of role that growth and exploratory experiences have led one to consider congenial and appropriate.*

The individual who finds pleasure and satisfaction in work does so because the position held permits characteristics and values to be used in a way that is seen as important. In other words, the experiences encountered in work are comparable with the individual's mental image of self—they give sufficient opportunity to be the kind of person one pictures oneself to be.

If the work performed does not provide the possibility to be the type of person one pictures oneself to be, one becomes discontented. This dissatisfaction usually causes a person to look for a work situation where the possibility to play the desired role seems likelier.

13. *The degree of satisfaction people attain from work is proportional to the degree to which they have been able to implement self-concepts.* The relationship of the work situation to the individual's role must be thought of in the broad sense. The professions and higher managerial positions probably provide the greatest opportunities, as viewed by most people, for the intrinsic satisfactions that come from work itself. But many individuals gain great satisfaction from work that to some appears boring and monotonous. Other workers find satisfaction in jobs that they too may consider routine and unchallenging but that provide them the chance to be the kind of people they want to be, to do the things they want to do, and to think of themselves as they wish to think. Super proposes that the amount of satisfaction is directly related to the extent the job fits the self-concept. Super and Kidd (1979) explore career change and modification in adults, recognizing the increase in midlife career change. They suggest that *career adaptability* may be an appropriate term to identify the individual's ability to face, pursue, or accept changing career roles.

14. *Work and occupation provide a focus for personality organization for most men and women, although for some persons this focus is peripheral, incidental, or even nonexistent. Then other foci, such as leisure activities and homemaking, may be central. (Social traditions, such as gender-role stereotyping and modeling, racial and ethnic biases, and the opportunity structure, as well as individual differences, are important determinants of preferences for such roles as worker, student, leisurite, homemaker, and citizen.)*

Essentially, this proposition says that most adults are what they do—the individual is a reflection of that person's job or major role. To a large degree this proposition relates to the Life-Career Rainbow proposed by Super (1980) as representative of life span, life space career development. As indicated in this proposition, Super believes that the various segments of his theory apply to both men and women, if modified slightly to provide for women's childbearing role.

Status and Use of Super's Theory

At the time of his death in 1994, Super had authored or co-authored nearly 200 articles, books, book units, monographs, and other publications, many of them dealing with his theory. His students and others have also contributed dozens, if not hundreds, of publications to the professional literature, all stimulated by his theory. His theory is, by his own admission (Super, 1990), not well constructed because the various segments are not cemented together. This is probably the reason that many of the research studies stimulated by the theory focus on some of the constructs (e.g., career maturity) contained in the theory as opposed to testing its assumptions directly (Super, Savickas, & Super, 1996).

Super's (1990) theory has a number of applications. For example, it has been used as the framework for career development programs for children and adolescents. Growth is the developmental stage that covers pre-K to middle school and is broken down into curiosity, fantasies, interests, and capacities (focusing on abilities). The exploration stage begins at about age 14 and continues until age 18, at which time a choice is crystallized. These stages are obviously approximations, but they can be useful when designing a career development program.

The theory can also be used as a basis for career counseling. The objective of the career counseling process would be the development of career maturity, which can be broken down into several components as measured by the Career Development Inventory (CDI) (Super, Thompson, Jordaan, & Myers, 1984). These are

- *Career planning (CP).* Career-mature individuals actively engage in the planning process and perceive themselves to be so engaged. The career planning scale is an effective scale that reveals how persons perceive themselves in relation to the planning process.
- *Career exploration (CE).* Career-mature individuals relate to the willingness of a client to engage in exploring careers, that is, their willingness to use materials. This scale is combined with the CP scale to produce a career development attitude (CDA) scale.
- *Decision making (DM).* Career-mature individuals know how to make decisions and have confidence in their abilities to do so.
- *World-of-work information (WWI).* The most obvious component of this scale involves having accurate information about work. Super believed that decision makers should have some knowledge of the time, developmentally speaking, in which people should acquire important information about work.
- *Knowledge of preferred occupations (PO).* Following, the CDI, people choose 20 occupations and answer questions about the jobs and qualifications needed to enter a particular occupation. WWI and PO are combined in the CDI to produce a career development knowledge and skill score (CDK).
- *Career orientation (COT).* The COT is the total score on the CDI, with the exception of the PO. In a sense this can be considered a global measure of career maturity.

Career counselors may or may not administer the CDI or another inventory, the Career Maturity Inventory (CMI) (Crites & Savickas, 1995), which also measures readiness to make a career decision and the amount of knowledge needed to make that decision. McDivitt (2002) suggests that the CMI can be used to teach clients the decision-making process, and the same can be said of the CDI. Counselors can raise some of the following issues to obtain some of the same information.

- *CP.* How would you rate your ability to make future plans on a scale of 1 to 10? How far along are you in the planning for your career?
- *CP.* Do you live in the past, focus on the present, or plan for the future? Why did you rate yourself as you did?
- *CE.* Estimate how many times you have sought information about careers by (1) talking to people, (2) reading occupational information, (3) using online sources of information about jobs, or (4) consulting other sources of information about jobs.
- *PO.* How much information do you have about your current occupational choice? What are the characteristics needed by successful workers in this occupation and how do these match your own characteristics?
- *DM.* Rate you ability to make a wise occupational choice on a scale of 1 to 10. Describe the process you followed when you last made a major decision.

Super's (e.g., 1980, 1981) early theorizing focused on what he perceived as the difference between the career development of men and women. It was and is a "white bread" theory because it was formulated based on research with white subjects. Sharf (2002) summarized the research on the career maturity of African Americans and concluded that they are likely to be lower in career maturity than white persons. However, stimulating career maturity, as defined by Super, and then helping clients develop and implement an occupational self-concept seems appropriate for most groups if they subscribe to an independence social value. Leong and Serifica (1995) questioned the application of Super's ideas to Asian American students because they are more likely to have a dependent decision-making style. It should be added that the dependent decision-making style is typical for individuals who subscribe to collateral social values. One of the goals implicit in the counseling process outlined here is the stimulation of an independent decision-making style.

Gottfredson's Theory of Circumscription and Compromise

Gottfredson's (1996) theory is concerned with how career aspirations develop. It is predicated on four basic assumptions: (1) The career development process begins in childhood; (2) career aspirations are attempts to implement one's self-concept; (3) career satisfaction depends on the degree to which the career is congruent with self-perceptions; and (4) people develop occupational stereotypes that guide them in the selection process. Obviously, these assumptions about self-concept have much in common with Super (1990), and Gottfredson's views on occupational stereotypes are identical to Holland's (1997).

Gottfredson departs from other theorists in that she believes the self-concept consists of a social self and a psychological self, with the former being the more important determinant of occupational aspirations. The social self is made up of those aspects of self-perceptions regarding intelligence, social status, and gender, whereas the psychological self is made up of variables such as values and personality variables. Gottfredson believes that the major thrust of choosing a career is to establish a social identity based on the choice. According to Gottfredson (1996), people develop cognitive maps of occupations that are organized along the following dimensions:

1. Masculinity/femininity of the occupation
2. The prestige of the occupation (see Table 4.2)
3. Fields of work

For Gottfredson, prestige goes beyond the social status of the occupation and includes an intellectual complexity or ability dimension. Of these dimensions, the sex-type assigned to the occupation and the prestige associated with it are the most important in the career choice–making process. In the choice-making process individuals estimate the degree to which they are compatible with a given occupation. In making these estimates, preserving one's self-perception regarding one's masculinity or femininity is the most powerful concern, followed in descending order by protecting one's social standing, and representing one's interests and personality. Obviously, in the consideration of potential occupational choices, the accessibility of the occupation also must be considered. Career aspirations are the result of the interaction between estimates of accessibility and compatibility estimates.

As children grow, and develop perceptions of themselves and occupational fields, they begin to narrow or circumscribe their range of occupations based on their estimates of compatibility (sex-type, prestige, and interests) and accessibility. Gottfredson believes that once self-perceptions are developed and occupations discounted as incompatible with them, it is unlikely that the process will be reversed unless some type of intervention occurs, such as an influential person telling them that they have the intellectual capacity to perform the tasks associated with entering the occupation.

Often the final occupational choice is a compromise as adolescents and adults give up their most preferred choices in favor of those that are more accessible. Compromise, that is, the process of selecting an occupation that is viewed as a less-than-optimal fit with the self-view, occurs as a result of many factors, including the availability of work in some fields (e.g., artistic jobs), availability and quality of educational and employment opportunities, and discrimination. When people are forced to compromise, they give first consideration to sex-type, second consideration to prestige, and third consideration to interests. Using these three variables and their knowledge about the accessibility of careers, individuals develop a zone of acceptable occupations within their cognitive map of the occupational structure.

TABLE 4.2   Social Status of 25 Occupations: 1925, 1946, 1967, 1975, and 1992

Occupation	1925	1946	1967	1975	1992
Banker	1	2.5	4	3	5
Physician	2	1	1	1	1
Lawyer	3	2.5	2	5	2
Superintendent of Schools	4	4	3	4	4
Civil Engineer	5	5	5	2	3
Army Captain	6	6	8	8	6
Foreign Missionary	7	7	7	9	NR
Elementary School Teacher	8	8	6	6	7
Farmer	9	12	19	7	16
Machinist	10	9	12	11	14
Traveling Salesperson	11	16	13	16	13
Grocer	12	13	17	13	18
Electrician	13	11	9	10	8
Insurance Agent	14	10	10	14	9
Mail Carrier	15	14	18	17	15
Carpenter	16	15	11	12	10
Soldier	17	19	15	19	11
Plumber	18	17	16	15	12
Motorman (Bus Driver)	19	18	20	22	19
Barber	20	20	14	18	17
Truck Driver	21	21.5	21	21	20
Coal Miner	22	21.5	23	20	21
Janitor	23	23	22	24	23
Hod Carrier	24	24	24	23	22
Ditchdigger	25	25	25	25	24

Source: From "Fifty Years of Stability in the Social Status of Occupations," by G. A. Kanzaki, 1976, *Vocational Guidance Quarterly, 25,* pp. 101–105; and from "Social Status Ranking of Occupations in The People's Republic of China, Taiwan, and the United States," by R. H. Frederickson, J. G. Lin, & S. Xing, 1992, *Career Development Quarterly, 40,* pp. 351–360. Used by permission of NCDA.

Gottfredson's Developmental Stages

Ages 3–5: Orientation to size and power. During this stage children are laying the groundwork for later sex-role stereotypes as they observe play activities, orient themselves to same-sex adults, and learn about adult activities, such as occupations.

Ages 6–8: Orientation to sex roles. Children are not aware of social class at this stage, but they are beginning to develop perceptions of what is "acceptable" for men and women.

Ages 9–13: Orientation to social valuation. Children perceive that occupations have different social statuses and become critical of lower-status occupations.

They also begin to recognize the symbols of social status. During this stage, they begin to develop ideas about their abilities, and using these perceptions, along with those associated with social class and sex typing (see case of Julio—Counselor's Report), they begin to develop tolerable boundaries of acceptable occupations. By the end of this period, or soon thereafter, numerous occupations will be eliminated as the circumscription process continues. Once eliminated, an occupation is unlikely to be considered without intervention.

Ages 14+: Choices explored. Occupational choices are explored but are limited to those jobs within the tolerable boundaries that have been constructed, beginning with the appropriateness of the sex-role associated with various occupations, the social status associated with occupations, and perceptions of their abilities. They reject occupational options perceived as being to be too difficult, either because of their perceptions of their abilities or accessibility. Compromises in preferred occupational choice are often made because of perceptions regarding accessibility.

Julio—Counselor's Report

Julio was a 19-year-old, single male of Cuban descent. He graduated from high school and, at the time he began counseling, was driving a bus that picked up and delivered guests to a large hotel. He was earning $7.50 per hour plus tips. His stated goal was to enter an occupation that would allow him to live well and support the family he expected to have in the future. He had been a good student and indicated when asked that attending the local community college either full or part time was something he had considered, but he didn't know what course of study to follow.

I suggested that, although we would go through a thorough complete process to identify alternatives, the hottest job that fit the description he had given was nursing. Big mistake! He sat up straight in his chair and declared, "You have to be kidding. My friends would crucify me."

Status and Use of Gottfredson's Theory

Gottfredson (1996, 2002) suggests that her theory has two uses. One of these is in the design of career development programs that break down sex-role stereotypes and limitations in occupational choice based on social status. She suggests that elementary school programs should focus on exploring a full range of occupations to prevent premature circumscription and to provide a basis for later occupational choice. Middle school programs should alert students that they already may be limiting their occupational choices and encourage their self-exploration. The process of identifying interests and abilities continues at the high school level and the issue of how to enter occupations should be introduced. In the author's view, the issue of breaking down occupation barriers should be a major part of this latter program

Clearly, Gottfredson's theory has implications for career counseling. The second major application in her model involves diagnosing developmental problems. She lists five problems that should be assessed. I have taken the liberty altering questions to make the framework useful with racial and ethnic minorities and persons who have other than heterosexual orientations. The areas to be assessed are

1. Does the client have occupational alternatives? If not, is the problem a lack of self-knowledge, lack of occupational knowledge, or unwillingness to choose from among acceptable alternatives? Is the unwillingness the result of sex-role or racial/ethnic group stereotypes or because persons who are gay, lesbian, or bisexual are likely to be discriminated against?
2. Do the demands of entrants into an occupation match the characteristics of the client? Are the choices being considered appropriate?
3. Is the client satisfied with the alternatives being considered? If not, is the dissatisfaction a result of the necessity of compromising interests, or sex-type or racial/ethnic perceptions? Does sexual orientation cause concern about the appropriateness of one or more of the occupations being considered?
4. Has the client unduly restricted his or her occupational choices because of a lack of self-knowledge, knowledge about occupations, or unexamined sex-role or racial/ethnic stereotypes? Has the client's sexual orientation resulted in undue restrictions on occupational choice?
5. Is the client aware of the pathways to the occupations chosen, and is she or he confident that she or he can negotiate those pathways? Have occupational alternatives been eliminated because of lack of skill or knowledge about these pathways?

Occupational information plays a major role in Gottfredson's approach to career counseling as it does in all the approaches outlined to this point. The strength of the theory itself is that it provides career counselors with a way to conceptualize how occupations may be limited by sex-role perceptions. Moreover, because it is likely that the process of circumscription and compromise may parallel the process that racial and ethnic minorities and persons with homosexual or bisexual orientations experience, it can be applied easily to these groups as well. However, Gottfredson's theory is based on the supposition that the client will be the decision maker and, thus, the application to clients who do not have independent social values is problematic.

SUMMARY

Five theories of career choice and development, three from the trait-and-factor perspective and two developmental theories, were discussed in this unit.

At the conclusion of each theory some of the applications of the theory were presented and the current status of the theory outlined. In each case, the application of the theory with multicultural populations was discussed. Although it was not pointed out specifically, one factor that limits the application of four of the five theories discussed in this unit was the social value held by the client or group. All of the theories except Brown's (2002a) value-based theory are predicated on the belief that the individual holds an independence social value and will choose his or her own occupation. This supposition is not accurate for some members of the white majority culture and is patently false for many minority group members. The application of a theory indiscriminately is inappropriate and unethical.

REFERENCES

Arbona, C. (1995). Theory and research on racial and ethnic minorities: Hispanic Americans. In F. T. L. Leong (Ed.), *Career development and vocational behavior of ethnic and racial minorities* (pp. 37–66). Mahwah, NJ: Erlbaum.

Arnold, J. (2004). The congruence problem in John Holland's theory of vocational decisions. *Journal of Occupational and Organizational Psychology, 77,* 95–113.

Astin, H. S. (1984). The meaning of work in women's lives: A sociopsychological perspective. *The Counseling Psychologist, 12,* 117–126.

Bandura, A. (1986). *Social foundations of thought and action: A social-cognitive theory.* Englewood Cliffs, NJ: Prentice-Hall.

Beck, A. (1976). *Cognitive therapy and the emotional disorders.* New York: International Universities Press.

Berry, J. W. (1990). Psychology of acculturation: Understanding people moving between cultures. In R. W. Brislin (Ed.), *Applied cross-cultural psychology* (pp. 232–253). Newbury Park, CA: Sage.

Blau, P. M., & Duncan, O. D. (1967). *The American occupational structure.* New York: Wiley.

Bloch, D. P. (2005). Complexity, chaos, and non-linear dynamics: A new perspective on career development theory. *Career Development Quarterly, 53,* 194–207.

Bordin, E. S. (1984). Psychodynamic model of career choice and satisfaction. In D. Brown, L. Brooks, & Associates, *Career choice and development* (pp. 94–136). San Francisco: Jossey-Bass.

Brenner, O. C., Blazini, A. P., & Greenhaus, J. H. (1988). An examination of race and sex differences in manager work values. *Journal of Vocational Behavior, 32,* 336–344.

Bright, J. E., & Pryor, R. G. L. (2005). The chaos theory of careers: A user's guide. *Career Development Quarterly, 53,* 291–305.

Brown, D. (1996). A holistic, values-based model of career and life role choice and satisfaction. In D. Brown, L. Brooks, & Associates, *Career choice and development* (3rd ed.). San Francisco: Jossey-Bass.

Brown, D. (2002a). The role of work values and cultural values in occupational choice, satisfaction, and success. In D. Brown and Associates, *Career choice and development* (4th ed., pp. 465–509). San Francisco: Jossey-Bass.

Brown, D. (2002b). The role of work and cultural values in occupational choice, success, and satisfaction. *Journal of Counseling and Development, 80,* 48–56.

Brown, D., & Brooks, L. (1996). Introduction to theories of career choice and development. In D. Brown, L. Brooks, & Associates. *Career choice and development* (3rd ed., pp. 1–32). San Francisco: Jossey-Bass.

Brown, D., & Crace, R. K. (1995). Values and life role decision making: A conceptual model. *Career Development Quarterly, 44,* 211–223.

Brown, M. T. (1995). The career development of African Americans: Theoretical and empirical issues. In F. T. L. Leong (Ed.), *Career development and vocational behavior of racial and ethnic minorities* (pp. 7–30). Mahwah, NJ: Erlbaum.

Carter, R. T. (1991). Cultural values: A review of empirical research and implications for counseling. *Journal of Counseling and Development, 70,* 164–173.

Casserly, M. (1982). Effects of differentially structured career counseling on the decision quality of subjects with varying cognitive styles. Unpublished doctoral dissertation, University of Maryland, College Park.

Chan, K. S., & Ostheimer, B. (1983). *Navajo youth and early school withdrawal.* Los Alamitis, CA: National Center for Bilingual Research.

Crites, J. D., & Savickas, M. L. (1995). Career Maturity Inventory. Ogdenburg, NY: Career ware.

Dawis, R. V. (1996). The theory of work adjustment and person–environment–correspondence counseling. In D. Brown, L. Brooks, & Associates, *Career choice and development* (3rd ed., pp.75–120). San Francisco: Jossey-Bass.

Dawis, R. V., England, G. W., & Lofquist, L. H. (1964). A theory of work adjustment. *Minnesota Studies in Vocational Rehabilitation No. XV.* Minneapolis: University of Minnesota.

Dawis, R. V., & Lofquist, L. H. (1984). *A psychological theory of work adjustment.* Minneapolis: University of Minnesota Press.

Dawis, R. V., Lofquist, L. H., & Weiss, D. J. (1968). A theory of work adjustment (A revision). *Minnesota Studies in Vocational Rehabilitation No. XXIII.* Minneapolis: University of Minnesota.

Day, S. X., Rounds, J., & Swaney, K. (1998). The structure of vocational interests for diverse racial-ethnic groups. *Psychological Science, 9,* 40–44.

Department of Defense (DOD). (2005). *Finding you interests.* Washington, DC: Author.

Feather, N. T. (1988). Values systems across cultures: Australia and China. *International Journal of Psychology, 21,* 697–715.

Fitzgerald, L. F., & Betz, N. E. (1994). Career development in a cultural context. In M. L. Savickas & R. W. Lent (Eds.), *Convergence in career development theories* (pp. 103–118). Palo Alto, CA: CPP Books.

Fouad, N. A. (1995). Career behavior of Hispanics: Assessment and intervention. In F. T. L. Leong (Ed.), *Career development and vocational behavior of racial and ethnic minorities* (pp. 165–192). Mahwah, NJ: Erlbaum.

Gottfredson, L. S. (1981). Circumscription and compromise: A developmental theory of occupational aspirations (Monograph). *Journal of Counseling Psychology, 28,* 545–579.

Gottfredson, L. S. (1996). A theory of circumscription and compromise. In D. Brown, L. Brooks, & Associates, *Career choice and development* (3rd ed., 2002, pp. 179–281). San Francisco: Jossey-Bass.

Gottfredson, L. (2002). Gottfredson's theory of circumscription and compromise. In D. Brown & Associates, *Career choice and development* (4th ed., pp. 85–148). San Francisco: Jossey-Bass.

Gould, R. (1972). The phases of adult life: A study in developmental psychology. *American Journal of Psychiatry, 129,* 521–531.

Hackett, G., & Betz, N. E. (1981). A self-efficacy approach to the career development of women. *Journal of Vocational Behavior, 24,* 326–339.

Hartung, P. G. (2002). Cultural context in career theory: Role salience and values. *Career Devel-opment Quarterly, 51,* 12–25.

Ho, D. Y. F. (1995). Internal culture, culturocentrism, and transcendence. *The Counseling Psychologist, 23,* 4–24.

Ho, M. K. (1987). *Family therapy with ethnic minorities.* Newbury Park, CA: Sage.

Holland, J. L. (1959). A theory of vocational choice. *Journal of Counseling Psychology, 6,* 35–45.

Holland, J. L. (1962). Some explorations of a theory of vocational choice: I. One- and two-year longitudinal studies. *Psychological Monographs, 76* (26, Whole No. 545).

Holland, J. L. (1963a). Explorations of a theory of vocational choice and achievement: II. A four-year prediction study. *Psychological Reports, 12,* 547–594.

Holland, J. L. (1963b). A theory of vocational choice: Part I. Vocational images and choice. *Vocational Guidance Quarterly, 11,* 232–239.

Holland, J. L. (1963c). A theory of vocational choice: Part II. Self descriptions and vocational preferences. *Vocational Guidance Quarterly, 12,* 17–24.

Holland, J. L. (1963d). A theory of vocational choice: Part IV. Vocational daydreams. *Vocational Guidance Quarterly, 12,* 93–97.

Holland, J. L. (1966a). A psychological classification scheme for vocations and major fields. *Journal of Counseling Psychology, 13,* 278–288.

Holland, J. L. (1966b). *The psychology of vocational choice.* Waltham, MA: Blaisdell.

Holland, J. L. (1968). Explorations of a theory of vocational choice: Part VI. A longitudinal study using a sample of typical college students. *Journal of Applied Psychology, 52* (Monograph Suppl.).

Holland, J. L. (1972). The present status of a theory of vocational choice. In J. M. Whiteley & A. Resnikoff (Eds.), *Perspectives on vocational development.* Washington, DC: American Personnel and Guidance Association.

Holland, J. L. (1973). *Making vocational choices: A theory of careers.* Englewood Cliffs, NJ: Prentice-Hall.

Holland, J. L. (1985). *Making vocational choices: A theory of vocational personalities and work environments* (2nd ed.). Englewood Cliffs, NJ: Prentice-Hall.

Holland, J. L. (1987). Current status of Holland's theory of careers: Another perspective. *Career Development Quarterly, 36,* 31–44.

Holland, J. L. (1994a). *The self-directed search technical manual* (4th ed.). Odessa, FL: PAR.

Holland, J. L. (1994b). *The occupations locator* (4th ed.). Odessa, FL: PAR.

Holland, J. L. (1997). *Making vocational choices* (3rd ed.). Englewood Cliffs, NJ: Prentice-Hall.

Holland, J. L., Daiger, D.C., & Power, P. G. (1980). *My vocational situation.* Palo Alto, CA: Consulting Psychologist Press.

Holland, J. L., & Gottfredson, G. D. (1976). Using a typology of persons and environments to explain careers: Some extensions and clarifications. *Counseling Psychologist, 6,* 20–29.

Holland, J. L., & Gottfredson, G. D. (1990). *An annotated bibliography for Holland's theory of vocational personality and work environment.* Baltimore: Johns Hopkins University.

Holland, J. L., & Lutz, S. W. (1968). The predictive value of a student's choice of vocation. *Personnel and Guidance Journal, 46,* 428–436.

Holland, J. L., & Nichols, R. C. (1964). Explorations of a theory of vocational choice: III. A longitudinal study of change in major fields of study. *Personnel and Guidance Journal, 43,* 235–242.

Hotchkiss, L., & Borow, H. (1996). Sociological perspectives on work and career development. In D. Brown, L. Brooks, & Associates, *Career choice and development* (3rd ed., pp. 137–168). San Francisco: Jossey-Bass.

Ibrahim, F. A. (1985). Effective cross-cultural counseling and psychotherapy: A framework. *The Counseling Psychologist, 13,* 625–638.

Jencks, C., Crouse, J. & Mueser, P. (1983). The Wisconsin model of status and attainment: A national replication with improved measures of ability and aspiration. *Sociology of Education, 56,* 3–19.

Kanzaki, G. A. (1976). Fifty years of stability in the social status of occupations. *Vocational Guidance Quarterly, 25,* 101–105.

Kluckhorn, F. R., & Strodtbeck, F. L. (1961). *Values in values orientations.* Evanston, IL: Row Peterson.

Krumboltz, J. D. (1994). Improving career development theory from a social learning theory perspective. In M. L. Savickas & R. W. Lent (Eds.), *Convergence in career development theory* (pp. 9–32). Palo Alto, CA: CPP Books.

LaFromboise, T. D., Trimble, J. E., & Mohatt, G. V. (1990). Counseling intervention and Native American tradition: An integrative approach. *The Counseling Psychologist, 18,* 624–628.

Lee, K. C. (1991). The problem of the appropriateness of the Rokeach Values Survey in Korea, *International Journal of Psychology, 26,* 299–310.

Lent, R. W., Brown, S. D., & Hackett, G. (1995). Toward a unifying social cognitive theory of career and academic interest, choice, and performance. *Journal of Vocational Behavior, 45,* 79–122.

Lent, R. W., Brown, S. D., & Hackett, G. (1996). Career development from a social cognitive perspective. In D. Brown, L. Brooks, & Associates, *Career choice and development* (3rd ed., pp. 373–422). San Francisco: Jossey-Bass.

Lent, R. W., Brown, S. D., & Hackett, G. (2002). Career development from a social cognitive perspective. In D. Brown, L. Brooks, and Associates, *Career choice and development* (4th ed., pp. 255–311). San Francisco: Jossey-Bass.

Leong, F. T. L. (1991). Career development attributes and occupational values of Asian American and white high school students. *Career Development Quarterly, 39,* 221–230.

Leong, F. T. L., & Gim-Chung, R. H. (1995). Career assessment and intervention with Asian Americans. In F. T. L. Leong (Ed.), *Career development and vocational behavior of racial and ethnic minorities* (pp. 193–226). Mahwah, NJ: Erlbaum.

Leong, F. T. L., & Serifica, F. C. (1995). Career development of Asian Americans: A research area in need of a good theory. In F. T. L. Leong (Ed.), *Career development and vocational behavior of ethnic and racial minorities* (pp. 67–102). Mahwah, NJ: Erlbaum.

Levinson, D. J. (1978). *The seasons of a man's life.* New York: Knopf.

Lofquist, L. H., & Dawis, R. V. (1991). *Essentials of person–environment–correspondence counseling.* Minneapolis: University of Minnesota Press.

Marin, G., & Marin, V. M. (1991). *Research with Hispanic populations.* Newbury Park, CA: Sage.

McDivitt, P. J. (2002). Career Maturity Inventory. In J. T. Kapes & E. A. Whitfield (Eds.), *A counselor's guide to career development instruments* (4th ed., pp. 336–342). Tulsa, OK: National Career Development Association.

McWhirter, J. J., & Ryan, C. A. (1991). Counseling the Navajo: Cultural understanding. *Journal of Multicultural Counseling and Development, 19,* 74–82.

Melamed, T. (1995). Career success: The moderating effects of gender. *Journal of Vocational Behavior, 47,* 295–314.

Melamed, T. (1996). Career success: An assessment of a gender-specific model. *Journal of Occupational and Organizational Psychology, 69,* 217–226.

Murphy, P., & Burck, H. (1976). Career development of men in middle life. *Journal of Vocational Behavior, 9,* 337–343.

Parsons, F. (1909). *Choosing your vocation.* Boston: Houghton-Mifflin.

Pedersen, P. B. (1991). Multiculturalism as a generic approach to counseling. *Journal of Counseling and Development, 70,* 6–12.

Peterson, G. W., Sampson, J. P., Jr., & Reardon, R. C. (1991). *Career development and services: A cognitive approach.* Pacific Grove, CA: Brooks/Cole.

Peterson, G. W., Sampson, J. P., Jr., Reardon, R. C., & Lenz, J. G. (1996). A cognitive information processing approach. In D. Brown, L. Brooks, & Associates, *Career choice and development* (3rd ed., pp. 423–476). San Francisco: Jossey-Bass.

Peterson, N., & Gonzalez. R. C. (2005). *The role of work in people's lives: Applied career counseling and vocational psychology* (2nd ed.). Belmont, CA: Brooks/Cole.

Phillips, S. D., & Imhoff, A. R. (1997). Women and career development: A decade of research. *Annual Review of Psychology, 48,* 31–60.

Pietromonaco, J. G., & Rock, K. S. (1987). Decision style in depression: The contribution of perceived risks versus benefits. *Journal of Personality and Social Psychology, 52,* 399–408.

Roe, A. (1956). *The psychology of occupations.* New York: Wiley.

Roe, A. (1984). Personality development and career choice. In D. Brown, L. Brooks, & Associates, *Career choice and development* (pp. 31–53). San Francisco: Jossey-Bass.

Roe, A., & Lunneborg, P. W. (1990). Personality development and career choice. In D. Brown, L. Brooks, & Associates, *Career choice and development* (2nd ed., pp. 68–101). San Francisco: Jossey-Bass.

Rokeach, M. (1973). *The nature of human values.* New York: Free Press.

Sharf, R. S. (2002). *Applying career development theory to counseling* (3rd ed.). Pacific Grove, CA: Brooks/Cole.

Smart, J. F., & Smart, D. W. (1995). Acculturative stress: The experience of the Hispanic immigrant. *The Counseling Psychologist, 23,* 25–42.

Sue, D. W., & Sue, D. (2000). *Counseling the culturally different* (3rd ed.). New York: Wiley.

Super, D. E. (1951). Vocational adjustment: Implementing a self-concept. *Occupations, 30,* 1–5.

Super, D. E. (1953). A theory of vocational development. *American Psychologist, 8,* 185–190.

Super, D. E. (1954). Career patterns as a basis for vocational counseling. *Journal of Counseling Psychology, 1,* 12–20.

Super, D. E. (1955). Personality integration through vocational counseling. *Journal of Counseling Psychology, 2,* 217–226.

Super, D. E. (1957). *The psychology of careers.* New York: Harper & Row.

Super, D. E. (1960). The critical ninth grade: Vocational choice or vocational exploration. *Personnel and Guidance Journal, 39,* 106–109.

Super, D. E. (1964a). A developmental approach to vocational guidance. *Vocational Guidance Quarterly, 13,* 1–10.

Super, D. E. (1964b). Goal specificity in the vocational counseling of future college students. *Personnel and Guidance Journal, 43,* 127–134.

Super, D. E. (1969). Vocational development theory. *The Counseling Psychologist, 1,* 2–30.

Super, D. E. (1972). Vocational development theory: Persons, positions, processes. In J. M. Whiteley & A. Resnikoff (Eds.), *Perspectives on vocational guidance.* Washington, DC: American Personnel and Guidance Association.

Super, D. E. (Ed.). (1974). *Measuring vocational maturity for counseling and evaluation.* Wash-ing-ton, DC: American Personnel and Guidance Association.

Super, D. E. (1977). Vocational maturity in mid-career. *Vocational Guidance Quarterly, 25,* 294–302.

Super, D. E. (1980). A life-span, life-space approach to career development. *Journal of Vocational Behavior, 16,* 282–298.

Super, D. E. (1981). A developmental theory: Implementing a self-concept. In D. H. Montros & C. J. Shinkman (Eds.), *Career development in the 1980s: Theory and practice.* Springfield, IL: Thomas.

Super, D. E. (1983). Assessment in career guidance: Toward truly developmental counseling. *Personnel and Guidance Journal, 61,* 555–562.

Super, D. E. (1984). Career and life development. In D. Brown, L. Brooks, & Associates (Eds.), *Career choice and development.* San Francisco: Jossey-Bass.

Super, D. E. (1990). A life-span, life-space approach to career development. In D. Brown, L. Brooks, & Associates (Eds.), *Career choice and development* (2nd ed.). San Francisco: Jossey-Bass.

Super, D. E., & Bachrach, P. B. (1957). *Scientific careers and vocational development theory.* New York: Teachers College, Columbia University.

Super, D. E., Crites, J. O., Hummel, R. C., Moser, H. P., Overstreet, P. L., & Warnath, C. F. (1957). *Vocational development: A framework for research.* New York: Teachers College, Columbia University.

Super, D. E., & Kidd, J. M. (1979). Vocational maturity in adulthood: Toward turning a model into a measure. *Journal of Vocational Behavior, 14,* 255–270.

Super, D. E., Savickas, M. L., & Super, C. (1996). A life-span, life-space approach to career de-velopment. In D. Brown, L. Brooks, & Associates, *Career choice and development* (3rd ed., pp. 121–178). San Francisco: Jossey-Bass.

Super, D. E., Starishevsky, R., Matlin, R., & Jordaan, J. P. (1963). *Career development: Self-concept theory.* New York: College Entrance Examination Board.

Super, D. E., & Sverko, B. (Eds.). (1995). *Life roles, values, and careers: International findings of the work importance study.* San Francisco: Jossey-Bass.

Super, D. E., Thompson, A. S., Jordaan, J. P., & Myers, R. (1984). Career Development Inventory. Palo Alto, CA: Consulting Psychologist Press.

Young, R. A., Valach, L., & Collin, A. (2002). A contextual explanation of career. In D. Brown, L. Brooks, & Associates (Eds.), *Career choice and development* (4th ed., pp. 206–254). San Francisco: Jossey-Bass.

UNIT 5

LEGISLATIVE FOUNDATIONS

WHAT IS PUBLIC POLICY?

This unit is about public policy. It is concerned with what governments do, why they do it, and what difference it makes. It is also about political science and the ability of this academic discipline to describe, analyze, and explain public policy.

Definition of Policy

Public policy is whatever governments choose to do or not to do.[1] Governments do many things. They regulate conflict within society; they organize society to carry on conflict with other societies; they distribute a great variety of symbolic rewards and material services to members of the society; and they extract money from society, most often in the form of taxes. Thus public policies may regulate behavior, organize bureaucracies, distribute benefits, or extract taxes—or all these things at once.

Policy Expansion and Government Growth

Today people expect government to do a great many things for them. Indeed there is hardly any personal or societal problem for which some group will not demand a government solution—that is, a public policy designed to alleviate personal discomfort or societal unease. Over the years, as more and more Americans

---

Taken from Dye, T. R. (2008). *Understanding Public Policy*, Twelfth Edition. Upper Saddle River, NJ: Pearson Prentice Hall. Chapter 1, pp. 1–10.

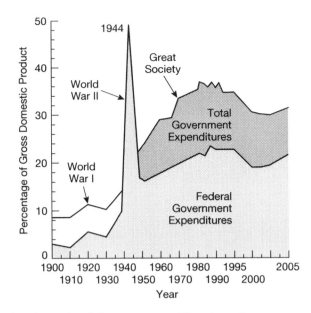

FIGURE 5.1   The Growth of Government The size of government can be measured in relation to the size of the economy. Total federal, state, and local government spending now exceeds 30 percent of the GDP, the size of the economy

turned to government to resolve society's problems, government grew in size and public policy expanded in scope to encompass just about every sector of American life.

Throughout most of the twentieth century, government grew in both absolute size and in relation to the size of the national economy. The size of the economy is usually measured by the gross domestic product (GDP), the sum of all the goods and services produced in the United States in a year (see Figure 5.1). Government spending amounted to only about 8 percent of the GDP at the beginning of the century, and most governmental activities were carried out by state and local governments. Two world wars, the New Deal programs devised during the Great Depression of the 1930s, and the growth of the Great Society programs of the 1960s and 1970s all greatly expanded the size of government, particularly the federal government. The rise in government growth relative to the economy leveled off during the Reagan presidency (1981–1989). The economy in the 1990s grew faster than government spending, resulting in a decline in the size of government *relative to the economy.* An economic downturn in 2000–2001, together with increased government expenditures for defense and homeland security, has caused government to grow relative to the GDP in recent years. Currently, total government spending—federal, state, and local—amounts to about 30 percent of the GDP. More than two-thirds of this government spending—about 20 percent of GDP—is accounted for by the *federal government* alone. The nation's fifty *state*

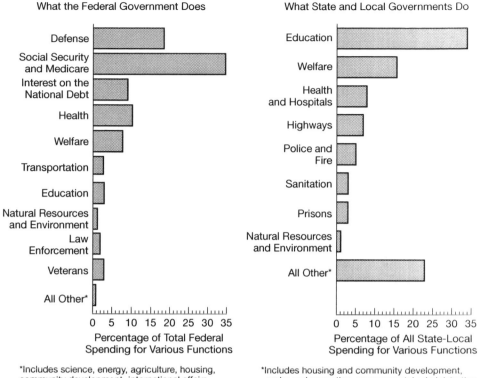

What the Federal Government Does

What State and Local Governments Do

*Includes science, energy, agriculture, housing, community development, international affairs, and general government.

*Includes housing and community development, parks and recreation, governmental administration, and interest.

FIGURE 5.2   Public Policy: What Governments Do Government spending figures indicate that Social Security and Medicare consume the largest share of federal spending, while education is the largest item in state and local government spending.

Sources: Budget of the United States Government, 2007; Statistical Abstract of the United States, 2005–2006.

governments and 87,000 *local* governments (cities, counties, towns and townships, school districts, and special districts) combined account for less than one-third of total government spending—about 10 percent of GDP.

Scope of Public Policy

Not everything that government does is reflected in governmental expenditures. *Regulatory activity*, for example, especially environmental regulations, imposes significant costs on individuals and businesses; these costs are *not* shown in government budgets. Nevertheless, government spending is a common indicator of governmental functions and priorities. For example, Figure 5.2 indicates that the *federal government* spends more on senior citizens—in Social Security and Medicare outlays—than on any other function, including national defense. Federal welfare and health programs account for substantial budget outlays, but federal financial support of education is very modest. *State and local governments* in the United States bear the major burden of public education. Welfare and health functions consume larger shares of their budgets than highways and law enforcement do.

WHY STUDY PUBLIC POLICY?

Political science is the study of politics—the study of "who gets what when and how."[2] It is more than the study of governmental institutions, that is, federalism, separation of powers, checks and balances, judicial review, the powers and duties of Congress, the president, and the courts. "Traditional" political science focuses primarily on these institutional arrangements as well as the philosophical justification of government. And political science is more than the study of political processes, that is, campaigns and elections, voting, lobbying, legislating, and adjudicating. Modern "behavioral" political science focuses primarily on these processes.

Political science is also the study of public policy—*the description and explanation of the causes and consequences of government activity*. This focus involves a description of the content of public policy; an analysis of the impact of social, economic, and political forces on the content of public policy; an inquiry into the effect of various institutional arrangements and political processes on public policy; and an evaluation of the consequences of public policies on society, both expected and unexpected.

WHAT CAN BE LEARNED FROM POLICY ANALYSIS?

Policy analysis is finding out what governments do, why they do it, and what difference, if any, it makes. What can be learned from policy analysis?

Description

First, we can describe public policy—we can learn what government is doing (and not doing) in welfare, defense, education, civil rights, health, the environment, taxation, and so on. A factual basis of information about national policy is really an indispensable part of everyone's education. What does the Civil Rights Act of 1964 actually say about discrimination in employment? What did the Supreme Court rule in the *Bakke* case about affirmative action programs? What is the condition of the nation's Social Security program? What do the Medicaid and Medicare programs promise for the poor and the aged? What agreements have been reached between the United States and Russia regarding nuclear weapons? What is being done to fight terrorism at home and abroad? How much money are we paying in taxes? How much money does the federal government spend each year, and what does it spend it on? These are examples of descriptive questions.

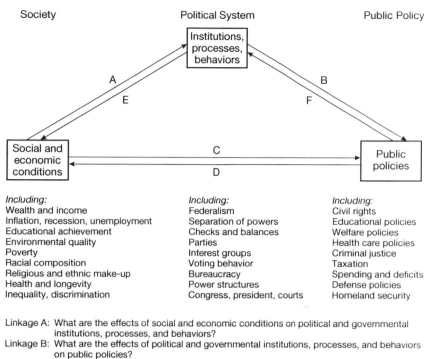

Society   Political System   Public Policy

Institutions, processes, behaviors

A   B
E   F

Social and economic conditions

C
D

Public policies

Including:
Wealth and income
Inflation, recession, unemployment
Educational achievement
Environmental quality
Poverty
Racial composition
Religious and ethnic make-up
Health and longevity
Inequality, discrimination

Including:
Federalism
Separation of powers
Checks and balances
Parties
Interest groups
Voting behavior
Bureaucracy
Power structures
Congress, president, courts

Including:
Civil rights
Educational policies
Welfare policies
Health care policies
Criminal justice
Taxation
Spending and deficits
Defense policies
Homeland security

Linkage A: What are the effects of social and economic conditions on political and governmental institutions, processes, and behaviors?
Linkage B: What are the effects of political and governmental institutions, processes, and behaviors on public policies?
Linkage C: What are the effects of social and economic conditions on public policies?
Linkage D: What are the effects (feedback) of public policies on social and economic conditions?
Linkage E: What are the effects (feedback) of political and governmental institutions, processes, and behaviors on social and economic conditions?
Linkage F: What are the effects (feedback) of public policies on political and governmental institutions, processes, and behaviors?

FIGURE 5.3   Studying Public Policy, Its Causes and Consequences This diagram (sometimes referred to as the "systems model") classifies societal conditions, political system characteristics, and public policies, and suggests possible linkages between them.

Causes

Second, we can inquire about the causes, or determinants, of public policy. Why is public policy what it is? Why do governments do what they do? We might inquire about the effects of political institutions, processes, and behaviors on public policies (Linkage B in Figure 5.3). For example, does it make any difference in tax and spending levels whether Democrats or Republicans control the presidency and Congress? What is the impact of lobbying by the special interests on efforts to reform the federal tax system? We can also inquire about the effects of social, economic, and cultural forces in shaping public policy (Linkage C in Figure 5.3). For example: What are the effects of changing public attitudes about race on civil rights policy? What are the effects of recessions on government spending? What is the effect of an increasingly older population on the Social Security and Medicare programs? In scientific terms, when we study the *causes* of public policy, policies become the *dependent* variables, and their various political, social, economic, and cultural determinants become the *independent* variables.

Consequences

Third, we can inquire about the consequences, or impacts, of public policy. Learning about the consequences of public policy is often referred to as *policy evaluation*. What difference, if any, does public policy make in people's lives? We might inquire about the effects of public policy on political institutions and processes (Linkage F in Figure 5.3). For example, what is the effect of the war in Iraq on Republican party fortunes in Congress? What is the impact of immigration policies on the president's popularity? We also want to examine the impact of public policies on conditions in society (Linkage D in Figure 5.3). For example, does capital punishment help to deter crime? Does cutting cash welfare benefits encourage people to work? Does increased educational spending produce higher student achievement scores? In scientific terms, when we study the *consequences* of public policy, policies become the *independent* variables, and their political, social, economic, and cultural impacts on society become the *dependent* variables.

POLICY ANALYSIS AND POLICY ADVOCACY

It is important to distinguish policy analysis from policy advocacy. *Explaining* the causes and consequences of various policies is not equivalent to *prescribing* what policies governments ought to pursue. Learning *why* governments do what they do and what the consequences of their actions are is not the same as saying what governments *ought* to do or bringing about changes in what they do. Policy advocacy requires the skills of rhetoric, persuasion, organization, and activism. Policy analysis encourages scholars and students to attack critical policy issues with the tools of systematic inquiry. There is an implied assumption in policy analysis that developing scientific knowledge about the forces shaping public policy and the consequences of public policy is itself a socially relevant activity and that such analysis is a prerequisite to prescription, advocacy, and activism.

Specifically, policy analysis involves:

1. *A primary concern with explanation rather than prescription.* Policy recommendations—if they are made at all—are subordinate to description and explanation. There is an implicit judgment that understanding is a prerequisite to prescription and that understanding is best achieved through careful analysis rather than rhetoric or polemics.
2. *A rigorous search for the causes and consequences of public policies.* This search involves the use of scientific standards of inference. Sophisticated quantitative techniques may be helpful in establishing valid inferences about causes and consequences, but they are not essential.

3. *An effort to develop and test general propositions about the causes and consequences of public policy and to accumulate reliable research findings of general relevance.* The object is to develop general theories about public policy that are reliable and that apply to different government agencies and different policy areas. Policy analysts clearly prefer to develop explanations that fit more than one policy decision or case study—explanations that stand up over time in a variety of settings.

However, it must be remembered that policy issues are decided not by analysts but by political actors—elected and appointed government officials, interest groups, and occasionally even voters. Social science research often does not fare well in the political arena; it may be interpreted, misinterpreted, ignored, or even used as a weapon by political combatants. Policy analysis sometimes produces unexpected and even politically embarrassing findings. Public policies do not always work as intended. And political interests will accept, reject, or use findings to fit their own purposes.

POLICY ANALYSIS AND THE QUEST FOR SOLUTIONS TO AMERICA'S PROBLEMS

It is questionable that policy analysis can ever "solve" America's problems. Ignorance, crime, poverty, racial conflict, inequality, poor housing, ill health, pollution, congestion, and unhappy lives have afflicted people and societies for a long time. Of course, this is no excuse for failing to work toward a society free of these maladies. But our striving for a better society should be tempered with the realization that solutions to these problems may be very difficult to find. There are many reasons for qualifying our enthusiasm for policy analysis.

Limits on Government Power

First, it is easy to exaggerate the importance, both for good and for ill, of the policies of governments. It is not clear that government policies, however ingenious, could cure all or even most of society's ills. Governments are constrained by many powerful social forces—patterns of family life, class structure, child-rearing practices, religious beliefs, and so on. These forces are not easily managed by governments, nor could they be controlled even if it seemed desirable to do so. Some of society's problems are very intractable.

Disagreement over the Problem

Second, policy analysis cannot offer solutions to problems when there is no general agreement on what the problems are. For example, in educational policy some researchers assume that raising achievement levels (measures of verbal and quantitative abilities) is the problem to which our efforts should be directed. But educators often argue that the acquisition of verbal and quantitative skills is not the only, or even the most important, goal of the public schools. They contend that schools must also develop positive self-images among pupils of all races and backgrounds, encourage social awareness and the appreciation of multiple cultures, teach children to respect one another and to resolve their differences peacefully, raise children's awareness of the dangers of drugs and educate them about sex and sexually transmitted diseases, and so on. In other words, many educators define the problems confronting schools more broadly than raising achievement levels.

Policy analysis is not capable of resolving value conflicts. If there is little agreement on what values should be emphasized in educational policy, there is not much that policy research can contribute to policymaking. At best it can advise on how to achieve certain results, but it cannot determine what is truly valuable for society.

Subjectivity in Interpretation

Third, policy analysis deals with very subjective topics and must rely on interpretation of results. Professional researchers frequently interpret the results of their analyses differently. Social science research cannot be value-free. Even the selection of the topic for research is affected by one's values about what is important in society and worthy of attention.

Limitations on Design of Human Research

Another set of problems in systematic policy analysis centers around inherent limitations in the design of social science research. It is not really possible to conduct some forms of controlled experiments on human beings. For example, researchers cannot order children to go to poor schools for several years just to see if it adversely impacts their achievement levels. Instead, social researchers must find situations in which educational deprivation has been produced "naturally" in order to make the necessary observations about the causes of such deprivation. Because we cannot control all the factors in a real-world situation, it is difficult to pinpoint precisely what causes educational achievement or nonachievement. Moreover, even where some experimentation is permitted, human beings frequently modify their behavior simply because they know that they are being observed in an experimental situation. For example, in educational research it frequently turns out that children perform well under *any* new teaching method or curricular innovation. It is difficult to know whether the improvements observed are a product of the new teaching method or curricular improvement or merely a product of the experimental situation.

Complexity of Human Behavior

Perhaps the most serious reservation about policy analysis is the fact that social problems are so complex that social scientists are unable to make accurate predictions about the impact of proposed policies. *Social scientists simply do not know enough about individual and group behavior to be able to give reliable advice to policymakers.* Occasionally policymakers turn to social scientists for "solutions," but social scientists do not have any. Most of society's problems are shaped by so many variables that a simple explanation of them, or remedy for them, is rarely possible. The fact that social scientists give so many contradictory recommendations is an indication of the absence of reliable scientific knowledge about social problems. Although some scholars argue that no advice is better than contradictory or inaccurate advice, policymakers still must make decisions, and it is probably better that they act in the light of whatever little knowledge social science can provide than that they act in the absence of any knowledge at all. Even if social scientists cannot predict the impact of future policies, they can at least attempt to measure the impact of current and past public policies and make this knowledge available to decision makers.

POLICY ANALYSIS AS ART AND CRAFT

Understanding public policy is both an art and a craft. It is an art because it requires insight, creativity, and imagination in identifying societal problems and describing them, in devising public policies that might alleviate them, and then in finding out whether these policies end up making things better or worse. It is a craft because these tasks usually require some knowledge of economics, political science, public administration, sociology, law, and statistics. Policy analysis is really an applied subfield of all of these traditional academic disciplines.

We doubt that there is any "model of choice" in policy analysis—that is, a single model or method that is preferable to all others and that consistently renders the best solutions to public problems. Instead we agree with political scientist Aaron Wildavsky, who wrote:

> *Policy analysis is one activity for which there can be no fixed program, for policy analysis is synonymous with creativity, which may be stimulated by theory and sharpened by practice, which can be learned but not taught.*

Wildavsky goes on to warn students that solutions to great public questions are not to be expected:

> *In large part, it must be admitted, knowledge is negative. It tells us what we cannot do, where we cannot go, wherein we have been wrong, but not necessarily how to correct these errors. After all, if current efforts were judged wholly satisfactory, there would be little need for analysis and less for analysts.*

There is no one model of choice to be found in this unit, but if anyone wants to begin a debate about different ways of understanding public policy, this unit is a good place to begin.

BIBLIOGRAPHY

Anderson, James E. *Public Policymaking*, 6th ed. Boston: Houghton Mifflin, 2006.

Cochran, Clarke E., et al. *American Public Policy: An Introduction*, 8th ed. Belmont, CA: Wadsworth, 2006.

Dunn, William N. *Public Policy Analysis*, 3rd ed. Upper Saddle River, NJ: Prentice Hall, 2004.

Heineman, Robert A., William T. Bluhm, Steven A. Peterson, and Edward N. Kearny. *The World of the Policy Analyst*. New York: Chatham House, 2000.

Kraft, Michael E., and Scott R. Furlang. *Public Policy: Politics, Analysis and Alternatives*, 2nd ed. Washington, DC: CQ Press, 2006.

Peters, B. Guy. *American Public Policy: Promise and Performance*, 6th ed. Washington, DC: CQ Press, 2006.

Rushefsky, Mark E. *Public Policy in the United States*, 3rd ed. Armonk, NY: M. E. Sharpe, 2002.

Wildavsky, Aaron. *Speaking Truth to Power*. New York: John Wiley, 1979.

FEDERAL WORKFORCE LEGISLATION

INTRODUCTION

Federal legislation has always been enacted in order to help solve the major problems facing the nation as a whole or to address a cultural need, such as ensuring the constitutional rights of all Americans. The Smith-Hughes Act of 1917 demonstrated the concern in Congress that the security and the welfare of a nation are dependent not only upon the nation's ability to govern itself, but also upon its ability to educate its people for productive work and meaningful lives. As skills needed for work and living became more complex (a trend that continues today), the training of skilled workers became a continuous identified need. Congress responded to the need by providing support for career and technical (CTE) education. This began with the passage of the Morrill Act of 1862, which supported college and university programs of vocational education. With current career and technical legislation, Congress continues that support today. It continues to affirm its belief that federal support for CTE is an investment in the future of the nation's workforce. A highly skilled workforce is viewed as essential to maintaining the nation's standard of living, defense preparedness, economic strength, and leadership position in the free world.

As the nation progressed from a predominantly agrarian society in its early years to a highly industrialized, technological society, vast social, religious,

Taken from Scott, J.L. and Sarkees-Wircenski, M. (2008) *Overview of Career and Technical Education*. Homewood, IL: American Technical Publishers. pp. 237–312.

philosophical, psychological, educational, and cultural changes took place requiring congressional action that could address the nation's needs. These needs were addressed over the years by educational legislation. The development of CTE has been influenced greatly by many federal enactments since the Smith-Hughes Act of 1917. A review of these enactments aids in understanding our present form of CTE and the need to continue some form of federal support in partnership with states and local communities.

OBJECTIVES

After completing this unit the reader should be able to accomplish the following:

1. Describe the relationship between the federal and state governments and local educational agencies with respect to CTE.
2. Describe the major provisions of legislation involving CTE from the passage of the Morrill Act of 1862, through the Workforce Investment Act of 1998, the Ticket to Work and Work Incentives Improvement Act of 1999, and the Carl D. Perkins Career and Technical Education Improvement Act of 2006.
3. Describe the provisions of federal legislation that involve students from special populations, including the civil rights act addressing special needs individuals and the many legislative acts that addressed the needs of special populations, up to the Individuals with Disabilities Act of 2004.
4. Describe the role of the federal government in improving education through partnerships with state and local educational agencies.

FEDERAL CAREER AND TECHNICAL EDUCATION LEGISLATION

The state of the nation in the early 1900s raised concerns among leaders, for it was faced with a shortage of skilled workers in agriculture and industry. A continuous flow of people came from rural America to the cities to fill vacant positions in manufacturing jobs. A growing number of European immigrants also flowed into the cities in search of employment. Urban areas grew so rapidly that they could not provide adequate housing or services. This in turn led to deplorable living conditions. Poor men and women entered agricultural and industrial jobs and left children unsupervised, which led to moral decay and an increase in youth crime. Workers were forced to work long hours for low pay at repetitive jobs that afforded little opportunity for them to use their talents and creativity.

Public high schools established in the late 1800s to provide classical education to only a small number of students were being forced to serve an increasing number of students from rural America and from foreign countries. The narrow curriculum offered in high schools to prepare students for the professions was deemed unsuitable for preparing the masses of students needed for the industrial age. Critics of public secondary schools were unhappy that only about 8%

of students graduated from high school, leaving many students without an adequate general education and few skills that prepared them for work.

Educational reformers began to advocate an expanded curriculum to include practical education—one designed to prepare workers for the type of jobs in which the masses of people could find employment. They wanted youth and adults to have a chance for better careers and for social and economic mobility. Business and industry leaders wanted a supply of young people to fill agricultural and industrial jobs so that they could compete in the market. They wanted individuals who had good attitudes, respected authority, followed directions, and could fit into the organization of the workplace.

Educational reformers, business and industry leaders, and government leaders began to form coalitions to press for federal legislation that would stimulate the development of a federal-state partnerships and lead to the inclusion of practical subjects into the school curricula to prepare young people for employment in the trade and industries, in agriculture, in commerce and commercial pursuits, and in occupations and roles related to home economics. A little over ten years later, the goal of this coalition of leaders was met with the passage of the Smith-Hughes Act of 1917.

The information in this section is a brief review of the federal acts that shaped CTE for over 130 years and is based in part on the scholarly work of Nystrom and Bayne (1979) and on the statutes themselves as listed in the *United States Statutes at Large*. Most career and technical educators associate the beginning of federal support for CTE with direct federal funding to programs as first provided by the Smith-Hughes Act of 1917, but federal support for CTE actually began with the passage of the Morrill Act of 1862, which authorized land grants for the establishment of educational institutions that included programs for agriculture and the mechanic arts.

Ever since the passage of the Smith-Hughes Act of 1917, which established the federal-state-local cooperative effort of providing CTE, the federal government has maintained an active interest in CTE. Federal policy from 1917 to the passage of the Vocational Act of 1963 focused on expanding and improving CTE programs and building CTE capacity to serve the corporate needs of business and industry.

Cohen and Besharov (2002) state that concerns of Congress in the early years were the economy and national defense in the 1920s, unemployment reduction in the 1930s, and a shift back to peacetime economic development after World War II. In the 1960s, the new concern of poverty emerged and federal legislation began to address this with set-asides to serve poor, disadvantaged, and disabled individuals.

From 1963 to the present, federal policy has continued its focus on improving and expanding programs to prepare people for work and has added a focus on meeting human needs by increasing access to high-quality CTE for all students, especially those from special populations.

Through the 1980s and into the 1990s, federal legislation emphasized service to special populations, but it also included a focus on improving the academic preparation of CTE students to facilitate transition to postsecondary education and to prepare workers for emerging high-tech occupations. In the early 1990s,

Congress was influenced by the success of European apprenticeship programs in preparing skilled workers, which led to the passage of legislation to encourage states and local school systems to implement work-based programs. Beginning in the late 1990s and continuing to the present, Congress continued its initiatives on improving CTE programs to include more academic rigor, which it felt was essential to preparing individuals for postsecondary education and meeting the ever-increasing technical jobs of the 21st century. Programs like Tech Prep and Career Pathways emerged and are still being emphasized today.

From the Smith-Hughes Act of 1917 to the current legislation, Congress has reaffirmed its belief that federal support for CTE is an investment in the future of the nation's workforce. In addition, many factors over the 84 years since Smith-Hughes have affected legislative priorities, including the following:

- several wars
- a major depression
- labor/management strife
- the "space race"
- continuous technological advancements
- changes in population demographics
- increased standards of living and economic security
- increased numbers of individuals in school and increased level of education for the populations as a whole
- social unrest and increasing incidence of crime
- high youth unemployment and high periods of unemployment and under-employment
- desegregation
- widespread discrimination
- gender-bias and gender-role stereotyping
- an increased number of women in the labor force
- multicultural diversity
- changes in educational psychology
- unacceptable levels of school dropouts
- the widening skill gap and shortage of highly skilled workers

The reader should note the progressive evolution and expansion of CTE legislation, which included new areas of study resulting from technological change. In addition, the reader should note the change from specific occupational programs designed to meet the needs of business and industry to programs designed to meet the needs of people. Finally, the increasing interest of Congress on meeting the needs of special populations through vocational programs should be noted.

The following information is provided to assist the reader interested in these legislative enactments. Federal enactments are first assigned a public law (PL) number. A PL number consists of a multidigit code number, with the first two or three digits standing for the session of congress, then a hyphen, then the last digits, which represent where the bill fell chronologically in the listing of the bills in that particular session. For Example, PL 85-864, the National Defense Education Act of 1958, is a law passed during the eighty-fifth Congress and assigned the number 864 indicating its sequence in the 85th session of Congress.

Once bills become law, they are assigned a volume number and a statute number for inclusion in the multivolume *United States Statutes at Large* resource. PL 85-864 was assigned the code of 72 Stat. 1580, which means it is in the 72nd volume of the *United States Statutes at Large* under law number 1580. Specific legislation can also be located in the Statutes at Large publications with only the public law number. It is necessary to identify the volume(s) labeled as the eighty-fifth Congress and sequentially locate the 864th order of legislation. The reader can obtain the PL number and the U.S. code number for federal and state laws in a multivolume publication entitled *Shepard's Federal and State Acts and Cases by Popular Names*, published by McGraw-Hill, Inc. and available in college and university libraries. See Appendix.

Morrill Act of 1862 (PL None)

Federal legislation for CTE at the college level began with the 1862 Morrill Act known as the Land-Grant Act in which states were given land that could be either sold or leased to raise money for establishing at least one college in the state. In this college, liberal and practical education studies were to be combined into a curriculum that was vocational without being viewed as inferior to a purely academic curriculum. The land-grant colleges and universities established by this act opened the doors to higher educational opportunities to a wide range of students and paved the way toward acceptance of vocational education in institutions of higher education and later in the high schools of America. The intent of congress was to call attention to the importance of the mechanical arts and agriculture in this country and to ensure that this form of education was accepted as vital to the national welfare and as a necessary incentive to spur economic growth.

Department of Education Act of 1867 (PL None)

The U.S. Department of Education was established in 1867 and was later known as the Office of Education. Over 100 years later in 1980, under PL 96-88, it became a cabinet-level department. The U.S. Office of Education would later be charged with the responsibility of conducting studies, investigations, and reports with particular reference to their use in aiding the states in the establishment of vocational schools and classes and in giving instruction in agriculture, trades and industries, commerce and commercial pursuits, and home economics.

Hatch Act of 1887 (PL None)

The Hatch Act was also known as the Experimental Stations Act in that it provided funds for each state to establish an agricultural experiment station in which agricultural research could be conducted and the results written in the form of useful information to inform people about the applications of agricultural science.

Morrill Act of 1890 (PL None)

The second Morrill Act was known as the Maintenance Act. It authorized additional funds from the sale or lease of public lands to more fully support and maintain the agriculture and mechanical arts programs established by the original Morrill Act. The act included a new provision that included the use of funds to establish and support at least one land-grant institution that served African-American students in agriculture and the mechanic arts.

The second Morrill Act gave real incentive to the establishment of land-grant colleges for African-Americans. Many graduates from these African-American land-grant colleges became teachers of manual training or vocational education and some were instrumental in establishing educational institutions for African-Americans.

Adams Act of 1906 (PL 58-74)

The Adams Act increased the appropriations of funds provided to states for the operation of experiment stations provided by the Hatch Act.

Nelson Amendments to Morrill Act of 1907 (PL 59-242)

The Nelson Amendments increased the amount of funds used to support land-grant colleges and designated that a portion of the monies should be spent in the preparation of instructors for teaching agriculture and the mechanical arts.

Smith-Lever Act of 1914 (PL 63-95)

The Smith-Lever Act, known as the Agriculture Extension Act, provided for a program of cooperative extension work in agriculture and home economics in which instruction and practical demonstrations in agriculture and home economics were to be given to persons not attending or resident in college. This act was a significant piece of legislation in that it provided needed training in demonstrations and project work at the farm and in the home for American farmers and homemakers as vocational education of less than college grade. The practice of 50–50 matching began with this act, for the state was required to finance half of the cost of the extension programs and the federal government the other half.

Smith-Hughes Act of 1917 (PL 64-347)

The Smith-Hughes Act, known as the Vocational Act of 1917, started the federal-state-local agency partnership for establishing and operating vocational education programs in public institutions of less than baccalaureate level. This act was the most specific and exacting of all the enactments in its requirement upon states in the use of federal money, which was provided in perpetuity for public schools. It represented national endorsement of vocational education in the public school system, a dream of many educational reformers and business and industry leaders. The Smith-Hughes Act contained the following provisions, which shaped the form of vocational education for many years:

- It created the Federal Board for Vocational Education.
- It provided categorical aid only within narrowly defined limits, thereby giving the board control over state programs.
- It provided for a designated amount of funds to be given to states annually until $7,000,000 was reached to promote vocational education programs in the areas of agriculture, trades and industry, and home economics.
- It provided annual appropriations for the following: (a) salaries of teachers, supervisors, and directors of vocational education areas, with states paying half of salaries and the federal government the other half, (b) teacher preparation in the areas of agriculture, home economics, and trade and industrial subjects, and (c) support for the activities of the Federal Board for Vocational Education.
- It mandated the creation of state boards to govern vocational education in cooperation with the federal board.
- It required the development of state plans describing the kinds of vocational education to be offered by each state.
- It required development of an annual report on the state vocational education system to be submitted to the federal board.
- It required states to bear half the cost of salaries for vocational education personnel and to cooperate with local schools to provide funds to support high quality vocational programs, facilities, equipment, and materials.
- It required federal funds to be under public supervision and control.
- It required that vocational training be provided to individuals who (a) had selected a vocational area and desired preparation in it, (b) had already been employed and sought greater efficiency in that employment, and (c) had accepted employment and wished to advance to positions of responsibility. Vocational education was to be less than college grade, for persons over 14 years of age, who desired daytime training, and for persons over 16 years of age who sought evening class training.

Smith-Sears Act of 1918 (PL 65-178)

The Smith-Sears Act (also called the Vocational Rehabilitation Act) authorized funds for establishing retraining programs for the returning disabled servicemen of World War I. Many of these veterans enrolled in vocational programs.

Smith-Bankhead Act of 1920 (PL 66-236)

The Smith-Bankhead Act, known as the Federal Rehabilitation Act, provided for the establishment of programs for the rehabilitation of nonmilitary disabled persons into civilian employment. This act created state rehabilitation boards and an assistant director for vocational rehabilitation at the federal level. Many rehabilitation students enrolled in vocational programs to prepare for new jobs.

Smith-Fess Act of 1920 (PL 66-236)

The Smith-Fess Act, known as the Industrial Rehabilitation Act, provided federal aid for the vocational rehabilitation of industry-disabled persons. This act only lasted four years, but established a precedent that would lead to other vocational rehabilitation acts years later.

PL 68-35 (1924) An Act to Extend Vocational Education to Hawaii

This act added the territory of Hawaii to share in the benefits and provisions of the Smith-Hughes Act of 1917.

Purnell Act of 1925 (PL 68-458)

The Purnell Act authorized money for the more complete endowment of agricultural experiment endowments. The research and development that came out of the land-grant colleges and agricultural experiment stations led to the second agricultural revolution.

Capper-Ketcham Act of 1928 (PL 70-475)

The Capper-Ketcham Act authorized money for the further development of agricultural extension work in land-grant colleges.

George-Reed Act of 1929 (PL 70-702)

The George-Reed Act was a supplemental authorization enactment that provided additional funds (besides those provided through previous legislation) for home economics and agricultural education with no additional funds authorized for trade and industrial education. This was not a popular law for industrial education leaders.

Territory of Puerto Rico Agricultural Experiment Station Act of 1931 (PL 71-856)

An act to coordinate the agricultural experiment station work and to extend the benefits of certain acts of Congress to the territory of Puerto Rico.

George-Ellzey Act of 1934 (PL 73-245)

The George-Ellzey Act increased the supplemental funds for agriculture and home economics and reinstated support for trade and industrial education that had ended with the termination of the George-Reed Act, which lasted only three years.

Bankhead-Jones Act of 1935 (PL 74-182)

The Bankhead-Jones Act authorized grants to states for the expansion of agricultural experiment stations in order to provide more endowment and support of the land-grant colleges in several states.

George-Deen Act of 1936 (PL 74-673)

The George-Deen Act was another supplemental authorization enactment for increasing funding to agriculture, home economics, and trade and industrial education. In addition, it responded to a societal need to provide vocational education for individuals engaged in distributive (marketing) occupations. Money was also authorized for teacher education programs. This act began to broaden the scope of vocational education—a trend that would continue for many years.

Vocational Education for National Defense (1940 to 1946)

A series of ten legislative acts were passed as war emergency measures that utilized the framework of vocational education for preparing people for the war effort. Vocational programs that were converted for national defense purposes were entirely funded by the federal government. The success of vocational education in preparing people for war industries firmly established vocational education as an important component of national defense. Some of the emergency acts included (1) PL 78-156, a joint resolution to appropriate money for the fiscal year of 1944 for emergency maternity and infant care for wives of enlisted men in the armed forces; (2) PL 78-248, an act to provide for the training of nurses for the armed forces, governmental, and civilian hospitals, health agencies, and the war industries; and (3) PL 78-338, amendments to the 1931 act to provide books for the adult blind.

Servicemen's Readjustment Act of 1944 (PL 78-346)

The Servicemen's Readjustment Act, known as the GI Bill of Rights, was passed to assist World War II veterans in making the adjustment to civilian life. One of the important stipulations of this act was that returning GIs had to declare a vocational objective in order to receive financial support to cover the cost of their education. This act encouraged the inclusion of occupationally oriented programs in higher education institutions of America. It also encouraged enrollment of veterans in adult vocational education programs, which helped to develop a network of postsecondary vocational-technical schools in every state. The GI Bill subsidized the cost of education and included subsistence for thousands of World War II veterans and, with subsequent legislation, provided the same services to veterans of the Korean and Vietnam wars.

The George-Barden Act or the Vocational Education Act of 1946 (PL 79-586)

The George-Barden Act, known as the Vocational Education Act of 1946, was another supplemental authorization bill that increased funding for existing vocational programs including agriculture, home economics, trade and industrial education, and distributive (marketing) education. Like the George-Deen Act, it added areas that could receive funds, such as allocations for the Office of Vocational Education in Washington and authorization to include vocational education for the fishery trades. This act relaxed tight federal control over how the money provided by the act could be spent, giving more decision-making control to the state and local education agencies—a trend that continues today.

Funds for the George-Barden Act could be spent for supervision and teacher training; for salaries and necessary travel expenses of teachers, teacher trainers, vocational counselors, supervisors and directors of vocational education, and vocational guidance; for securing information necessary for improvement of vocational programs and vocational guidance; for training and work-experience training programs; for rental of equipment and supplies required to support instruction; and for supervision of Future Farmers of America and the New Farmers of America student organizations by vocational agriculture teachers.

The National School Lunch Act of 1946 (PL 79-396)

The National School Lunch Act authorized assistance to states through grants-in-aid and other means to assist in providing adequate foods and facilities for the establishment, maintenance, operation, and expansion of nonprofit school lunch programs. The school lunch program continues today and is an important part of the social services provided by schools as links have been established between nutrition and learning.

Federal Property and Administrative Services Act of 1949 (PL 81-152)

This act provided for the donation of surplus property of the federal government to educational institutions and for other public purposes. This act benefited schools with vocational programs by providing them with free or low-cost machines, equipment, tools, and supplies.

An Act to Incorporate the Future Farmers of America of 1950 (PL 81-740)

Congress officially chartered the vocational student organization of Future Farmers of America as a vital part of vocational agricultural education. The act spelled out in great detail the purposes and objectives of the Future Farmers of America and how it would be organized and administered.

Health Amendments Act of 1956 (PL 84-911)

The Health Amendments authorized funds to address the need to provide more nurses for a growing health care system and added practical nursing as one of the vocational areas that could be supported with federal funds.

Fishery Amendment, George-Barden Act of 1956 (PL 84-911)

An amendment to the George-Barden Act was enacted to further promote the fishing industry and to include the distribution aspects of that industry. The way money was to flow to support vocational education for fishery trades was changed to a system based on the size of each states's fishing industry and was to be regulated by the U.S. Commissioner of Education and the Secretary of the Interior.

National Defense Education Act (NDEA) of 1958 (PL 85-864)

The National Defense Education Act is an excellent example of Congress responding to a critical need in society and enacting legislation to address this need. The launching of the Russian satellite, Sputnik I, raised great concern about the standing of America in technical and scientific areas. A quick review of our space program revealed huge manpower shortages in electronics, aerospace engineering, mathematics, foreign languages, and other highly technical occupations. Congress acted quickly by passing the comprehensive National Defense Education Act (NDEA) of 1958. The NDEA was the first act to stress the importance of science, mathematics, foreign language, and technical competencies, and subsequent legislation would continue this focus as occupations became more complex, requiring higher levels of applied academics and technical skills. Unlike most previous legislation, which supported vocational education programs for secondary students, the focus of this legislation was on postsecondary training.

Title VIII of the act created the area school concept and provided funds for the operation of these postsecondary area schools in each state. The intent of Congress was to extend vocational education to residents of areas inadequately served and to encourage the development of postsecondary vocational programs. These programs would emphasize a combination of manipulative skills and related technical knowledge including mathematics, science, and applied technology and would enable graduates to work effectively as technicians, aiding engineers and scientists. The focus of this act was on providing vocational and related training for youth, adults, and older persons and included related instruction for apprentices, designed to fit them for employment as technicians or skilled workers in scientific or technical fields.

This act impacted both traditional as well as vocational education and aroused public interest in all students going to college. The NDEA included ten titles, with nine of them outlining and authorizing funds for different programs to receive federal aid. These titles did the following:

1. Authorized loans to qualified students in institutions of higher learning that were intended to encourage them to prepare for teaching in elementary and secondary schools or to prepare as specialists in science, mathematics, engineering, and foreign languages. Graduates who entered elementary or secondary teaching were eligible to have one-half of their loans forgiven. Many capable students were given an opportunity to complete a higher education degree that they would not have otherwise completed because of the high cost of a college education.
2. Strengthened instruction and promoted enrollments in America's secondary schools in the areas of science, mathematics, and modern foreign languages by providing for the purchase of equipment, the remodeling of buildings, and the employment of qualified state supervisors.
3. Provided for fellowships to be awarded through institutions of higher learning to promote research, the extension of knowledge, and the training of college teachers.
4. Provided funds for state departments of education to aid in testing, counseling, and guidance in elementary and secondary schools as well as funds for counselor training through regular courses and short-term institutes in colleges and universities.
5. Provided for federal aid for research and instruction in modern foreign languages through research studies and language institutes for teachers.
6. Provided funds for research and experimentation on the more effective utilization of television, radio, motion pictures, and related media for instructional purposes.
7. Provided funds for a science information service administered by the National Science Foundation.
8. Provided funds to assist state educational agencies for statistical services to improve their educational records and reports.
9. Provided funds to establish and maintain vocational schools on an area-wide basis to serve individuals, geographic regions, and occupations not being adequately served by existing vocational education programs.

Captioned Films for the Deaf Act (PL 85-905)

The Captioned Films for the Deaf Act authorized a loan service of captioned films for the deaf.

Education of Mentally Retarded Children Act of 1958 (PL 85-926)

The Education of Mentally Retarded Children Act authorized federal assistance for training teachers of the handicapped.

Manpower Legislation

The 1960s were years of social unrest and instability for our country. The Vietnam War had caused internal social problems and the rapid march of technology was displacing unskilled workers, causing widespread unemployment and underemployment. A growing number of people who had no skills and had lost their self-respect plagued the nation's inner cities and countryside. Ironically, at the same time that there were high periods of unemployment, industry was in need of skilled workers. The number of economically depressed areas was beginning to rise. There was growing public sentiment that government needed to act to solve problems of unemployment, the rising cost of living, the rights of minority groups, and the shortage of skilled workers for business and industry. The federal government took action by implementing a number of acts directed toward retraining underemployed or unemployed adults through the Department of Labor. These acts created a number of programs that have been collectively called manpower programs. The current manpower act is the Workforce Investment Act of 1998.

Area Redevelopment Act of 1961 (PL 87-27)

The Area Redevelopment Act (ARA) was directed at providing retraining opportunities to individuals in economically depressed areas of the United States. Subsistence payments were given to trainees, which served to encourage them to enroll and stay in training programs. Forty-five million dollars was allocated to support vocational training, and existing vocational education programs provided training for some of the participants.

Manpower Development and Training Act (MDTA) of 1962 (PL 87-415)

The Manpower Development and Training Act provided training opportunities for underemployed and unemployed individuals based on training needs as determined by the Department of Labor and local employment services agencies. Three hundred seventy million dollars was authorized to be spent over a three-year period. A number of training programs were administered through existing state agencies for vocational education. Many MDTA trainees were enrolled in area vocational schools in day and evening programs.

Health Professions Educational Assistance Act of 1963 (PL 88-129)

The Health Professions Education Assistance Act provided federal funds for expanding teaching facilities for health programs and for loans to students in the health professions.

Higher Education Facilities Act (HEFA) of 1963 (PL 88-204)

The Higher Education Facilities Act authorized a five-year program of federal grants and loans to colleges and universities for the expansion and development of physical facilities. In the early 1960s, college enrollment had reached an all time high due, in part, to the influence of the National Defense Education Act, and resulting in a critical need for the federal government to assist institutions of higher learning in providing housing for these students. The HEFA provided money to public institutions on a 40% federal to 60% state matching ratio and to private institutions on a 33.3% federal matching basis. This act provided much-needed assistance to junior colleges, undergraduate programs, and graduate programs involved in training skilled technicians. Many of the existing occupational programs in various community colleges owe a large part of their physical facilities to this legislation.

Vocational Education Act of 1963 (PL 88-210)

As stated earlier, the early 1960s was a stressful period in our history, characterized by a dramatic increase in youth unemployment and underemployment, a critical shortage of technicians and skilled workers, a constant need to retrain workers displaced by automation, and a growing need to provide new educational opportunities at the secondary and postsecondary levels. Congress had already enacted manpower legislation through the Department of Labor to deal with the problems of adults who were underemployed and unemployed, but something needed to be done to reduce the pool of people exiting from the high schools without the skills needed to find employment.

President John F. Kennedy, in his message to Congress in 1961 on American education, called for an examination of existing vocational education legislation with a view toward modernizing the acts currently in force. He appointed an advisory board, known as the Panel of Consultants, to conduct a study of the current national vocational acts and to make recommendations for improving and redirecting vocational education programs. The panel released its report entitled *Education for a Changing World of Work* in November of 1962. The report contained a number of findings and recommendations, including the need to drastically increase the amount of federal money allocated to support vocational education programs and the need to eliminate funding by occupational categories in favor of a more flexible organizational structure that would better serve the needs of students (U.S. Department of Health, Education, and Welfare, Office of Education, 1963).

The Vocational Act of 1963, also known as the Perkins-Morse Bill, was signed into law by President Lyndon Johnson, marking a new era for vocational education. It affirmed the federal governments' commitment to vocational education as an essential program for the common welfare and national defense of the country. The central theme of this enactment was to broaden the conceptions of education for work to better meet the needs of different groups of people. The purpose of this act was to "authorize federal grants to states to assist them to maintain, extend, and improve existing programs of vocational education, to develop new programs for vocational education, and to provide part-time employment for youths who need the earning from such employment to continue their vocational training on a full-time basis, so that persons of all ages in all communities of the state—those in high school, those who have completed or discontinued their formal education and are preparing to enter the labor market but need to upgrade their skills or learn new ones, and those with special education handicaps—will have access to vocational training or retraining which is of high quality, which is realistic in the light of actual or anticipated opportunities for gainful employment, and which is suited to their needs, interests, and ability to benefit from training (Nystrom & Bayne, 1979).

Under the Vocational Act of 1963, 90% of the funds were allocated on the basis of a state's population, and these funds were to be spent for the following purposes:

- vocational education for high school students
- vocational education for individuals who have completed or discontinued their high school education but are available for full-time study to prepare for employment.
- vocational education for persons who are already employed and need training or retraining to achieve employment stability or advancement in employment
- vocational education for persons who have academic, socioeconomic, or other handicaps that prevent them from succeeding in the regular vocational education program (Ten percent of the funds provided by this act were to be spent on research and development of experimental programs to better serve the needs of handicapped individuals who could not succeed in regular vocational education programs.)
- construction of area vocational schools
- ancillary services—teacher training, vocational guidance, job placement, curriculum development, state leadership, etc., and activities to assure quality in all vocational education programs

The act also included a number of important provisions that affected vocational education:

1. An advisory committee on vocational education was established in the Office of Education for the purpose of advising the Commissioner of Education on the national administration of vocational education programs with respect to actual training requirements.
2. For the first time in federal vocational education legislation, states were permitted to transfer or combine categorical training allotments to meet their unique needs, thus ending specific categorical funding to most programs.

3. An advisory council was to be appointed in 1966 for the purpose of reviewing the progress of vocational education programs and making recommendations for improvement. This council was to reconvene periodically, with intervals of no less than five years, and prepare reports on the state of vocational education in the nation. These advisory council reports have significantly influenced other federal vocational legislation.
4. Work-study programs for vocational students were created by this act to allow students with financial need to become employed in order to begin or continue their vocational education.

Finally, the Vocational Act of 1963 broadened the definition of vocational education and defined the different types of area vocational schools. Vocational education meant "vocational or technical training or retraining which is given in schools or classes under public supervision and control, or under contract with a State board or local educational agency, and is conducted as a part of a program designed to fit individuals for gainful employment as semi-skilled or skilled workers or technicians in recognized occupations. This includes, in addition to the programs under the Vocational Act of 1946, as amended, any program designed to fit individuals for gainful employment in business and office occupations" (Nystrom & Bayne, 1979).

The definition of area vocational education schools of this act was instrumental in developing the delivery system of vocational education used today. Area vocational education schools meant "(a) a specialized high school used exclusively or principally for the provision of vocational education to persons who are available for full-time study in preparation for entering the labor market; or (b) the department of a high school exclusively or principally used for providing vocational education in no less than five different occupational fields to persons who are available for full-time study in preparation for entering the labor market; or (c) a technical or vocational school used exclusively or principally for the provision of vocational education to persons who have completed or left high school and who are available for full-time study in preparation for entering the labor market; or (d) the department or division of a junior college or community college or university which provides vocational education in no less than five different occupational field under the supervision of the state board for vocational education leading to immediate employment, but not leading to a baccalaureate degree" (The House Committee on Education and Labor and the Senate Committee on Labor and Public Welfare, 1975).

Civil Rights Act of 1964 (PL 88-352)

The Civil Rights Act of 1964 dealt with basic human rights and responsibilities in the workplace. Its major purpose was to ensure that individuals, regardless of race, gender, national origin, or handicap, would receive equal treatment and that selection for employment, education, apprenticeship, or membership in a labor organization would be based solely on qualifications. Issues addressed by this act included equal employment opportunities, voting rights, equal education, fair housing, and public accommodation. Provisions of this act regarding handicapped individuals were to be revisited later in the Americans with Disabilities Act of 1990.

The Civil Rights Act provided federal grants to institutions of higher education to conduct special institutes for training elementary and secondary teachers to deal more effectively with special education problems resulting from desegregation. It also provided grants to local school boards to conduct in-service training for instructional staff to deal with problems arising from desegregation. School boards could also apply for technical assistance to comply with desegregation mandates of this act.

Economic Opportunity Act of 1964 (PL 88-452)

The Economic Opportunity Act, another manpower legislative enactment, was established to strengthen and supplement existing legislation in order to increase the opportunity for everyone to receive education and training for work and to live with dignity. This act included provisions that impacted vocational education including the establishment of the following:

- a Job Corps preparing young men and women between sixteen and twenty years of age for the responsibilities of citizenship and for employment through residential training centers. (This program is still in operation today under the WIA.)
- work-training programs providing young people between the ages of sixteen and twenty-one with useful work experiences in public and other types of state and local work-study programs
- work-study programs providing youth from low-income families enrolled in higher education part-time employment so they could continue their education
- work-experience programs providing opportunities for work and other types of training to individuals unable to support or care for themselves or their families

Nurse Training Act of 1964 (PL 88-581)

The Nurse Training Act included amendments to the Public Health Service Act and was designed to increase opportunities for training professional nursing personnel.

Elementary and Secondary Education Act (ESEA) of 1965 (PL 89-10)

The Elementary and Secondary Education Act was designed to provide sound educational opportunities to children and youth between the ages of five and seventeen with particular emphasis on the education of students from low-income families. This enactment was in response to the alarming degree of illiteracy that existed in urban and rural areas of the country. It was also deemed necessary to supplement the educational effort of states and local communities to improve the quality of elementary and secondary education nationwide. Title I of the ESEA strengthened local educational agencies and provided additional assistance to areas serving low-income and educationally deprived youngsters. Title II provided resources in the areas of school libraries, textbooks, and other instructional materials. Title III provided financial assistance to agencies developing exemplary programs and projects that could serve as models for regular school programs.

This idea of funding exemplary programs as models to be incorporated in regular school programs was incorporated into the Vocational Act of 1963, a practice that would appear again and again in subsequent federal vocational legislation. In the ESEA, Congress established a precedent of letting state and local school educational leaders make decisions regarding which programs to offer and discontinued their practice of mandating specific programs through federal legislation.

National Technical Institute for the Deaf Act of 1965 (PL 89-36)

The National Technical Institute for the Deaf Act provided for the establishment, construction, equipping, and operation of a residential school for postsecondary educational and technical training of the deaf.

Higher Education Act of 1965 (PL 89-329)

The Higher Education Act was a companion bill to the ESEA, with the same focus of assisting local agencies in solving local educational problems. Previous legislation, such as the NDEA, placed emphasis on national control of education, which led to placing less priority on solving local educational problems. This neglect at the local level contributed to the unrest, turmoil, and rioting that existed in many communities of the country. What was needed was a partnership between federal, state, and local educational agencies to address specific local problems.

The Higher Education Act provided assistance to colleges and universities in solving local problems. Among its important provisions were: (a) the establishment of community service and continuing education programs that would serve the needs of the community, (b) educational opportunity grants and subsidized low-interest, insured-loan payments to assist students without adequate financial support in enrolling and continuing their education, and (c) the establishment of the National Teacher Corps to ensure an adequate source of qualified teaching personnel.

Adult Education Act of 1966 (PL 89-750)

The Adult Education Act authorized grants to states to encourage the expansion of educational programs for adults, including the training of teachers of adults and demonstrations in adult education.

Elementary and Secondary Education Amendments (ESEA) of 1966 (PL 89-750)

The ESEA Amendments modified existing elementary and secondary programs and provided for state grants to initiate, expand, and improve programs and projects for the education of handicapped children at the preschool, elementary, and secondary school levels.

Education Professions Development Act (EPDA) of 1967 (PL 90-35)

The Education Professions Development Act was created when the Higher Education Act of 1965 was amended. It was intended to combine into one act all the elements of previous legislation regarding teacher education. This act was instrumental in providing a vital source of college and university vocational teacher educators. Title V included five personnel preparation programs covering the following areas: the National Teacher Corps; teachers in areas of critical shortage; fellowships for teachers and other educational professionals; improved opportunities for training for personnel serving in areas other than higher education; and training programs for higher education personnel and, after the passage of the Vocational Amendments of 1968, training for vocational education personnel.

Elementary and Secondary Education Amendments of 1967 (PL 90-247)

The ESEA amendments authorized support of regional centers for the education of handicapped children; model centers and services for deaf-blind children; recruitment of personnel and dissemination of information on the education of the handicapped; technical assistance for education in rural areas; support for dropout prevention programs; and support for bilingual education programs.

Vocational Education Amendments of 1968 (PL 90-576)

The Vocational Amendments of 1968 was a significant piece of legislation in that it virtually canceled all previous vocational legislation except the Smith-Hughes Act, which was retained because it was the first federal legislation for vocational education at the secondary level. Congress recognized the need to consolidate vocational legislation in order to eliminate duplication of effort and to improve administrative efficiency. This act was essentially a rewrite of the Vocational Act of 1963.

The overriding purpose of these amendments was to provide access to all citizens to appropriate training and retraining, which was nearly the same purpose as the Vocational Education Act of 1963. The major differences were that these amendments emphasized vocational education in postsecondary schools and broadened the definition of vocational education to bring it closer to general education. This act authorized the appropriation of millions of dollars for vocational education in an attempt to find solutions to the nation's social and economic problems.

Under the amendments, federal funds could be used for the following:

- high school and postsecondary students
- those who had completed or left high school
- those in the labor market in need of retraining
- those who had academic, socioeconomic, or other handicaps
- those who were mentally retarded, deaf, or otherwise handicapped
- construction of area vocational school facilities
- vocational guidance for all persons mentioned
- training in private schools under contract with public schools
- ancillary services (preparation of state plans, administration, evaluation of programs, teacher education, etc.)

Special provisions of the Vocational Amendments of 1968 included the following:

- It created a 21-member national advisory council with members to be appointed by the president. This council has been very influential in subsequent federal legislation.
- It created state and local advisory councils to be involved in state and local plan development and to give guidance to vocational education at the state and local school levels.
- It required more detailed state plans taking more control over local plans.
- It earmarked funds for new exemplary programs and projects, which were aimed at finding new ways to bridge the gap between school and work—a current focus of the School-to-Work Opportunities Act of 1994.
- It provided funds for state-based research.
- It provided funds for programs and projects designed to broaden or improve vocational education curricula.
- It provided funds for vocational education leadership and professional development for experienced vocational educators who wanted to engage in full-time study for a period not to exceed three years.
- It provided funds to support a teacher/industry worker exchange program to update the occupational competencies of vocational teachers.
- It earmarked funds for the support of cooperative vocational education programs to cover the additional cost that it takes to operate these program. Cooperative education programs have been an important part of the CTE delivery system for many years and are viewed as essential in today's diverse labor market.
- It provided funds for consumer and homemaking education.
- It provided funds to support work-study programs for vocational students in need.

Nurse Training Act of 1971 (PL 92-158)

The Nurse Training Act was an amendment to the Public Health Services Act. It provided funds for increasing and expanding provisions for nurse training facilities.

Education Amendments of 1972 (PL 92-318)

The passage of the omnibus bill, the Education Amendments of 1972, reflected the attempt by Congress to further consolidate previously enacted legislation. This act amended the Higher Education Act of 1965, the Elementary and Secondary Education Act of 1965, the Vocational Act of 1963, and several others. It extended portions of the Vocational Act of 1963 and its amendments of 1968 until fiscal year 1975 and made a number of adjustments to assist vocational education to better serve people in need of training and retraining for productive employment.

The Education Amendments of 1972 continued support of programs begun in the Vocational Act of 1963 including exemplary programs and projects, residential vocational schools, consumer homemaking education, cooperative vocational education, curriculum development, work-study programs, and the National Advisory Council of Vocational Education. The council continued monitoring the status of vocational education and issuing reports that identified issues to be addressed in new legislation. This act also introduced some new provisions important to vocational education, such as special programs for the disadvantaged and a new definition of vocational education that allowed federal funds to be spent for industrial arts programs and for training volunteer firefighters.

There were two other portions of this act that were significant for vocational education: Title III, which established the National Institute of Education (NIE), and Title X, which expanded community colleges and occupational education at the postsecondary level. The NIE was created to conduct educational research for the improvement of the quality of education for every American regardless of race, color, religion, gender, national origin, or social class. Title X provided funds for community colleges and the expansion of occupational education offerings at the postsecondary and adult levels. States were required to complete a comprehensive plan for the establishment and operation of occupational programs at the postsecondary level. To provide leadership to the expansion of postsecondary and adult occupational education, the Bureau of Occupational and Adult Education was established in the U.S. Office of Education.

Rehabilitation Act of 1973 (PL 93-112)

The Rehabilitation Act of 1973, sections 503 and 504, affirmed the rights of handicapped persons in the workplace. There were no funds provided in this act for its mandates, so this enactment is viewed more as a civil rights act, extending the Civil Rights Act of 1964. Section 503 required employers with federal contracts of more than $2500 to initiate affirmative action to hire handicapped individuals. Employers were to make reasonable accommodations for all interested handicapped persons.

Section 504 prohibited discrimination on the basis of handicap in any private or public program or activity receiving federal funds and was designed to provide opportunities for handicapped persons to enter mainstream life. Under this section, agencies receiving federal funds were required to (1) provide opportunities, benefits, aids, or services for handicapped persons equal to those provided for the non-handicapped, (2) provide aids, benefits, and services for the handicapped in the same setting as the non-handicapped except in cases where effectiveness would be compromised, (3) provide barrier-free environments to ensure facility and program accessibility, and (4) provide equal treatment and services in recruitment, training, promotion, and compensation for the handicapped.

Comprehensive Employment and Training Act (CETA) of 1973 (PL 93-203)

The Comprehensive Employment and Training Act was a consolidation of earlier manpower legislation that began in the early 1960s and marked the beginning of the federal government's involvement in establishing training programs for the unemployed and underemployed. The purpose of this new law was to decentralize and streamline manpower programs, to make them more administratively efficient, and to make them more responsive to local employment and manpower needs. This act nearly eliminated the practice of categorical manpower programs and introduced the concept of prime sponsors who, after careful planning, would receive block grants to operate training programs to meet local labor market needs. These prime sponsors often turned to established vocational education programs to provide training for their constituents.

Education Amendments of 1974 (PL 93-380)

The Education Amendments of 1974 were primarily adjustments made to the Elementary and Secondary Education Act of 1965. The amendments, however, included some important provisions that impacted vocational education. One of these provisions was encouragement in the development of a written Individualized Education Plan (IEP) for each child participating in Title I of the 1965 Act, who were children with special needs. This provision encouraged the involvement of parents and guardians, as well as vocational teachers, in the development of the IEP for handicapped students enrolled in vocational classes.

One of the provisions of the 1974 Amendments, Title IV, was the Women's Educational Equality Act of 1974. Congress found that educational programs in the U.S. were inequitable as they related to women and frequently limited full participation of all citizens. This act provided the financial incentive for states to develop the programs specified in the act to help achieve educational equity for women.

Another provision of Title IV of the 1974 Amendments was support for career education. Sidney Marland Jr., U.S. Commissioner of Education, introduced the concept of career education to express a major reform needed in secondary education and promoted this concept through the funds he had available in his discretionary grants. In a short period of time, this concept became a major education movement in the country and attracted the attention of the educational world and Congress. The concept of career education was viewed not as another program, but as a continuum that began in early childhood and extended into old age and it was felt that its mission was primarily job- or work-related. Vocational educators were quick to recognize the potential of career education in the early years by helping youngsters select occupations and eventually vocational programs that would prepare them for their chosen careers. Congress added its sanction of career education by establishing an office of career education to carry out provisions relating to the definition and to assist in the implementation of career education programs in the nation's schools. Career education was defined in the 1974 Amendments as an educational process designed to do the following:

- increase interaction between schools and society
- provide opportunities for counseling, guidance, and career development for all children
- relate the subject matter of the curricula of schools to the societal needs of persons
- extend the concept of the educational process beyond the school into the area of employment and the community
- foster flexibility in attitudes, skills, and knowledge in order to enable persons to cope with accelerating change and obsolescence
- make education more relevant to employment and to the need to function in society
- eliminate any distinction between education for vocational purposes and general or academic education

The career education movement was actually receiving federal support before the 1974 Amendments through exemplary programs and projects of previous legislation. Congress had simply recognized its importance and provided separate funding for expansion of the movement. With federal support, career education was the "hot topic" of the 1970s but had all but disappeared by 1981. The need to provide students with awareness and orientation for careers had not diminished, however, and was an important part of the School-to-Work movement of the 1990s.

The Amendments established a National Center for Educational Statistics (NCES) in the Office of the Assistant Secretary for Education and charged it with the responsibility for the collection and diffusion of educational statistics. Also, the 1974 Amendments made provision to conduct research into the problems of providing bilingual vocational education. Congress discovered that many youth and adults could not profit completely from vocational education programs because of their limited ability to deal with the English language. These persons were then unable to fill the need for more and better-trained personnel in critical occupational areas.

Emergency Jobs and Employment Assistance Act of 1974 (PL 94-505)

The Emergency Jobs and Employment Assistance Act of 1974 was passed to maximize efforts to produce jobs and job training for individuals who served in the armed services and to inform all veterans about employment, job training, on-the-job training, and educational opportunities under the Comprehensive Employment and Training Act of 1973.

Education for All Handicapped Children Act of 1975 (PL 94-142)

The Education for All Handicapped Children Act of 1975 marked the beginning of a national effort to provide free and appropriate education for all handicapped children ages 3–21. In this act, Congress was affirming the belief that if adequate funds were provided to state and local agencies, they could provide the services required to meet the needs of handicapped children. This act specified a number of assurances or protective measures for handicapped learners and their parents in making public education free and appropriate for all youngsters. These assurances included the following:

- a complete due process procedure
- the development and maintenance of written IEP for each handicapped student
- placement of handicapped students in the least restrictive environment and whenever possible, placement with non-handicapped students (which marked the beginning of the mainstreaming concept)
- assessment of handicapped students for placement purposes through bias-free testing and evaluation procedures
- development and implementation of policies and procedures to protect the confidentiality of student records

This act replaced Title IV of the Elementary and Secondary Education Act. It provided grant programs to states to help educate disabled students and added new programs and funding areas including research, early intervention, and personnel training. These state grants were to assist in providing special education services to all disabled individuals from ages 3–21. Grants were also awarded to public agencies and nonprofit organizations for preschool and early intervention demonstration programs. These programs were meant to (a) facilitate the intellectual, emotional, physical, mental, social, speech, and language development of disabled children; (b) encourage parent or guardian participation; (c) inform the community about disabled preschool children; and (d) offer training about model programs to state and local personnel who provided services for disabled children to age eight (*Education of the Handicapped*, 1991).

This act also did the following:

- It defined handicapped individuals to include mentally retarded, hard of hearing, deaf, speech-impaired, visually impaired, seriously emotionally disturbed, orthopedically impaired, and other health impaired or learning disabled.

- It defined special education as "specially designed instruction provided in classrooms, in physical education, at home and in hospitals."
- It defined related services as "transportation and other support services, including speech pathology, psychological services, physical and occupational therapy, recreation and medical services needed for a disabled child to benefit from special education."
- It defined an individual education program (IEP) as "a written statement drawn up by the teacher, parent, and a school representative that must include the child's present educational level; annual goals, including short-term instructional objectives; the specific educational services to be provided and the extent to which the child will participate in regular education programs; initiation date and length of services; and evaluation procedures."
- It authorized the establishment of six regional resource centers that were to provide technical and training assistance to state agencies and the establishment of one federal technical assistance center to deal with national priorities.
- It authorized grants to states and agencies to assist in providing special education, vocational, and transition services to deaf-blind individuals.
- It authorized grants to public and nonprofit agencies for research, development of new techniques, personnel training, and information dissemination to better meet the needs of severely disabled children.
- It provided grants to agencies to assist the transition of disabled youth to postsecondary education, vocational training, employment, and continuing education. These grants were aimed at improving secondary special education programs and the vocational skills of disabled students.
- It authorized grants to assist universities and nonprofit agencies in training personnel for careers in special education. These grants could be used to provide training as well as for fellowships for trainees. In addition, grants could be obtained to conduct special projects and develop new approaches for preservice and in-service training of personnel who served disabled children.
- It authorized grants to agencies for improving special education and related services through the development of teaching techniques, effective curricula, technologies, model programs, and instruments for measuring progress.
- It established a service to loan films and other educational media to deaf students and helped establish the National Theater of the Deaf, Inc. to provide experiences for deaf individuals.
- It authorized grants, contracts, and cooperative agreements for local and state agencies and universities to advance the use of instructional technology and mediated materials to teach disabled children.
- It authorized grants to states for establishing interagency systems to provide early intervention services to all disabled children from birth to age three (*Education of the Handicapped*, 1991).

Education Amendments of 1976 (PL 94-482)

The Education Amendments of 1976 were a continuation on the part of Congress to write omnibus and comprehensive legislation that extended and revised existing legislation. These amendments came out of a desire of Congress to redirect American education in an attempt to correct some of the nation's problems and change the prevailing attitudes regarding the roles of men and women in society. One of its major thrusts was to extend and further revise the Vocational Act of 1963 to meet the following purposes: (a) to extend, improve, and maintain existing programs of vocational education; (b) to develop new programs of vocational education; (c) to overcome gender discrimination and gender stereotyping; and (d) to provide part-time employment to youths who need earnings to continue their vocational training on a full-time basis.

There were a number of new directions for vocational education specified in the Education Amendments of 1976, which included the following:

- It required the development of programs to eliminate gender discrimination and gender stereotyping.
- It required the development of a five-year state plan that involved all agencies dealing in vocational education and its development.
- It required an annual program plan and accountability report for each fiscal year.
- It required each state to name a state board or agency to be the state agency responsible for administration of all public vocational programs within the state.
- It established programs for the handicapped, for disadvantaged individuals, for persons of limited English proficiency, for persons who had completed or left high school and were enrolled in organized programs of study for which credit was given toward an associate or other degree not leading to a baccalaureate or higher degree, and for persons who had already entered the labor market or who were employed. Ten percent of the funds from the act were to be spent for programs for the handicapped.
- It continued funding for exemplary and innovative programs, particularly those in urban centers with high concentrations of economically disadvantaged individuals, unskilled workers, and unemployed workers; those that provided training for persons in sparsely populated rural areas; those that provided training to limited English-proficiency persons; those designed to awaken occupational aspirations of youth with academic, socioeconomic, or other handicaps; and those that focused on discovering new ways to bridge the gap between school and work—a current concern of vocational education.
- It encouraged improvement in vocational guidance and counseling programs.
- It continued support of consumer and homemaking education and placed special emphasis on the changing roles of men and women as workers and homemakers.
- It required the development of a national vocational education date reporting and accounting system.

- It extended federal assistance for programs of career education and for the National Institute of Education.
- It required states to develop an evaluation system to determine effectiveness of all vocational programs in the state.
- It established the National Occupational Information Coordinating Committee (NOICC) and a system of State Occupational Information Coordinating Committees (SOICCs) to improve communication among vocational and manpower administrators and to develop and implement an occupational information system to meet the common occupational information needs of vocational education and manpower training programs at the national, state, and local levels.
- It changed the professional development focus for vocational education personnel to provide opportunities for experienced vocational educators to enter into full time advanced study of vocational education; for certified teachers of other subjects to become vocational teachers if they had work experience in a vocational field; and for persons from industry with experience in a vocational field to become vocational teachers in areas needing additional instructors.
- It continued the emphasis on improving bilingual vocational education through training programs for teachers and programs for students who had limited ability in English.
- It provided emergency assistance for remodeling vocational facilities in order to comply with the Architectural Barriers Act of 1968 and make educational facilities accessible to handicapped persons.

Youth Employment and Demonstration Projects Act of 1977 (PL 95-93)

The Youth Employment and Demonstration Projects Act established youth employment training programs that promoted education-to-work transition; literacy and bilingual training; attainment of certificates of high school equivalency; job sampling including vocational exploration in the public school sector; and institutional and on-the-job training including development of basic skills and job skills.

Career Education Incentive Act of 1978 (PL 95-207)

The Career Education Incentive Act authorized the establishment of career education programs for elementary and secondary schools. A unique feature of the act was the stipulation that state departments of education disburse 85% of the federal funds provided them to local education agencies, thereby starting the trend of subsequent federal legislative acts placing greater responsibility at the state and local level for federal programs supporting vocational education. An experienced state coordinator of career education had to be employed and given the responsibility of assisting in developing a state plan for career education, monitoring the progress of career education at the local level, and compiling a report on the progress local schools were making in implementing career education a the k-12 level. In addition, a school district coordinator of career education who did not reside at the school building had to be employed to develop proposals to the state for career education grants and to provide leadership and accountability for career education.

Comprehensive Employment and Training Act (CETA) Amendments of 1978 (PL 95-524)

The 1978 Amendments to CETA represented a major revision of previous manpower legislation to connect manpower training programs with other related programs involved in preparing people for work. Greater emphasis was to be placed upon utilization of existing services and facilities for manpower training if appropriate. Such services would include state employment services and state and local vocational schools as well as the services of the state vocational rehabilitation agencies. Greater emphasis was also to be placed on the utilization of public vocational education facilities.

This act provided funds for the following programs: (1) comprehensive employment and training services, (2) youth programs, (3) National Commission on Employment Policy, (4) a counter-cyclical public service employment program, (5) private sector opportunities for the economically disadvantaged, and (6) a young adult conservation corps.

A significant provision of this act to vocational education was that vocational boards and prime sponsors were required to consult with other agencies, such as vocational rehabilitation, the Bureau of Education for the Handicapped, and state employment services, in formulating the five-year plan for vocational education and training. This requirement resulted in prime sponsors identifying the services to be provided to handicapped individuals in their five-year and annual training plans.

Educational Amendments of 1978 (PL 95-561)

The Educational Amendments established a comprehensive basic skills program aimed at improving student achievement in reading, mathematics, and written and oral communication. This act also established the community schools concept, which encouraged the use of public buildings, including schools, to function as community centers for the education of adults.

Department of Education Organization Act of 1979 (PL 96-88)

This act established a Department of Education with responsibilities formerly assigned to the Education Division of the Department of Health, Education, and Welfare.

Job Training Partnership Act of 1982 (PL 97-300)

The Job Training Partnership Act (JTPA) of 1982 was an extension and major revision of the Comprehensive Employment and Training Act as amended in 1978, marking a new era in which vocational education and the private sector could collaborate in providing job training and related services. The intent of Congress in this act was to increase the role of private business and industry in the training and employment of unskilled adults and disadvantaged youth and adults. For the first time in manpower training legislation, the JTPA gave states and localities substantial choice in the direction of their employment and training policies. Under this act, a working partnership was formed between the public and private sectors with federal funds flowing down to states and on to local or regional service areas, each of which had to utilize a private industry council (PIC) to determine what training programs were needed and how these programs would be implemented. The PICS were to be widely representative of individuals knowledgeable about training needs and training programs in the service areas and consist of the following partners: (a) business and industry leaders and officials, and (2) representative from organized labor, rehabilitation, employment services, economic development, and education. The PICs had the responsibility for determining the training agencies most suited to conducting training and for establishing programs to prepare eligible youth and adults for entry into the labor force.

The JTPA was a training enactment with no funds to support employment subsistence programs. Seventy percent of the funds were to be spent on training with 30% to be divided between administrative cost and support services. The training programs were targeted for unskilled youth and adults who were economically disadvantaged or had serious problems gaining employment. This act included special provisions for summer youth employment and training programs, dislocated and older workers, Native Americans, migrants and seasonable farm workers, and veterans. The act also renewed authorization of the successful Job Corps program—a program directed toward improving the employability prospects of economically disadvantaged youth through residential training centers.

According to Griffin (1983), the JTPA provided benefits to vocational education in the form of the following:

- additional funds to reach out and serve more disadvantaged individuals and groups
- additional services to those disadvantaged individuals currently in the programs including such services as job search assistance, job counseling, remedial education and basic skills training, on-the-job training, vocational exploration, literacy and bilingual training, and follow-up services
- new programs offered by vocational educators and by professionals not formerly part of the school system
- more active interest from the private sector in vocational education
- more local planning for vocational education that stimulated more local involvement of the community in vocational education

Education Handicapped Act Amendments of 1983 (PL 98-199)

The Education Handicapped Act Amendments of 1983 included an important section entitled "Secondary Education and Transitional Services for Handicapped

Youth," which was designed to support and coordinate educational and service programs to assist handicapped youth in the transition from secondary to post-secondary education, employment, or adult services. The act provided incentives to expand preschool special education programs and early intervention programs. Responsibility for administering and monitoring all Education of the Handicapped Act programs was transferred to the Office of Special Education Programs (OSEP).

The act also provided funds to support the development of demonstration projects for postsecondary educational programs for handicapped persons and the development of cooperative models for planning and development.

Rehabilitation Act Amendments of 1984 (PL 98-221)

The Rehabilitation Act Amendments changed the Rehabilitation Act of 1973 by authorizing demonstration projects to address the problems encountered by youth with disabilities in making the transition from school-to-work.

Carl D. Perkins Vocational Education Act of 1984 (PL 98-524)

The Carl D. Perkins Vocational Education Act, known as the Perkins Act, continued the affirmation of Congress that effective vocational education programs are essential to the nation's future as a free and democratic society. The act had two interrelated goals: one economic and one social. The economic goal was to improve the skills of the labor force and prepare adults for job opportunities—a longstanding goal traceable to the Smith-Hughes Act. The social goal was to provide equal opportunities for adults in vocational education. These two goals are reflected in the nine stated purposes of the act, which are as follows:

1. Assist the states to expand, improve, modernize, and develop quality vocational education programs in order to meet the marketable skill needs of the nation's existing and future workforce, improve productivity, and promote economic growth.
2. Ensure that individuals who are inadequately served under vocational education programs have access to quality vocational education programs, especially those who are disadvantaged, handicapped, entering nontraditional occupations, in need of training and retraining, individuals single parents or homemakers, limited in English proficiency, and incarcerated in correctional institutions.
3. Promote greater cooperation between public agencies and the private sector in preparing individuals for employment, in promoting the quality of vocational education in the states, and in making the system more responsive to the labor market in the states.
4. Improve the academic foundation of vocational students and aid in the application of newer technologies (including the use of computers) in terms of employment or occupational goals.

5. Provide vocational education services to train, retrain, and upgrade employed and unemployed workers with the new skills demanded in that state or in the employment market.
6. Assist the most economically depressed areas of a state to raise employment and occupational competencies of its citizens.
7. Assist the states to utilize a full range of supportive services, special programs, and guidance and placement to achieve the basic purpose of this act.
8. Improve the effectiveness of consumer and homemaking education and reduce the limiting effects of sex-role stereotyping on occupations, job skills, levels of competency, and careers.
9. Authorize national programs designed to meet designated vocational education needs and strengthen the vocational education research process.

Under the Perkins Act, each state was required to provide educational services and activities designed to meet the special needs of, and to enhance the participation of (a) handicapped individuals, (b) disadvantaged individuals, (c) adults who were in need of training and retraining, (d) individuals who were single parents or homemakers, (e) individuals who participated in programs designed to eliminate sex bias and stereotyping in vocational education, and (f) criminal offenders who were serving in a correctional institution.

Title II, Part B of the Perkins Act—Vocational Education Program Improvement, Innovation, and Expansion—identified 24 different areas where states could use funds to meet the needs identified in their state plans. This list is too exhaustive to present here, but an example area is the improvement of vocational education programs within the state designed to improve the quality of vocational education, including high-technology programs involving an industry-education partnership, apprenticeship training programs, and the provision of technical assistance.

Of particular interest is the Criteria For Services and Activities for the Handicapped and for the Disadvantaged, spelled out in Title II, Part A, Section 204, State boards providing vocational services and activities for handicapped and disadvantaged individuals had to provide the following assurances:

1. Equal access will be provided to handicapped and disadvantaged individuals in recruitment, enrollment, and placement activities.
2. Equal access will be provided to handicapped and disadvantaged individuals to the full range of vocational programs available, including occupationally specific courses of study, cooperative education, and apprenticeship programs.
3. Vocational education programs and activities for handicapped individuals will be provided in the least restrictive environment, and will, whenever appropriate, be included as a component of the IEP cooperatively developed between vocational education and special education personnel.
4. Information will be provided to handicapped and disadvantaged students and parents of such students concerning the opportunities available in vocational

education at least one year before the students enter the grade level in which vocational education programs are first generally available in the state, but no later than the beginning of the ninth grade, together with the requirements for eligibility for enrollment in such vocational education programs.

5. Each student who is enrolled in vocational programs shall receive (a) assessment of their interests, abilities, and special needs with respect to successfully completing the vocational program, (b) special services, including adaptation of curriculum, instruction, equipment, and facilities, designed to meet student needs, (c) guidance, counseling, and career development activities conducted by professionally trained counselors, and (d) counseling services designed to facilitate the transition from school to post-school employment and career opportunities (The Carl D. Perkins Vocational Education Act of 1984).

Significant changes in this act from previous vocational education legislation included the following:

- It provided for the formation of 13-member state councils on vocational education consisting of seven members from the private sector; five representatives of business, industry and agriculture; two representatives of labor organizations; and representatives from secondary and postsecondary vocational institutions. The chairperson had to come from the private sector. State councils had more responsibilities than the old advisory committees including the responsibility of developing a report every two years on the effectiveness of the vocational education delivery system funded under the Perkins Act and the JTPA.
- It provided for the formation of state technical committees from the private sector to advise the state boards and councils on the development of model curricula to address state labor market needs.
- It created provisions that allowed states to use funds to strengthen the academic foundations of vocational education through courses or special strategies designed to teach the fundamental principles of mathematics and science through practical applications.
- It specified certain services to be provided for handicapped and disadvantaged individuals including: (a) information about local vocational education opportunities; (b) assessment of student interests, abilities, and special needs; (c) guidance, counseling, and career development activities; (d) counseling services to facilitate the transition from school to employment; and (e) other special services, such as adaptation of curriculum, instruction, equipment, and facilities.
- It provided for the creation of a full-time state sex equity coordinator to assist in eliminating sex bias and stereotyping in vocational education and to administer the funds for single parent and homemaker programs and sex equity activities.
- It eliminated the requirement that states prepare a separate accountability report. Instead, each state was required to produce an annual progress report

based on stated objectives and use this report as a tool in planning and improving programs. Thus the focus of state reports to the federal government had switched from "financial accountability" to "program outcomes."

- It required the development of state plans covering a two-year period instead of the annual plan and five-year plan required in previous legislation.
- It created the National Council on Vocational Education, consisting of 17 members appointed by the president, nine of whom were representatives of the private sector.
- It required the coordination of the Perkins Act with the Job Training Partnership Act (JTPA) in order to provide programs of assistance for dislocated workers funded under title III of the JTPA.
- It developed measures for the effectiveness of programs under the Perkins Act, including such evaluative measures as the following: the occupations to be trained for—again reflecting an assessment of the labor market needs of the state; the levels of skills to be achieved in particular occupations—reflecting the hiring needs of employers; and the basic employment competencies to be used in performance outcomes—reflecting the hiring needs of employers.
- It specified a national assessment of vocational education to be conducted by the National Institute of Education, with the results reported to Congress in the form of interim reports in January and July of 1988 and the final report submitted by January 1, 1989.

The Carl D. Perkins Act reflected the philosophy of Congress that vocational education programs are best administered by local communities who are in the best position to make educational decisions and that nongovernmental alternatives promoting linkages between public school needs and private sector sources of support should be encouraged and implemented to strengthen vocational education and training programs.

Handicapped Children's Protection Act of 1986 (PL 99-372)

The Handicapped Children's Protection Act provided for monetary support for parents and guardians who found themselves in administrative hearings or in court with a school system over a dispute concerning their child's right to a free appropriate special education and related services.

Education Handicapped Act Amendments of 1986 (PL 99-457)

The Education Handicapped Act Amendments of 1986 continued and expanded discretionary programs and transition programs. This act also changed the age of eligibility for special education and services for all children to age three and established the Handicapped Infant and Toddler Program designed to meet the needs of children from birth to their third birthday who needed early intervention services.

Rehabilitation Act Amendments of 1986 (PL 99-506)

The Rehabilitation Act Amendments authorized funding for programs in supported employment services for individuals with disabilities.

Technology-Related Assistance for Individuals with Disabilities Act of 1988 (PL 100-407)

The Technology-Related Assistance Act provided assistance to states in developing needed programs of technology-related assistance to individuals with disabilities and their families. Technology-related assistance was broadly defined in the act as giving states flexibility in providing technology services to meet the unique needs of disabled consumers and their families.

Children with Disabilities Temporary Care Reauthorization Act of 1989 (PL 101-127)

This act authorized funds to provide temporary child care (respite care) for children who had a disability or chronic illness and crisis nurseries for children at risk of abuse or neglect.

Americans with Disabilities Act (ADA) of 1990 (PL 101-336)

The Americans with Disabilities Act furthered the provisions that began in the Rehabilitation Act of 1973, banning discrimination based on disability and guaranteeing equal opportunities for individuals with disabilities in employment, public accommodation, transportation, state and local government services, and telecommunications. This act was the most comprehensive enactment ever written to identify and protect the civil rights of Americans with disabilities.

The act applied to public and private organizations, regardless of whether they received federal funds, and covered the three areas of services, physical accessibility, and employment. Employers who had 15 or more employees could not discriminate in hiring and promoting workers with disabilities, and they were required to make reasonable accommodations to enable disabled persons to work for their companies. Public accommodations and transportation were required to be accessible to people with disabilities. This mandate required public and private transportation carriers, and a myriad of public and private entities such as hotels, restaurants, bars, theaters, libraries, parks, and schools to make reasonable accommodations, remove architectural barriers, and provide auxiliary assistance so that individuals with disabilities could use public accommodations and transportation services.

The essential elements of the ADA in the areas of services, physical accessibility, and employment were as follows:

- The ADA affected services including integration, program accessibility, safety, communication, and the provision of aids, services, and preparation of self-evaluations.

- The ADA affected physical accessibility including accessibility audits, removal of barriers both inside and outside a facility, alterations of new construction, and preparation of transition plans.
- The ADA affected employment including areas of posting of job notices, setting of job qualifications, interviewing, testing of applicants, hiring, the provision of reasonable accommodations and training and other areas of employment.

This act required public and private schools to (a) make any program, service, or activity readily accessible to and usable by students with disabilities, (b) provide information so students with disabilities can act on information about a program, service, or activity, (c) ensure that when evaluating disabled students, screening and testing procedures are fair, accurate, and nondiscriminatory, and (d) provide an opportunity for disabled students to participate in any activity, service, or program school offered (Morrissey, 1993).

Carl D. Perkins Vocational and Applied Technology Education Act of 1990 (PL 101-392)

The Carl D. Perkins Vocational and Applied Technology Education Act amended and extended the Carl D. Perkins Vocational Act of 1984, authorizing the largest amount of funds ever for vocational education. The act was designed to assist states and local schools in teaching the skills and competencies necessary for students to acquire work in a technologically advanced society. A major goal of this enactment was to provide greater vocational opportunities to disadvantaged persons. Basic state grants were exclusively devoted to special populations. These grants were specifically earmarked for programs addressing the vocational needs of poor and handicapped students and those with limited English proficiency.

In addition to basic grants primarily devoted to improving programs for special populations, the act included 11 other categories as follows:

1. Tech Prep—the Perkins Act of 1990 authorized funds for Tech Prep programs, which were cooperative arrangements that combine two years of technology-oriented preparatory education in high school with two years of advanced technology studies at a community college or technical institute. Tech Prep programs were designed to integrate academic and vocational education, which was a priority of this new act.
2. Supplementary grants for facilities and equipment—states and local districts with the highest concentration of disadvantaged students could obtain funds to improve vocational education facilities and equipment under this provision.
3. Consumer/homemaking education—Congress continued its emphasis on preparing people to live effectively in the family by providing funds for states to develop or improve instruction in nutrition, health, clothing, consumer education, family living and parenthood, child development, housing, and homemaking.

4. Career guidance and counseling—the act, like other legislation of this period, placed emphasis on helping students make the transition from school to employment. The act provided for career development programs that helped people make the transition from school-to-work, maintain current job skills, develop skills needed to move into high-tech careers, develop job search skills, and learn about other job training programs such as the JTPA.
5. Community-based organizations—the act provided funding for local non-profit and other community groups to carry on vocational education programs and services to disadvantaged people.
6. Bilingual vocational education—the act authorized funds for programs specifically designed to provide bilingual vocational education and English language instruction for those persons with limited English language proficiency.
7. Business/labor education partnerships—the act provided funds for support of business/labor/education partnerships that could improve the quality of vocational education and assist in upgrading minimal standards in key occupational areas.
8. Community education and lighthouse schools—the act authorized funds to establish and evaluate model high school community education employment centers in urban and rural areas that serve disadvantaged persons and lighthouse schools or model vocational institutions that provide information and technical assistance to the field of vocational education about curriculum; develop linkages with other providers of vocational education and training; and disseminate model approaches to meeting training needs of special populations and for eliminating sex bias.
9. State councils on vocational education—this act extended support for state councils on vocational education established in the original Perkins Act because of the key role these councils play in advising state agencies that establish vocational education policy.
10. Tribally controlled postsecondary institutions—the act authorized funds to assist in the operation and improvement of tribally controlled postsecondary vocational institutions.
11. National Council of Vocational Education—the act provided temporary support for the activities of the National Council on Vocational Education created in earlier legislation until September 30, 1992 when the Council was disbanded (Wilcox, 1991).

The Carl D. Perkins Vocational and Applied Technology Act placed strong emphasis on improving vocational programs for the disadvantaged, integration of academic and vocational education, Tech Prep, accountability, and increased flexibility of state and local educational agencies. The act required each state to create a set of core standards and performance measures to form a benchmark for Perkins-mandated evaluations. Each state had to conduct an initial assessment of its programs, submit a three-year state plan detailing how it planned to administer Perkins funds, and make regular statewide assessments of vocational education programs as part of the accountability process.

The act eliminated set-asides (targeted funds) for support services for special populations in an effort to allow flexibility for state and local agencies to design and deliver services that better met the needs of special populations. The act continued all the assurances of due process, equal access, least restrictive environment, supplementary services, etc., of previous legislation and added a new provision requiring local educational agencies to provide appropriate information about vocational programs to special populations prior to entry into eighth grade (West & Meers, 1992).

Education of the Handicapped Amendments of 1990 (PL 101-476)

This act, which began in 1975 as The Education of All Handicapped Children Act, was revised in 1983 and 1986 as Education Handicapped Act Amendments and amended again in 1990 when its name was changed to the Individuals with Disabilities Education Act (IDEA). This act, as amended, was the most important piece of legislation passed by Congress for educating disabled children and youth. The IDEA enactment expanded many of the discretionary programs authorized by previous legislation and created a number of new ones. Provisions of the IDEA included the following:

- It required schools to provide assistive devices (any item or piece of equipment or product system that is used to increase, maintain, or improve the functional capabilities of children with disabilities) to students who fall under the 11 categories of disabilities specified in the IDEA.
- It established special programs on transition.
- It established a new program to improve services for children and youth with serious emotional disturbances.
- It established a research and dissemination program on attention deficit disorders.
- It expanded the list of nine conditions that children may have in order to be eligible for special education and related services to 11, adding the conditions of autism and traumatic brain injury.
- It required that transition services and assistive technology services be made available for disabled children and youth and specified in their IEPs.
- It expanded the definition of related services to include rehabilitation counseling and social work services.
- It expanded the definition of special education to include instruction in all settings, including workplace and training sites.
- It placed emphasis on meeting the needs of traditionally neglected populations to include minority, poor, and limited English proficient individuals with disabilities.
- It provided a new structure to develop IEPs and ITPs based on multidisciplinary assessments and added new assurances for each disabled student in the IEP and ITP planning process.

Developmental Disabilities Assistance and Bill of Rights Act of 1990 (PL 101-496)

The Developmental Disabilities Assistance and Bill of Rights Act authorized grants to support the planning, coordination, and delivery of specialized services to persons with developmental disabilities. The act also provided funds for the operation of state protection and advocacy systems for persons with disabilities.

Job Training Reform Amendments of 1992 (PL 102-367)

The Job Training Reform Amendments revised the JTPA of 1982, changing the focus of JTPA programs toward improving services to those facing serious barriers to employment; enhancing the quality of services provided; improving the accountability of funds and the programs they support; linking services provided to real labor market needs; and facilitating the development of a comprehensive and coherent system of human resources service. Many of the revisions were administrative in nature, but there were some provisions of importance to vocational educators:

- New requirements for on-the-job training (OJT) included (a) development of an OJT contract to specify the type and duration of training to be developed and other services to be provided in order to ensure that proposed costs are reasonable, (b) OJT was to be conducted in the highest skill occupations appropriate for the eligible participant and should not be viewed as subsidized employment for low-skill occupations that need very little training time, and (c) the length of OJT training time supported with JTPA funds was limited to six months.
- Eligible participants were to undergo an objective assessment that was to be a client-centered, diagnostic approach to evaluation of the needs of the participant without regard to services or training programs already available in the service delivery area (SDA). This assessment was to be a multifaceted ongoing process, making use of the full array of options including such items as structured group interviews, paper and pencil tests, performance tests, behavioral observations, interest inventories, career guidance instruments, aptitude tests, and basic skill tests.
- An individual service strategy (ISS) or an employability development plan was to be developed for each JTPA participant based on an objective assessment. The ISS was to include the appropriate mix and sequence of services with justification for each, indicate any need for supportive services, and develop the individual continuum of services to lead to an employment goal.
- Performance standards were to be developed for older worker programs, adult and youth programs, and dislocated workers. These standards may include standards for employment competencies, which were to be based on such factors as entry-level skills and other hiring requirements.
- The Nontraditional Employment for Women (NEW) Act is part of the Amendments of 1992 and had the purpose of providing a wider range of training opportunities for women under existing JTPA programs; providing

incentive for the establishment of programs that train, place, and retain women in non-traditional fields; and facilitating coordination of JTPA and vocational education resources available for training and placing women in nontraditional employment. Non-traditional employment is defined as occupations or fields or work where women comprise less than 25% of the individuals employed in such occupations or fields of work.

- A new year-round youth program was established consisting of various activities that could be used to address the needs of in-school and out-of-school youth, with priority given to youth currently out of any formalized school system, including dropouts.

- The amendments emphasized targeting services to the hard to serve, and they recognized the need to provide appropriate supportive services to allow participants to stay in a JTPA program longer. Therefore, the amendments provided for several types of payments, all of which had to be charged to the training-related and supportive services category.

- The amendments included new guidelines for the make-up and duties of the private industry councils (PICs). The act required that no less than 15% of the PIC membership be from organized labor organizations and community-based organizations.

- The amendments required that SDAs operating adult programs and year-round youth programs establish appropriate linkages with other federal human resource programs and other agencies providing service to JTPA populations to avoid duplication and to enhance delivery of services.

- The Youth Fair Chance program was established to provide comprehensive services to youth living in high poverty areas in urban and rural communities. The purpose of this program was to provide all youth living in designated target areas with improved access to the types of services and support necessary to help them acquire the skills and knowledge they needed to succeed. Services include employment, training, education, child care, transportation, and social services.

Technology-Related Assistance for Individuals with Disabilities Act Amendments of 1994 (PL 103-218)

The Technology-Related Assistance for Individuals with Disabilities Act Amendments of 1994, known as the Technology-Related Assistance Act or Tech Act, amended the Technology-Related Assistance for Individuals with Disabilities Act of 1988. The purposes of the Tech Act amendments included (a) to provide discretionary grants to states to assist them in developing and implementing a "consumer-responsive, comprehensive, statewide program of technology-related assistance for individuals with disabilities of all ages, (b) to fund programs of national significance related to assistive technology, and (c) to establish and expand alternative financing mechanisms to allow individuals with disabilities to purchase assistive technology devices and services." In passing this act, Congress acknowledged the powerful role that assistive technology can play in maximizing the independence of individuals with disabilities. When fully implemented, this act has the potential to open many new opportunities for individuals with disabilities. When fully implemented, this act has the potential to open many new opportunities for individuals with disabilities and their families to receive needed assistive technology services (Learning Disabilities Research and Training Center, 1994).

Goals 2000: Educate America Act of 1994 (PL 103-227)

The Goals 2000: Educate America Act was a blueprint for improving the nation's schools through establishing national goals and standards and assisting state and local agencies in helping every child meet these standards. The act emphasized high standards for all students, support for comprehensive efforts at all levels, the development of a framework for a Goals 2000 plan, and the development of a process for building a broad partnership (U.S. Department of Education, 1994).

Goals 2000 identified eight national education goals; authorized funds for the improvement of schools k-12; established a framework to encourage state and local education agencies to develop comprehensive plans for integration and implementation of federal education programs; and provided for the development of national education performance standards and content standards, which states were encouraged to adopt. The act did the following:

- It established eight national education goals.
- It created the National Education Goals panel to build public support for the goals, report on the nation's progress toward meeting the goals, and review standards submitted to the National Education Standards and Improvement Council.
- It created the National Education Standards and Improvement Council to oversee achievement standards in mathematics, science, and other academic subjects and certify voluntary national standards; state standards for content, student performance, and opportunities to learn; and student assessment systems.
- It established the State and Local Education Systemic Improvement Program.
- It created a National Skills Standards Board to stimulate the development of a voluntary national system of occupational standards and certification. The board identifies clusters of major occupations in the U.S. and encourages development of skill standards in each cluster. Voluntary standards submitted to the board that meet established criteria will be certified (U.S. Department of Education, 1994).

The focus of Goals 2000 was on improving student learning by establishing goals for students and schools and encouraging states and local school systems to adopt high standards and form partnerships to improve the educational delivery system. The act contained a suggested framework identifying ten elements that should be included in a Goals 2000 plan:

1. Teaching and learning, standards, and assessments
2. Opportunity-to-learn standards or strategies and program improvement and accountability.
3. Technology

4. Governance, accountability, and management of schools
5. Parent and community support and involvement
6. System-wide improvements
7. Promotion of grassroots efforts
8. Dropout strategies
9. Creation of a coordinated education and training system
10. Milestones and time lines (U.S. Department of Education, 1994).

School-to-Work Opportunities Act (STWOA) of 1994 (PL 103-239)

The School-to-Work Opportunities Act was passed to address the national skills shortage by providing a framework to build a highly skilled workforce through partnerships between educators and employers. The STWOA emphasized preparing students with the knowledge, skills, abilities, and information about occupations and the labor market that would help them make the transition from school to post-school employment. This would be done through school-based and work-based instructional components supported by a connecting activities component. Key elements of the STWOA included (a) collaborative partnerships, (b) integrated curriculum, (c) technological advances, (d) adaptable workers, (e) comprehensive career guidance, (f) work-based learning, and (g) a step-by-step approach. This act promised to play a key role in the educational reform of our nation's secondary schools and in expanding postsecondary programs and services to include a wider audience. It was hoped that the school-to-work transition programs would redirect the focus of high schools toward integrating academic and vocational course work, teaching all aspects of an industry, integrating school-based and work-based learning, and establishing functioning partnerships among elementary, middle, secondary, and postsecondary schools (Brustein & Mahler, 1994).

The act provided funds to states and local agencies that met the requirements established by the STWOA. Basic program requirements fell under three major components: schools-based learning, work-based learning, and connecting activities. See Figure 5.4

The intent of Congress in passing the STWOA was to encourage states and local schools to work together to establish a school-to-work opportunities system by providing "seed money" of venture capital to help underwrite the cost. Funding for the STWOA ended in 2001, but some states were able to request funds in 2001 for the next year. The programs and initiatives begun under the act were to be maintained with other federal, state, and local funds once the act expired. State and local educators and policy makers knew from the start that federal funds for the STWOA would end in 2001, and they developed post-federal funding strategies to maintain their school-to-work programs. All 50 states and the District of Columbia and Puerto Rico received federal implementation grants from the national School-to-Work office of the Departments of Labor and Education. It was estimated that around two billion dollars in federal monies was dispersed to states to support school-to-work programs, and most educators agree that school-to-work was a real success story (Cutshall, 2001).

KEY COMPONENTS AND ELEMENTS OF STWOA

SCHOOL-BASED LEARNING COMPONENT

- Career Counseling
- Selection of a Career Major
- Program of Study (Goals 2000)
- Integration of Academic and Vocational Education
- Evaluation
- Secondary/Postsecondary Articulation

WORK-BASED LEARNING COMPONENT

- Paid or Non-Paid Work Experience
- Job Training
- Workplace Mentoring
- Instruction in Workplace Competencies
- Instruction in All Aspects of the Industry

CONNECTING ACTIVITIES COMPONENT

- Matching Students with Employers
- Establishing Liasons Between Education and Work
- Technical Assistance to Schools, Students, and Employers
- Assistance to Integrate School-Based & Work-Based Learning
- Encourage Participation of Employers
- Job Placement, Continuing Education of Further Training
- Collection & Analysis of Post-Program Outcomes of Participants
- Linkages with Youth Development Activities and Industry

Source: Brustein, M., & Mahler, M. (1994). *AVA Guide to the School-to-Work Opportunities Act.* Alexandria, VA: American Vocational Association.

FIGURE 5.4   Key program components and elements of STWOA have been identified by Brustein and Mahler in the *AVA Guide to the School-to-work Opportunities Act*, 1994.

Improving America's Schools Act of 1994 (PL 103-382)

The Improving America's Schools Act was a reauthorization of the Elementary and Secondary Education Act (ESEA), which placed primary emphasis on serving disadvantaged students. The overriding goal of Title I was revised to improve the teaching and learning of children in highly impoverished schools to enable them to meet the challenging academic and performance standards being established by the Goals 2000 Act.

The Safe and Drug-Free Schools and Community Act is part of this enactment. It provided funds to school districts and schools in support of a comprehensive effort to combat problems of violence and drug use in schools. The act established a new Dwight D. Eisenhower Professional Development Program, which provided support for school districts and schools to develop plans for improving instruction and gave school personnel opportunities to determine the type of training and retraining they needed. The act assisted schools in gaining access to the Internet and other technological advances in order to transform classrooms and improve student learning through the application of technology. The act provided an opportunity for states to obtain grants to support the planning and initial implementation of public charter schools.

According to the American Vocational Association's *Legislative Update* (1994), the Improving America's Schools Act increased opportunities for vocational education input into state and local educational plans and strengthened vocational education in the following areas:

- States had to coordinate the activities under the act with school-to-work, vocational education, cooperative education, mentoring, and apprenticeship programs involving business, labor, and industry.
- Targeted Assistance School Programs had to include applied learning techniques; college and career awareness and preparation and teaching methods, which could include applied learning and team teaching; and services to prepare students for the transition from school-to-work, including the formation of partnerships and the integration of school-based and work-based learning.
- Grants for professional development were available for developing curricula and teaching methods that integrated academic and vocational instruction, including applied learning, and team teaching strategies.
- Education of Migratory Children grants to states had to include assurances that, when possible, programs would provide for the transition of secondary students to postsecondary education or employment.
- Dropout prevention programs had to contain descriptions of the program goals, objectives, and performance measures used to assess the effectiveness of the program in improving vocational skills.
- Demonstration of Innovative Practices programs could include grants to public or private partnerships involving business that emphasized the integration of academic and vocational learning and made school relevant to the workplace through applied and interactive teaching methodologies, team-teaching strategies, and learning opportunities connecting school, workplace, career exploration awareness, and career guidance opportunities.
- Funds made available through the Dwight D. Eisenhower Professional Development Program could be used to train teachers in innovative instructional methods, including the integration of academic and vocational learning and applied learning and other teaching strategies that integrate real-world applications into the core academic subjects.
- National Programs for Technology made funds available to develop demonstration and evaluation programs of applications of existing technology in pre-school education, elementary and secondary education, training and lifelong learning, and professional development of educational personnel.

- Funds were made available through the Star Schools Program for activities that provided information about employment opportunities, job training, and professional development for vocational education teacher and staff.
- The Magnet Schools Assistance provision provided state and local education agencies with assistance in providing instruction within magnet schools that would result in strengthening the vocational skills of students.
- The Women's Educational Equity program provided funds for leadership training for women and girls to develop professional and marketable skills, improve self-esteem, and benefit from exposure to positive role models; for school-to-work transition programs, and programs that increased opportunities for women and girls to enter the technologically demanding workplace and high skilled, high paying careers in which they had been under represented; and for the development of guidance and counseling activities, including career education programs.
- Bilingual Education Language Enhancement and Acquisition programs grants now included vocational education.
- The Indian, Native Hawaiian and Alaska Native Education Program provided funds for school-to-work transition activities including Tech Prep, mentoring and apprenticeship.
- Urban and Rural Education Assistance grants now included in-school youth employment, vocational education, and career education programs that improved the transition from school to work.

The Personal Responsibility and Work Opportunity Reconciliation Act of 1996 (PL 104-193)

The Personal Responsibilities and Work Opportunity Reconciliation Act (PRWORA) was signed into law by President Clinton in August 1996 with the promise of dramatically changing the nation's welfare system into one that required work in exchange for time-limited assistance. The PRWORA contained strong work requirements combined with supports for families moving from welfare to work, including increased funding for child care and continued eligibility for medical coverage. It encouraged states to meet PRWORA goals by awarding a bonus to states that met or exceeded them. The Department of Health and Human Services (HHS) was the federal agency that oversaw this comprehensive bipartisan welfare reform plan.

According to the HHS Fact Sheet (2001), the PRWORA included a wide range of provisions designed to encourage and support efforts by states to help transition individuals from welfare to work. Some of these provisions were as follows: (1) the act redefined how government agencies were to assist low-income families with the primary basis for assistance established on ability to work instead of need; (2) states and local communities were responsible for the development of work that would assist families to meet their needs; (3) the act eliminated the Aid to Families with Dependent Children (AFDC) and created a new program; TANF (Temporary Assistance to Needy Families); (4) the act affected a number of federal programs designed to help low income families; (5) families were allowed to receive cash assistance for a maximum of five years in a lifetime with families permitted to go off assistance for a period of time and come back on, but not to exceed five years; (6) after receiving assistance for two years, recipients were required to participate in a work activity, with work activity defined as subsidized or unsubsidized employment, on-the-job training, work study, internships, apprenticeships, community service, up to 12 months of vocational training, or providing child care services to individuals participating in community service. Teen parents were required to attend school and live in an adult supervised setting; (7) there was a reduction in financial support, particularly as people went to work. Recipients between the ages of 18 and 55 who were not working or looking for work would be able to receive food stamps only three months out of three years; (8) there was a small reduction in the school lunch program; (9) there was a new definition of eligibility for recipients, including individuals with drug and alcohol dependency and children with disabilities; and (10) there was a separate application process for families.

This act was scheduled to be reauthorized in 2002. The House of Representatives passed a welfare bill similar to the Bush administration's plan. The bill sought to impose greater restrictions on work requirements (40 hours per week) and even more severe limitations on education and training (four months of vocational education instead of the 12-month time limit in the 1996 act). This welfare bill provided few resources to states facing budget shortfalls across the country for such services as childcare (Association for Career and Technical Education [ACTE], 2003).

The Finance Committee of the Senate developed a plan to make modest improvements to the TANF program of the PRWORA, including increasing the time recipients could spend in education and training, such as vocational education for 24 months, and expanding the definition of work activities to include additional categories, including postsecondary education. This bill never made it to the full Senate and action was delayed until the 108th Congress convened in 2003. Since no new authorization legislation was passed, the PRWORA was extended in its previous form (ACTE, 2003).

In September 2003, the Senate Finance Committee marked up legislation to reauthorize the TANF program, increasing the number of required work hours to 34 and maintaining the 12-month limit on vocational education imposed in the original act along with the 30% cap on the number of recipients that can be engaged in education and training activities. The committee plan did include a provision allowing postsecondary education to count as a work activity for 10% of a state's caseload (ACTE, 2003).

The Balanced Budget Act of 1997 (BBA), (PL 105-33)

The Balanced Budget Act of 1997 (BBA) was signed into law by President Clinton and contained the most significant changes to the Medicare and Medicaid programs since their inception. It also contained provisions designed to move people from welfare to work and modified provisions in the welfare reform law passed in 1996. Specific provisions of the act regarding welfare inform included the establishment. Specific provisions of the act regarding welfare inform included the establishment of a Welfare-to-Work Jobs Challenge Fund to help states and local communities move long-term welfare recipients and certain non-custodial parents of children on welfare into lasting, unsubsidized employment. These funds could be used for job creation, job placement, and job retention efforts, including wage subsidies to private employers and other critical post-employment support services. The act also provided a welfare-to-work tax credit provision that gives employers and added incentive to hire long-term welfare recipients. The credit was for two years per worker to encourage not only hiring, but job retention as well. Amendments in 1999 to the BBA of 1997 expanded the definition of eligible non-custodial parents to include those who were unemployed or under-employed and having difficulty meeting child support obligations or had children receiving or eligible to receive food stamps, supplemental security income (SSI), Medicaid, or SCHIP. The amendments also required parents receiving services to enter into and comply with a personal responsibility contract that included cooperation with child support efforts. The BBA and the Noncitizen Technical Amendments Act of 1998 provided billions of dollars to restore disability and health benefits to 380,000 legal immigrants who were in this country before welfare reform became law. Other provisions extended SSI and Medicaid eligibility periods for refugees and people seeking asylum from five years to seven years to give these individuals more time to naturalize. Finally, the Act modified some food stamp provisions by creating work slots and preserving food stamp benefits for those single, able-bodied recipients without dependents who were willing to work but, through no fault of their own, were not been able to find employment (U.S. Department of Health and Human Services, 2001).

The Individuals with Disabilities Education Act Amendments of 1997 (PL 105-17)

The original act on which the Individuals with Disabilities Education Act Amendments of 1997 was based was The Education of All Handicapped Children Act of 1975 (PL 94-142), which was amended in 1983 and 1986 and amended again in 1990 as PL 102-19, when its name was changed to the Individuals with Disabilities Education Act (IDEA). The IDEA, with its amendments signed into law in June 1997, was the most important piece of federal legislation passed by Congress for educating children and youth with disabilities. This act strengthened academic expectations and accountability for the nation's 5.8 million children with disabilities and bridged the gap that had frequently existed between what children with disabilities learn and what is expected in a regular curriculum. Other legislative acts that had provisions for serving children with disabilities like the School-to-Work Act, Perkins III, and the Americans with Disabilities Act (ADA) only provided limited guidance as to how to design the support services, modifications, and accommodations that individual students in curricular experiences needed. The Individuals with Disabilities Act as amended, however, provided for individual planning and service design that helped accomplish the goals established by other supporting legislation.

The purposes of the IDEA as described in the act are (1) to ensure that all children with disabilities have available to them a free appropriate public education that emphasizes special education and related services designed to meet their unique needs and prepare them for employment and independent living. (2) to assist states in the implementation of a statewide, comprehensive, coordinated, multidisciplinary, interagency system of early intervention services for infants and toddlers with disabilities and their families, (3) to ensure that educators and parents have the necessary tools to improve educational results for children with disabilities by supporting systemic-change activities; coordinated research and personnel preparation; coordinated technical assistance, dissemination, and support; and technology development and media services; and (4) to assess, and ensure the effectiveness of, efforts to educate children with disabilities.

Ordover and Annexstein (1999) identified the key provisions of the IDEA. They report that the IDEA was written to ensure that special education and related services were provided to eligible individuals under the age of 22 in addition to the general curriculum and not separate from it. The IDEA provided for individualized planning and service. It provided federal funds for children and youth with disabilities and delimited who was covered under the laws by identifying 13 types of disabilities, any of which could make a person eligible for special education. The IDEA reaffirmed the right to a free appropriate education, including transition and planning services to eligible persons with disabilities. Special education was defined in the IDEA as "specially designed instruction. . . to meet the unique needs of a child with a disability," including instruction conducted in the classroom and other settings. The IDEA emphasized that special education was a package of instructional techniques and services, not a place. Related services were to be provided that were defined as "any developmental, corrective, and other support services that a child may need to benefit from his or her education." Examples included transportation, rehabilitation counseling, physical and occupational therapy. Transition services, which are a set of activities that promote movement from school to postschool activities, were to be provided and included such things as employment, postsecondary education and vocational training. The IDEA required annual individualized education programs (IEPs) containing detailed requirements for planning the education of individual students. Each individual student had to be provided with a comprehensive evaluation of educational needs at least once every three years. Transition planning had to begin by age 14, and the IEPs needed to include transition service needs. Schools were responsible for ensuring transition services, including those from outside agencies. The IDEA clarified who participated in transition planning, including parents, student, and agency participation. Finally, the IDEA provided detailed procedures to deal with any disputes occurring between parents and schools regarding the planning and delivery of services.

Knoblauch and McLane (1999) reported the following changes that affected special education practice nationwide as a result of the IDEA amendments: (1) participation of students with disabilities in state and district-wide assessment (testing) programs (including alternative assessment) with appropriate accommodations where necessary, (2) development and review of the IEP, including increased emphasis on participation of children and youth with disabilities in the general education curriculum and involvement of general education teachers in developing, reviewing, and revising the IEP, (3) enhanced parent participation in eligibility and placement decisions, (4) streamlined student evaluation/reevaluation requirements, (5) identification of transition service needed within a child's course of study beginning at age 14 and updated annually, (6) availability of mediation services as a means of more easily resolving parent-school differences, (7) disciplinary procedures for students with disabilities, including allowance for an appropriate interim alternative educational setting up to 45 days, and (8) allowing children ages 3–9 to be identified as developmentally delayed; previously, it was 3–5.

There is a large body of literature regarding the IDEA in published form and on the Internet to assist CTE teachers in providing services to students with disabilities. One very good source of information is the textbook by Taymans, J.M., West, L.L. and Sullivan, M. (Eds.). (2000). *Unlocking Potential That Promotes the Concept of Self-Determination—An Individual's Ability to Define and Achieve Goals Based on Knowing and Valuing Him or Herself.*

The Carl D. Perkins Vocational and Technical Education Act of 1998 (PL 105-332)

On October 31, 1998, President Clinton signed into law the Carl D. Perkins Vocational and Technical Education Act of 1998. This five-year authorizing law replaced the 1990 Perkins Act and gave states and local school districts greater flexibility to develop vocational education programs while making them more accountable for student performance. In fact this last feature, greater accountability, was the hall-mark of the new legislation. Congress listened to a field that was demanding greater flexibility in administering programs and allocating federal funds and honored its request. In return for granting this flexibility, however, Congress established procedures that required the field to demonstrate results in terms of student achievement, program completion, placement in postsecondary education and the workforce, and improved gender equity in program offerings. Educators would have to devise new state plans for administering vocational-technical education and develop systems to track students more extensively than in the past. The new law was expected to strengthen academic and vocational-technical instruction, place more emphasis on professional development, and support career guidance activities along with other desirable outcomes (Hoachlander & Klein, 1999).

The 1998 Perkins Act was a direct response by Congress to the national concern that high school graduates lack the basic skills necessary to succeed in the global marketplace. Congress identified these skills for the new century as (1) strong basic and advanced academic skills, (2) computer and other technical skills, (3) theoretical knowledge and communication, (4) problem-solving, teamwork, and employability skills, and (5) the ability to acquire additional knowledge and skill throughout a lifetime. Congress wanted the Perkins funds to serve all students at the public secondary and postsecondary levels who were interested in vocational and technical education programs. Section 2 of the act revealed the purpose or Congressional intent of the legislation. The purposes of the legislation were "to further develop the academic, vocational, and technical skills of vocational and technical education students through high standards; link secondary and postsecondary programs; increase flexibility in the administration and use of funds provided under the act; disseminate national research about vocational and technical education; and provide professional development and technical assistance to vocational and technical educators." The new Perkins Act continued federal support for vocational and technical education that assists youth and adults to prepare for and make successful transitions to postsecondary education, employment and independent, satisfying adult life (American Vocational Association [AVA], 1998).

The road leading to the Perkins Act of 1998 was long and tiresome. Congress began work on a new Perkins reauthorizing bill in 1995 but failed to reauthorize vocational education before the October 1995 deadline when the 1990 Perkins Act officially expired. The 1990 Perkins Act was extended and funding was appropriated pending completion of a reauthorized act. In 1997, the one hundred and fifth Congress introduced the Perkins Act reauthorization and began the process all over again with two different bills approved by the house and senate. A long process of negotiation ensued between proponents of the house and senate bills for nearly two years until the bill was finally passed and signed into law on October 31, 1998. Congress appeared to be preoccupied with other concerns including political scandals, reauthorization of higher education, and revamping the nation's job training system. Along the way, vocational educators feared that vocational legislation might become part of a job training block grant, attached to welfare reform, and even given over to governors to control vocational funds. In the end, however, the new act left control of vocational education in the hands of educators and gave vocational education separate authorizing legislation. The new law introduced a number of changes, some presenting real challenges to vocational leaders, but the overall reaction among most leaders was that they overwhelmingly approved the new law and said that changes introduced were long overdue (Hettinger, 1999).

According to the Association for Career and Technical Education (ACTE), there were a number of political issues and trends that were addressed in the 1998 Perkins Act. While both republican and democratic leaders desired legislation that would better prepare high school students for the global marketplace, there was considerable disagreement as to how the legislation should be framed so that it could serve all students well. Republicans viewed the 1990 Perkins Act, with its numerous set-asides and directives focusing on specific segments of the population, as problematic for serving all student well. They argued that the focus of the 1990 Act was on providing narrow services to specific categories of individuals and that students and their parents who were not members of targeted categories viewed CTE as primarily a program to meet the needs of special populations, which tended to discourage other students from enrolling in these programs.

In other words, republicans viewed vocational education as primarily serving students from special populations and not serving other students, who were left to flounder in general education programs that neither prepared them for work or for postsecondary education. Democrats countered that it was essential to maintain a focus on serving students from special populations or these students would be left out of the system. They argued that federal legislation beginning in the early 1960s and continuing through the 1990s had made a difference in serving youth and adults from special populations and that it was necessary for this focus to continue in order to ensure that these individuals would be successful in schooling and in the workplace. These two conflicting views were satisfied in a compromise in the 1998 act that eliminated unintentionally harmful provisions, which hurt rather than helped students with special needs. Contrary to the popular perception that the new Perkins Act would de-emphasize serving special populations and discontinue providing essential support services, the focus of the act was on improving CTE programs while providing equal access, rights, and protection for all learners. The 1998 Perkins Act emphasized that all learners in CTE programs, including special population learners, needed to obtain skills in order to participate successfully in the modern economy.

Another issue was the fear that the School-to-Work Opportunities Act of 1994 had paved the way for a government supported system of tracking students into job training programs by forcing them to choose careers at a very young age. A similar concern was that the government was involved in forcing students into CTE programs. The response of Congress to these issues was to include wording in the new law that stated that students must voluntarily choose CTE and that Perkins funds could not be used to support any School-to-Work Opportunities Act provisions.

One final issue of the act focused on gender equity for members of a targeted group consisting of single parents, single pregnant mothers, parenting teens, displaced homemakers, and those involved in nontraditional training and employment. Gender equity advocates nearly caused the legislation to die as they pushed for a greater allocation of funds for their cause. A compromise was reached in the new legislation that listed all the different types of individuals needing equity services as part of the definition of special populations that are to be served with other students. The 1990 Perkins Act gender equity set-aside provision was allowed to continue, although modified, but the provision for a state gender equity coordinator was eliminated (AVA, 1998).

There are similarities between the 1990 Perkins Act and the 1998 Perkins Act, such as the continuing focus on integrating academic and vocational education and expanding Tech Prep. There are also a number of striking differences in the two piece of legislation, especially with regard to increased state and local education agency flexibility in designing, delivering and funding CTE programs and the requirement of increased accountability for providing results in terms of improved student learning and increased numbers of student who continue their education beyond high school. The following are distinguishing features of the 1998 Perkins Act sometimes called Perkins III, which were identified by Hettinger (1999).

Accountability

States would have to develop new data collection and reporting systems that differed significantly from those used in the past. States would have to report data on student achievement using a common language that allowed for nation-wide comparisons. States would have to shoulder the burden of greater follow-up CTE programs and be able to document the impact of their programs. In particular, states would have to work with the U.S Department of Education in setting expected performance levels for four categories: (1) student attainment of vocational, technical, and academic skill proficiencies; (2) acquisition of secondary or postsecondary degrees or credentials; (3) placement and retention in postsecondary education or employment; and (4) completion of vocational and technical programs leading to nontraditional training and employment. The performance indicators had to include percentages or numbers that could be used to make data objective, quantifiable, and measurable. State would have to show progress toward improving the performance of CTE students and would have to publicize their progress in a manner that allowed state-by-state comparisons.

Funding Formulas

Perkins III established the formula of 85% of state grants being allocated to local school districts, with states able to keep 10% for leadership activities and 5% or $250,000 (whichever was greater). States could reserve up to 10% of funds sent to local districts for rural areas, regions that had high numbers or percentages of CTE students, and areas that received less money because of changes made to the within-state secondary funding formula. The first year funding remained the same as the 1990 Perkins Act, but the second year funding formula would switch to one based 70% on poverty and 30% on population.

Tech Prep

Tech Prep programs were strengthened in Perkins III by requesting the use of consortia to develop longer-range plans, to use technology more in instruction, to improve communication among Tech Prep partners, and to extend their plans outlining the development and implementation of their programs from three to five years. The expectation of the new legislation regarding Tech Prep was that consortia would develop more thorough and complete plans to serve students from high school through an associate's degree, and on to work or even a four-year college. Specific instructional activities that could be offered through the new Tech Prep regulations included preparing students for the information technology field and using technology for the professional development and distance learning of CTE teachers involved in Tech Prep activities.

School-to-Work

Congress sought to prevent Perkins Act funds from being used for School-to-Work programs unless those funds were used for activities serving only students eligible for CTE. Since there was considerable overlap between activities funded through the School-to-Work Act of 1994 and Perkins III, it was somewhat difficult for states and local school districts to determine what was legal in the use of funds for activities such as curriculum integration, professional development, and career guidance. Most state and local school CTE administrators interpreted this portion of the law as continuing to allow Perkins III funds to enable learners to continue with work-site learning, career guidance, and other activities.

Gender Equity

Perkins III reduced required gender equity activities, eliminating the requirement that states retain a full-time equity coordinator, the requirement that states spend $60,000 on related activities, and the 10.5% set-aside for sex equity and programs serving single parents, single pregnant women, and displaced homemakers. The act did give states the flexibility to continue equity programs if they chose and mandated that states spend between $60,000 and $150,000 of their leadership money on programs to prepare people for nontraditional training and employment.

Students with Disabilities

Perkins III contained several important changes from earlier Perkins Acts, which were intended to better serve students with disabilities by ensuring that they were not placed in CTE programs in order for school districts to receive federal funding. Perkins II had established a funding formula that unintentionally became a quota system and led to the placement of students with disabilities in vocational programs whether or not this was the best decision for the students. Perkins III eliminated the quota for students with disabilities in area vocational schools. Gone also was a loophole that allowed cities to strike deals with area vocational schools to distribute funding, which resulted in some area vocational schools being underfunded.

Perkins III intended for school systems to better serve students with disabilities who choose CTE programs by eliminating specific requirements, which the school systems believed did not work well, and replacing them with greater flexibility for states to determine the best strategies for serving student with disabilities. While some special education teachers believed that Perkins III reduced the emphasis on serving students from special populations, the intent of the act was to force state and local school district educators to rethink how to best serve these students in a more flexible manner while preserving accountability. Accountability provisions in the Perkins Act required states to report in quantifiable terms the progress that CTE students with disabilities were making toward the new, state-established, academic and career and technical skill proficiencies. States also had to track how many students with disabilities obtained diplomas and advanced to postsecondary education. In addition, state plans had to describe how special populations were being provided equal access to vocational education programs and how they were being prepared for high-skill, high-wage careers.

The Perkins Act of 1998 ushered in a new area for federal funding of CTE, relaxing some of the specific requirements while giving states and local school districts considerable flexibility in determining how best to serve all students who chose to enroll in the programs. In exchange for greater flexibility, however, states and local school districts would be held accountable for favorable results for all students, including contribution to student achievement, program completion, placement in postsecondary education and the workforce, and improved gender equity in program offerings.

Federal funds provided by the Perkins Act of 1998 were provided to state for secondary and postsecondary education. The states were responsible for allocating the funds according to a state-developed formula to secondary and postsecondary schools. States received two grants under the Perkins Act: basic state grants and Tech Prep. States had to distribute at least 85% of the basic state grant funds to local programs using either a needs-based formula described in the law or an alternate formula targeting resources to disadvantaged schools and students. According to ACTE information on the background of the Perkins Act, the types of activities that state and local funds could be used for included the following:

- serving as a catalyst for change through program improvement
- developing an accountability system that ensures quality and improved results
- strengthening the integration of academic education and CTE
- ensuring access to CTE for students with special needs, including those with disabilities
- developing and improving relevant curricula
- purchasing equipment to ensure that classrooms and laboratories have the latest technology
- providing career guidance and academic counseling services
- providing professional development and technical assistance to teachers, counselors, and administrators
- supporting career and technical student organizations that are an integral part of the curriculum (ACTE, 2003).

The Workforce Investment Act (WIA) of 1998 (PL 105-220)

The Workforce Investment Act (WIA) was signed into law August 7, 1998, repealing the Job Training Partnership Act as of July 1, 2000. The WIA provided increased flexibility for state and local officials to establish broad-based labor market systems using job training funds for adults, dislocated workers, and youth. It was designed to establish a framework for a unique national workforce preparation and employment system that would better meet the needs of the nation's businesses, the needs of job seekers, and those who wanted to further their careers. The overall goal of the WIA was to provide workforce development services to employers and workers through a highly accessible, information driven, one-stop career center system.

Specifically, the goals of the WIA were (1) increase the employment, retention, and earnings of participants, (2) increase occupational skill attainment by participants, (3) improve the quality of the workforce, (4) reduce welfare dependency, and (5) enhance the productivity and competitiveness of the nation. Key principles of the WIA included (1) streamlining services, (2) empowering individuals, (3) providing universal access, (4) increasing accountability, (5) creating new roles for local boards, (6) providing state and local flexibility, and (7) improving youth programs.

According to former Secretary Alexis M. Herman of the U.S. Department of Labor, the WIA brought a new emphasis and substantive reform to how youth are served within the workforce investment system. It provided the structure to prepare the nation's young people and offered an array of services so that they were able to successfully transition to the workforce and to continued education and training. The act challenged local communities to reach a higher level of collaboration among local workforce training providers, schools, community organizations, and others in an effort to align and leverage resources and to create community youth assistance strategies. The reforms of youth services were organized under the following four major themes: (1) the establishment of the local youth council, (2) comprehensive services based on individual assessment, (3) youth connections and access to the one-stop delivery system, and (4) performance accountability.

The road to the WIA is filled with a long history of legislation and movements to create jobs and to provide income assistance for needy individuals. Kaufmann and Wills (1999) provide an historical account of the events and legislation that began with the Smith-Hughes Act of 1917 and the creation of the vocational rehabilitation system three years later to provide targeted services to individuals with disabilities, and ending with the Workforce Investment Act of 1998, which replaced the Job Partnership and Training Act passed in 1982.

From the 1930s through the 1950s, the focus of federal support was on income support and job creation, such as with the Civilian Conservation Corps and the Work Progress Administration. Training was only incidental to these programs. Two pieces of legislation that did support training during this time were the National Apprenticeship Act of 1937 and the GI Bill.

In the 1960s and 1970s, government workforce programs expanded significantly to address the high level of unemployment that persisted after the Korean War. Two of the major workforce preparation acts that refocused federal support for training were the Manpower Development and Training Act of 1962 and the Comprehensive Employment and Training Act of 1973. These acts attempted to consolidate several War-on-Poverty programs and decentralize control of the programs to better serve the manpower needs of local governments.

In the period between 1980 and 1984, President Ronald Reagan sought to eliminate costly and ineffective programs and reduce federal expenditure, which resulted in the passage of the Job Training and Partnership Act (JTPA) of 1982, which eliminated job creation efforts and emphasized support for training and related services. The JTPA gave state governments and the business community stronger roles in deciding how federal funds could be spent and established private industry councils (PICs) to coordinate all job preparation programs within a given state's geographic area.

The WIA of 1998 replaced the JTPA while retaining some of its strong components, but placed the overall responsibility of managing the workforce preparation component of the welfare system under the Department of Labor. The WIA made some significant changes in the nation's employment and training programs and built on themes that had emerged in past manpower legislation. The WIA was a very comprehensive act, with five main titles and many provisions in each. Kaufmann and Wills (1999) present nine key features of the act:

Designation of One-Stop Centers for Delivery of Services

The WIA made the U.S. Department's one-stop career centers the central player of the workforce delivery system. These centers made it possible for job-seekers and employers to obtain information and services in one location instead of having to go from place to place to receive information and services as in the past. One-stop centers helped individuals and employers determine who was eligible for various programs by providing services such as assessment and job search and placement.

Consolidation of Workforce Development Activities

President Reagan began the movement to consolidate federal programs to assist the underemployed or unemployed with the creation of the JTPA of 1982, but the General Accounting Office reported on 154 programs or funding streams designed to assist the unemployed, enhance worker skills, or create employment opportunities. The WIA still did not consolidate all the federal initiatives, but it did eliminate the JTPA, the Adult Education Act and the National Literacy Act of 1991 and consolidated their activities, along with activities of vocational rehabilitation.

Re-alignment of Existing Programs

Legislation and programs not eliminated by the WIA were re-aligned in various ways through an optional state plan or through the designation of local areas by the governor of each state. For example, Job Corps, one of the successful programs of the JTPA, could be represented on youth councils and was a vital part of the state plan.

Emphasis on Youth Programs

A separate title of the WIA was youth programs. In some cases under the JTPA, out-of-school youth did not receive enough attention from the local service delivery area, which was responsible for both youth and adults. The WIA had a separate section for youth activities and created a youth council to coordinate activities and services. The summer youth employment and training programs that had been offered under the JTPA became allowable services that had to be balanced with other youth services. Youth programs had to have the following assessments: (1) individual assessment, (2) service strategies, (3) preparation for postsecondary educational opportunities, (4) linkages between academic and occupational learning, (5) preparation for jobs, and (6) connections to the job market for area employers.

There were a number important provisions relating to youth: (1) eligible youth had to be below income: (2) 5% of youth served had to be other than low income if they faced other barriers to school completion and employment; (3) categories under which the 5% with other barriers were identified were school dropout, basic literacy skills deficient, homeless, runaway or foster child, pregnant or parenting, offender, or in need of help completing an educational program or securing and holding employment; (4) programs had to link academic and occupational learning and skill development; (5) programs had to include tutoring, study skills and instruction leading to the completion of secondary school, mentoring, paid and unpaid work, leadership development, and other appropriate services; (6) participants were to receive follow-up services for a minimum of one year; and (7) programs had to provide summer employment opportunities linked to academic and occupational learning.

Emphasis on Customer Information and Choice

The WIA used a service delivery system that included individual training accounts with vouchers, allowing those seeking services to make informed choices among service providers regarding education and training. To ensure that those needing services were provided with them in an efficient manner, customer satisfaction surveys were part of the accountability measures in the law.

New Focus on Program Accountability

The demand for accountability of federal programs, which began in the Nixon administration and was emphasized even more in the Reagan administration, was a major consideration of the WIA. More responsibility for setting performance measures and providing accountability data was placed on state and local agencies. Providers of services were to be chosen based on their track records of performance.

Difference in Individual Outcomes

The WIA established different outcomes depending on who was being served. The appropriate outcome for youth was basic attainment or work readiness occupational skills and education. The outcomes for older youth and adults included both attainment of educational and occupational credentials as well as employment.

The WIA provided different types and levels of services, depending on the individual's skills and needs as they related to workplace demands.

Role of Employers

The WIA, as with previous workforce preparation programs like the JTPA, recognized the role of employers in the workforce development system. State employers' associations were recognized as important participants on the workforce investment board (WIB) at the state level. Likewise, local workforce investment boards had to involve private sector employers in providing connecting, brokering, and coaching activities along with other services.

Longer Periods of Time for Planning and Service

The WIA recognized that individuals with disabilities and other barriers to employment needed assistance for longer periods of time than was provided by previous education/employment and training programs. Under the provisions of the WIA, individuals were provided with extended mentorship services, longer follow-up on services, and longer planning periods. States had to submit five-year plans for providing services in both job training and adult education and literacy sections of the WIA.

The WIA ushered in a new approach to the development of amore complete workforce development system. The act built on the most successful elements of previous federal legislation and adjusted or eliminated legislation that was not effective. It was based on extensive federal, state, and local research and evaluation studies of successful training and employment innovations. The law made changes to funding streams, target populations, systems of delivery, long-term planning, labor market information systems, and the governance structure.

According to the ACTE, implementation of the WIA worked well in some local areas, but overall there was a reduction in the prevision of employment services, particularly in the number of job seekers being referred to training programs. Cited causes include local agencies diverting funds to the development of the one-stop system infrastructure, complicated negotiations among partner agencies, and limited business engagement in the system (ACTE, 2003).

Adult Education and Family Literacy Act of 1998 (PL 105-220)

Adult education was an important component of the Workforce Investment Act (WIA) and Title II of the WIA is the Adult Education and Family Literacy Act (AEFLA) of 1998. This act restructured and improved programs previously authorized by the Adult Education Act as amended by the National Literacy Act of 1991. The AEFLA gave states greater flexibility in administering adult education programs. It was designed to improve adult education programs by requiring states to give priority to local programs that were based on a solid foundation of research, that addressed the diverse needs of adult learners, and that utilized other effective practices and strategies.

In addition, states were to determine whether programs provided learning in real-life contexts, employed advances in technology, and staffed well-trained instructors, counselors, and administrators. To promote accountability and continuous program improvement, states had to establish a performance accountability system that required adult education programs to meet core indicators specified in the law.

The 1998 Amendments to the Higher Education Act of 1965 (PL 105-244)

The Amendments to the Higher Education Act of 1965 extended authorization of programs under the Higher Education Act of 1965 and contained a number of new provisions to strengthen higher education. The act contained provisions lowering the student loan interest rate, preparing more students for college, recruiting and training well-qualified teachers, modernizing student-aid delivery, and promoting high-quality distance learning options for students. The House passed the Ready to Teach Act of 2003 in July, which addressed Title II of the current HEA and focused on grants to states and partnerships that can be used to strengthen teacher education programs and recruit highly qualified teachers (ACTE, 2003).

The Assistive Technology Act of 1998 (PL 105-394)

Congress was well aware that disability is a natural part of the human experience and in no way diminishes the right of individuals to benefit from an education and pursue meaningful careers. It recognized that technology had come to play an increasingly important role in the lives of all Americans and could have a significant impact on individuals with disabilities. The Assistive Technology Act of 1998 supports states in providing assistive technology to individuals with disabilities. There are three major purposes of the act, each with several specific actions, but the thrust of the act is to provide financial assistance to the states so that they can provide permanent, comprehensive statewide technology-related assistance programs.

The Ticket to Work and Work Incentives Improvement Act of 1999 (PL 106-170)

President Clinton signed the Ticket to Work and Work Incentives Improvement Act (TWWIIA) into law in December 1999. This landmark legislation increased employment opportunities for people with disabilities. According to the Social Security Administration (2000), this law had three major thrusts: (1) increasing beneficiary choice in obtaining rehabilitation and vocational services, (2) removing barriers requiring people with disabilities to choose between health care coverage and work, and (3) assuring that more Americans with disabilities had the opportunity to participate in the workforce and lessen their dependency on public benefits.

Specific provisions of the act did the following: (1) provided expanded availability of health care services to more people with disabilities who work; (2) established a ticket to work and self-sufficiency program in which Social Security and Supplemental Security Income (SSI) disability beneficiaries could use a ticket to obtain vocational rehabilitation and employment support services from an approved provider of their choice; (3) established employment networks or public or private entities approved by the SSA through which recipients could receive ticket services; (4) charged the Social Security Administration (SSA) with the tasks of creating a mechanism for resolving disputes; (5) expanded services provided under Individual Work Plans (IWPs) to include case management, work incentive planning, supported employment, career planning, career plan development, vocational assessment, job training, placement, follow-up services, and other services specified by the SSA under the program; (6) gave networks opportunities to establish outcome payment systems; (7) changed the way individuals using a ticket had to undergo regularly scheduled disability reviews; (8) created the Work Incentives Advisory Panel within Social Security to report to the commissioner and to Congress on the implementation of the ticket program; (9) directed Social Security to establish a community-based work incentives planning and assistance program for disseminating accurate and current information about work incentives; and (10) authorized Social Security to make payments to protection and advocacy systems established in each state to provide information, advice, and other services to disability beneficiaries.

According to the U.S. Department of Labor, Office of Disability Employment Policy (2000), the Ticket to Work program administered by the SSA modernized employment-related services offered to Americans with disabilities so they would be able to obtain job-related training and placement assistance from an approved provider of their choice. It also expanded health care coverage so that individuals with disabilities would be able to become employed without fear of losing their health insurance. Ticket services were provided to beneficiaries by providers who were part of an approved employment network, and service providers were rewarded through an incentive-based system, ensuring that individuals received the ongoing services needed to maintain employment and succeed at work.

No Child Left Behind (NCLB) Act of 2001 (PL 107-110)

The No Child Left Behind (NCLB) Act of 2001 made a sweeping change to the Elementary and Secondary Education Act (ESEA) of 1965, which was amended in 1966, 1967, 1972, 1974, 1978, and in 1994 as the Improving America's Schools Act. President George W. Bush signed the NCLB Act into law in January of 2002. In signing the act, President Bush said "Today begins a new era, a new time for public education in our country. Our schools will have higher expectations—we believe every child can learn. From this day forward, all students will have a better chance to learn, to excel, and to live out their dreams." (News from the Committee on Education and the Workforce, 2002).

The NCLB was the result of a bipartisan debate of a plan submitted by the Bush administration to Congress in January of 2001 that contained the challenge of discovering how the federal role in education could close the achievement gap between disadvantaged and minority students and their peers. The president's plan included the four principles of stronger accountability for results, expanding flexibility and local control, expanding options for parents, and an emphasis on teaching methods that have proven effective (U.S. Department of Education, n.d.).

The NCLB Act had nine Titles with Title I addressing basic programs; Title II directed at improving teaching; Title III addressing Language Instruction for LEP and immigrant students; Title IV focusing on safe and drug-free schools; Title V addressing innovative programs; Title VI dealing with state assessments; Title VII addressing Indian, Native Hawaiians, and Alaska Native Education; Title VIII dealing with impact aid; and Title IX addressing general provisions (U.S. Department of Education, n.d.). According to the fact sheet on No Child Left Behind from the Department of Education, the NCLB Act, commonly known as H.R.1, included the following major provisions:

Accountability for Results

H.R.1 will result in the creation of assessments in each state that measure what children know and learn in reading and math in grades three to eight. Student achievement must be measured with tests that are given to every child every year. The results will be reported to parents, citizens, and others in the form of annual report cards on school performance and statewide progress. Statewide reports must include data that show not only how well students are doing overall but also the progress in closing the achievement gap between disadvantaged and other groups of students (U.S. Department of Education, n.d.).

Creating Flexibility at the State and Local Levels and Reducing Red Tape

The overall number of ESEA programs at the Department of Education will be reduced from 55 down to 45. H.R.1 will allow local schools to transfer 50% of the federal dollars they receive to several programs without separate approval. In a similar fashion, states will have the freedom to transfer up to 50% of non-Title I state activity federal funds among an assortment of ESEA programs without separate approval. H.R.1 will provide for the creation of up to 150 local flexibility demonstration projects that allow consolidation of funds so long as they are held accountable for higher academic performance. H.R.1 will give local school officials serving rural schools and districts more flexibility and a greater determination in how federal funds can be used in their schools (U.S. Department of Education, n.d.).

Expanding Options for Parents for Children from Disadvantaged Backgrounds

The NCLB Act provides options for parents whose children are enrolled in failing schools, allowing them to transfer their children to better-performing public or charter schools immediately after a school is identified as failing. Title I funds can be used to provide supplemental services (tutoring, after school services, summer school programs) for children enrolled in failing schools. The act also expands federal support for parents and community leaders to create charter schools to improve educational options for students (U.S. Department of Education, n.d.).

Ensuring Every Child can Read with Reading First

H.R.1 authorizes increases in federal funds for reading programs that link scientifically proven methods of reading instruction that are in line with the president's Reading First program (U.S. Department of Education, n.d.).

Strengthening Teacher Quality

The NCLB Act provides direction and support for local schools to recruit and retain excellent teachers. It asks states to employ highly qualified teachers in every classroom. The act defined highly qualified teacher as "one who obtains full state certification as a teacher; holds at least a bachelor's degree; and has demonstrated subject matter competence in each academic subject in which the teacher teaches." According to the ACTE, this standard was designed to apply to only teachers of core subjects, but the language was unclear and could have been applied to all teachers. This would have initiated a huge problem because in the trade and industrial, technical, and health education programs, teachers can have less than a bachelor's degree and be employed on the basis of competence based on work experience and licensure. The U.S. Department of Education issued a policy on June 7, 2002 that allowed the hiring of CTE teachers who do not have a bachelor's degree so long as they are not teaching core academic subjects for which students receive academic credit. While this policy provided some relief for employing some CTE teachers, there remains the problem for some CTE teachers who offer a class for which students receive academic credit, such as science credits for health occupations. H.R.1 simply requires that any teacher offering a class for which a student receives academic credit must have a bachelor's degree (in any area) and demonstrate subject matter competence in an academic area that is being offered. States are actively recruiting CTE teachers who hold a minimum of a bachelor's degree and are using a variety of strategies for ensuring academic competence in the areas in which academic credit is granted for a CTE class (ACTE, 2003).

The NCLB Act consolidates smaller programs within the U.S. Department of Education and creates a new Teacher Quality program that allows greater flexibility for local school districts. It provides specific funds for teacher quality and allows local schools to use up to 50% of their non-Title I funds for hiring new teachers, increasing teacher salaries, improving teacher training, and other development efforts (U.S. Department of Education, n.d.).

Confirming Progress

The act provides for a small sample of students in each state in the fourth and eighth grades to participate every year in the National Assessment of Educational Progress (NAEP) in reading and math. This allows the U.S. Department of Education to verify the results of statewide assessments required under Title I (U.S. Department of Education, n.d.).

Promoting English Proficiency

H.R.1 consolidates the U.S. Department of Education's bilingual and immigrant education program to streamline program administration, increase flexibility, and focus support on enabling all limited English proficient (LEP) students to learn English as soon as possible. A major thrust of this part of the act is to assist LEP students in learning English through scientifically based teaching methods. To ensure LEP students are learning, students will be tested for reading and language arts in English after they have attended U.S. schools for three consecutive years. Another provision is that parents will be notified if their child demonstrates limited English proficiency and is in need of English language instruction (U.S. Department of Education, n.d.).

Keeping Schools Safe and Drug Free

The NCLB Act supports state and local efforts to keep schools safe and free from drugs, while at the same time ensuring that students who are enrolled in dangerous schools and have been victimized are able to transfer to a safer school. States are required to report safety statistics to the public on a school-by-school basis and local school leaders must use federal Safe and Drug-Free Schools and Communities funding to implement drug and violence prevention programs that are effective (U.S. Department of Education, n.d.).

According to the ACTE (2003), all 50 states are currently in the early stages of the implementation of the provisions of NCLB and have submitted plans for compliance that have been approved by the federal government. Unfortunately the amount of federal funds provided to states and local school systems to implement mandates has not kept pace with the amounts authorized by the law, which has left many states and school districts struggling to fund new testing programs, accountability strategies, and supplemental services required under the act.

The Nurse Reinvestment Act of 2002 (PL 107-205)

The Nurse Reinvestment Act was signed into law by President George W. Bush in July 2002. This act amended the Public Health Services Act (PHSA). Its major focus was to assist schools of nursing in reducing the shortage of nurses at hospitals, nursing homes, and other health practice sites. The American Association of Colleges of Nursing provided the following analysis of major provisions of the act. The act established nurse scholarships to nursing students in exchange for a commitment to serve in a public or private non-profit health facility determined to have a critical nurse shortage. It provided funds to help health care facilities retain nurses and improve patient care services through improved collaboration between nurses and other health care professionals, thereby giving nurses more power in the decision-making process.

The act provided for funds to train and educate nurses in the field of geriatric care. A faculty loan cancellation program was established under the act allowing practicing nurses to begin full-time study and complete advanced degrees in a more timely manner. To be eligible for the loan cancellation program, recipients would have to agree to spend a designated amount of time in a faculty position at a school of nursing. A career ladder grant program was established under the act to assist individuals in the nursing workforce in obtaining more education. Under the career ladder program, partnerships were to be formed between health care providers and schools of nursing for advanced training. The act established a public service announcement program that was designed to increase the number of advertisements educating the public about the rewards of a nursing career and promoting the nursing profession (American Association of Colleges of Nursing, 2002).

The Assistive Technology Act Amendments of 2004 (PL 108-364)

The 2004 amendments to the Assistive Technology Act of 1998 continue the support of state efforts to improve the provisions of assistive technology to individuals with disabilities through comprehensive statewide programs and to provide states with the financial assistance needed to support programs to maximize the ability of individuals with disabilities and their families, guardians, advocates, and authorized representatives to obtain assistive technology devices and assistive technology services. The amendments included several changes to the 1998 act including authorizing the program for 6 years (2005–2010); halting the direct payment for assistive technology devices for an individual with a disability; ensuring that funds received through the grant will be used to supplement, not supplant, funds available from other sources for technology-related assistance; establishing an advisory council to provide "consumer-responsive, consumer-driven advice" for the planning and implementation and evaluation of programs; and extending coverage to people with disabilities of all ages, all disabilities, in all environments (early intervention, K-12, postsecondary, vocational rehabilitation, community living, aging services, etc.).

The Individuals with Disabilities Education Improvement Act (IDEA) of 2004 (PL 108-446)

The Individuals with Disabilities Education Improvement Act (IDEA) is the nation's special education law in force today. It was first enacted three decades ago and it provides billions of dollars of federal funding to assist states and local communities in providing educational opportunities for approximately 6 million students with disabilities. The IDEA requires states to provide a free and appropriate education for individuals with disabilities in the least restrictive environment.

On December 3, 2004, the U.S. Congress passed a reauthorization act to the Individuals with Disabilities Act as amended in 1997 and cited this bill as the Individuals with Disabilities Education Improvement Act of 2004. This new act includes a number of changes to the previous act, including changes to the due process provisions, provisions relating to the education of school-aged and preschool children, funding formulas, evaluation of services, eligibility determinations, individualized education programs (IEPs), and educational placement.

Part C of the new act provides early intervention services for infants and toddlers with disabilities and their families (from birth through age 3). This early intervention program has initiated the development of an individualized family service plan (IFSP) that guides the integration of services to address the needs of the family, as well as the child (U.S. Department of Education, 2004).

This act vigorously enforces its provisions by giving the U.S. Secretary of Education and state education agencies greater power and new tools to measure compliance and impose sanctions when schools fail to meet standards. It requires states to develop a plan, establish targets, and meet the targets in the areas of appropriate public education, general supervision, transition services, and disproportionate representation of minorities. It also makes agreements in dispute resolution and due process binding and establishes competency standards for the training of hearing officers.

Carl D. Perkins Career and Technical Education Improvement Act of 2006 (PL 109-270)

The Carl D. Perkins Career and Technical Education Improvement Act of 2006 was signed into law on August 12, 2006 by President George W. Bush. This legislation marked the beginning of the 109th Congress' efforts to reauthorize the Carl D. Perkins Vocational and Technical Education Act of 1998, a process that began in the 108th Congress. This act, extending through 2012, provides almost $1.3 billion in federal support for CTE programs in all 50 states. The act provides an increased focus on the academic achievement of CTE students, strengthens the connections between secondary and postsecondary education, and improves state and local accountability. The purpose of this act is to develop more fully the academic and career and technical skills of secondary and postsecondary students who elect to enroll in CTE programs.

The most notable provisions of the act are that it uses the term "career and technical education" instead of "vocational education" throughout, it maintains the Tech Prep program as a separate federal funding stream within the legislation, and it maintains state administrative funding at 5% of a state's allocation.

The four purposes of the 1998 Perkins law have been expanded, and two new purposes added, resulting in seven purposes as follows:

1. build on the efforts of states and localities in developing challenging academic and technical standards and assisting students in meeting such standards including preparation for high-skill, high-wage, or high-demand occupations in current or emerging professions
2. promote the development of services and activities that integrate rigorous and challenging academic and career and technical instruction and that link secondary education and postsecondary education for participating CTE students
3. increase state and local flexibility in providing services and activities designed to develop, implement, and improve CTE, including Tech Prep education
4. conduct and disseminate national research and disseminate information on best practices that improve CTE programs, services, and activities
5. provide technical assistance that promotes leadership, initial preparation, and professional development at the state and local levels and that improves the quality of CTE teachers, faculty, administrators, and counselors
6. support partnerships among secondary schools, postsecondary institutions, baccalaureate degree granting institutions, area CTE schools, local workforce investment boards, business and industry, and intermediaries
7. provide individuals with opportunities throughout their lifetime to develop, in conjunction with other education and training programs, the knowledge and skills needed to keep the United States competitive

The Association for Career and Technical Education (2006) describes the major provisions of The Carl D. Perkins Career and Technical Education Improvement Act of 2006. The act maintains the same structure of the within-state allocation as the former law—85% of funds must be distributed to local programs, 10% can be used for state leadership activities, and 5% for state administration activities. Developing and supporting state data systems to be used for CTE is added as an allowable use of administrative funds.

Of the 85% of funds for local programs, the reserve fund is maintained at the allowable 10% (or 8.5% of the state's total allocation) and can be used in rural areas or areas with high numbers or high percentages of CTE students. The option to spend reserve funds on areas negatively impacted by the 1998 formula change was eliminated, as was the special rule requiring funds to be spent on serving at least two of the allowable categories.

Accountability

The act requires that eligible recipients agree to accept the state levels of performance or negotiate performance measures with the state the same way that states negotiate with the federal government, and report student progress in achieving these performance levels on an annual basis, with the data being disaggregated by special populations. Under the six-year authorization of the act, states and locals will be required to negotiate adjusted levels of performance three times—for the first and second years, third and fourth years, and fifth and sixth years.

The act also creates separate core performance indicators for secondary and postsecondary students. Several changes were made to the specific performance indicators that states and local programs will have to report. At the secondary level, academic attainment will now have to be measured by the academic assessments a state has approved under No Child Left Behind (NCLB). Graduation rates will also have to be reported as defined in NCLB, and technical proficiency should include student achievement on technical assessments that are aligned with industry-recognized standards when possible.

At the postsecondary level, academic attainment will no longer have to be reported as a separate measure, but technical skill proficiency should include student achievement on technical assessments that are aligned with industry-recognized standards when possible. Also at the postsecondary level, student placement in high-wage, high-skill, or high-demand occupations or professions should be measured.

National Activities

The act adds several groups to the list of those that should be represented on the independent advisory panel, including state directors of CTE, chief executives, those with expertise in academic and technical integration, experts in evaluation and assessment, and representatives of small business, economic development, and workforce investment entities. The panel will submit an independent analysis of findings and recommendations to the Secretary of Education and Congress. The act also clarifies that the assessment shall include, to the extent practical, evaluation of the implementation of the new law. The act provides for only one national center. It is specified that the national research center must carry out "scientifically based research and evaluation."

State Administration and Plan

Each state must submit a six-year plan, although a state may submit a transition plan for the first year of that six. States must submit a single state plan to fulfill the requirements of the basic state grant and the Tech Prep program.

Regarding input to the state plan, the act specifies that charter school authorizers and organizers, employers, labor organizations, parents, students, and community organizations must be afforded an opportunity during the state-plan hearing process to present their views and adds that the following groups must be consulted on the state plan development: faculty, administrators, career guidance and academic counselors, charter school authorizers and organizers, institutions of higher education, Tech Prep coordinators and representatives of consortia (if applicable), entities participating in WIA, parent and community organizations, and representatives of small businesses. The act also specifies that both academic and CTE teachers must be involved.

There are several new requirements for information to be added to the state plan. Information that must be added to the state plan includes the following:

- a description of the career and technical programs of study, which may be adopted by local educational agencies and postsecondary institutions to be offered as options to students when planning for and completing future coursework for career and technical content areas
- a description of how the eligible agency, in consultation with eligible recipients, will develop and implement the career and technical programs of study
- a description of how the eligible agency will support eligible recipients in developing and implementing articulation agreements between secondary education and postsecondary education institutions
- a description of how the eligible agency will make available information about career and technical programs of study offered by eligible recipients
- a description of criteria that will be used to assess the extent to which local plans will promote continuous improvement in academic achievement and technical skill attainment and identify and address current or emerging occupational opportunities
- a description of how programs at the secondary level will prepare students, including those from special populations, to graduate with a diploma
- a description of how new courses at the secondary level will be aligned with rigorous and challenging academic content and achievement standards under NCLB, and at the postsecondary level, will be relevant and challenging and will lead to employment in high-skill, high-wage, or high-demand occupations
- a description of how the state will facilitate and coordinate communication of best practices among successful recipients of Tech Prep program funds and local CTE programs
- a description of how the state will report the integration of academics in CTE programs in order to evaluate the quality of such integration
- a description of how professional development will be provided that for CTE teachers, faculty, administrators, and career guidance and academic counselors
- a description of efforts to improve the recruitment and retention of CTE teachers, faculty, and counselors
- a description of efforts to facilitate the transition of subbaccalaureate CTE students into baccalaureate degree programs
- a description of how the state, in consultation with local recipients, will develop a process for the negotiation of local performance measures

Improvement Plans

In the act, the state and local improvement plans are separated into subsections. If a state or local program fails to meet at least 90% of an agreed-upon target for any of the indicators of performance, it will have to develop and implement an improvement plan, with special consideration to performance gaps between population subgroups. If no improvement is made, or the state or local program fails to meet at least 90% of a performance level for three years in a row, then the Secretary of Education or the state could withhold a portion of the funding for that state or local program.

If funds are withheld from a state, the funds must be used to provide technical assistance, for the development of a new state improvement plan, or for other improvement activities in the state. If a state withholds funds from a local program, it must use them to provide, through alternative arrangements, services and activities to students within the area served by the local program.

State Leadership Activities

Changes to the professional development requirements were the most extensive in this section. There is now a requirement to ensure that professional development is provided at both the postsecondary and secondary levels, and the details related to this professional development are much more prescriptive than in the previous legislation. Professional development must

- provide inservice and preservice training to CTE teachers;
- be high-quality, sustained, intensive, and classroom-focused in order to have a positive and lasting impact on classroom instruction and the teacher's performance in the classroom, and not be one-day or short-term workshops or conferences;
- help ensure teachers and personnel can effectively develop rigorous and challenging, integrated academic and CTE education curricula jointly with academic teachers;
- develop a higher level of academic and industry knowledge and skills in CTE; and
- ensure teachers can effectively use applied learning that contributes to the academic and career and technical knowledge of the student.

Minor changes were made to the current state permissible uses of funds. New permissible uses of funds include the following:

- support for initiatives to facilitate the transition of subbaccalaureate CTE students into baccalaureate degree programs
- awarding incentive grants to eligible recipients for exemplary performance in carrying out programs or for pooling with other recipients for innovative initiatives
- providing for activities to support entrepreneurship education and training
- developing valid and reliable assessments of technical skills
- developing and enhancing data systems to collect and analyze data on secondary and postsecondary academic and employment outcomes
- improving the recruitment and retention of CTE teachers, faculty, administrators, and career guidance and academic counselors, including individuals in

groups underrepresented in the teaching profession; and the transition to teaching from business and industry, including small business
- support for occupational and employment information resources

Local Plan

The state-to-local formula for secondary programs remains basically the same, with an update to the language, and at the postsecondary level, the state-to-local formula remains the same. Additional information that must be included in the local plan includes the following:

- description of how the eligible recipient will meet its own negotiated levels of performance
- description of how the recipient will offer the appropriate courses of at least one program of study
- description of how secondary recipients will encourage CTE students to enroll in rigorous and challenging core academic subjects
- description of how professional development will promote the integration of academic and technical education
- description of how activities will be provided to prepare special populations, including single parents and displaced homemakers, for high-skill, high-wage, or high-demand occupations that will lead to self-sufficiency
- description of how career guidance and academic counseling will be provided to CTE students, including linkages to future education and training opportunities
- description of how to improve the recruitment and retention of CTE teachers, faculty, and career guidance and academic counselors, including individuals in groups underrepresented in the teaching profession, and the transition to teaching from business and industry

Additional emphasis is added to the requirement for funds to be spent on professional development. Locals must ensure professional development is provided to both secondary and postsecondary professionals, and require professional development in effective integration of academic and technical education and the effective use of scientifically based research and data to improve instruction. Several new options are added to the permissive uses of funds including the following:

- developing and expanding postsecondary program offerings at times and in formats that are accessible to students, including working students, and including the use of distance education
- developing initiatives that facilitate the transition of subbaccalaureate CTE students into baccalaureate degree programs
- providing activities to support entrepreneurship education and training
- developing and supporting small, personalized career-themed learning communities

- providing support for training programs in automotive technologies
- pooling a portion of funds with another portion of funds from at least one other eligible recipient for innovative initiatives, which may include improving the initial preparation and professional development of CTE teachers, faculty, administrators, and counselors; establishing, enhancing, or supporting systems for accountability data collection or reporting; implementing career and technical programs of study; or implementing technical assessments

Tech Prep

While the Tech Prep program is maintained as a separate title and federal funding stream under the act, states will have the flexibility to consolidate all or part of their Tech Prep grants with funds received under the basic state grant. States must make this choice in their state plans.

The definition of a Tech Prep program is incorporated in the program description section and is very similar to current law. Tech Prep programs must lead to technical skill proficiency, an industry-recognized credential, a certificate, or a degree in a specific career field. The program must utilize CTE program of study to the extent practical and must coordinate with activities conducted with basic state grants. Additional language is added to authorized activities to strengthen career guidance and counseling provisions and encourage transition between secondary and postsecondary education.

A new section was added to Perkins III to strengthen accountability for the implementation of Tech Prep programs. Each consortium that receives a Tech Prep grant must establish and report on the following indicators of performance and enter into agreement with the state to meet a minimum level of performance on each of these indicators:

- the number of secondary and postsecondary Tech Prep students served
- the number and percentage of secondary Tech Prep students who enroll in postsecondary education; enroll in postsecondary education in the same field; complete a state or industry-recognized certification or licensure; complete courses that earn postsecondary credit; and enroll in remedial math, writing, or reading courses upon entering postsecondary education
- the number and percentage of postsecondary Tech Prep students who are placed in a related field of employment within 12 months of graduation; complete a state or industry-recognized certification or licensure; complete a two-year degree or certificate program within the normal time; and complete a baccalaureate degree program within the normal time

To aid in specifying which students should be included in this accountability reporting, two new definitions are included in the Definitions section of the act. A "secondary education tech prep student' is defined as a student who has enrolled in two courses in the secondary component of a Tech Prep program. A "postsecondary education tech prep student" is defined as a student who has completed the secondary component of a Tech Prep program and has enrolled in the postsecondary component at an institution of higher learning.

CURRENT LEGISLATION AFFECTING WORKFORCE PREPARATION PROGRAMS AND OUTLOOK

There are only a few acts that are currently in force that impact CTE. These include the original Smith-Hughes Act of 1917, which is a perpetual act that has been in force since its inception; the Education for All Handicapped Children Act of 1975 as amended in 1990, 1997, and 2004, which changed the name of the act to the Individuals with Disabilities Act (IDEA); the Developmental Disabilities Assistance and Bill of Rights Act of 1990; the Technology-Related Assistance Act for Individuals with Disabilities Act Amendments of 1994; the Goals 2000: Educate America Act of 1994; the School-to-Work Opportunities Act of 1994; the Personal Responsibility and Work Opportunities Act of 1996; the Balanced Budget Act of 1997; the Workforce Investment Act of 1998; the Ticket to Work and Work Incentives Act of 1999; the No Child Left Behind Act of 2002; the Nurse Reinvestment Act of 2002; and the Carl D. Perkins Act of 2006. See Appendix.

From the passage of the Smith-Hughes Act of 1917 to the Carl D. Perkins Act of 2006, Congress has attempted to solve some of the nation's most pressing social, political, and economic problems by enacting workforce legislation. The federal government has a long history of continuing support for CTE, and they understand the importance of investing in workforce education in order to ensure the career futures of American students.

At first, federal legislation was highly prescriptive; however, since the Vocational Education Act of 1963, most federal legislation has specified basic requirements but has given states and local agencies considerable flexibility on how to meet legislative mandates. Recent federal legislation has also sent more money to the local level, believing that local educational agencies are in the best position to identify problems and make adjustment to maximize learning for students. In exchange for increased flexibility for states and local educational and training agencies, there is increased emphasis on accountability.

Congress wants to see the results of CTE programs in terms of performance measures established by states for students and clients. Congress has also attempted to consolidate many separate enactments affecting vocational education and workforce preparation programs into only a few that are active today. The Workforce Investment Act of 1998 consolidated a number of separate federal job training programs, but there are still others that will probably be targeted for consolidation in future congressional action.

CTE programs are supported by a combination of federal, state, local and private funds, with most funding coming from state and local education budgets. The amount of federal financial support has remained fairly constant for many years at around 10% (Cohen & Besharov, 2002). While the federal share of financing for CTE is relatively small, federal support has driven much of the needed changes in programs to prepare people for work over the years. Federal legislation is not solely generated in Washington. Considerable input comes from individuals and groups that have a vested interest in workforce preparation at the state and local levels. Federal and state legislation can expand opportunities to improve CTE, or it can severely limit the ability of career and technical educators to prepare students for the highly advanced workplace. It is important now more than ever for career and technical educators to become advocates for legislation and to provide input to the political leaders who will make the decisions that will affect CTE programs, opportunities for students, and the careers of educators (Dykman, 1995).

It is difficult to predict what changes will be made in federal support for CTE, but many leaders believe that continuing federal support is dependent upon data provided to Congress that reports progress in terms of performance measures established by states. Congress wants to see data on student achievement reported by states in a way that has never been done before. In other words, Congress has removed a number of reported barriers confronting CTE and has given states and local educational agencies considerable flexibility to improve services to students, but they want to see evidence of the effects that CTE programs have on preparing students for productive employment or lifelong learning.

Policy makers continue to examine the field of career and technial education and the social, economic, and educational issues that affect it. It is important that career and technical educators understand the intent of federal legislation as well as the rules and regulations designed to implement Congressional intent. It is only through a full understanding of content and context of legislation that educators can ensure that expected outcomes of legislation are fully realized.